DIAGRAMMATIC REASONING IN AI

DIAGRAMMATIC REASONING IN AI

Robbie Nakatsu

A JOHN WILEY & SONS, INC., PUBLICATION

Published by John Wiley & Sons, Inc., Hoboken, New Jersey
Published simultaneously in Canada

For general information on our other products and services or for technical support, please contact our Customer Care Department within the United States at (800) 762–2974, outside the United States at (317) 572–3993 or fax (317) 572–4002.

Wiley also publishes its books in a variety of electronic formats. Some content that appears in print may not be available in electronic formats. For more information about Wiley products, visit our web site at www.wiley.com.

Library of Congress Cataloging-in-Publication Data:

Nakatsu, Robbie T., 1964–
  Diagrammatic reasoning in AI / Robbie T. Nakatsu.
     p. cm.
  ISBN 978-0-470-33187-3 (cloth)
  1. Arti cial intelligence–Graphic methods. 2. Arti cial intelligence–Mathematics. 3. Reasoning–Graphic methods. I. Title.
  Q335.N355 2009
  006.3–dc22

                                                                              2009015920

10 9 8 7 6 5 4 3 2 1

CONTENTS

PREFACE

This book is really the end product of over a decade of work, on and off, on diagrammatic reasoning in artificial intelligence (AI). In developing this book, I drew inspiration from a variety of sources: two experimental studies, the development of two prototype systems, an extensive literature review and analysis in AI, human–computer interaction (HCI), and cognitive psychology. This work especially contributes to our understanding of how to design the graphical user interface to support the needs of the end user in decision-making and problem-solving tasks. These are important topics today because there is an urgent need to understand how end users can cope with increasingly complex information technologies and computer-based information systems. Diagrammatic representations can help in this regard. Moreover, I believe that reasoning with diagrams will become an important part of the newest generation of AI systems to be developed in the future.

I began investigating the topic of diagrammatic reasoning several years ago as a doctoral student while working on research on user interface design. Almost serendipitously, I stumbled on a concept in cognitive psychology known as *mental models*. This is the idea that we construct models of the world in our minds to help us in our daily interactions with the world. I was intrigued by the idea and wanted to learn more about how, when, and why people do this. I believed that if we could better understand what these mental models are about, then we might use this knowledge to design computer user interfaces and aids, such as tutorials and explanations that might support people in complex tasks, and in their everyday lives. I devote an entire chapter (Chapter 2) to the subject of mental models.

It turns out that my investigation on mental models naturally and gradually evolved into a more general investigation on diagrams. This is because I soon came to view mental models, in many cases, as nothing more than diagrams in the mind's eye. By *diagram* I mean a graphical representation of how objects in a domain are interconnected or interrelated to one another. (In Chapter 3 I try to pin down the concept of *diagram* by defining it more precisely. I also provide a taxonomy of diagram types.) In the process of researching and studying diagramming, I made a few key discoveries. The first is that diagramming is really a basic human activity—most of us do it quite naturally, even if in an informal and adhoc way. On occasion, we do it more formally and explicitly and will spend time to create the "right" diagram, especially if we need to present it to others. I was surprised at how often the need to diagram appeared in my own daily life; it was not at all difficult to come up with several examples of diagramming. The second discovery is that diagramming can take on numerous incarnations and forms, more than I could ever imagine. It was overwhelming to keep track of all the different notations and techniques. Yet, underlying all these variations in notation were a few underlying principles and themes. I will address what these principles and themes are later on in Chapter 3 and in the concluding chapter, Chapter 9. The third discovery is that a diagram is more than just a static picture or representation. Diagrams can be used in more dynamic and interesting ways. Indeed, a theme of this book is that diagrams can be a central part of an intelligent user interface, meant to be manipulated and modified and, in some cases, used to infer solutions to difficult problems. All in all, there is much more to diagramming than meets the eye.

What were my motivations for writing this book and what message do I want to convey to the reader? First, I wanted to understand how diagrams can be used to help learners understand complex ideas. As a teacher at an institution of higher education, I am particularly interested in the pedagogical function of diagrams—to teach and communicate complex ideas with precision and clarity. I am keenly aware of the difficulties that students face in the classroom in trying to understand course material. Textbooks, all too often, contain explanations that confuse more than edify, and classroom lectures often fail to communicate effectively because instructors make too many assumptions about what students are supposed to know or what they already know. In the end, the classroom environment fails to create an effective mental model of the course material for the learner. Moreover, interconnections and interrelationships among concepts are not reinforced strongly enough, so that retention of the material is short lived. Throughout this book, I present many examples of how diagramming can be used to convey information more effectively to learners.

A second motivation is to understand how to make AI systems easier to understand and use. This is really one of the primary objectives of the book. Many critics of AI systems have argued for more transparency and flexibility in the user interface if users are to embrace and accept these systems. Traditional intelligent systems are black box systems that provide little or no opportunity to actively probe and question system conclusions and recommendations. Therefore, I argue that a diagrammatic user interface can help users better understand and visualize system actions.

To this end, I borrow heavily from AI and hence the title of the book is *Diagrammatic Reasoning in AI*. I could just as easily have titled the book simply "Diagrammatic Reasoning" or "The Visualization of Expertise," but these titles do not adequately capture how much I have borrowed from the AI discipline. I look, specifically, at expert systems, model-based reasoning, and inexact reasoning (including certainty factors and Bayesian networks)—three important AI areas that have attempted to create programs capable of emulating human thinking and problem solving in various ways. I also cover logic reasoning (Chapter 4), which is a topic that has also been dealt with extensively in the AI literature.

A third motivation for writing this book is that there are no books that I know of on the marketplace today that address diagrammatic reasoning in a coherent or unified way. I hope to fill this void by providing a more cohesive treatment of the subject. While there are a number of books about information design and graphic design that deal with the topic of diagramming, they explore the topic primarily from the perspective of illustrating principles of good graphic design. There are also several books that deal with specific diagramming notations. For instance, there are books on Unified Modeling Language (UML), a diagramming standard used to model software systems and aid in systems development. Another diagramming technique that is well covered in the literature is the decision graph and other notations used for decision analysis. All these books do a fine and nimble job of describing and illustrating one specific type of diagramming technique, but they are limited because they deal with only one type of diagram or focus on one type of reasoning methodology. This book, on the other hand, is intended to cover a diverse range of diagrams and reasoning methodologies, thereby exposing the reader to the larger issues surrounding diagrams. I hope that by presenting many different types of diagrams and many types of applications, the reader will come away with a deeper appreciation of the power of diagrams.

The targeted audiences of this book are practitioners and researchers in AI and human–computer interaction, programmers and designers of graphical user interfaces (including designers of web applications), and business and computing professionals who might be interested in deploying intelligent systems in their organizations. This book is also suitable for noncomputing professionals who are interested in learning more about the power of diagrams. Indeed, unlike many AI texts on the marketplace today, I assume no prior knowledge of AI or mathematics beyond high school algebra. (The one exception is when I discuss Bayesian networks, a topic that requires a basic understanding of probability theory; in Chapter 8, I provide a brief introduction to probability theory for the reader who has no prior knowledge of the subject.) This book may be used as a self-learner's guide to diagrammatic reasoning and intelligent user interfaces. Furthermore, the diagrammatic applications developed in this book are not targeted to any one particular audience but were created to represent diversity and to demonstrate that diagramming can be a powerful technique for everyone.

The book consists of nine chapters, each of which is more or less self-contained, so that the reader can easily read any one of them, in any order, without any knowledge of the prior chapters. One exception is Chapter 5, which describes the fundamentals of rule-based expert systems; this information serves as background knowledge for Chapter 6. The other exception is the final chapter, Chapter 9, which is meant to serve as a culmination of the previous eight chapters.

Chapter 1 begins with a discussion of the difficulties of AI and the limitations of creating machines that can solve problems like humans (the so-called thinking machine that Alan Turing proposed decades ago). I argue in this chapter that we need to be more accepting of the limitations of AI by finding work-around solutions. In particular, I suggest that we need to look at the role the user interface plays in an intelligent system: How can we make intelligent systems more transparent and more flexible so that we are more accepting of their limitations?

Chapter 2 looks at mental models, or internal models, that we create in our minds to understand a complex phenomenon or system. I have subtitled this chapter "Diagrams in the Mind's Eye" to reflect the idea that a mental model often involves the creation of an adhoc diagram, created on the fly, to help us solve problems and respond to the real world. I will look at several examples of how this occurs and why mental models are useful for problem solving. The discussion will center on two types of mental models:

- **Internal connections**. A description of how the components of a system causally interact to produce outputs or behaviors.
- **External connections**. The connections between a person's prior knowledge and a complex target system to be understood (e.g., the use of analogical representations to understand a complex domain).

I illustrate mental models with several examples, including a mental model of an electromechanical thermostat (an original example) and several well-known examples from the cognitive science literature, including the use of analogies to help with creative problem solving.

Chapter 3 classifies the great variety of diagrams in use today. The classification scheme consists of six categories of diagrams according to their function:

- System topology.
- Sequence and flow.
- Hierarchy and classification.
- Association.
- Cause and effect.
- Logic reasoning.

Throughout this chapter, I illustrate diagrams in a wide range of application areas: everything from network diagrams that show how the hardware components in a computer network are interconnected to one another, to flowcharts that help doctors classify heart attack patients, to semantic networks that illustrate how the characters of Shakespeare's play *Hamlet* are related. Even with such a tremendous diversity of usage, these six categories cut across all these types of diagrams and serve as a unifying framework for understanding and organizing a great variety of diagramming notations.

Chapter 4 is about the use of diagrams in formal logic reasoning. This chapter demonstrates how complex logic problems can be made more comprehensible through the use of diagrams. I look especially at dynamic Venn diagrams that can be used to construct logic proofs for a subset of logic problems.

The discussion of Venn diagrams takes the reader, step by step, through a procedure that enables one to construct logic proofs in a graphical and visual way. The Venn diagrams described in this chapter go far beyond the conventional Venn diagram used in mathematics and set theory: They are not merely static diagrams that depict the relations between two or three sets, rather they are meant to be modified, updated, and combined in many different ways. In fact, I show how Venn diagrams can be used to construct valid logic proofs. I then consider how a linguistic representation system, such as first-order logic, compares to a nonlinguistic system, such as Venn diagrams.

Chapter 5 describes expert systems, which are AI programs that emulate the decision-making ability of a human expert, a person who has expertise in a certain area. In many respects, this entire book is about capturing expertise in some form or another, and thus expert systems play a central role in the discussion. The most common form of expert system stores knowledge as a collection of if–then rules; hence they are referred to as rule-based expert systems. In this chapter, I describe the components of a traditional rule-based expert system, including its two most important parts, the knowledge base and the inference engine. I then illustrate how to create a rule-based expert system using the specialized programming language CLIPS. Finally, I consider some of the benefits and problems of expert system technology.

Chapter 6 explores some of the techniques that may be employed to increase the transparency and flexibility of rule-based expert systems. Specifically, I look at a number of diagrams that can serve as the central component of the user interface itself, including

- Flowchart diagrams that allow one to visually trace the line of reasoning through the knowledge base, taking the user step by step through the reasoning process.
- Diagrams in which a complex knowledge base is partitioned into meaningful segments that can be organized in a hierarchic way.
- Rule trace diagrams that graphically show the interrelationships between the conditions and actions in a rule trace.
- Diagrams that model strategic knowledge, the methods and approaches used for problem solving, so that users have a high-level sense of how the expert systems is reaching its conclusions.

These diagrammatic user interfaces enable a user to more effectively visualize how a system is reaching its conclusions and recommendations. Further, these user interfaces are highly flexible because they allow the user to explore and test out different scenarios and assumptions.

Chapter 7 discusses model-based reasoning techniques and how they may be employed to create more interactive intelligent systems. This technique offers a powerful alternative to more traditional rule-based representational systems. By model-based reasoning, I am referring to a class of AI techniques that involves the analysis of both the structure and the behavior of a system. Model-based reasoning systems start out with some kind of diagram and then reasons with the diagram to help solve difficult problems. We will look at two applications of model-based reasoning. First, we will look at how model-based reasoning can be used to aid in the fault diagnosis of a simple device. Second, we will look at how model-based reasoning can be used to help in the design of business logistics networks.

Chapter 8 delves into the problem of inexact reasoning or how to represent and process uncertainty in AI. This chapter describes two different approaches to processing uncertainty—namely, certainty factors and Bayesian networks. The first approach, certainty factors, was developed as a practical and convenient way for processing uncertainty. Although it is easy to compute certainty factors, this approach lacks rigor and theoretical justification. Therefore, Bayesian networks, an approach that has become increasingly popular today, is described as an alternative that offers a more technically correct approach. Its calculations are based on probability theory and Bayes' theorem.

In addition, I look at how these two approaches can be modeled using belief networks and causal diagrams. These diagrams are not merely static but are dynamic because they can change based on the introduction of new data and evidence.

Finally, in Chapter 9, I summarize and integrate the discussion of the previous eight chapters. I attempt to address the following questions: What is the essence of diagramming? What are the criteria for good diagrams? How do we classify the diagrammatic reasoning techniques covered throughout the book? By answering these questions, I hope to provide a framework for understanding diagrammatic reasoning.

An important part of the book is the development of applications and graphical illustrations throughout. I draw on such diverse areas as physical science, macroeconomics, finance, business logistics management, and medicine to illustrate some of the key ideas. For example, I use diagrams and graphical illustrations to illustrate what factors affect the unemployment rate in the United States. (What are the variables and how do you graphically depict causal relationships among the variables?). In the medical domain, I illustrate a decision flowchart that predicts what factors predict a heart attack. The decision flowchart is meant to be used by emergency room personnel who must quickly make decisions about what to do with patients who come to the emergency room with symptoms of a heart attack.

Unless otherwise noted, most of the diagrams in the book are original examples. I thought that it was very important, if I was going to write a book on diagrams, to develop original examples and applications. I also believed that it was important for me to actually draw the diagrams—only then would I be fully aware of the benefits and limitations of a particular diagramming technique. Hence all of the original diagrams were manually drawn (with the help of Microsoft Visio). In drawing the diagrams, I learned that only through the active creation of diagrams is one able to appreciate that diagramming is a process, sometimes requiring iteration and refinement. This is especially true for more complex diagrams, many of which do not fit on a single page. The end product, the diagrams that you see in the pages of this book, were sometimes arrived at through a consideration of difficult design trade-offs. I discovered very quickly and early on that no one diagramming notation is perfect or complete and that, in the end, what you see in this book is a final result of these trade-offs.

ROBBIE NAKATSU

February 2009
Los Angeles, California

ACKNOWLEDGMENTS

I am grateful to a number of individuals who assisted in the publication of this book. Thanks to Chris Green, who designed the book cover, and the cover department at Wiley for producing the final book cover that you see. A number of individuals read portions of the manuscript and offered their useful suggestions and comments. I am especially grateful to Peder Fedde, who read through some of the diagrams and chapters in the book to ensure that they were accurate and clear. He was extremely supportive and helpful throughout; his support was especially valuable during those times when the progress of the book seemed to move very slowly. Izak Benbasat of the University of British Columbia supported the development of the prototype systems (TransMode Hierarchy and LogNet) discussed in the book while I was a doctoral student there.

I am fortunate to be a part of a very supportive network of colleagues at Loyola Marymount University. They have been a source of support and inspiration to me through these years. I am grateful to the Summer Research Grant Committee of the College of Business for awarding me a grant to pursue the writing of this book. I would also like to thank my students, both graduate and undergraduate, for their support. Two in particular, Timothy Lui and Nathan Peranelli, served as my undergraduate research students. Glenn Grau-Johnson and Ted Tegencamp helped research some of the copyright issues related to the publication of this book. Diana Asai provided excellent administrative support. Tony Patino and his marketing class provided valuable comments on how to market and promote the book.

The staff at Wiley have been very helpful and professional throughout the process. I want to thank George Telecki, Associate Publisher, for having confidence in the book, even when it was in its initial, unformed stages. Kristen

Parrish, Senior Production Editor, was outstanding in overseeing the production of the book, and was always patient, responsive, and helpful to any concerns that I had. Lucy Hitz, Editorial Assistant, unfailingly fielded all my questions and took the time to oversee many aspects of the book. I would also like to thank Candace Levy, the copy editor, who offered many useful suggestions on how the manuscript could be improved. I feel fortunate to have had the opportunity to work with such a team of professionals.

Finally, I am most grateful to my parents, Ron and Yoshiko Nakatsu, for their support throughout the years. This book is dedicated to them.

CHAPTER 1

INTRODUCTION: WORKING AROUND THE LIMITATIONS OF AI

At the dawn of the new millennium, there was much to marvel about in the world of computing and technology. PCs, cell phones, and other digital devices were everywhere and commonplace, enabling an unprecedented amount of digital processing and communication. The Internet had morphed, in a few short years, from a communications medium known only to a chosen few, mostly in academia and government, to a global repository of information exchange known the world over. Global positioning systems (GPS) provided everyday car drivers turn-by-turn instructions with an amazing degree of precision and accuracy. Digitization proceeded at a feverish pace, and everything from music, to videos, to the world's books were transmitted as digitized bits over miles and miles of networks, increasingly in a wireless fashion. Some would say a technology revolution had taken place, resulting in an explosion of innovative applications and ideas in the technology marketplace, unlike anything we had seen before.

Unfortunately, the trajectory of progress in arti cial intelligence (AI) would be much less dramatic, and many would argue, ultimately disappointing. Amid the wild successes of the Internet and wireless communications, we would hear far less talk about machines that could think and solve problems like humans. For the most part, in recent years, AI has taken a back seat to Internet and wireless applications. Indeed, after a speculative boom in the 1980s, a time in which many of its far-out ideas did not pan out, and starting in the 1990s AI lost much of its sex appeal and dazzle. Its image and reputation as a eld of promise have not recovered to this day. (It is interesting that the new overhyped application of today is nanotechnology, another eld with outsized expectations that is also likely to generate disappointing results out of alignment with public perceptions.)

It was not always so. There was once a time when AI was viewed as the wave of the future, the eld that would generate the most transformative computer systems known to humankind. Perhaps no gure in the history of AI represents this promise better than Alan Turing, who in 1950 wrote the article titled "Computing Machinery and Intelligence"[1] in which he considered the question, Can machines think? In this paper, Turing formulated his famous Turing Test, a test in which a human interrogator poses questions to both a computer program and a real person. The computer passes the test if the interrogator cannot tell whether the responses come from the computer or the person. Turing was optimistic that we would have such thinking machines in the near future:

> The original question "Can Machines Think?" I believe to be too meaningless to deserve discussion. Nevertheless, I believe that at the end of the century the use of words and general educated opinion will have altered so much that one will be able to speak of machines thinking without expecting to be contradicted.

As of 2009, we do not yet have machines that pass the Turing Test, let alone machines that can think.

The huge chasm between public perception and actual accomplishment in AI has only been exacerbated by science ction and Hollywood. Many science ction writers, such as Jules Verne and, more recently, Isaac Asimov, have long written about human-like thinking robots and have contributed to the fantasy, the hope, and to some the fear of thinking machines. Perhaps the most iconic image of our time belongs to HAL, the human-like supercomputer in Stanley Kubrick's 1968 movie *2001: A Space Odyssey*. HAL is not so much a robotic machine with a human-like physical form but a machine with a super-human red eye. It is capable of carrying on a natural conversation with other humans but can also play chess and notably possesses superior visual recognition capabilities. In one of the lm's most memorable sequences, HAL reads the quick-moving lips of two of the crew members carrying on a conversation out of earshot.

The science ction image of HAL can be contrasted to the real-life image of Grace (which stands for Graduated Robot Attending Conference), an actual robot that was created by researchers and was asked to perform at the 18th annual conference for the American Association for Arti cial Intelligence held in 2002.[2] Grace took the combined efforts of ve educational and research institutions to create. See Figure 1.1 for a photograph of Grace. The challenge presented to Grace was to start at the entrance to the conference center, take the elevator to the registration desk, register for the conference, and then report to the auditorium at a set time to deliver a speech.

How did Grace perform? Despite the thunderous applause that she received at the conference, an observer familiar with the hopes and dreams of AI would have been greatly disappointed. Throughout, she made a lot of mistakes. About 30 feet into her assigned task, Grace began to misinterpret the spoken commands she was getting. She bumped into walls, repeatedly stopped, or did nothing. In large part,

Figure 1.1. Grace the robot. (Reprinted with permission from Endnote 2.)

her poor performance was due to her limited voice-recognition capabilities. But more fundamentally, Grace lacked that elusive and extremely hard-to-program quality known as autonomy. Autonomy is the ability of a machine (or program) to act on its own without constant supervision. "Take the elevator to the second oor" is a command that most of us could easily execute without much effort and without constant supervision. For a robotic machine to execute such a command on its own would be a monumental and (at this point in time) impossibly dif cult task.

The image of HAL vs. that of Grace is a stark one and provides us with a reality check. We are nowhere close to creating thinking machines, even by the limited standards proposed by the Turing Test. If Grace represents the state of the art, then we have a long way to go before we have designed a machine that even remotely resembles a thinking machine—one that can converse with humans, one that can recognize objects and act on them accordingly, one that possesses the motor skills required to navigate through an unknown terrain, or one that is capable of general problem-solving skills requiring only the commonsense knowledge of a child.

Why is it so hard to create a machine that can think like a human? This is a decades-old question that has plagued AI researchers from the very beginning of the eld. Part of the problem lies in understanding what is meant by arti cial intelligence. De nitions such as "the art of creating machines that perform functions that require intelligence when performed by people"[3] raise more questions than they provide answers about what the eld is about. Perhaps a better de nition is provided by Bellman: "[The automation of] activities that we associate with human thinking, activities such as decision-making, problem solving, learning."[4] But again this de nition too is couched in ambiguity: What exactly do we mean by *human thinking*?

Another problem is that the de nition seems to be a perpetually moving target. There is an old adage in AI that a problem is an AI problem if it hasn't been solved yet. Once some AI function is successfully programmed, it is no longer considered an AI program anymore. Unfortunately, such an attitude means that we will always be disappointed and disillusioned because "real" AI topics will be unattainable as researchers chase ever-more unpractical ideas about thinking machines and human-like robots—the AI community's version of chasing after the Holy Grail. In the meantime, real and concrete accomplishments—in areas such as expert systems, speech/voice recognition, Bayesian networks, neural networks, and other applications—will go underappreciated and even scorned by AI researchers because they will be tainted as easily solvable problems that couldn't possibly be of real interest to AI.

Such thinking is misguided and damaging to the eld of AI, both to its perception as a viable research area, as well as an area full of promising applications. This book argues that we need to have a clear-sighted understanding of the current limitations of AI and the dif culties of creating thinking machines. Rather than bemoaning these limitations and simply giving up, or pursuing unrealistic AI agendas to the exclusion of all others, we need to design AI systems, in particular the user interface, to take into account these limitations and dif culties. Indeed, we need to be more embracing of the shortcomings by nding workaround ways to make AI systems more useful and usable given these inherent shortcomings.

THE DIFFICULTIES OF CREATING A THINKING MACHINE

One common view that explains the dif culty of creating a thinking machine is that AI programs lack commonsense knowledge. Commonsense knowledge, as opposed to specialized expert knowledge, refers to the things that most people can do, often without conscious thought.[5] In fact, when you ask people to explain their commonsense reasoning, they are often at a loss to do so because such knowledge has become so automatized that they lose conscious access it.

As an example, interpreting English sentences such as the following will happen automatically to an average reader of English:

> Last night Mary and Jane went out to dinner. It was Mary's birthday, so Jane paid for dinner. When the check came, she offered to pick up the tab.

A reader of the above three sentences is likely to infer the following:

1. Yesterday was Mary's birthday.
2. It is customary, according to culture and tradition, for the person having a birthday to be treated for dinner.
3. *She* in the third sentence refers to Jane, not Mary.
4. A *tab* is the same thing as a check. To *pick up the tab* refers to paying the bill.
5. The check came at the end of the dinner, not at the beginning.

When one considers all the knowledge that is required to interpret English sentences, it is no wonder that we have been unable to create a reliable language translation program. The irony is that even though a child early on learns to use and understand thousands of words, no computer is capable of understanding what those words mean and cannot even carry on a simple conversation. (The Turing Test, it turns out, has been a tough nut to crack!) To create a language translation program, say from French to English, a programmer might start by creating a simple dictionary look-up program, mapping French words to English words, and rearranging the words according to the laws of English grammar and usage. In fact, that is just what early efforts at language translation programs were. However, such a program is bound to generate a translation that is rife with errors and awkward constructions. (The famous mistranslation of *"the spirit is willing, but the flesh is weak"* into "the vodka is good, but the meat is rotten" illustrates this point well.) One obvious problem is that the program does not contain knowledge of all the idiomatic expressions of the English language. But a bigger problem is that the program lacks a mental model* of the world being discussed. A language translation program, unlike a human, makes no use of models of the world to understand language and will thus easily become over-whelmed by ambiguities and multiple meanings. Indeed, early efforts at creating language translation programs failed miserably and disappointed AI researchers.[6]

What kinds of models might a language translation program contain? For one, it might contain a knowledge structure known as a semantic network, a kind of diagrammatic representation that is composed of nodes and links that interconnect the nodes. Many kinds of semantic networks are possible. See Figure 1.2 for one type of semantic network. In one simple form, the nodes are represented by rectangles and can be anything from a physical object (such as a book, house, tree) to a person (such as Abraham Lincoln, Mary, a waiter), to a concept (such as happiness, religion, crime) or to an event (such as yesterday, Fourth of July, the first day of school). The links interconnect two or more nodes and show the relationship between the nodes (sometimes a verb or other piece of descriptive text is added to describe the relationship). Figure 1.2 represents a simple semantic network of the "Mary and Jane went out to dinner" scenario described earlier.

---

*Mental models are discussed in Chapter 2.

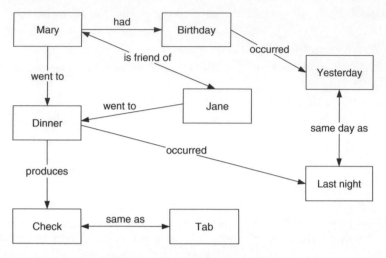

Figure 1.2. A semantic network.

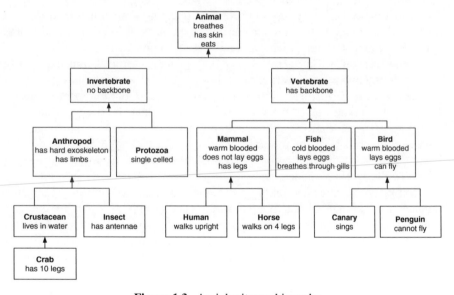

Figure 1.3. An inheritance hierarchy.

A second type of of model is an inheritance hierarchy that can represent a taxonomy or classi cation scheme. See Figure 1.3 for an example of this type of mode. In this hierarchy three pieces of information are represented:

- **Units**. The thing or object.
- **Properties**. Characteristics of the unit.
- **Pointers**. Class associations among the units.

In this example, knowledge about animals can be illustrated as a hierarchy of nodes, represented as rectangles in the diagram. A node connected to another node is either on the top (a superclass or parent node) or on the bottom (a subclass or a child node). For example, the superclass *animal* is connected to two subclasses, *invertebrate* and *vertebrate*. Under this scheme, subclasses inherit all properties of their superclasses. (Properties are indicated below the class name in each of the nodes in the gure.) For example, while *canary* inherits properties from *bird, vertebrate*, and *animal*, it does not inherit properties from *fish*. Note also that a particular unit on the hierarchy can override a property it inherits: *Penguin* inherits the property *can fly* from its superclass *bird*, but it is overridden by the property *cannot fly*.

A third type of model that might be included in a language translation program might be a script, a well-known knowledge structure described by Schank and Abelson.[7] A script can be de ned as a stereotyped sequence of events that together de ne a well-known situation. The best-known example is the one for going to a restaurant. A restaurant script might include the following sequence of events:

1. Enter the restaurant.
2. Be greeted by the host, who seats you at a table and gives you a menu.
3. Read menu and decide what you want.
4. Order when the waiter comes.
5. Wait for food to come.
6. Eat when food comes.
7. Ask for the check.
8. Pay the check.
9. Exit the restaurant.

The advantage of having a set of scripts is that they can give an AI program the ability to infer actions and predict what will happen in conventional situations.

It is a rather trivial matter to construct semantic networks, inheritance hierarchies, and scripts for very simple situations and problem solving contexts. However, to construct them for all of a typical human adult's knowledge about the world would be a colossal undertaking. Consider for example that if a typical adult knows thousands of words, each of those words would be linked to hundreds of knowledge structures, which in turn are linked to hundreds of other knowledge structures, and so on, resulting in a very intricate and elaborate network. Moreover, these semantic networks are not static but typically change over time as a person acquires experience and more knowledge about the world. A more practical use of semantic networks, inheritance hierarchies, scripts, and other knowledge structures would be to construct them for more well-de ned contexts and problem solving tasks.

Lack of Commonsense Reasoning

Several AI researchers have tackled the problem of understanding commonsense reasoning. Among some of the components that are frequently brought forth as essential components of commonsense reasoning are the following:[8]

- The ability to use different representations to describe the same situation.
- The ability to recognize when a problem solving method is failing.
- Self-re ection at a higher level.
- Ef cient knowledge retrieval.

Let us look at each of the four issues and consider what is wrong with the current generation of AI systems. Further, let us suggest some possible remedies for these limitations. These four components of commonsense reasoning serve as a framework for how to evaluate the effectiveness of an intelligent user interface.

The Ability to Use Multiple Representations. A conventional program is built such that it approaches a problem in a single way. Such a program is likely to be rigid and not very robust to changing assumptions and to different ways of using the program. We need AI programs that are built to work around multiple representations, so that when one representation fails, the program is easily able to switch over to nd an alternative. For a human problem solver to really comprehend a problem-solving situation, he or she must possess not only a set of representations on the problem but also an ability to understand how they are related to one another, a kind of integrated view of the set. Likewise, an AI program should be able to understand how to process multiple representations effectively.

The topic of knowledge representation is a central one in AI, one that has occupied the attention of AI researchers from the very beginning, and one that remains a central challenge today. One goal of this book is to address how to approach the topic of knowledge representation as refracted through the prism of diagrammatic representations. In the chapters to follow, we look at many different types of knowledge representation schemes, all of them represented diagrammatically. We investigate how to reason with and draw inferences on many different kinds of graphical diagrams. Some examples include decision trees and in uence diagrams that help us make better decisions (Chapter 3), directed graphs to aid us in understanding mechanisms of cause and effect (Chapter 3), Venn diagrams that can be used to perform logic reasoning (Chapter 4), diagrams to represent the problem-solving strategies used in expert system (Chapter 6), model-based reasoning systems that can help us with fault diagnosis (see Chapter 7), and Bayesian networks that perform probabilistic reasoning (or reasoning with inexact and imperfect data) (Chapter 8). Others have looked at neural networks, scripts (brie y discussed earlier), frame-based representations, logic, object-oriented approaches, and other techniques and formalisms for representing knowledge. Because the focus of this book is on reasoning with diagrams, many of these additional knowledge representation techniques will not be covered insofar as they do not deal with diagrammatic representations.

The Ability to Deal with Errors. Traditional AI user interfaces have long been criticized for being extremely brittle—that is, they are programmed to do only one speci c thing, but when you try to push the system beyond what it was programmed to do (i.e., beyond its bounds of ignorance), the system will completely malfunction. Indeed, the AI landscape is littered with thousands of highly specialized programs that can each do some well-circumscribed task: diagnosing bacterial skin infections, playing chess, determining what drug to take and in what dosage for patients with high cholesterol. Such programs can perform their speci c task very well, sometimes even surpassing the level of a human expert. However, if even one underlying assumption is unmet, if one piece of data is missing, or if some piece of evidence is not known with complete certainty, the system will completely break down. Human problem solvers, by contrast, degrade more gracefully when faced with uncertainty, incompleteness in data, or noisy information. Moreover, human problem solvers are better equipped to know when failure occurs and can employ adaptive strategies to deal with such situations.

We need to do better job when designing our AI systems. In great part, the ability to deal with error and failure can be vastly improved with a better user interface, today this being primarily the graphical user interface. In general, we need user interfaces that are exible enough to process errors and uncertain information. We deal with the subject of system exibility at the end of this chapter and throughout this book.

Self-Reflection at a Higher Level. A conventional program executes a pre-programmed set of instructions but no attempt is ever made by the program to stop and re ect on its own actions, even when it is pursuing a blind alley or veering wildly off track. Such a program is badly in need of some kind of over-all plan of attack, a model of how to approach a problem-solving situation. A human problem solver often possesses higher-level strategies on how to approach a problem. He or she will often need to stop and re ect on the current state of the problem and decide whether a change of course is in order. Having strategic knowledge and the ability to adapt in midstream are important characteristics of effective problem solvers and decision makers.

We need AI programs that possess strategic knowledge and can re ect on whether they are pursuing the right problem-solving methods. Strategic knowledge is about understanding the methods used for problem solving and about how those methods are ordered to reach a goal.[9] Strategic knowledge and how to diagrammatically represent such knowledge are addressed more extensively in Chapter 6.

Efficient Knowledge Retrieval. The ability to retrieve relevant information from a person's vast storehouse of knowledge is, of course, an important function for effective performance and problem solving. AI programs also need to do to be able to do this effectively, so that it is relatively easy to get at the right information quickly (an exhaustive and linear search through the memory, or knowledge base, of an AI program will just not cut it). Moreover, knowledge retrieval requires that AI programs can recognize patterns and features of a current problem-solving context so that the program knows which problem context stored in its knowledge base will best match the current context.

A number of knowledge representation schemes have been proposed to deal with the knowledge retrieval problem. One popular method is known as case-based reasoning. This type of system organizes knowledge into cases, which are problem solving experiences used for inferring solutions to future problems. An example of an application is a technical support system that provides help desk operators guidance on how to troubleshoot a customer's problems. For instance, a customer calls a help desk to report a problem with her printer. She reports that she is receiving error message 908, that her printer does nothing, and that the orange light is ashing. A case-based reasoning system will search through its database of historical cases to nd the one that best matches the features of the current problem. At times, there will not be a perfect match to an historical case, so the system must know how to adapt the previous solution to t the current problem. In addition, a new case that does not perfectly match any of the previous cases is added to the knowledge base of historical cases, so that a case-based reasoning system adapts and grows over time as it acquires more and more experiential knowledge.

This book investigates a variety of diagrammatic representations, one of whose primary functions will be to serve as "organizational scaffolds"[10] that enable more ef cient knowledge retrieval. Indeed, a very important function of diagrams is to organize information more effectively so that it is easier to retrieve. For example, one common and natural way to organize a lot of information is as a hierarchy. These diagrams, whether hierarchy or some other form, can be part of the user interface itself, enabling an end user to interact with the diagram to better understand the system. Hence in addition to their role as ef cient knowledge retrievers, they will also serve in the role of helping us understand the components of a system and their interrelationships—that is, the underlying mechanism of a complex system.

Intractability

Another explanation for the dif culty of AI and the dif culty of creating thinking machines is the intractability of many of its problems. These are problems that are computationally dif cult, if not impossible to solve, with currently known algorithms. Whereas the problems of AI programs lacking commonsense reasoning concentrate on general problem-solving skills that almost everyone possesses (even a child), intractable problems can involve more complex and specialized problem-solving tasks (such as playing chess).

Early on in the history of AI, most research efforts were centered on very simple, toy problems, also known as microworlds, so that computational complexity was not a primary concern. A good example is the **blocks world**, a domain that consisted of a set of blocks (e.g., rectangular blocks, cones, balls, etc.) placed

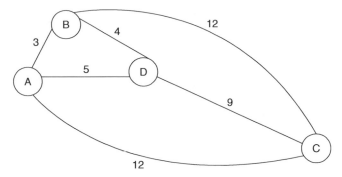

Figure 1.4. Traveling salesman problem. What is the solution to this problem given four cities, A, B, C, and D? Answer: One solution is ACDBA (28 miles).

on a tabletop. A typical task in this domain was to command a robotic arm to rearrange the blocks in a certain way. For example, "place the cone on top of the large block." SHRDLU was a natural language program that allowed user interaction with the blocks world.[11] The user instructed SHRDLU to manipulate the various objects in the blocks world. The program was computationally feasible because the blocks world was so simple: The entire set of objects could be described by perhaps 50 words, from nouns like *block* and *cone* to adjectives like *small* and *red*. Unfortunately, researchers at the time failed to realize that such simple toy problems would not scale up to more realistic and complex problem-solving domains without becoming computationally intractable.

Intractability has had a great impact on the eld of AI and computer science. Many problems, to the consternation of many early AI prognosticators, have turned out to be too dif cult to solve, a turn of events that has greatly limited the progress of AI. One classic example that illustrates the nature of intractability is the well-known traveling salesman problem. In this problem, we are given *n* cities, and for each pair of cities, the distance between the two cities. The problem is to nd the shortest round-trip route that visits each city once and returns to the starting city. An example is given in Figure 1.4.

One way to solve this problem is simply by brute force search—that is, try out every possible ordering of the cities and select the one with the minimum total number of miles. This approach will work ne only when the problem size is small but quickly becomes intractable. For $n = 4$, you would need to try out 4! permutations or 24 possibilities.* In general, you would need to try out n! permutations, for a problem size of *n* cities. The problem quickly grows in size as *n* increases. For example, for $n = 10$ cities you would need to try out 3.6 million permutations and for $n = 20$ cities, the time complexity of the problem grows to

*In the case of 4 cities, there are 4 possible cities to be chosen as the rst city. Once this city has been selected, there are $(n - 1)$ or 3 cities to choose from the remaining cities. Once this city has been removed from the list, there are now $(n - 2)$ or 2 cities. Hence, in general, for a problem of size *n* there are n! or $n(n - 1)(n - 2) \cdots 1$ permutations.

2.4×10^{18} permutations. Obviously, a brute force search strategy would quickly bog down even the fastest computers of today for suf ciently large values of n.

How does one de ne intractability? One de nition is that a problem is intractable if the time required to solve the problem grows exponentially with the size of the problem.[12] By exponential time, mathematically we mean that computation time $T(n)$ is a function of problem size n and there exists a constant $c > 1$ such that:

$$T(n) = O(c^n)$$

Polynomial time functions, by contrast, are much more desirable in terms of time complexity. Mathematically they can be written as:

$$T(n) = O(n^k)$$

Examples of exponential time functions include 2^n and 3^n. Examples of polynomial time functions include n (linear time), n^2 (quadratic time), and n^3 (cubic time).

A side-by-side comparison of polynomial time functions versus exponential time function is given in Table 1.1.[14] In the table, the functions express execution times in terms of microseconds. The interesting thing to observe here is the extremely rapid growth rates of the exponential time functions, compared to the polynomial time functions. It is quickly evident that polynomial time functions are much more desirable than exponential time functions. As Gary and Johnson state, "Most exponential time algorithms are merely variations on exhaustive search, whereas polynomial time algorithms generally are made possible only

Table 1.1. Comparison of several polynomial and exponential time complexity functions. Adapted from Endnote 13

Time complexity function	Size n					
	10	20	30	40	50	60
n	.00001 second	.00002 second	.00003 second	.00005 second	.00005 second	.00006 second
n^2	.0001 second	.0004 second	.0009 second	.0016 second	.0025 second	.0036 second
n^3	.001 second	.008 second	.027 second	.064 second	.125 second	.216 second
n^5	.1 second	3.2 seconds	24.3 seconds	1.7 minutes	5.2 minutes	13.0 minutes
2^n	.001 second	1.0 second	17.9 minutes	12.7 days	35.7 years	366 centuries
3^n	.059 second	58 minutes	6.5 years	3855 centuries	2×10^8 centuries	1.3×10^{13} centuries

through the gain of some deeper insight into the structure of a problem. There is wide agreement that a problem has not been 'well-solved' until a polynomial time algorithm is known for it."[14] (It is worthwhile to note that using dynamic programming, a mathematical method for solving problems with a sequential decision structure, the traveling salesman problem can be solved in time $O(n^2 *$ $2^n)$. Although still exponential, it is better than $O(n!)$).

It is beyond the scope of this book to identify and address the problem of intractability. The theory of NP-completeness,[15] which is not addressed in this book, was developed for this purpose and is discussed in many standard texts covering AI algorithms. We do not deal with issues of intractability any further in this book. Certainly, diagrammatic approaches may be used to better understand the structure of a problem and suggest ways to develop heuristics, or rules of thumb, to make some of these problems more manageable, by suggesting good-enough solutions, but not necessarily optimal solutions. In Chapter 7, we employ model-based reasoning, a technique that starts with a diagrammatic model of some kind and reasons from this model to help us solve an intractable problem. Hence diagrammatic methods may help us better understand intractable problems as well as provide insight as to how to nd work-around solutions.

EXPLANATORY POWER OF INTELLIGENT SYSTEMS

It is obvious that there arc huge dif culties that need to be overcome before AI programs resemble thinking machines. Many of these obstacles will remain insurmountable for the foreseeable future at least, despite all the best efforts of AI researchers and the business community to create more robust AI programs. Breakthroughs in areas such as computer vision, language understanding, and machine learning as well as better AI algorithms to deal with intractability will all contribute to the progress of AI, and hopefully narrow the gap that exists between the clunky programs and robots of today and the AI programs of tomorrow. It is not the goal of this book to address what needs to be done to bridge this gap and create machines and programs that can more closely resemble human thinking. Rather, this book turns its attention to what will increasingly become an important and central component of AI systems: **the user interface**, in particular the graphical user interface, which will increasingly use diagrams and various other graphical representations to aid in system understanding.

As AI technologies become more widely used in the future, the graphical user interface is likely to take on a more prominent role. There are at least two reasons for this prediction. First, given the limitations of AI systems—and the unlikelihood of their being resolved in the near future—there will be a more urgent need to create user interfaces that are better able to cope with an AI system's weak spots. As discussed earlier, AI systems that are rigid dialogues are unable to deal gracefully with their lack of commonsense reasoning—such as, their inability to process uncertain and incomplete data and their inability to retrieve knowledge ef ciently. A user interface that can, at least in part, deal with these weaknesses is far more likely to be effective and accepted by the user community. Second, the AI systems of the future are likely to tackle increasingly complex tasks, capable of solving problems in domains as diverse as medical diagnosis, computer design/con guration, and loan portfolio analysis, just to name a few examples. If users are to trust and accept the advice and recommendations that these systems generate, the user interface will need to be able to comfortably explain itself.

What do we mean by a system that can explain itself? It is useful at this point to limit our discussion to advice-giving systems that provide recommendations on how to solve problems or help us make the right decisions. Hereafter, such systems are referred to as **intelligent systems**. Such intelligent systems are said to be endowed with **explanatory power** when they are capable of explaining their own actions through a user interface.[16] Two system characteristics are relevant to understanding explanatory power: **transparency** or the ability to see the underlying mechanism of the system so that it is not a black box and **flexibility** or the ability of the user interface to adapt to a wide variety of end-user interactions so that it is not a rigid dialogue but an open-ended interaction that allows the user to explore and understand the system more fully. While system transparency is a quality related to the informational content of the system itself—that is, information that helps us understand a system's actions— exibility is more related to the nature of the end-user interaction with the system. More exibility in the user interface can lead to more transparency—having a more open-ended interaction can enable a user to seek out more ways to better understand the system. By the same token, having a more restrictive interface can impair a user's ability to seek out more transparency, even it does already exist. Hence exibility is treated as a separate quality of the user interface that exists independently of interface transparency.

System Transparency

How can we render an intelligent system more visible for inspection so that its internal mechanism is no longer a black box? System transparency involves providing users with information about how a system functions. In general, as typical users of computers and technology, we are often plagued by a computer's lack of transparency. We usually aren't bothered by this state of affairs until the system malfunctions or when we wish to use a system in a novel or nonroutine way. If this is the case, we may yearn for some kind of deeper system understanding that will help us cope with the error or novelty. Most times, we receive no information at all regarding what a system is doing. If we are fortunate enough to get any message at all, it will oftentimes make no sense to us, or will not contribute to a deeper understanding of the system. For example, suppose an unusual error message pops up on your computer screen: "Buffer over ow. Please restart computer." What does the message mean? What is a buffer? What was the cause of the error? And what does restarting the computer do to resolve the problem? Unless there is system transparency, we are relegated to the role of passive user, unable to do anything but blindly accept the system's recommended action.

To provide system transparency, a number of questions could conceivably be asked by a user and answered by an intelligent system:

* How did you reach that conclusion?
* Why did <such and such> an event occur?
* What if I tried <such and such>?
* Why not <such and such>?

It would be a very dif cult task indeed to devise a system that could answer all these questions in a satisfactory manner, even for a relatively simple domain. Questions of the last type (*Why not?*), in particular, are notoriously dif cult to answer because they require an anticipation of alternative hypotheses. One approach would be to create a database of questions and their corresponding answers, a kind of FAQs (frequently asked questions) for the situation at hand. A problem with this approach is that a system designer would need to anticipate all questions and their responses beforehand. Yet it is highly unlikely that all the relevant questions will be thought out ahead of time. Furthermore, the responses to the questions would be canned text, or prefabricated responses, which would ignore context and contain no model of system behavior. This approach, while certainly better than having no explanations at all, is limited in effectiveness and cannot scale up to more complex domains or anticipate future scenarios, particularly novel situations that have not been encountered before.

A second possibility, one that may provide more exibility than an enumeration of questions and answers, and one that can provide a more expansive and global view of a system, is to provide the end-user with a conceptual model of the domain. A good conceptual model can provide one with a deeper understanding of a system. The conceptual model may, for example, contain a description of the components of a system, how they are interconnected to one another and how they may causally interact to produce outputs. A conceptual model is typically rendered as a graphical diagram of some kind. One simple example is given in Figure 1.5, which portrays the causal chain of events that causes a car to move. It is based on the following description of how an internal combustion engine moves an automobile forward:

> In an internal combustion engine, gasoline is ignited by a spark plug, causing a small explosion, which generates work. The work pushes a piston, which in turn drives a crankshaft connected to an axle. The axle is connected to wheels, which turn to drive the automobile forward.

We will address the topic of conceptual models and causal models more fully in Chapter 2. Then, in Chapter 3, we will look at a wide range of diagrams, and attempt to provide a classi cation of their different forms, by how they are used, and what they are suitable for. There are many possible ways for promoting deep understanding with a diagram of some kind.

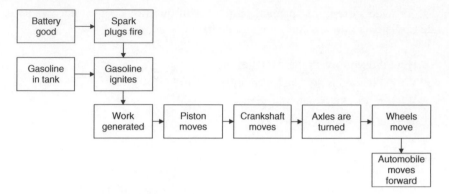

Figure 1.5. Causal model of how a car moves.

For now, we note that a good conceptual model can facilitate system understanding—for example, an understanding of mechanisms of cause and effect. By possessing such an understanding, a user is better equipped to deal with system errors and problems. Moreover, a good conceptual model can predict the effects of our actions. Without a conceptual model, a user must operate by rote, blindly accepting a system's recommendations.

System Flexibility

The careful selection of features of the user interface may also enhance its explanatory power. A highly exible system may encourage exploration and experimentation, which means that users will more likely seek out explanations and deeper meanings in the system recommendations. A rigid interface, by contrast, discourages them from seeking out more information because the effort to do so would be too great and not worth it. Moreover, highly exible systems can adapt to different problem-solving contexts and to different informational needs. Let us look at, speci cally, six desirable user interface characteristics[17] that may lead to greater system exibility: (1) natural mappings, (2) feedback, (3) recoverability, (4) granularity, (5) ability to handle errors, and (6) multiple representations to the same knowledge.

Natural Mappings. The term *natural mappings* refers to the ability to represent the user's domain so that it maps as closely as possible to his or her mental model. In his book *The Design of Everyday Things*, Donald Norman[18] provides a number of examples of everyday objects that are easy and natural to use. One reason that these objects are so easy to gure out is that they possess a natural mapping that is visible and intuitive enough to understand. For example, when we look at a knob, we assume that it is for turning and adjusting something (e.g., the ame on a stove). Likewise we assume a slot is for inserting things, a switch turns something on or off, and a handle on a cabinet door is used to pull it open. In these examples, the physical appearance of the object, by itself, naturally suggests to us what its purpose is, and how it is to be used.

We should expect the same for intelligent user interfaces. For example, a text-based, question-and-answer dialogue may be the primary vehicle for entering inputs and displaying outputs. Such an interface would work well enough if all we wanted to do was enter inputs and have an intelligent system display a recommendation. However, the rigidity of the question-and-answer format may not be a natural way to foster explanation-seeking behaviors. For more exibility, a graphical user interface could allow users to perform actions directly on a graphical diagram of the domain. Such an interface could facilitate a more naturalistic interaction with the system. Throughout this book, we will look at a number of diagrammatic user interfaces and consider how they may be used to support a more naturalistic dialogue with the user.

Feedback. The ability to send back information about what action has been performed and what has been accomplished is *feedback*. It is a well-established principle in user interface design, and for good reason: Without feedback, a user may wonder whether anything has happened yet. Feedback is missing in all too many systems. For example, we often experience the frustration of receiving no feedback when we click on a button in a web page to perform some kind of action (such as downloading software) and nothing happens. Sometimes we end up repeating the mouse-click, and the operation, to our dismay, is performed twice. Or we refresh the web page, thinking erroneously that the web page is stuck.

Feedback is critical in intelligent systems. It may give us comfort that we are on the right track; it may guide us toward system understanding; it may help in building system trust. For maximum effectiveness, feedback should be provided immediately, and whenever there is a change in system state.

Recoverability. Recoverability is the ability to back out of changes made to the system. This capability may encourage a user to explore and experiment with a system, without having to start all over again when an error is made. There are many possible ways to build recoverability into an interface. As users of today's most popular software products today, we are familiar with many of them: a back button, undo facilities, history lists of the most recent actions performed, hypertext links that enable a user to jump directly to a relevant portion of a problem-solving situation.*

Another approach to promoting exploratory behaviors is to create special modes of operation. For example, a protected mode might be created in which user actions are shielded from harmful consequences. A user could turn on protected mode and system commands are simulated without actually affecting the

---

*A good example of software that has these features is TurboTax. The software allows you to jump to a speci c portion of your tax return—such us your deductions—so that you do not have to search sequentially through every portion of your tax return if you are interested in seeing and modifying only one portion of it.

data.[19] Another possibility is control blocking. This means that a portion, or subset, of a system's functions is made inaccessible to the user to prevent their accidental usage. These and other techniques can be used to encourage system exploration: Users are freer to actively experiment with a system's features, without fear of destroying data, or producing irreparable damage to the system.

Granularity. The ability to display different levels of detail depending on the situation the user is currently in is granularity. Especially in complex systems composed of multiple components, this capability is very useful in addressing the cognitive limitations of a user. Such a user can become overwhelmed by the enormous amount of information required to understand the system. An interface that supports granularity may be one that allows the creation of multileveled, hierarchic descriptions of a system. A user can drill down the branches of the hierarchy to obtain more detail, or go up the branches to obtain a higher-level view. An interface endowed with granularity would enable a user to change the level of detail frequently and with ease during a user session.

Ability to Handle Errors. As discussed previously, traditional AI programs are unable to handle errors well. In such programs, the user is required to enter a set of inputs in a prescribed sequence, and there may be no tolerance for uncertainty in the data, or missing data. A flexible system might possess the following desirable characteristics:

- We should be allowed to enter data in any order, and the system recommendation should not be affected by the order (invariance to data entry order).
- We should be able to enter incomplete data, and the system should make its best guess as to what the system recommendation should be given what it does know (ability to process incomplete information).
- We should be able to attach certainty factors* to our data inputs if we are uncertain about the accuracy of the data (e.g., we may have an imprecise test result, or we may have a data sensor that is not 100% accurate); the system will accordingly adapt its recommendation (ability to process noisy data).
- We should be able to perform sensitivity analysis on the data, to test how robust a system recommendation is to a range of values (ability to test for the robustness of the system recommendation).

Beyond these specific measures and recommendations, it is important for designers of intelligent systems to design for error. Having such a design philosophy

---

*A certainty factor expresses how certain we are about the data inputs. There are different methods used to assign certainty factors and process them. For now, we may think of a certainty factor as being in the range from 0 (completely uncertain) to 1.0 (completely certain). We will have more to say about certainty factors in Chapter 8.

will predispose designers to the idea that people will misuse intelligent systems, misconstrue its features, and sometimes get lost when using these systems. Designers aware of these human tendencies can plan for them ahead of time and alleviate their adverse consequences. This could make all the difference in terms of whether these systems are ultimately embraced or not by the user community.

Better still, it is highly recommended to perform extensive end-user testing before systems are implemented and deployed to the larger user population. One goal of such testing would be to come up with a list of errors that users commonly make. Having knowledge of the most common types of errors could be used to redesign the user interface so that committing errors does not result in complete system breakdown. This important step, regrettably, is all too often neglected and ignored in the development of intelligent systems.

Multiple Representations to the Same Knowledge. Because different tasks and different users may have different requirements for using knowledge, a system that enables multiple representations to the same knowledge would permit greater exibility. We have already identi ed the ability to use multiple representations as a component of commonsense reasoning and have noted that this book will address many types of diagrammatic representations. We will see throughout this book how these graphical representations can be employed to support different kinds of users and different kinds of tasks.

THE FUTURE OF AI: TOWARD INTERACTIVE DIAGRAMS

We began the chapter by observing the huge discrepancy that exists between the futuristic thinking robots so vividly portrayed in science ction and the current reality of limited AI machines and programs that can solve only well-circumscribed tasks. We further noted that this has been the cause of disillusionment and disappointment to many in the eld who got caught up in the hype and excitement of robots and thinking machines. However, such an unrealistic outlook on the future of AI downplays the real and concrete achievements that have occurred in the past decades since AI was born in the 1950s. Here are just a few notable success stories:

- The chess program Deep Blue, created by IBM, defeated Gary Kasparov in 1997 (the program was capable of evaluating some 200 million board positions per second).
- Neural networks are now capable of recognizing speech, albeit in well-structured domains with limited vocabularies.
- Expert system technology has been successfully implemented in many business organizations and has resulted in higher productivity and better and more consistent decision making, not to mention that it has shed considerable light on the nature of expertise and how humans solve problems in complex domains.

- NASA sent autonomous vehicles (rovers) into space to act as robots that could perform on-site geological investigations on Mars.

All these applications illustrate a few key commonalities about what makes an AI program successful. First, they deal with well-de ned domains, as opposed to tackling general problem solving. This is an important point, because all these programs focus their efforts on resolving one speci c problem, not creating a machine that can do everything a human can. Second, they recognize the limitations of AI, but nonetheless manage to work around them. Their successes are highly attributable to having a well-grounded understanding of the practical issues involved in implementing AI programs and machines. A central tenet of this book is that the designers of the next generation of AI programs will require a good grasp of the dif culties of AI to nd work-around solutions. In this chapter, we have discussed two frameworks for dealing with the dif culties of intelligent systems.

The rst framework explores an AI program's lack of commonsense reasoning. We looked speci cally at four constituents of commonsense reasoning—namely, the use of multiple representations, the ability to deal with failure, self-re ection, and knowledge retrieval. Intelligent systems in the future will increasingly need to be able to deal with these four problem areas if they are to have any chance of solving complex problems in realistic settings.

The second framework explores the concept of explanatory power, or the ability of a system to explain itself. The focus of the discussion here turned squarely on the user interface, which will increasingly assume a central role in AI systems. We looked speci cally at two characteristics of the user interface: transparency and exibility. Intelligent user interfaces of the future that are endowed with these characteristics are more likely to be embraced and accepted because users are more likely to understand and, therefore, trust their recommendations. Moreover, these systems will be able to handle a greater variety of problems and degrade more gracefully when faced with errors and uncertainty. AI systems, in general, have long been regarded as in exible and poorly adaptable in dealing with new situations.

One solution to these limitations is to develop some kind of diagram or graphical model that serves as the central part of the user interface, the primary means by which an end-user will interact with a system. A diagram is de ned as a graphic representation that shows how something works or makes something easier to understand. This book focuses not only static diagrams, such as the type that might exist in the pages of a book, but also on dynamic diagrams that can be part of an intelligent user interface. An end-user can explore and manipulate these more dynamic diagrams in a variety of ways.

In the chapters that follow we investigate a wide variety of diagrams that can be used in intelligent user interfaces. One important characteristic of the diagrammatic interfaces that we will explore is that they are meant to *serve in an advisory capacity* to human decision making and problem solving. This is an important point to underscore, because these systems are not meant to replace the human, contrary to futuristic AI notions of robots and programs working autonomously, on their own without any kind of supervision. Indeed, the user remains rmly behind the steering wheel, in the decision making loop, throughout. The belief here is that a collaboration between human and machine is much more effective than either one working alone, and that each party brings different capabilities to the table. In effect, this means that a human user need not blindly accept an intelligent system's recommendations and conclusions, but can actively question, probe, and try to understand rationales underlying system actions. It is the interactive diagram that will make the partnership between human and machine possible.

ENDNOTES

1. Alan M. Turing, "Computing Machinery and Intelligence," *Mind* 59, no. 236 (1950), 433–460.
2. Curtis Gillespie, "Charmed by Six Feet of Circuitry," *New York Times*, Aug. 8, 2002. Photo by Rick MacWilliam. Reprinted with permission from Edmonton Journal.
3. Raymond Kurzweil, *The Age of Intelligent Machines*. Cambridge, MA: MIT Press, 1990.
4. Richard E. Bellman, *An Introduction to Artificial Intelligence: Can Computers Think?* San Francisco, CA: Boyd & Fraser, 1978.
5. Marvin Minsky, "Commonsense-Based Interfaces," *Communications of the ACM* 43, no. 8 (Aug. 2000), 67–73.
6. Douglas R. Hofstadter, *Gödel, Escher, Bach: An Eternal Golden Braid*. New York: Vintage Books, 1979.
7. Roger C. Schank and Robert P. Abelson, *Scripts, Plans, Goals, and Understanding*. Hillsdale, NJ: L. Erlbaum Associates, 1977.
8. See Minsky, pp. 69–70, for a discussion of some of the components of commonsense reasoning.
9. William J. Clancey, "The Epistemology of a Rule-Based Expert System—A Framework for Explanation," *Artificial Intelligence* 20 (1983), 215–251.
10. The phrase *organizational scaffold* is from Bower, 41. He remarked: "a hierarchy is an extremely familiar and ef cient organizational scaffold." Gordon H. Bower, "Organizational Factors in memory," *Cognitive Psychology* 1 (1970), 18–46.
11. Terry Winograd, "Understanding Natural Language," *Cognitive Psychology* 3, no. 1 (1971), 1–191.
12. Stuart Russell and Peter Norvig, *Artificial Intelligence: A Modern Approach*, 2nd ed. Upper Saddle River, NJ: Prentice Hall, 2003.
13. Michael R. Garey and David S. Johnson, *Computers and Intractability: A Guide to the Theory of NP-Completeness*. New York: W.II. Freeman, 1979.
14. Ibid., p. 8.
15. For a good introduction to the theory of NP-completeness see Garey and Johnson. See also S. A. Cook, "The Complexity of Theorem-Proving Procedures," in *Proceedings New York: ACM of the 3rd Annual ACM Symposium on Theory of Computing*.

New York: ACM, (1971), pp. 151–158; and R. M. Karp, "Reducibility Among Combinatorial Problems, in *Complexity of Computer Computations*. New York: Plenum Press, 1972, pp. 85–103.

16. For more details on explanatory power see Robbie T. Nakatsu, "Explanatory Power of Intelligent Systems," in *Intelligent Decision-Making Support Systems: Foundations, Applications and Challenges*. London: Springer, 2006, pp. 123–143.

17. The framework for these interface characteristics is borrowed and adapted from Marilyn Stelzner and Michael D. Williams, "The Evolution of Interface Requirements for Expert Systems," in *Expert Systems: The User Interface*. Ablex Pub. Corp.: Norwood, NJ, 1988, pp. 285–305.

18. Donald A.Norman, *The Design of Everyday Things*. New York: Basic Books, 2002, pp. 1–9.

19. A. P. Jagodzinski, Theoretical Basis for the Representation of On-Line Computer Systems to Naïve Users, *International Journal of Man-Machine Studies*, 18, no. 3 (1983), 215–252.

CHAPTER 2

MENTAL MODELS: DIAGRAMS IN THE MIND'S EYE

The notion of mental models has great intuitive appeal. The idea that we create and "run" internal models in our minds when we interact with the real world seems grounded in commonsense experience. Imagine, for example, any complex system or phenomenon that you may have encountered during your lifetime: an automobile, spreadsheet software, a computer, an economic theory of in a-tion, the political environment of the company you work for. To develop a deep understanding of these systems, you require some kind of internal representation, one that you can simulate in your mind's eye. Such a representation can help you predict how the system will behave under a wide variety of circumstances. Otherwise, without a mental model, you would be very limited in your interactions with the real world. Kenneth Craik expressed it well when he wrote in 1943:

> If the organism carries a "small-scale model" of external reality and of its own possible actions within its head, it is able to try out various alternatives, conclude which is the best of them, react to future situations before they arise, utilize the knowledge of past events in dealing with the present and future, and in every way to react in a much fuller, safer, and more competent manner to the emergencies which face it.[1]

In this chapter we explore what is meant by mental models, and why they are useful and relevant to what we are studying—namely, the design of dynamic diagrams and representations. We look at several examples of how they are used by human problem solvers. This understanding should provide us with guidance on how to design intelligent user interfaces in which a diagram plays a central role. A central theme of this chapter is that a diagram of some kind can foster the appropriate development of a mental model of a complex system.

A de nition of mental models would be useful before we proceed any further in our discussion. In this chapter, *mental models* is used in a narrow sense to mean an internal representation of knowledge or expertise about a system. In this sense, there is a surprising similarity and overlap in the de nitions that various cognitive scientists have offered. One de nition of a mental model is "knowledge of how the system works, what its components are, how they are related, what the internal processes are, and how they affect the components."[2] Another de nition is given by the following: "A mental model is a collection of 'connected' autonomous objects. Running a mental model corresponds to modifying the parameters of the model by propagating information using the internal rules and speci ed topology."[3] Both de nitions use the notion of interconnectedness of components of a system, a notion that is further developed later on in the chapter.

Important in the both de nitions is the notion of one having the ability to run a mental model. A mental model, according to this perspective, is not a static structure but a dynamic one that can be modi ed accordingly for a speci c context and situation. Parameter passing and propagation are the mechanisms that allow a mental model to be used in an adaptable manner. The prediction of future states or the prediction of how a system will respond to a novel situation may be implemented through these mechanisms. The expression "simulating the machine (or system) in the mind's eye" captures this idea well.

Why do people use mental models? First, they are used as inference tools to predict the behavior of a system under novel conditions. They enable us to predict system outcomes from system parameters: We may run our mental model by modifying the system parameters and observing how the behavior of the system changes. Second, mental models can be used to produce explanations and justi cations. Such explanations may give us con dence in using the system and enable us to more readily trust the results of the system. Third, mental models can be used as mnemonic devices to facilitate remembering and long-term retention of information. Here, a mental model may provide one with a "cover story" to make the understanding of the system more memorable and easier to recall.

Underlying these three reasons, is the assumption that we use mental models for system understanding: "The psychological core of understanding, I shall assume, consists in your having a 'working model' of the phenomenon in your mind."[4] Hence a mental model enables a user to develop a deeper understanding of a system, which a user may consciously or unconsciously choose to use when interacting with a system. Such deep understanding helps with prediction, explanation, and long-term retention and, therefore, can enhance the problem-solving capabilities of users.

In this chapter, we distinguish a mental model from a conceptual model, which is typically represented by a diagram of some kind.[5] We look at examples of conceptual models, represented diagrammatically, later on in the chapter. A mental model is the user's model of a target system; it is a model of a system that exists in a person's head. Through interaction with a complex system, it is a naturally evolving model. As a person develops more experience with a system, the model develops and becomes more re ned. Hence, at any given point in time, the mental model, as seen through the eyes of the user, is a dynamic, usually incomplete speci cation of the target system. A conceptual model, on the other hand, is typically the designer's complete speci cation of a target system. As such, it is intended to be an accurate, consistent, and complete representation of a target system. Ideally, we would want the user's mental model to be the same as the system designer's conceptual model.

Many of the experimental studies that have investigated mental models report on how users often develop mental models that are ill-formed: They are typically incomplete, incorrect, inconsistent, unstable in time, and oftentimes rife with superstition. For example, one study looked at the mental models of people using calculators.[6] Users would frequently have a distrust of some of the calculator features, even when they were fully aware of their existence. Often, they would take extra steps or fail to take advantage of a calculator's features. For example, they would repeatedly clear the display (sometimes hitting the clear button several times) or write down partial results on a piece of paper, even when they were aware that intermediate results could be stored in the calculator's memory.

Another experimental study[7] showed that users' mental models evolve over time. This study investigated the mental models that individuals developed in trying to understand and justify the behavior of a simple heat exchanger, a device used to cool down a hot uid. In the think-aloud protocols,* one subject appeared to develop a series of three progressively more powerful models. Each succeeding model made more predictions than the preceding model and provided more nearly correct predictions where the prior model failed. The subject appeared to be driven by questions from the experimenter to produce partially correct system models that could account for only the phenomenon observed. When the subject was unable to answer a question, a new and more comprehensive model was constructed to account for the unexplained behavior.

This experimental investigation illustrates that a mental model is a dynamic construct. Over time and with more exposure to a system, a person can develop progressively more powerful mental models. (Conversely, with disuse or misuse of a system, a mental model may deteriorate). The development of a mental model, then, can be chronicled, much like the development of a cognitive skill. Three developmental processes[8] seem to be at play when a mental model evolves. First, *generalization* means that mental model becomes more powerful because it works for a wider variety of situations. Second, *discrimination* means that a mental model is more sensitive to variations in a given situation so that a mental model may add an important new condition where previously it had been overlooked. Third, *strengthening* means that those aspects of a mental model that

---

*This technique is frequently employed in studies attempting to capture mental models. It requires that the subject verbalize his or her thought processes while engaged in a problem-solving task (concurrent verbalizations).

have been successfully applied in the past are strengthened and rendered more salient and signi cant.

How are mental models developed and shaped by individuals? Sometimes a complete and accurate mental model is hard, if not impossible, to come by. Einstein and Infeld liken the acquisition of a mental model to a person trying to understand the mechanism of a closed watch:

> In our endeavour to understand reality we are somewhat like a man trying to understand the mechanism of a closed watch. He sees the face and the moving hands, even hears its ticking, but he has no way of opening the case. If he is ingenious he may form some picture of a mechanism which could be responsible for all the things he observes.[9]

Indeed, it may very well be the case that most individuals will never acquire an appropriate mental model: The system under consideration, much like the proverbial closed watch, is impenetrable and not visible for inspection. Such individuals must content themselves with having but a shallow understanding of the system. That kind of understanding may suf ce for most purposes. On the other hand, mental models can be actively constructed and acquired by the learner. Through personal observation, trial and error, other people's explanations, and one's simple ability to construct models for oneself either from a set of basic components or from analogous models that one may already internally possess, a person is able to create and develop his or her own mental models.[10]

In contrast to the active learning view, or the idea that individuals will proactively construct their own mental models, is the approach of being explicitly provided with a conceptual model of the system to be understood. This approach is the one advocated by this book. In this chapter we will see a number of examples of diagrammatic aids that serve as conceptual models for a system. Such diagrams may aid a user in attempting to learn how to better understand a system—in effect, to develop a richer mental model, and in a shorter amount of time, than by way of the active learning approach. Furthermore, as the research in mental models amply illustrates, learners, left to their own devices, will often develop highly inappropriate mental models.

THE ORGANIZATION OF KNOWLEDGE

In attempting to de ne and delineate the domain known as mental models, many researchers have noted with frustration that *mental models* is a fuzzy concept, lacking a core set of de ning features, and widely agreed-on constructs. To their dismay, mental models seems to take on a variety of incarnations and names in the literature: cognitive mappings, conceptual frameworks, schemata, scripts, semantic networks, generalized knowledge, analogical representations, and here's an interesting one, ideational scaffolding (just to name a few of the monikers that researchers have employed). As a result, the concept of mental models appears confusing and incoherent. Collaboration among the different disciplines is dif - cult because terminology has different meanings, depending on where you are coming from and who you are talking to.

Although it is undoubtedly true that many have used the term *mental models* rather loosely without a clear understanding of what it means, there have also been remarkable similarities in the way that researchers have de ned and used the term. One important theme that emerges is that a mental model can organize knowledge in some meaningful way. As many of the studies have demonstrated, without a meaningful representation of knowledge, the human mental processing system would be incapable of making sense of a complex system. An effective organization of knowledge allows one to comprehend complexity and to more effectively use a system in novel ways.

In this section, we focus on how mental models organize knowledge in a complex domain. In particular, we look at how mental models interconnect the components of a complex system, to help us better understand it. To organize the discussion, two types of interconnections will be considered: **Internal connections** are the links among the components of a complex system; **external connections** refer to the links between an individual's prior knowledge and a complex target system to be understood.[11]

Internal Connections

The experimental studies of Kieras and Bovair (1984)[12] on how to operate a device provide a good example of how problem solvers employ mental models involving internal connections. This study illustrates well some of the basic ideas underlying mental models. Kieras and Bovair devised a simple control panel of a device that consisted of a toggle switch, a three-position rotary selector switch, two push buttons, and four indicator lights (to give the individual an indication of what state the device was in). See Figure 2.1 for a sketch of the control panel. The control panel was presented on a computer screen, and the computer monitored

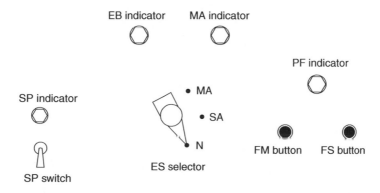

Figure 2.1. Sketch of the control panel of the device. Adapted from Endnote 12.

the settings of the switches and push buttons. The device was   ctitious, and its operation was simulated on a computer.

Two groups of subjects (40 subjects total, 20 in each group) learned a set of procedures on how to operate the device. The *device model group* was provided with a description of how the components of the system were interconnected (i.e., the device model). The *rote group* received no model training, but learned how to operate the device by rote.

Figure 2.2 shows the diagram that was provided to the subjects in the device model group. In addition they were provided with written materials that described what process acted on the components of the device. An excerpt of the written materials follows:

The energy booster takes in power from the ship and boosts it to the level necessary to   re the phasers. Power that has been boosted by the energy booster is fed into the two accumulators. Both accumulators store large amounts of power ready to be discharged to the phaser bank whenever the phasers are   red.

Because the accumulators handle such large amounts of power, if they are used continuously they are liable to overload and burn out. To prevent continuous use of one accumulator, the system has two: the main accumulator (MA) and the secondary accumulator (SA).

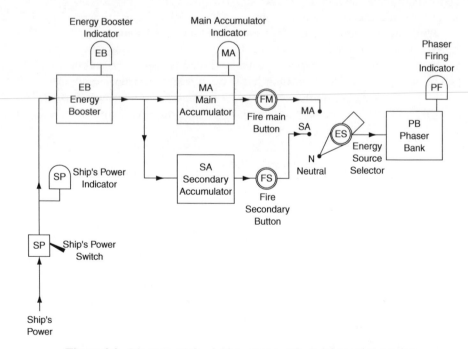

Figure 2.2. Diagram of the device model. Adapted from Endnote 12.

The power coming in from the shipboard circuits is controlled by the ship's power (SP). When this switch is off, no power is being drawn from the ship. When the switch is turned on, power is drawn from the ship into the energy booster. The boosted power is then fed into the accumulators. The accumulator whose energy will be discharged to the phaser banks is selected by the energy source selector (ES). While the ES selector is set to neutral (N), no energy can be discharged from either accumulator to the phaser bank.[13]

These materials provide a description of how the components of the device relate to one another and how the controls on the device panel regulate the ow of energy from one component to another. Moreover, the materials were related in a fantasy context—namely described in terms of a phaser bank from the *Starship Enterprise* (from the television series *Star Trek*).

Both groups of subjects received exactly the same training on the operating procedures. They were given instruction on both normal and malfunction procedures. For example, a normal procedure included the following steps: Turn SP switch on, set ES selector to MA (or SA), press button FM (or FS), wait until PF indicator nishes ashing, set ES selector to N, turn SP off. After learning the normal procedures, subject were told that the device would sometimes malfunction and could be made to work using an alternative procedure (i.e., a malfunction procedure). One example of a malfunction is that in some situations the PF indicator would not ash, so subjects were instructed to shut down the system by setting the ES indicator to N and turning the SP switch off. Some of the procedures, both normal and malfunction, were intentionally designed to be inef cient. By including such procedures, it was possible to test whether subjects would be able to short-cut the inef cient procedures.

As expected and hypothesized, the device model group outperformed the rote group on all measures. Table 2.1 summarizes the experimental results. All results reported are statistically signi cant at or beyond the. 05 level. First, subjects in the model group learned the procedures faster than subjects in the rote group. Second, a retention test was given to subjects after all procedures were learned and 1 week after the experiment to test for long-term retention. In both cases, subjects in the model group remembered more about device operation than did subjects in the rote group. Third, subjects in the model group short-cut inef cient procedures four times more often than did subjects in the rote group. Finally, the model group executed procedures signi cantly faster.

A second experiment, conducted with a different set of subjects, also employed a device model group and a rote group. In this experiment, however, subjects were not instructed on procedures. Instead they were asked to infer the procedures. The experimenter prompted the subjects to think out loud while performing this task, with all statements and activities of the subject recorded on videotape. Again, the device model group performed signi cantly better. Through trial and error, the rote group subjects tried a very large number of actions on their rst attempt to infer the procedures. By contrast, almost all of the device model subjects inferred the correct procedures on their rst attempt. Clearly, the device model facilitated the task of inferring procedures.

Table 2.1. Summary of Results on Learning Procedures with and without a Device Model

	Group		
	Rote	Model	Improvement
Mean device model training time (s)	—	1141	—
Mean procedure training time (s)	270	194	28%
Mean correct procedure retention (over all tests)	67%	80%	19%
Mean correct retention after 1 week	71%	78%	11%
Proportion of short-cuts	8%	40%	400%
Mean execution time of retained instructed procedures (s)	20.1	16.8	17%

Adapted from Endnote 12.

A third experiment con rmed that it was information about the system topology (knowledge of how components are interconnected and the how power ows through the system) rather than the fantasy context given to the device model group that facilitated inference of procedures. The condition that Kieras and Bovair wanted to test in this experiment was whether placing the device in a stimulating and interesting context (i.e., through the use of the *Star Trek* story) was an important factor in helping subjects to infer the procedures. They employed a 2 × 2 factorial design experiment,* with the two factors being the presence or absence of a fantasy context and the presence or absence of a device model. The results revealed that being provided with the device model is what facilitated inference, not the provision of the fantasy context. In a later section, however, we will look at an experimental study that shows how providing a meaningful context to a problem can improve problem-solving performance.

The Kieras and Bovair studies demonstrate, in a convincing way, that having an appropriate mental model can help users understand complex systems and interact with them more effectively. Although the system is a very simple toy device, the study was effective in conveying just what kind of mental model facilitates problem-solving performance. (Many other experimental studies involving more complex domains have failed to demonstrate signi cant and conclusive results). In addition, their study succeeds in demonstrating what kind of diagram and what kind of associated descriptive information is useful for developing an appropriate mental model. An important result was that having knowledge about internal connections, or how one component is connected to another (system topology), was critical for enhancing problem solving. But that by itself was not enough. The device model group was also provided with knowledge of power

---

*The 2 × 2 factorial design, in effect, creates four conditions: (1) device model, fantasy context; (2) device model, no fantasy context; (3) no device model, fantasy context; and (4) no device model, no fantasy context. The device model, fantasy context is the same as the device model group in experiment 1 and the no device model, no fantasy context is the same as the rote model group in experiment 1.

ow, information related to how power ows through the system topology, and information on how users could manipulate the controls in the model to control power ow. In short, the device model was useful only to the extent that it provided information to support inferences about how to use the system. (One can easily imagine that some device models would be useless in that they convey information that is super cial and incomplete or do not support a user's needs very well.)

A Mental Model of an Electromechanical Thermostat. Let's take a look at a more realistic example, a device more familiar to us, a typical home thermostat. This device is used to maintain a room temperature so that it turns on the heater whenever the temperature falls below a certain set level and will likewise turn on the air-conditioner whenever the temperature rises above a certain set level. Without a mental model of the thermostat, the device is a black box, and one can understand it only on the most super cial level. Most end users are probably quite content having just this super cial understanding, so long as the device performs according to expectation. For them, knowledge about how user actions (e.g., adjust temperature up, adjust temperature down) map to system behaviors (e.g., heater on, air-conditioner on) should suf ce in most cases.

More curious users may seek a deeper understanding of the thermostat. As a rst step, such an individual may attempt to gain insight about the device by looking under the hood, so to speak, and taking the device apart. See Figure 2.3 for the three main pieces of a typical electromechanical thermostat. Below the cover is the top layer, which contains the mercury switch and thermometer coil. The bottom layer contains the circuit card. Unfortunately, unless one possesses prior knowledge of similar devices and components, it is extremely dif cult to infer how the device works. If an individual is mechanically minded and ingenious enough, he or she might experiment with the device to observe what happens when the thermostat settings are adjusted and manipulated. For most of us without prior knowledge of such devices, it would be very dif cult, if not impossible, to acquire a suitable mental model by self-experimentation and observation of the device alone.

A diagram or pictorial representation could greatly aid in understanding, but a picture by itself is often dif cult to comprehend (a picture often does *not* paint a thousand words!). A more effective strategy would be to provide a pictorial representation, together with descriptive information. One technique would be to annotate a picture with the descriptive information and to associate the descriptions with locations on the picture itself. Such a technique is illustrated in Figure 2.4.

In this picture, the components of the device are appropriately labeled A, B, and C to denote the main components of the thermostat. The descriptive text is broken into six callouts, or boxes, each of which references a different part of the picture and tells one part of the story. The callouts are meant to provide a kind of running narrative to the device, meant to be read sequentially, in clockwise order from callout 1 to callout 6, as a way to understand how the components of the

Figure 2.3. Three pieces of an electromechanical thermostat. Image provided courtesy of howstuffworks.com.

device causally interact to turn on the heater. Much of the description involves relating how the action of one component affects a neighboring component. For example in callout 1, the sentence "When the lever is adjusted upward (i.e., temperature is set higher), it rotates the coil to the right" describes how the action of adjusting the temperature affects the coil. Callout 3 describes how rotating the coil, in turn, affects its neighboring component: "When the coil is rotated to the right, the mercury switch, which is attached to the coil, tips to the right, and the mercury thereby makes contact with the right wire." Hence the text provides a description of a cascading series of events in which one action (adjusting the lever) results in a series of causal events until, ultimately, the heater is activated and turned on.

In Figure 2.4, not all of the textual description is about causal knowledge in the form *If A occurs, Then B occurs*. Some of it is purely descriptive, to give the novice user an understanding of the underlying physics of the device, and to provide a rationale for why the device does what it is supposed to do. For example, callout 2 describes a mercury switch (this component by itself could be modeled as a device containing four components—namely, the mercury and the three wires). It is a smaller device within a larger device. Later, in callout

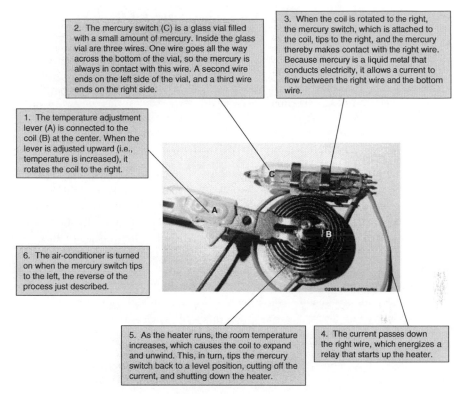

2. The mercury switch (C) is a glass vial filled with a small amount of mercury. Inside the glass vial are three wires. One wire goes all the way across the bottom of the vial, so the mercury is always in contact with this wire. A second wire ends on the left side of the vial, and a third wire ends on the right side.

3. When the coil is rotated to the right, the mercury switch, which is attached to the coil, tips to the right, and the mercury thereby makes contact with the right wire. Because mercury is a liquid metal that conducts electricity, it allows a current to flow between the right wire and the bottom wire.

1. The temperature adjustment lever (A) is connected to the coil (B) at the center. When the lever is adjusted upward (i.e., temperature is increased), it rotates the coil to the right.

6. The air-conditioner is turned on when the mercury switch tips to the left, the reverse of the process just described.

5. As the heater runs, the room temperature increases, which causes the coil to expand and unwind. This, in turn, tips the mercury switch back to a level position, cutting off the current, and shutting down the heater.

4. The current passes down the right wire, which energizes a relay that starts up the heater.

Figure 2.4. How an electromechanical thermostat works. Image provided courtesy of howstuffworks.com.

3, the user learns that mercury is a liquid metal that conducts electricity. Such information furnishes the user with the mental model that when the glass vial tips to the right, the mercury touches the right wire and the bottom wire at the same time, and therefore, the current is able to pass through both wires.

This account of the type of mental model a person might form of the thermostat, is stated rather loosely and informally. It would be useful to understand how these ideas of internal connections and causality could be applied and generalized to other domains, be they simple devices, more complex devices, or abstract systems (e.g., having a causal model of what macroeconomic forces in uence in ation). We need some kind of formalism, or a set of rules and guidelines, on how to capture and document mental models so that system structure and causal knowledge are rendered more explicit. Indeed, without such a formalism, a person's mental model could easily devolve into vagueness and fuzziness. By making a person's mental model as explicit as possible, we can openly criticize it, and devise ways to make it more accurate and complete.

We rst consider system structure (also known as system topology), which is typically rendered as a diagrammatic conceptual model of some kind that shows what the components are and how they are interconnected. De Kleer and Brown state it well when they describe the topology of a machine:

> A machine consists of constituents. Some of these constituents represent parts which themselves can be viewed as smaller machines (e.g., resistors, valves, boilers). Other constituents represent connections (e.g., pipes, wires, cables) through which the parts communicate by transmitting information. These connections can be thought of as conduits through which "stuff" ows, its ow captured by conduit laws.[14]

The conceptual model of the electromechanical thermostat is shown in Figure 2.5. There are ve component parts represented in this diagram: temperature adjustment lever, coil, mercury switch, air-conditioner, and heater. In this diagram, ellipses are used to represent components of the thermostat itself, and rectangles are used to represent components external to the thermostat, in this case the air-conditioner and the heater (one can use different shapes to represent the different types of components). In addition, there are two connections, a left wire that connects the mercury switch to the air-conditioner, and a right wire that connects the mercury switch to the heater. We also model temperature because this variable will in uence the state the coil is in. These connections (indicated by a solid line) represent conduits through which an electrical current ows. The dotted lines, by contrast, are not actual physical conduits (i.e., "stuff" does not ow between these components) but indicate that a component affects a neighboring component. For example, the temperature adjustment lever is attached to

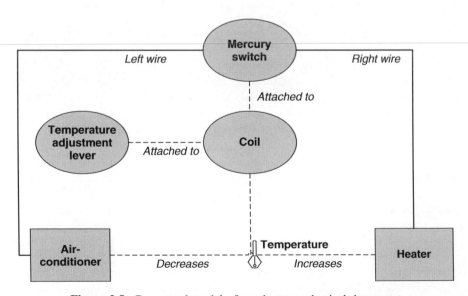

Figure 2.5. Conceptual model of an electromechanical thermostat.

the coil, and the air-conditioner and heater both affect the coil by changing the room temperature. The temperature itself is represented by a thermometer icon.*

The conceptual model of the device shows the physical organization of its components but does not determine the device behavior. For this, we need to create a causal model that expresses how the components causally interact to produce the device behaviors. Determining how the device behaves from its structure requires that we have an understanding of how each component acts individually. Equipped with this knowledge, we can piece together the speci c local behaviors of each component part, and how they interact with a neighboring component. Our mental model will be a series of such component interactions.

First, we need to de ne each component part in the model. The notation that we will use to describe each component part takes the following form:

```
<component>
      <state 1>:  <rule A>
                  <rule B>
                    . . .
      <state 2>:  <rule A>
                  <rule B>
                    . . .


      <state n>:  <rule A>
                  <rule B>
                    . . .
```

The rst step in de ning a component part is to de ne all possible states that the part can assume. Because we are dealing with mental models, the states should be qualitative values such as *increasing, decreasing, high, average, and low*. Our mental models should not use precise quantitative values and complex mathematical calculations because they should be easy enough to run in our mind's eye. Given the human limitations on short-term memory capacity, a mental model that uses ne-grained distinctions could easily bog down even the most expert individuals. In our thermostat example, the coil assumes four states: rotates-left, rotates-right, expands, and contracts. The mercury switch assumes three states: level, tips-left, and tips-right.

The rule portion of the component description speci es an IF–THEN rule that indicates how the component will reach that state. The IF part of the rule (the antecedent) provides the conditions under which the component reaches the given state, while the THEN part of the rule (the consequent) speci es the state

---

*The conceptual model of the electromechanical thermostat depicted in Figure 2.5 is a simpli cation of the physical organization of a thermostat. It does not show how the mercury switch works (one could create a separate conceptual model for this component alone), nor does it show how the wires connect to the circuit card, relays, and other components that play a role in turning on the heater and air-conditioner.

itself. For example, if the temperature adjustment lever is adjusted downward, then the coil will rotate to the left. This is expressed by the rule: IF temperature-adjustment-lever down THEN coil rotates left. Conditions in the antecedent and the state reached in the consequent are expressed in the form <component state> as in <temperature-adjustment-lever down> and <coil rotates-left> in the preceding rule.

One important point to note about this rule is that it is expressed based on the state of a neighboring component. The *principle of locality*, an important concept in the speci cation of a causal model, means that a component in a model can causally interact only with its neighboring components, so that, for example, it would not be possible to state a rule such that the *coil* affects the state of the *left wire* because these two components are not directly connected to one another. *The conditions in the antecedent must refer to neighboring components only*.

The one exception to this notation is in the speci cation of the temperature adjustment lever rules. This is because the temperature adjustment lever is an **active device component**. This means that the only way that the state of this component changes is when a human user manipulates the component. A user can adjust the lever either upward or downward to change the component's state. All the other components in the thermostat are passive because their states are always determined by the states of their neighboring components.

The full causal model for the thermostat follows. It consists of total of seven components— ve component parts, plus two connections. Because temperature also in uences the device, it is also included in the causal model.

```
Temperature-adjustment-lever
     up:
            IF (user adjusts the lever upwards)* THEN
               temperature-adjustment-lever up
     down:
            IF (user adjusts the lever downwards)* THEN
               temperature-adjustment-lever down


Coil
     rotates-left:
            IF temperature-adjustment-lever down THEN
               coil rotates-left
     rotates-right:
            IF temperature-adjustment-lever up THEN
               coil rotates-right
     expands:
            IF temperature increases THEN
```

*This antecedent refers to a human user intervention. The only way the state of the temperature adjustment lever changes is when a human user adjusts it upward or downward.

```
                  coil expands
      contracts:
            IF temperature decreases THEN
            coil contracts
```

Mercury-switch

```
    tips-left:
            IF mercury-switch level AND coil contracts THEN
            mercury-switch tips-left
            IF mercury-switch level AND coil rotates-left THEN
            mercury-switch tips-left


    tips-right:
            IF mercury-switch level AND coil expands THEN
            mercury-switch tips-right
            IF mercury-switch level AND coil rotates-right THEN
            mercury-switch tips-right


    level:
            IF mercury-switch tips-left AND coil contracts THEN
            mercury-switch level
            IF mercury-switch tips-left AND coil rotates-right THEN
            mercury-switch level
            IF mercury-switch tips-right AND coil expands THEN
            mercury-switch level
            IF mercury-switch tips-right AND coil rotates-left THEN
            mercury-switch level
```

Left-wire

```
    on:
            IF mercury-switch tips-left THEN
            left-wire on
    off:
            IF mercury-switch level OR mercury-switch tips-right THEN
            left-wire off
```

Right-wire

```
    on:
            IF mercury-switch tips-right THEN
            right-wire on
    off:
            IF mercury-switch level OR mercury-switch tips-left THEN
            right-wire off
```

Air-conditioner

```
    on:
            IF left-wire on THEN
            air-conditioner on
```

```
    off:
            IF left-wire off THEN
              air-conditioner off
Heater
    on:
            IF right-wire on THEN
              heater on
    off:
            IF right-wire off THEN
              heater off


Temperature
    increases:
            IF heater on THEN
              temperature increases
    decreases:
            IF air-conditioner on THEN
              temperature decreases
    neutral:
            IF heater off THEN
              temperature neutral†
            IF air-conditioner off THEN
              temperature neutral†
```

The mercury switch is perhaps the most interesting and complicated of the components described. It can assume three possible states: level, tips-right, and tips-left. In this model, we assume that the mercury switch can tip right or tip left only when it is in a level state (i.e., it cannot move directly from state tips-right to state tips-left, but must move rst from state tips-right to state level and then, from state level to state tips-left). The two rules for state tips-left signify that there are two ways in which the mercury switch can tip left if it is in a level state: The coil can contract or the coil can rotate to the left. Likewise, the two rules for state tips-right signify that there are two ways in which the mercury switch can tip right: The coil can expand or the coil can rotate to the right.

Now that we have speci ed a causal model of the thermostat with our chosen notation and formalism, we are ready to simulate the model to see how the thermostat would work under a variety of circumstances. The process begins with an input that produces some kind of disequilibrium in the device. We next observe how the input propagates in the causal model. One input would be to observe what happens when we turn the temperature lever upward. Running the causal model yields the following sequence of events:

1. Temperature-adjustment-lever up.

---

†We assume here that the outside air temperature does not in uence the temperature.

2. Coil rotates-right.
3. Mercury-switch tips-right (we assume here that the mercury switch is initially level).
4. Right-wire on.
5. Heater on.

Together these ve causal events describe what happens when we set the temperature level to a higher setting. We could continue the narrative to see what happens after the heater is turned on:

6. Temperature increases.
7. Coil expands.
8. Mercury-switch level.
9. Right-wire off.
10. Heater off.
11. Temperature neutral.

The second half of the narrative describes how the system reaches a state of equilibrium again. When the heater is turned on, the temperature increase, and eventually the coil expands enough until the mercury-switch is leveled, cutting off the current in the right wire and shutting down the heater.

In effect, what we have created is a kind of story explaining how the device operates when we set the temperature adjustment lever to a higher level. We have simulated a cascading series of causal interactions in the device that provides a coherent explanation for why the device behaved the way it did. Moreover, we can predict future behaviors of the device from this causal model. For example: What would happen when we set the temperature to a lower level? What would happen when the room temperature increases or decreases?

Let us summarize the components of a mental model and what makes it useful for problem solving. First, to acquire an appropriate mental model, we often require some kind of conceptual model, one that is typically rendered as a graphical diagram. This diagram provides information about system organization, by depicting system components and how they are interconnected to one another. Second, it helps to have information about domain principles, whether they involve the physics of a device, or theory that explains system behavior (i.e., provides a system rationale). In the thermostat example, we employed a picture together with textual description (callouts) associated with each component of the device, describing, for example, how mercury is a liquid metal that conducts electricity and therefore when it touches two wires at the same time, an electrical current is able to ow between the two wires.* Third, we created a causal model,

---

*We do not really need to have domain principles, but they provide a user with deeper system understanding. A causal model by itself provides us with a mechanistic mental model (how one component causes the behaviors of another component) but does not answer the question; Why did the component do what it did?

or a description of how the components causally interact with one another. In the formalism that we have chosen, we construct the causal model as a collection of IF–THEN rules that describe how a system component can reach different states. Finally, we run the mental model by introducing an input that produces some kind of disequilibrium in the system. By using the causal model we are able to determine how the disequilibrium sets off a cascading series of causal events that together describe system behavior.

The account of mental models described here is generalizable to a wide variety of applications and systems. We are not limited to describing physical devices such as the electromechanical thermostat, but we could just as easily describe mental models of more abstract systems. For example, we could create a conceptual model of how a federal bill gets passed into law by Congress and its likelihood of successful passage. Or we could create a conceptual model of how a manufacturing process works and what could go wrong. The notation described in this section would work equally well for both these situations.

External Connections

Whereas internal connections focus on the interconnections among the components of a complex system, external connections attempt to draw on a person's prior knowledge to understand a new target system. As we will see in this section, sometimes internal connections are not enough, and it is helpful to draw on a person's vast storehouse of prior knowledge to understand a complex system. Two issues will be addressed here: (1) the reframing of problems so that they are related in a more meaningful context, and (2) the use of analogical representations to facilitate the understanding of a complex target system or phenomenon.

Providing a Meaningful Context. Many experimental investigations have demonstrated that the way you frame a problem will have a large affect on how well individuals understand a problem. A good example is the Wason card selection task,[15] in which an experimenter lays out four cards on the table, displaying the following symbols:

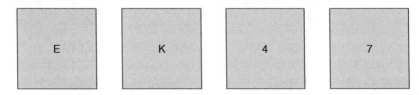

The experimenter then states the following rule: "If a card has a vowel on one side then it has an even number on the other side." The subject's task is to turn over only those cards that are necessary to determine whether the rule is true or false. (The reader is advised to perform this task before reading any further).

Although the task is very easy to understand, most people have a hard time with it. The correct answer is that E and 7 should be turned over. Most people realize that E should be turned over: if it has an odd number on the other side, then the rule is disproved. Likewise, most people correctly realize that K does not need to be turned over. One common error is that some people turn over the 4. However, this too is unnecessary because even if the card contains a consonant on the other side, then the rule would still be unhurt. The most common error arises with the 7. Very few subjects elect to turn this card over, despite the fact that if the card has a vowel on the other side, then the rule is disproved.

A variation of this selection task was created in a study conducted by Johnson-Laird, Legrenzi, and Legrenzi in 1972.[16] The task was logically identical to the Wason card selection task except that it was framed in a more meaningful context. Subjects in this study were shown four envelopes: Envelope A was sealed and back facing, envelope B was unsealed with no stamp, and front facing, envelope C was front facing with a 5d stamp on it, and envelope D was front facing with a 4d stamp on it.

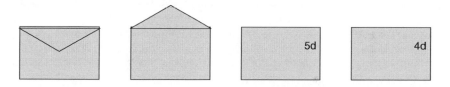

Subjects were asked to assess the rule: "If a letter is sealed, then it has a 5d stamp on it." Like the Wason task, the experimenter asked the subject to turn over only those envelopes which would validate or disprove the rule. The correct answer was that rst and fourth envelopes should be selected.

How did the subjects fare this time around? Whereas only 15% of the subjects correctly answered the problem in the original abstract Wason context, 81% of the subjects correctly answered the problem correctly when framed in the envelope context. These results strongly suggest that providing a more meaningful and concrete context can facilitate one's problem solving and reasoning capabilities.

But there is one more twist to this problem. Many Americans, when faced with the envelope context, still have a hard time with this problem. In a follow-up to the envelope problem, Griggs and Cox noted that concrete materials are not enough to improve performance in the Wason card selection task.[17] They conducted a study in which American students, who were unfamiliar with British postal rules, performed no better using the envelope context than the abstract Wason context. In an attempt to show the importance of familiarity with the context, they devised yet another card selection task that a typical American might be more familiar with.

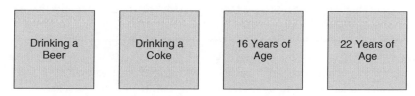

In this task, students were told that on one side of a card is a person's age and on the other side is what the person is drinking. The rule to assess is: "If a person is drinking beer, then the person must be over 19 years of age." Subjects were asked to select the card or cards that de nitely need to be turned over to determine whether people are violating this rule. In this task, the American students were able to perform much better. (The correct answer is to select the rst and third cards.) In sum, the results of the envelope study and the drinking age problem together suggest that the concreteness of the materials, together with the familiarity with the materials (which can be culture based) will affect how well people are able to solve these problems.

Analogical Representations. Human problem solvers are constantly faced with novelty. In our daily lives, we must confront and deal with new problems and situations that we had never faced before. If it weren't for the ability of analogical reasoning, we might easily become overwhelmed by this perpetual novelty—every time we faced a new problem we would be required to start from scratch and problem solving would become painstakingly slow. Fortunately for us, the human mind is endowed with the ability to detect similarities between past experiences and new problems, and apply what is already known to the new situation. Analogical thinking, it turns out, is quite pervasive and often proceeds unconsciously in our everyday thinking.

What do we mean by *analogical thinking*? Can we de ne it more precisely, and how does it help us solve problems and understand complex phenomena? In this section we de ne analogical reasoning more precisely and look at examples of how it occurs. It turns out that there are several excellent examples of analogical thinking in the cognitive science literature. Our rst example will investigate how analogies can be used to understand science. Gentner and Gentner[18] look at how analogies can be employed to make the concepts of electricity clearer for novice learners. Our second example considers how a seemingly intractable problem can be solved if a suitable analogy is provided. Gick and Holyoak's study on the tumor problem[19] provides not only a memorable example of analogical problem solving but also moves us toward a more precise de nition of what analogy is. Both of these examples involve experimental studies that have become classics in the cognitive science literature.

Let us begin this discussion by providing a working de nition of analogy. When we use analogical representations to understand complex phenomena, we make inferences about how properties of something known can be applied to something unknown. Hence we make use of two domains of knowledge: a base domain and a target domain. The base domain, or source domain, is the area that we are familiar with, whereas the target domain is the new domain that we are attempting to understand.

The essence of analogical thinking is the transfer of knowledge from a base domain to a target domain by a process of mapping—that is, nding a set of one-to-one correspondences between the two domains of knowledge. We often employ such analogical thinking when it is dif cult to understand a system whose mechanism is invisible or cannot easily be inferred. A famous example is Rutherford's analogy between the solar system (base domain) and the structure of the atom (target domain): "The structure of an atom is like the solar system."[20] Because the structure of an atom is invisible to the human eye, and its structure is dif cult to infer, Rutherford creates a mental model of something more concrete and familiar to all of us. Like the planets of our solar system orbiting the sun, he creates a mental model of electrons orbiting a nucleus in an atom. We take it for granted today, but Rutherford's solar system model of an atom was revolutionary for its time:

> Prior to Rutherford the best model of the atom was J.J. Thomson's plum pudding which pictured it in a thin cloud of positive charges, with electrons dotted amongst it, like so many raisins in a plum pudding.
>
> Rutherford's experiments showed the pudding idea was wrong, replacing it with a solar system model. An incredibly dense positively charged nucleus lay at the centre which was tiny compared to the whole atom; like a postage stamp in a football eld.[21]

What are the mappings that Rutherford employs in this analogy? In terms of component mappings, Rutherford maps the sun to the nucleus of the atom and he maps the planets of the solar system map to the electrons of an atom. In addition, Rutherford creates *relational mappings*, or relationships in the base system that can be mapped to relationships in the target system (See Figure 2.6 below for some of the relational mappings that he creates.)

An important point to note about analogy is that it re ects structural similarity but not surface similarity.[22] Whereas structural similarity refers to the similarity in the relations among the components, surface similarity refers to similarity in attributes of the components. In our solar system atom example, we have structural similarity, as given by the relational mappings depicted in Figure 2.6, but

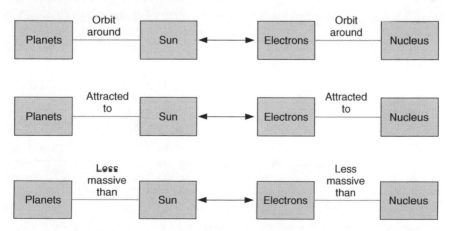

Figure 2.6. Relational mappings between solar system and hydrogen atom.

we certainly do not have surface similarity—the two domains deal with quite different objects (a sun has very different attributes from the nucleus of a hydrogen atom). Hence analogical representations can be drawn from vastly dissimilar domains—and indeed some of the most effective and powerful analogies are.

What makes for a good analogical representation? That depends, to a great extent, on who is using the representation and for what purpose. Obviously, the base domain must be understood by the user—if one does not have knowledge about the base source, the analogy is useless. Hence different people, depending on their levels of expertise, will understand analogies to varying degrees. Another important characteristic is the ability to draw attention to certain critical elements in a target domain. A useful analogy need not map every element to the target domain, but it certainly should map the important elements that require careful consideration. Again, different task situations will require different analogies, depending on what the problem solver wishes to focus on. Often, an obstacle in problem solving is the inability to attend to the relevant information in a problem. An analogy can help in this regard by making the less salient more salient or the less visible more visible.

It is interesting that qualities that make for good conceptual models, such as the type that describe the internal connections in a system, do not make for good analogies. Indeed, analogies are inherently open-ended, incomplete, and even indeterminate.[23] Returning to the solar system analogy of an atom, no one would ever mistake the solar system analogy to be a literal description of an atom. This is always the case in analogical reasoning: Relations between two dissimilar domains never map completely to one another. In fact, it is often the salient dissimilarities between the base and target domains that provoke thought and increase the usefulness of an analogy as a problem-solving tool.

This point underscores a fundamental difference between the function of conceptual models that depict internal connections and analogical representations that use mappings to prior knowledge. On the one hand, a conceptual model seeks to faithfully represent the components, the connections, the relations, and the processes that act on the components. On the other hand, a mental model that employs analogical representations is chosen to invite comparisons between two dissimilar domains, never to faithfully and completely represent the target domain.

Examples of Analogical Problem-Solving. Gentner and Gentner discuss electricity in analogical terms. The domain of electricity is a good illustration of how analogical reasoning can be used to teach novice learners its concepts. For one, it is a tractable phenomenon, one that is subject to the laws of physics. Second, because its mechanism is invisible, it is an ideal candidate for analogical thinking—that which we cannot observe, we might infer through something more familiar and visible to us.

Gentner and Gentner compare a hydraulic system to an electrical system. Because water and its properties are familiar to all of us, it is chosen as the base domain to make the concepts of electricity clearer. Their analogy draws a number of mappings between the two domains: Water ows through the pipes of a hydraulic system, just as electricity ows through the wires of an electrical system. A reservoir or pump is a source of water, just as a battery is a source of electricity. Voltage is the electrical force that moves the electrons through wires, just as water pressure is the force that moves the water through the pipes. Electrical current, which is the rate of electron ow, is analogous to water ow rate, as in liters of water that ow through a pipe per minute. Finally, resistance is the property of a resistor, a device that restricts electrical current, and this is analogous to narrowing a pipe to restrict water ow. Table 2.2 summarizes the mappings between a hydraulic system and an electrical circuit.

One function of this analogy is that it helps differentiate two related properties: electrical current and electrical pressure (voltage). As Gentner and Gentner point out, new learners of electricity often fail to differentiate between current and voltage; they seem to merge the two concepts into some kind of generalized strength concept. The hydraulic system analogy can serve to help novices better understand the difference: Electrical current is analogous to the amount of water that passes a point per unit time, whereas electrical pressure is analogous to the forced exerted by the water on the pipes per unit area. In learning a new domain, novices often mix up such related concepts. Hence an important function of analogical thinking is that it provides one with a mental model to make more salient the differences among concepts that may appear similar and confusing to novice learners.

In addition to these mappings, the water analogy can also facilitate understanding of the relationships among current, voltage, and resistance. Just as water ows through a hydraulic system due to a pressure difference produced by a reservoir, electrons ow through an electrical circuit because of a voltage difference produced by a battery. Ohm's law expresses the relationships as the following equation:

$$I = \frac{V}{R}$$

where I = current, V = voltage, and R = resistance.

Table 2.2. Mappings between Hydraulic System and Electrical Circuit

Base Domain: Hydraulic System	Target Domain: Electrical Circuit
Object Mappings	
Pipe (conduit)	Wire (conduit)
Reservoir (source)	Battery (source)
Narrow pipe	Resistor
Property Mappings	
Water pressure	Voltage (V)
Water ow rate	Electrical current (I)
Narrowness of pipe	Resistance (R)

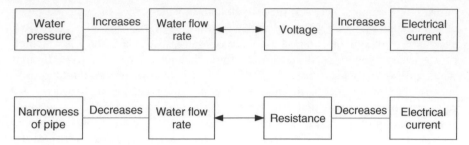

Figure 2.7. Relational mappings between hydraulic system and electrical circuit.

A very simple way to understand the relationships expressed in this law is by understanding the following: "More force, more ow. More drag, less ow." In other words, current is directly proportional to voltage and inversely proportional to resistance. The relational mappings between the hydraulic system and electrical system are given in Figure 2.7.

Up to this point, we have created a very simple conceptual model for the naive learner of electricity. How can we extend our analogical reasoning to cover more complex cases, and promote a deeper understanding of electricity? In fact, this is what Gentner and Gentner wanted to accomplish. Speci cally, they wanted to teach novices about more complex electrical circuits through the use of more sophisticated analogies. To do so, they looked at ve different types of electrical circuits (Figure 2.8).

In a simple circuit, there is one battery and one resistor (Figure 2.8a). What would happen if an additional battery or an additional resistor were added to an electrical circuit? More to the point, what would happen to electrical current—would it increase, decrease, or stay the same? This was the question that was posed to novice learners of electricity to test their understanding of the arrangement of components in an electrical circuit. The answer to the question, it turns out, depends on how the components are arranged—whether in serial arrangement, one on top of the other (as in Figure 2.8b and 2.8d) or in parallel arrangement, side by side (as in Figure 2.8c, 2.8e).

Understanding the serial combinations are relatively straightforward: two batteries arranged serially would lead to more current, and two resistors arranged serially would lead to less current. This prediction would follow even if one possessed only a naive understanding of electrical circuits—this is in line with the observation "more force, more ow; more drag, less ow."

However, this naive understanding would be insuf cient in understanding the behaviors of the parallel arrangements. In the case of the parallel arrangement of the batteries, the current does not change, and in the case of the parallel arrangement of the resistors, the current actually doubles. How then does one explain these results, which may appear counter intuitive to naive learners of electricity? Gentner and Gentner postulated that the use of two different mental

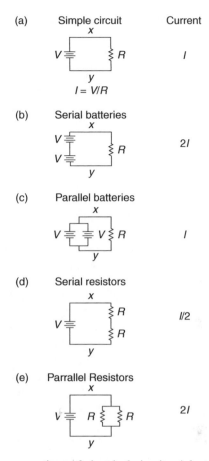

Figure 2.8. Five con gurations of electrical circuits. Adapted from Endnote 18.

models (the water model, and a new model) would help to explain separately the behaviors of the batteries versus that of the resistors.

First, in the case of the batteries, they further developed the water analogy by considering how two reservoirs, one stacked on top of the other, would affect water pressure. They write:

> Consider what happens when two reservoirs are connected in series, one on top of the other. Because the pressure produced by the reservoirs is determined by the height of the water and height has doubled, two reservoirs in series produce *twice* the original pressure, and thus *twice* the original ow rate.[24]

They further reasoned that if two reservoirs are connected in parallel, the height would not be changed. Therefore, because water pressure depends on height (not on total amount of water), the water pressure and water ow rate would remain unchanged. By mapping this result to the electrical circuit, two serial batteries would double electrical current, but two parallel batteries would have no effect on electrical current.

Second, a completely different analogy was employed to explain the behaviors of the resistors. In this case, they likened electrical current as masses of objects moving through passageways, which they refer to as the moving-crowd model. In one version of the moving-crowd model, they describe the electrons as cars moving on a highway:

> If you increase resistance in the circuit, the current slows down. Now that's like a highway, cars on a highway where . . . as you close down a lane . . . the cars move slower through the narrow point.[25]

Using this model, the behaviors of the resistors can easily be explained. In the serial case, that is much like having the cars travel down a single highway in which they must pass through two narrow sections, thus traf c ow rate is decreased by half. In the parallel case, the traf c ow splits into two separate highways, thus doubling the traf c ow.

In an experimental study[26] conducted on 36 high school and college students, all of whom were screened so that they were fairly naive about electricity, Gentner and Gentner tested whether one analogy would be more effective than the other in their understanding of electrical circuits As predicted, the participants who used the hydraulics model performed better on understanding the battery arrangements, whereas the participants who used the moving crowd model performed better on understanding the resistor arrangements. The results of this study provide evidence that people can make use of analogies to help them understand complex domains. In addition, the results support the contention that it is bene cial to use more than one analogy, because some analogies are better than others at emphasizing speci c aspects of a problem.

A second example of analogical reasoning is provided by Gick and Holyoak.[27] They pose a seemingly intractable problem:

> Suppose you are a doctor faced with a patient who has a malignant tumor in his stomach. It is impossible to operate on the patient, but unless the tumor is destroyed the patient will die. There is a kind of ray that can be used to destroy the tumor. If the rays reach the tumor all at once at suf ciently high intensity, the tumor will be destroyed. At lower intensities the rays are harmless to healthy tissue, but they will not affect the tumor either.[28]

The difference between this problem and the electrical circuit problems described earlier is that this problem is more ill-structured and complex, and a solution is not readily forthcoming. Indeed, it is not readily apparent whether there is even a solution at all. Most problem solvers faced with this seemingly impossible problem will need some guidance. One approach would be to provide an analogy that might spark an insight into how to approach the problem. Let's look at an analogous problem that is intended to shed some light on the problem:

A small country fell under the iron rule of a dictator. The dictator ruled the country from a strong fortress. The fortress was situated in the middle of the country, surrounded by farms and villages. Many roads radiated outward from the fortress like spokes on a wheel. A great general arose who raised a large army at the border and vowed to capture the fortress and free the country of the dictator. The general knew that if his entire army could attack the fortress at once it could be captured. His troops were posed at the head of one of the roads leading to the fortress, ready to attack. However, a spy brought the general a disturbing report. The ruthless dictator had planted mines on each of the roads. The mines were set so that small bodies of men could pass over them safely, since the dictator needed to be able to move troops and workers to and from the fortress. However, any large force would detonate the mines. Not only would this blow up the road and render it impassable, but the dictator would then destroy many villages in retaliation. A full-scale attack on the fortress therefore appeared impossible.[29]

Before we consider a solution to the tumor problem and its analogy, the military problem, let's consider how the two problems are similar in structure. That is, what kind of mappings can we create between the two stories? In Table 2.3, the mappings are described into three types: problem description, desired goal, and problem constraints. As illustrated in the mappings, the two stories, while drawn from vastly different domains, have a number of one-to-one correspondences. They both involve the destruction of an object located in the center of an area. In both cases, the use of a large force to destroy the object would be harmful to the surrounding area (on the one hand, destroying the healthy tissue surrounding the tumor, and on the other hand, detonating the mines surrounding the fortress). Because the two problems have similar structures, analogical thinking suggests that if we can nd a solution to the military problem, then we might be able to map that solution to the tumor problem.

One solution to the military problem, known as the dispersion solution, recommends that the general divide his troops into smaller groups and send them up multiple roads:

Table 2.3. Mappings between Tumor Problem and Military Problem

Tumor Problem	Military Problem
Problem Description	*Problem Description*
Patient has tumor	Country has dictator in fortress
Tumor surrounded by healthy tissue	Fortress in center of country
Desired Goal	*Desired Goal*
Destroy tumor with rays	Bombard fortress with army
Problem Constraints	*Problem Constraints*
Rays must be of high intensity to destroy tumor	Army force must be large enough to capture fortress
High intensity rays will destroy healthy tissue	Large army will detonate mines

The general, however, was undaunted. He divided his army up into small groups and dispatched each group to the head of a different road. When all was ready he gave the signal, and each group charged down a different road. All of the small groups passed safely over the mines, and the army then attacked the fortress in full strength. In this way, the general was able to capture the fortress and overthrow the dictator.[30]

What, then, is the analogous solution to the tumor problem? (Before reading any further, the reader is encouraged to try to come up with the solution on his or her own). Like the dispersion solution suggested by the military problem, the solution to the tumor problem involves a dispersion. In this case, the solution is to simultaneously apply multiple low-intensity rays in different directions all directed at the tumor. The result would be that the rays can converge in suf cient strength to destroy the tumor, while preserving the surrounding healthy tissue. The mappings between the two solutions are given in Figure 2.9.

In essence, both of these solutions require the possession of a spatial image involving a central object surrounded by many different routes (Figure 2.10).[31] The reference in the military story to "many roads radiated outward from the fortress like spokes on a wheel" creates a kind of spatial mental model that might help one come up with the analogous dispersion solution in the tumor problem.

A different analogy might induce a different solution to the tumor problem. For example, a different solution to the military problem might be to dig an underground tunnel beneath the mines following the route of the road to the fortress. The army could thus move all its forces underground through the tunnel, gather at the fortress, and launch a full-scale attack. Using this analogy instead, a problem solver might come up with an alternative solution to the tumor problem—for

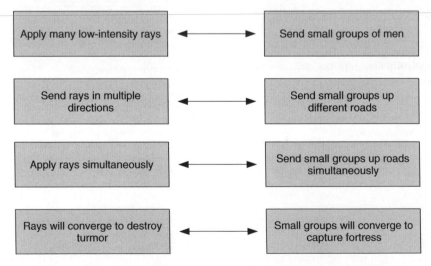

Figure 2.9. Mappings between tumor solution and military solution.

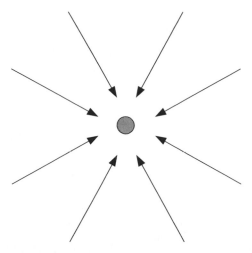

Figure 2.10. A spatial mental model to help solve the tumor problem.

example, to insert a tube through the stomach wall and send rays through it to the tumor.[32]

The important lesson here is that there is usually not only one way to solve a problem. Creative problem solving of ill-structured problems sometimes requires us to think outside the box so that we can come up with a variety of solutions. A useful analogy oftentimes can help us in this regard when we are feeling at a loss as to how to solve a problem. Many people who are faced with the tumor problem are simply stymied into thinking that there is no possible solution. As the military story demonstrates, an analogy can trigger a creative spark that can open up our minds, if not to come up with an outright solution, at least to free us up to think outside the box.

Thermostat Revisited. Earlier, we formulated a conceptual model of how an electromechanical thermostat works. We described the organization of the components of the thermostat (the system topology) and how the components causally interact to turn the heater on and off (the causal model). In effect, we provided a conceptual model of internal connections. How might we also use external connections, more speci cally analogical reasoning, to promote understanding of a thermostat?

It turns out that many users of home thermostats possess incorrect mental models that might not be recti ed by knowledge of internal connections alone. In particular, many users incorrectly believe that a thermostat controls the *amount* of heat that is released into a room.[33] That is to say, they believe that a higher temperature setting will cause a higher rate of ow. A user who holds this erroneous mental model might turn the temperature up on a cold day so that the house would heat up faster. The correct mental model is to think of the thermostat as a switch that senses temperature and turns a furnace on or off to maintain a

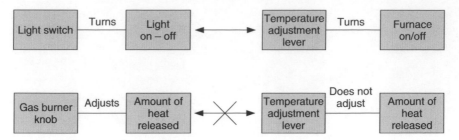

Figure 2.11. Analogies to thermostat behavior: light switch and gas burner knob.

set temperature. Therefore, setting the temperature to a higher level will have no affect on the amount of heat that is released (although the furnace will run for a longer time to reach the higher setting).

An analogy that can highlight the difference would be to compare a thermostat to two devices, both familiar to all of us: an on–off light switch versus a gas burner knob. A thermostat will turn a furnace on or off like an on–off light switch—it is either on or off, and there are no intermediate states. On the other hand, a gas burner knob allows you to adjust the size of the ame (and therefore the amount of heat released) on the stove. The mappings between the two analogies are depicted in the diagram in Figure 2.11. The *X* across the line on the gas burner analogy indicates an invalid mapping. This example illustrates how it is not only the correct mappings that can help us understand how a system behaves but also the counterfactual mapping or analogous counterexample that can shed much light, and clear up common misconceptions.

DISCUSSION

We have looked at a number of examples of mental models in this chapter. We framed the discussion in terms of how mental models organize knowledge. First, we looked at internal connections, or the interconnections among the components of a system. Second, we explored how prior knowledge can also be mapped to understand a complex system. We referred to this as external connections.

Throughout the discussion, we have seen several examples of how a diagrammatic representation can help in the development of an appropriate mental model. We looked at how a diagram that portrays system topology, or the organization of components in a system, can be extremely useful in promoting deeper system understanding (Figure 2.5). However, a diagram, in and of itself, is usually insuf cient in conveying information that will be useful to an end user. To make a diagram more useful and more user-friendly, we demonstrated how we might annotate a picture with textual descriptions (see the example of the electromechanical thermostat in Figure 2.4). The annotations we used were associated with different locations on the picture, and provided a kind of running narrative to how the device worked. Furthermore, we introduced a formalism for describing a causal model of the device, one that employed a set of IF–THEN rules that explained how the individual components causally interacted to produce the device behaviors. Our causal model not only provided an explanatory account of how the system worked but also enabled us to make predictions about the system: We were able to run our causal model on a different set of parameters to predict other system behaviors. Our diagram, together with our causal model, proved very useful to the extent that it provided the necessary information to support inferences on how to use the system.

We also discussed how the way you present and frame a problem could have implications on one's ability to understand a problem. The Wason selection task illustrates this idea well. When the problem is stated in an abstract way, using letters and numerals, people experience dif culty in coming up with the right solution. However, when the problem is framed in a more meaningful context, one more concrete and familiar to an end-user, the problem becomes much easier to solve. The implication of this result is that our materials, both diagrams and written materials, should be designed so that it promotes understanding. One strategy is to frame the materials in a more meaningful context. Indeed, many of the diagrams and system descriptions that we use today are couched in terms too abstract to be of much use to end-users.

Another strategy to make a dif cult problem more tractable is to employ analogical reasoning. We looked at two examples in the literature: rst, the use of analogy to understand electricity, and second, the use of analogy to foster creative problem solving of very dif cult problems. In essence, analogical reasoning involves an understanding of mappings between two domains of knowledge. To make good use of analogy, one must perceive these mappings, otherwise one may miss the point of the analogy. Hence our diagrams in this discussion were intended to draw attention to the mappings between the analogy (or base domain) and the dif cult-to-understand target domain (Figures 2.6, 2.7, 2.9, and 2.11). Second, a spatial diagram can help in analogical thinking by helping us see the similarity in structure between the two domains. In the tumor problem, we illustrated structural similarity to the military problem with a diagram of several arrows all converging on a single object (Figure 2.10). We could have also drawn a spatial diagram to depict the structural similarity an atom to the solar system (a larger center object with smaller objects orbiting around the center object). It turns out that diagramming is a useful tool that can facilitate analogical thinking.

We conclude this chapter with a brief discussion on the limitations and problems associated with mental models research. The primary dif culty is that we can never be sure what a user's mental model is—that is to say, how do we capture a mental model? In experimental studies, subjects are asked to perform some kind of problem-solving task. To gain insight into a person's mental models, the researcher may simply observe the subject. Direct observation, however, may reveal little about the underlying thought processes of the subject.

One solution to this problem is to interview the subject upon completion of the problem-solving task. Because interviews occur after the fact, many people have dif culty remembering what their thought processes were and may actually embellish their explanations in an interview. Because interviews suffer from this retrospective bias, think-aloud protocol analysis[34] is a technique that is frequently employed in studies of mental models. These techniques require that a subject verbalize his or her thought processes while engaged a problem-solving task (also known as concurrent verbalizations). When employing this technique, social interaction between the experimenter and the subject should be kept to a minimum. This is done so that the subject does not engage in explanation or verbal description. A researcher attempting to capture an individual's mental model should be more interested in trying to elicit the ways in which a subject engages in problem solving and the cognitive structure employed in performing a task. Such verbalizations, ideally, should be devoid of socialized explanations.

Another problem with concurrent verbalizations is that they can be quite obtrusive and some subjects will have a hard time working on a task and verbalizing at the same time. (Experimenters may have to keep reminding subject to talk out loud). To partially address this problem, subjects are videotaped while performing some task. The videotape is then replayed to the subject, and the subject is asked to give commentary on actions taken, with the video stopped at critical points, or at points when the subject's behavior is confusing to the researcher. However, this technique still suffers from the same biases as after-the-fact explanations given during interviewing.[35]

In the end, there is no perfect way to capture a person's mental models. We must content ourselves with doing the best we can, as the possibility of totally capturing a mental model is near impossible: "The search for mental models will never completely eliminate uncertainty; the black box will never be completely transparent."[36]

ENDNOTES

1. Kenneth Craik, *The Nature of Explanation* (1943); cited in Philip N. Johnson-Laird, *Mental Models*. New York: Cambridge Univ. Press, 1983, p. 3.

2. John M. Carroll and Judith R. Olson, "Mental Models in Human-Computer Interaction," in *Handbook of Human-Computer Interaction*. Amsterdam; New York: North Holland, 1988, pp. 45–65.

3. Michael D. Williams, James D. Hollan, and Albert L. Stevens, "Human Reasoning about a Simple Physical System," in *Mental Models*. Hillsdale, NJ: L. Erlbaum Associates, 1983, pp. 131–153.

4. Johnson-Laird, p. 2.

5. I adopt the distinction made between mental models and conceptual models from Donald A. Norman, "Some Observations on Mental Models," in *Mental Models*. Hillsdale, NJ: L. Erlbaum Associates, 1983, pp. 7–14.

6. Ibid., pp. 9–10.

7. Williams et al., op. cit.

8. For a discussion of cognitive skill acquisition, see Richard E. Mayer, *Thinking, Problem Solving, Cognition*, 2nd ed. New York: W.H. Freeman, 1992, pp. 196–201.

9. Albert Einstein and Leopold Infeld, *The Evolution of Physics*. New York: Simon and Schuster, 1938, p. 31.

10. Philip N. Johnson-Laird, "Mental Models," in *Foundations of Cognitive Science*. Cambridge, MA: MIT Press, 1989, p. 487.

11. Richard E. Mayer makes the distinction between internal connections and external connections in "Information Processing Variables in Learning to Solve Problems," *Review of Educational Research* 45, no. 4 (fall 1975), 525–541.

12. David E. Kieras and Susan Bovair, "The Role of a Mental Model in Learning to Operate a Device," *Cognitive Science* 8 (1984), 255–273.

13. Ibid., p. 261.

14. Johan de Kleer and John Seely Brown, "Assumptions and Ambiguities in Mechanistic Mental Models," in *Mental Models*. Hillsdale, NJ: L. Erlbaum Associates, 1983, p. 161.

15. P. C. Wason, "Reasoning," in *New Horizons in Psychology*. Baltimore: Penguin Books, 1966.

16. Philip N. Johnson-Laird, Paolo Legrenzi, and Maria S. Legrenzi, "Reasoning and a Sense of Reality," *British Journal of Psychology* 63 (1972), 395–400.

17. Richard A. Griggs and James R. Cox, "The Elusive Thematic-Materials Effect in Wason's Selection Task," *British Jounal of Psychology* 73 (1982), 407–420.

18. Dedre Gentner and Donald R. Gentner, "Flowing Waters or Teeming Crowds: Mental Models of Electricity," in *Mental Models*. Hillsdale, NJ: L. Erlbaum Associates, 1983, pp. 99–129.

19. Mary L. Gick and Keith J. Holyoak, "Analogical Problem Solving," *Cognitive Science* 12 (1980), 306–355.

20. For a discussion of the Rutherford analogy see Gentner and Gentner, pp. 101–107.

21. Nigel Costley, "Crocodile" Launched World into Atomic Age," *Sunday Star Times*, Oct. 17, 1999.

22. Dedre Gentner, "The Mechanisms of Analogical Reasoning," in *Similarity and Analogical Reasoning*. Cambridge; New York: Cambridge University Press, 1989.

23. See John M. Carroll and Robert L. Mack, "Metaphor, Computing Systems, and Active Learning," *International Journal of Man-Machine Studies* 22 (1985) for a discussion on the inherent incompleteness of analogies. pp. 39–57.

24. Gentner and Gentner, p. 113.

25. Ibid., p. 111.

26. See ibid., pp. 117–119 for results of the experimental study.

27. Gick and Holyoak (1980), pp. 306–335.

28. Ibid., pp. 307–308.

29. Ibid., p. 351.

30. Ibid.

31. See Mary L. Gick and Keith J. Holyoak, "Schema Induction and Analogical Transfer," *Cognitive Psychology* 15 (1983), pp. 1–38. They propose the use of a visual diagram of several converging arrows to help problem solvers come up with the dispersion solution to the tumor problem.

32. Gick and Holyoak (1980), p. 318.

33. See Willett Kempton, "Two Theories of Home Heat Control," *Cognitive Science* 10 (1986), pp. 75–90, for a study that looks at the incorrect mental models that people hold of home thermostats.

34. See K. A. Ericsson and Herbert A. Simon, *Protocol Analysis: Verbal Reports as Data*. Cambridge, MA: MIT Press, 1993, for a thorough and detailed discussion of think-aloud protocol analysis.

35. Judith R. Olson and K. J. Biolsi, "Techniques for Representing Expert Knowledge," in *Toward a General Theory of Expertise: Prospects and Limits*. Cambridge; New York: Cambridge University Press, 1991.

36. William B. Rouse and Nancy M. Morris, "On Looking into the Black Box: Prospects and Limits in the Search for Mental Models," *Psychological Bulletin* 100, no. 3 (1986), 360.

CHAPTER 3

TYPES OF DIAGRAMS

One possible solution to a system's lack of transparency is to provide a graphical diagram to aid in visualization. By visualization we mean a process by which numerical data and information are converted into meaningful images. One de - nition of visualization is "the process of forming a mental model of data, thereby gaining insight into the data."[1] In the last chapter, we looked at mental models that people can run in their minds when they are trying to understand the behavior of a complex system. In many ways, this chapter is a continuation of the discussion. Now, we broaden our discussion to consider many more types of diagrammatic representations. This topic is particularly relevant today given the advances in computer displays and the rise of the Internet as the medium of choice today. Without a doubt, the graphical user interface will assume a more prominent role in intelligent systems in the future. Now is a ripe time to explore the issue of how to provide graphical aids to customers and end users that assist in the visualization of data and information.

We de ned earlier (in Chapter 1) a diagram as a graphic representation that shows how something works or makes something easier to understand. It may seem fairly obvious and intuitive what a diagram is, but de ning it more precisely will help us focus our attention on speci c types of representations. Furthermore, we will consider the question of what is not a diagram, as this will eliminate from consideration many types of representations. First of all, a diagram is not a sentential or linguistic representation. In a sentential representation, we form system descriptions by employing the sentences of a language. A diagram, by contrast, is a type of **information graphic** that "preserves explicitly the information about

Diagrammatic Reasoning in AI, by Robbie Nakatsu
Copyright © 2010 John Wiley & Sons, Inc.

topological and geometric relations among the components of the problem."[2] In other words, an information graphic indexes information by location on a plane.* Because of this, an information graphic can be used to group related pieces of information together and can support a large number of perceptual inferences, in particular by tapping into the very powerful visual information processing system that most humans possess. For example, a graphical hierarchy can help humans sort through information much more ef ciently and understand how the objects of a domain are classi ed much more rapidly than a verbal description, which must be processed sequentially.

Not all information graphics are diagrams. Figure 3.1 is a tree that illustrates a taxonomy of information graphics. There are four main types of information graphics shown: (1) quantitative charts and graphs, (2) maps, (3) diagrams, and (4) tables.[3] *Quantitative charts and graphs* are used to show patterns and/or relationships of quantitative data. We are all familiar with the main types including line graphs, bar charts, pie charts, and *XY* scatterplots. *Maps* show spatial and directional relationships. A good example is a topographic map that shows the shape and elevation of the earth's surface. Another good example includes building layouts and oor plans. *Tables*, of course, are information graphics with information arranged in rows and columns in some meaningful way. Figure 3.1 also includes an *Other* category for information graphics that do not really t neatly into any of these four types. Some examples include pictorial illustrations, how-to charts, and cross-sectional displays. None of these types of information graphics is addressed in this book.

Diagrams are information graphics that are made up primarily of geometric shapes, such as rectangles, circles, diamonds, or triangles, that are typically (but not always) interconnected by lines or arrows. One of the major purposes of a diagram is to show how things, people, ideas, activities, etc. interrelate and interconnect. Unlike *quantitative charts and graphs*, diagrams are used to show interrelationships in a qualitative way. Many examples will be provided in this chapter, and throughout this book, to demonstrate how this can be accomplished.

What advantages do diagrams have over verbal descriptions in promoting system understanding? First, by providing a diagram, massive amounts of information can be presented more ef ciently. A diagram can strip down informational complexity to its core—in this sense, it can result in a parsimonious, minimalist description of a system. Second, a diagram can help us see patterns in information and data that may appear disordered otherwise. For example, a diagram can help us see mechanisms of cause and effect or can illustrate sequence and ow in a complex system. Third, a diagram can result in a less ambiguous description than a verbal description because it forces one to come up with a more structured description. By necessity, the notations of the diagramming language, which serve as its vocabulary, circumscribe what is and what is not allowed in the diagrammatic representation.

---

*Three-dimensional information graphics are also possible, but we consider only two-dimensional diagrams in this book.

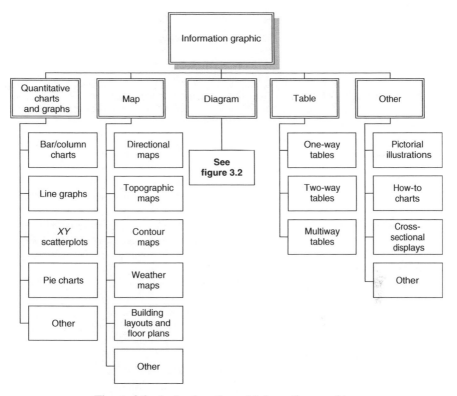

Figure 3.1. A classi cation of information graphics.

One dif culty in creating diagrams is that there are such an enormous variety of types. One can easily become overwhelmed by the huge number of notations and techniques that are employed in the different domains. There are literally hundreds of examples in speci c domain areas, including circuit and logic diagrams employed by electrical engineers to help them design and troubleshoot circuit boards; entity-relationship diagrams that later serve as blueprints for how a database application is created; Pert charts that project managers can use for scheduling and planning complex projects composed of many different tasks, some of which can be executed concurrently; and website maps that illustrate the structure of websites that web designers are planning to build. Indeed, in many different elds and walks of life, diagramming is an important skill that aids in understanding, communicating, and in many cases, implementing complex systems and ideas. See Table 3.1 for a sampling of some domain areas that use diagramming today.

One family of techniques that has become important in recent years among the software engineering community is known as UML (Uni ed Modeling Language). These techniques are used primarily to aid in the software design task but are useful for other reasons, which we will see later on in this chapter. There

Table 3.1. Some Domain-Specific Diagramming Techniques

Domain Sample Diagram(s)	Description
Engineering Circuits and logic diagrams Industrial control systems diagrams Fluid power diagrams Part and assembly diagrams Process ow diagrams	Show how the components of a physical system are interconnected to one another (system topology) and/or system process and ow
Database and systems design Entity-relationship diagrams	Used to model database applications; show entities (or tables) and how they are related to one another
Data ow diagrams	Show how data move from external entities into a system as well as the ow of data within a system and where they gets stored
Systems operation Fault tree analysis diagrams	Tree diagrams; illustrate what the causes of failure are (start with a topmost node, the failure itself, and use event shapes and logic gates to illustrate, top-down, how a sequence of events may lead to failure)
Networking and telecommunications Network topology diagrams	Show a network con guration (e.g., how the devices, cabling, servers, routers, switches, etc. are arranged in a network)
Project management PERT charts	Used to analyze activities needed to complete a complex project (create a network diagram by identifying sequence of activities and their dependencies); used to determine the critical path of a project
Web design Website maps	Show how web pages are hyperlinked to other web pages.

are 13 of cial diagram types in UML,* which can be classi ed into two types: structure diagrams that model the structural relationships of objects in a system; and behavior diagrams that model system behavior.[4] The most important structure diagram is the class diagram, a diagram that describes the types of objects in a system and the kinds of relationships that exist among them.[5] For example,

---

*The 13 types are 6 structure diagrams (class diagram, component diagram, composite structure diagram, deployment diagram, object diagram, and package diagram), and 7 behavior diagrams (activity diagram, use case diagram, state machine diagram, sequence diagram, communication diagram, interaction overview diagram, and timing diagram).

using the class diagram, a designer can construct a classi cation hierarchy of objects. An example of a behavior diagram is the activity diagram, which is used to describe procedural logic, business process, and work ow.[6] These diagrams are very similar to owcharts, and we will explore them in more detail later on in this chapter when we discuss diagrams that illustrate sequence and ow. Other than the activity diagram, we will not explore any of the UML diagramming techniques.

Given the vast number of techniques that have been employed by the different domain areas, it would be impossible to cover all the different types of diagramming within a single chapter or even within a single book. However, it is also clear from a survey of these techniques that a number of themes cut across the great diversity of diagrams in use today. One purpose of this chapter, then, is to provide a classi cation of the major types of diagrams that are possible, organized around six major themes. Speci cally, we will investigate the following categories of diagramming:

1. System topology
2. Sequence and ow
3. Hierarchy and classi cation
4. Association
5. Cause and effect
6. Logic reasoning

Figure 3.2 illustrates the classi cation hierarchy for these six categories as well as the different types of diagrams under each category that will be covered in this chapter and the next. The gure serves as the outline for our discussion. Obviously, the choice of speci c diagramming techniques and notations will necessarily be biased and selective. Therefore, every attempt has been made to select diagramming techniques that are drawn from the extant literature and, in many cases, have become de facto standards in their own right. Unless necessary, we will not invent new techniques and notations. Furthermore, although the selection of speci c diagramming techniques can be questioned and criticized (your favorite technique may be absent from the discussion), the examples were chosen carefully so that they are representative of the themes addressed in this book.

We conclude the chapter with a discussion on decision graphs to illustrate in more detail how some of these diagramming techniques can be used in a more speci c and concrete way. In particular, we explore two well-known techniques: the decision tree and the in uence diagram. These diagrams are used to help us make better decisions.

In this chapter we assume that the diagrams that are drawn are meant to faithfully represent the domain of interest to promote system understanding and communication. We focus on static diagrams that are not really meant to be manipulated and modi ed by an end user. In the next chapter, we consider logic

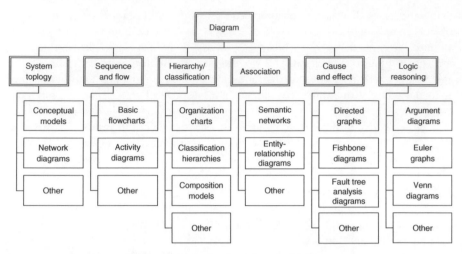

Figure 3.2. A classi cation of diagrams.

reasoning with diagrams that are meant to be more dynamic and can be used to support a number of inferences and logic reasoning tasks. Therefore, we consider only the rst ve categories of diagrams in this chapter and leave logic reasoning for later. In later chapters, we consider other techniques, including rule-based reasoning, model-based reasoning, and Bayesian networks. These techniques add a more dynamic and interactive quality to many of the diagramming techniques that are discussed in this chapter.

SYSTEM TOPOLOGY

System topology was addressed in Chapter 2, when we discussed the internal connections of a mental model. System topology was de ned as the organization of components in a system. It is typically rendered as a conceptual model of some kind (see Figure 2.5 for an example). It consists of components as well as connections among the components. In addition, as we discussed in considerable detail in Chapter 2, the conceptual model can be augmented with a causal model that describes how the components of the system causally interact to produce system outputs and observable behaviors. The conceptual model, by itself, does not furnish us with this description. We will have little more to add to the discussion of system topology in this section.

A good example of a diagram used to illustrate system topology is a network diagram, which shows how the hardware components of a network are intercon- nected. Figure 3.3 is a network diagram that shows how the computers, printers, servers, etc. are con gured in a company. In this diagram, there are two separate networks (sales network and nance network) and in between them sits a router, a device which routes traf c between the two networks as well as to the Internet.

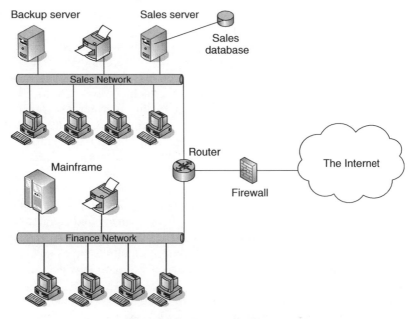

Figure 3.3. A network diagram.

This network diagram employs different icons to represent the different types of components (PCs, printers, servers, routers, rewalls, and the like). One could also represent different types of components by more abstract shapes such as rectangles, circles, and diamonds, as was the case in the conceptual model given in Figure 2.5. In fact, many different domain areas such as electrical engineering, mechanical engineering, and software design employ their own unique notations to describe system components.

SEQUENCE AND FLOW

Flowcharts are diagrams that are used to show sequence and ow—a temporal or chronological ordering of steps in a process of some kind. One example is a owchart that graphically depicts the sequenced activities, together with the decision points, which make up an organizational process. Another good use is to illustrate the steps of an algorithm (a sequence of instructions used for performing a task). For instance, a computer programmer may create a owchart that illustrates the steps of a computer algorithm.

There are several variations of owcharts in use today. PERT charts, for one, are used to show the sequencing of activities in a project and can help project managers monitor projects to ensure that activities are completed in a timely matter and milestones are met. Data ow diagrams (DFDs), another type of owchart, are used by systems designers to help them better understand how data ows into a system from external entities, how it moves from one process to another within a system, and where and when it gets stored. We will not be looking at any of these more specialized owcharts in this section.

Rather, we consider more generic owcharting techniques that can be employed across many types of domains and can illustrate many types of situations. We begin with the basic owchart, which is very easy to construct and understand because it uses so few diagramming conventions. Most of us have seen owcharts many times before so we are already familiar with their conventions (even if you have not, they are easy enough to gure out). A basic owchart is presented in Figure 3.4, which illustrates and describes the prototyping process.

Prototyping is a method of developing systems rapidly by creating a quick-and-dirty mockup of a system, called a prototype. Once created, the prototype is given to end users so that they can provide their feedback and suggestions for improvement. Based on this feedback, you modify and enhance the prototype. It is an iterative process in that you can get feedback multiple times and enhance the prototype accordingly. Figure 3.4 shows a feedback loop in which you obtain feedback and improve a prototype until you are satis ed with it.

There are three shapes used in the basic owchart, as shown in the prototyping diagram. The terminator shape (the ellipse) begins and ends a owchart (sometimes the terminators are left out of the owchart, because it is obvious where the beginning and end points are). The rectangle, the most common shape on a owchart, represents the action that needs to be taken. The diamond denotes a decision point. Typically, there is a question in the diamond, the answer to which leads you to the appropriate path out of the diamond. All the shapes are connected with arrows so that you can easily follow the sequence of activities, in the order in which they are supposed to occur. By convention, the owchart is either read from top to bottom (vertically) or from left to right (horizontally).

A diamond-shaped symbol allows for one input arrow and typically has two exit points (as in Figure 3.4), but can allow for three as well. If you need more than three exit points, you can draw a decision point like that shown in Figure 3.5. That is really all you need to know to construct a basic owchart. People who construct more specialized owcharts might use a wider range of symbols. For example, in software engineering there are symbols used to represent subroutines, databases, input/output, tapes, and the like (Figure 3.6).

Admittedly, many simple owcharts are not really that useful because they do not add greatly to our understanding of sequence and ow. Indeed, the prototyping process could just as easily have been described using sentences alone, numbered to represent the sequenced ordering:

1. Identify basic requirements.
2. Develop working prototype.
3. Get feedback from end users.
4. Revise and enhance prototype.
5. Repeat steps 3 and 4 until the end user is satis ed.

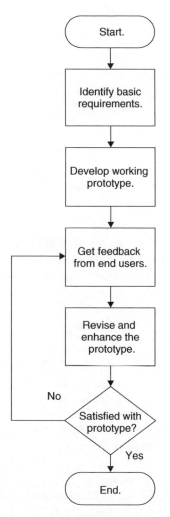

Figure 3.4. A Basic flowchart illustrating the prototyping process.

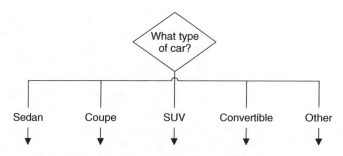

Figure 3.5. A decision point with multiple exit points.

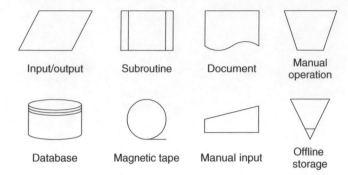

Figure 3.6. More flowcharting shapes used in software engineering.

One might argue that these numbered sentences describe the prototyping process quite adequately and more compactly than a flowchart does. Therefore, a flowchart is not really needed. In this section we look at examples in which flowcharting helps us better visualize process and sequence, over and above a simple numbered textual sequence could.

Activity Diagrams

An alternative to the basic flowchart is the activity diagram. The activity diagram is part of the UML family of graphical notations that are employed primarily to aid in software design. However, the activity diagram can be used more broadly to model many different types of problems—their usage is in no way restricted to software development problems. They are similar to basic flowcharting techniques, and serve the same basic purpose of illustrating sequence, but they also allow you to illustrate parallel behavior.

To see how this works, we will look at another example, slightly more complicated than the prototyping example. Figure 3.7 shows a basic flowchart that illustrates the sequence of steps you would take to make muffins. In this diagram, there are two decision points: (1) whether to make lowfat muffins: if yes, then halve the butter to 3 tablespoons and replace with 3 tablespoons of yogurt; and (2) what kind of fruit to use: blueberries, bananas, or strawberries. Note also the use of the *on-page reference* symbol (the circle with the letter *A*). This notation is very useful when you are dealing with larger flowcharts that cannot easily fit across a page either from top to bottom, or from left to right. You simply draw as much of the flowchart as you can (in this example, from top to bottom), and use the on-page reference symbol to indicate where the flowchart is to continue. An alternative to the on-page reference is the *off-page reference*—it's the same idea, except that the flowchart continues on a new page.

We can transform the basic flowchart into an activity diagram. Figure 3.8 shows the activity diagram, which is annotated to show the different types of

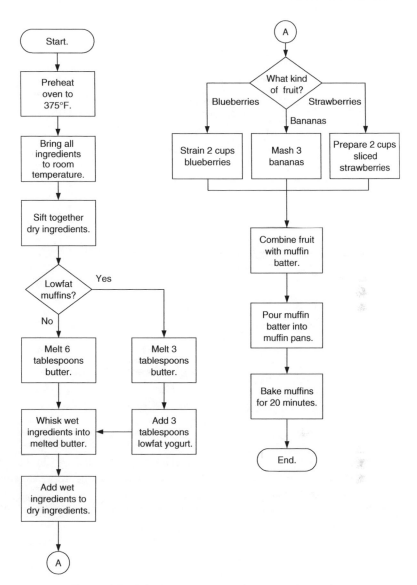

Figure 3.7. A basic flowchart on how to make muffins.

nodes and notations that are used. Like in the basic flowchart, there are terminator nodes to represent the start and the end of the flowchart:

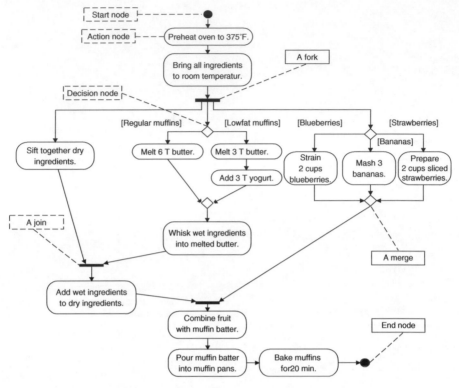

Figure 3.8. An activity diagram on how to make muf ns.

Action nodes, represented by the ellipse, describe the activities, or steps of the muf n recipe. Decision points, like in the basic owchart, are represented by diamond-shaped symbols like the following:

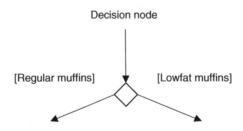

The notation used in the activity diagram is that each outbound ow must have what is known as a **guard**, which is a Boolean condition placed in square brackets: [Regular muf ns] and [Lowfat muf ns].

Junctions are used to either split one path into two or more paths, or merge two or more paths into a single path. Three types of junctions can be used: a fork, a join, and a merge:

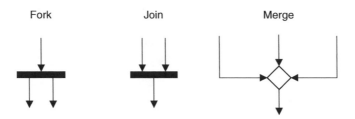

A fork splits an arrow into multiple paths. It is used to specify parallel actions. In Figure 3.8 the main fork indicates that three branches of activities can occur in parallel: (1) the sifting of the dry ingredients, (2) the processing of the wet ingredients, and (3) the selection and processing of the fruits. The activity diagram shows graphically that the three separate activities are independent of one another—that is to say, one activity does not precede another activity in time. For example, you do not need to sift the dry ingredients before you process the wet ingredients. The basic owchart, as given in Figure 3.7, seems to imply that the processing of the wet ingredients depends on the completion of the sifting of the dry ingredients, which is not the case. In this respect, the activity diagram has more expressive power than the basic owchart because the basic owchart does not allow the expression of parallel processing.

A join involves two separate paths merging into one, and it signi es that the outgoing ow can be taken only when all the incoming ows reach the join. For example, in Figure 3.8, the node "Add wet ingredients to dry ingredients" is not activated until both the action "Sift together dry ingredients" and the action "Whisk wet ingredients into melted butter" are completed.

A merge is not the same as a join, although in both cases several paths merge into one. Like a join, a merge has multiple in ows that merge into one out ow; visually they appear to be performing the same function. However, unlike a join, a merge is used to mark the end of multiple paths that lead from a decision node. Semantically, a merge is not a join because it is always the case that **only one** of the in ow paths is taken, whereas in the case of a join, **all** in ow paths must be taken for the out ow path to be activated.

In sum, you can always transform a basic owchart into an activity diagram, and vice versa. But the two diagrams are not equivalent in terms of their ability to represent sequence or ow. The most important difference is that the basic owchart is more limited because it cannot represent parallel actions, so that in the transformation from activity diagram to basic owchart, you may lose information. On the other hand, the basic owchart is a more compact representation that does not involve forks, joins, and merges—you can therefore represent larger sequences and ows. If you do not need to represent parallel actions, or if you need to represent a large sequence of activities more compactly, then a basic owchart may be the better diagramming choice.

Swimlanes: Partitioning an Activity Diagram. You can also add swim-lanes, also known as partitions, to an activity diagram. See Figure 3.9 for a three-swimlane activity diagram. The swimlanes in this diagram indicate who is responsible for what. In this example, we are looking at the customer order and ful llment process in a company. The partitions represent three departments that are a part of this process: Customer Service, Accounts Receivable, and Ful-llment. Actions are placed in the appropriate partition, depending on which department is responsible for the activity. For instance, the action "Customer places order" is the responsibility of the Customer Service Department, but the action "Look up customer account" is the responsibility of the Accounts Receiv-able Department.

Although swimlanes can be used to add another dimension of useful infor-mation to an activity diagram, they must be used carefully or not at all. The use of swimlanes can restrict you from creating larger activity diagrams because they are not as freeform or open ended to create—you have to be sure to place your actions into the appropriate partition, and the more partitions you create, the more dif cult it is to maneuver and place your objects appropriately. If your goal is to illustrate the sequence of activities in a process all on a single page and the process is rather complex, you probably should not add swimlanes to you diagram.

Case Study: Triage in an Emergency Room. We conclude this section by considering a case study in which a owchart aided in real-life decision-making task. The case involves the diagnosis of heart attack patients in a big

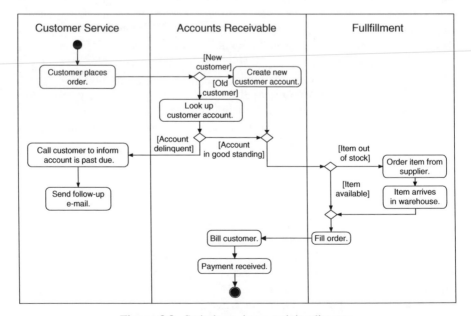

Figure 3.9. Swimlanes in an activity diagram.

public hospital in Chicago. Cook County Hospital was the place of last resort for hundreds of thousands of Chicagoans without health insurance, and it desperately needed a better procedure for determining how to treat heart attack patients.[7] In many ways this case shines a light on the great potential for diagrammatic representations to help solve many of the most dif cult problems that our society faces today.

In 1996, the emergency department at Cook County Hospital was stretched to the limit and ill-equipped to handle the huge number of patients who streamed in daily to seek emergency medical treatment. A signi cant number of these patients were people who were worried they were having a heart attack. Heart attack patients, in particular, were dif cult to treat because the treatment protocol for handling their symptoms was lengthy, subjective, and oftentimes inconclusive. Patients complaining of chest pain were often misdiagnosed and given inappropriate treatments.

The problem could be framed as a classic triage problem: In a resource-constrained environment, one in which quick decisions need to be made, how do you prioritize and sort patients according to the severity of their condition, using the limited patient data that you have? Once sorted and prioritized, the emergency department can assign an appropriate treatment to the patient. To solve this problem, we rst classify treatments in terms of their costs and the resources that they consume. A single bed in the intensive care unit cost roughly $2000 a night, with a typical heart attack patient staying for three nights. An intermediate care unit was a little cheaper to run than intensive care—about $1000 a night—because it is are staffed by nurses instead of cardiologists and is a little less intensive in terms of its level of care.[8] A third level of treatment would be an observation unit, in which a patient is observed for 12 h, under the most basic care and is either released (if there are no further complications) or reassessed to a higher level of care later on. The triage problem is really about the correct assignment of the patient to the level of treatment, according to the severity of the patient's condition. Two adverse consequences could occur if the assignment is wrongly made: (1) a patient is underserved, a patient dies or is severely harmed because more intensive care was required; or (2) a patient is overserved, in which case the patient wastes the resources of the hospital and also denies treatment to more critical patient cases because there are only a limited number of hospital beds and doctors who can tend to the most serious cases.

The triage problem, it turns out, was not an easy one to solve. It was not immediately clear to the doctors and staff at Cook County Hospital in 1996 how to assign patients to a treatment level. The traditional approach is to gather as much information as you reasonably can from the patient to assess the criticality of the patient's need for urgent care. Staff would interview the patient and ask any number of questions such as:

- What is you age?
- Where does it hurt and describe the pain?
- Have you experienced this pain before?

- Do you have a history of heart attacks in your family?
- What is your cholesterol reading?
- Do you have high blood pressure?
- Do you have diabetes?

The problem is that doctors, given the exact same patient data and symptoms, often came to different conclusions regarding the seriousness of a patient's condition. Moreover, it was not clear which factors were most predictive of a life-threatening heart attack.

To improve the likelihood of a correct diagnosis, a hospital could also perform a number of procedures and tests. For example, a doctor (or a nurse) might use a stethoscope to listen to a patient's chest for signs that he has uid in his lungs—a sign that his heart is having problems keeping up with its pumping function. The doctor may also administer an electrocardiogram (ECG), a test that reads the electrical activity of the heart to determine if there are any abnormalities in a patient's heart.

The problem, and dif culty, however, is that doctors are often wrong in their estimates, and often collect the wrong data. The ECG,* perhaps the best diagnostic tool available for emergency room situations, can identify damaged heart muscle and, therefore, the possible presence of acute myocardial infarction (i.e., a heart attack). Unfortunately, the ECG is an imperfect gauge: Someone with a normal ECG may actually be in need of serious attention, whereas someone with an abnormal ECG may be perfectly ne or at least not in need of immediate attention. The determination of severity, therefore, can be fraught with error and uncertainty.

It was against this backdrop of uncertainty and limited resources that Cook County Hospital decided to experiment with an algorithm developed by the cardiologist Lee Goldman.[9] Goldman and his colleagues treated the problem of triage as an empirical question: They looked at hundreds of actual patient cases to see what factors best predicted a heart attack. By doing so, they wanted to take out much of the guesswork in determining the severity of the patient's condition. The algorithm that they came up with is summarized in Figure 3.10.

The activity diagram shows how a patient is classi ed into one of four types: high risk, moderate risk, low risk, and very low risk. Based on this classi cation, an appropriate treatment is assigned.† One of three assignments is possible: (1) admit patient to intensive care, (2) admit patient to intermediate care, and (3) admit patient to observation unit.

The determination of patient risk is based on two factors. First, the ECG indicates whether a patient is suspected of having myocardial infarction (a heart

---

*In fact there are ways to determine for certain whether a patient is having a heart attack or not, but those tests can take hours for the results to come in, an unacceptable time lag in an emergency room that is forced to make quick decisions.

†This owchart is based on Ref. 9. The treatments are entirely made up, but the rest of owchart is reproduced directly from this paper.

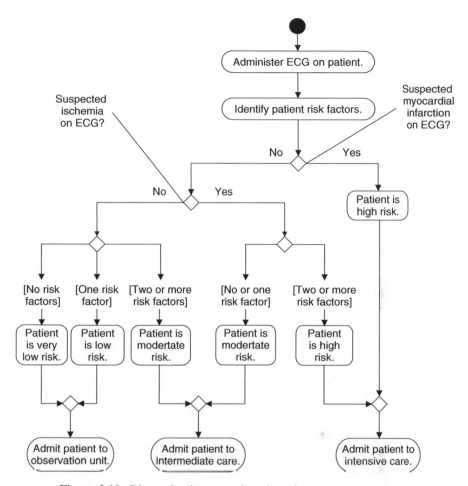

Figure 3.10. Diagnosing heart attack patients in an emergency room.

attack) or ischemia (a condition in which the heart isn't getting enough blood). Second, the algorithm also considers the number of risk factors that a patient has. For example:

- Is the chest pain unstable angina?
- Is there uid in the patient's lungs?
- Is the patient's systolic blood pressure <100?

Based on the ECG test results and these risk factors, the patient's need for urgent care is assessed.

Having a diagrammatic representation greatly helped the staff at Cook County Hospital focus on what the most important factors are in determining the seriousness of a patient's symptoms. Doctors, relying on their own best judgment and intuition, were unable to do this reliably and accurately on their own. The algorithm eliminated from consideration many irrelevant factors and helped them focus on what was really important (Figure 3.10). This case study nicely illustrates how diagrams can be employed to help people make dif cult decisions: it reduces a complex decision-making task to its essence by stripping away the all the variables that have little or no bearing on the task at hand.

HIERARCHY AND CLASSIFICATION

The bene ts of hierarchic organizations are well documented in the research literature. Researchers[10] have long known about the cognitive limitations of human problem solvers in numerous experimental studies. In particular, a human information processing system operates from a well-known short-term memory limitation, which can only hold a few chunks of information at a time. Moreover, the human information processor is largely serial in nature—we are capable of processing only a few symbols, one at a time. Given these limitations on our short-term memory and the serial processing of information, hierarchic organizations may be employed by people to retrieve large amounts of material more systematically. Because information cannot be received *en masse*, but rather must be funneled through the short-term memory bottleneck, a hierarchic structure can be used to process this information more effectively. As Bower[11] remarks, "a hierarchy is an extremely familiar and ef cient organizational scaffold."

What do we mean by a hierarchy? A hierarchy is a diagram that shows how various components of a system are related, often with a downward direction (or alternatively a left-to-right direction) that moves from more general to more speci c. One way to envision a hierarchy is as an inverted tree: We start with a single component (referred to as the root node or topmost node), typically denoted by a square, and then we draw one or more paths leading from it to other nodes. Each of these nodes, in turn, may subdivide into additional subpaths to other nodes. This process may be repeated any number of times to arrive at a multitiered, tree-like structure.

Another way to view hierarchy is as a description of a complex system. From this perspective, a complex system is composed of interrelated subsystems, each of which, in turn is hierarchic. A strict de nition of hierarchy assumes that "each of the subsystems is subordinated by an authority relation to the system it belongs to."[12] In other words, a formal hierarchy consists of a "boss" and a set of subordinate subsystems. Please note that system topology, as described earlier, is different from hierarchy. While both are used to describe system structure, topology involves how components are interconnected to one another in a more physical sense (i.e., how one neighboring component is connected or attached to another), which is different from a boss/subordinate description that a hierarchic speci cation would entail.

Hierarchies, it turns out, arise quite naturally in the real world and serve as a convenient way to view and organize a complex system. Biologists, for instance, classify all living things in a ranked hierarchy, starting at the top with kingdoms. Kingdoms, in turn, are divided into phyla (singular is phylum) for animals, which are then divided into classes, and they in turn into orders, families, genera (singular is genus), and nally species, in that order. Auto mechanics, as another example, may view an automobile as containing different subsystems: a cooling system, a fuel system, an exhaust system, and electrical system. These systems, in turn, are made up of components: the exhaust system contains an exhaust pipe, catalytic converter, muf er, etc. Historians who study the French Revolution may organize its causes into a hierarchic structure as well. At a high level, they may organize its causes into economic, social, and political factors. These high-level factors may, in turn, be further broken down into more speci c causes. Indeed, in many disciplines and walks of life, hierarchies are useful for organizing and making sense of a lot of information. It is not surprising, therefore, that hierarchic representations are one of the most popular forms of diagrams.

We will look at three different uses of hierarchy in this section. We will explore how hierarchies can be used (1) to represent organizational structure (organizational charts), (2) to depict a taxonomy or classi cation of items (inheritance hierarchy), and (3) to show the composition of a system, that is, whole-to-part relationships (composition models).

Organizational Charts

Organizational charts, also known simply as org charts, are diagrams that show how people, functions, divisions, activities, and the like are structured and arranged in an organization. One of the most widely used organizational charts shows who reports to whom in an organization (Figure 3.11).

In the gure, a number of conventions are employed. Each element has at most one parent; this means that every employee in this company (with the exception of the president and CEO who reports to no one) reports to one and only one other employee. The nodes, as represented by the rectangles, have different outlines to indicate the different types of employees in the company. Rectangles that are double-boxed represent employees who are managers—that is, they have subordinates who report to them. Single-boxed nodes represent nonmanagers. There is also a dashed-line box to represent employees who are consultants (because they are not employees in the company), as well as a very light dashed line to represent vacancies in the company. Finally, employees who do not have an of cial title are not given any separate box at all—in this example, these employees include the procurement staff and the production staff.*

In terms of node placement, the subordinates can be arranged either horizontally or vertically. This is to allow for the effective use of the space. For example, all nonmanager employees (the fourth tier on the hierarchy) are arranged vertically. Had we arranged the fourth tier horizontally, we would have quickly run out of space—the hierarchy would have become unnecessarily wide and unwieldy.

*These notations are adopted from Microsoft Visio 2003.

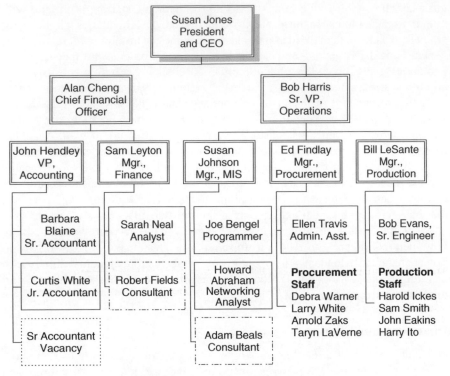

Figure 3.11. An organizational chart.

Inheritance Hierarchy

An important and common application of hierarchies is to illustrate a classi cation of items, also known as a taxonomy. Figure 3.1 and 3.2, for instance, represent classi cation schemes for information graphics and diagrams, respectively. Both diagrams start with a topmost node, or root node, and branch downward to more speci c types (the direction of these hierarchies is from top to bottom, from more general to more speci c). Like in the organizational chart described earlier, we employ a vertical arrangement of nodes on the third tier so that the diagram doesn't become too wide.

One form of a classi cation hierarchy is known as an inheritance hierarchy. They are much like classi cation hierarchies, but with one important difference: They include a speci cation of attributes to describe the items, as well as a scheme for inheriting attributes. Figure 3.12 shows an example.

Each node on the inheritance hierarchy represents a class (the class name, as indicated on each node, identi es the class). Each class contains a collection of attributes that describe the members of the class. Classes are structurally related by means of supertype-subtype relationships, also referred to as parent-child relationships. A supertype-subtype relationship is indicated by the upward pointing arrow, with subtypes pointing to its supertype.

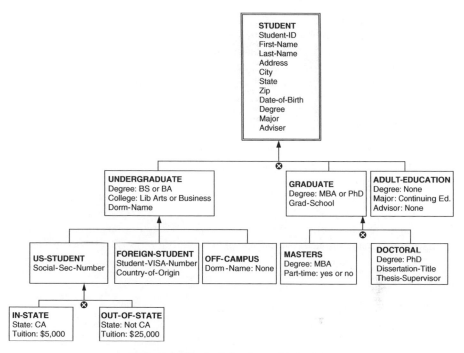

Figure 3.12. An inheritance hierarchy.

A supertype node contains attributes common to all its subtypes. In Figure 3.12, classes "undergraduate," "graduate," and "adult education" all inherit attributes from the "Student" class. In addition, subtype nodes may also include attributes and attribute values unique to that class. For example, in addition to inheriting all the "Student" attributes, the "Undergraduate" class contains two additional attributes, "College" and "Dorm Name." Furthermore, a subtype may specify a speci c value for an attribute that dc nes the class. For the "Undergraduate" class, the "Degree" attribute is either "BA" or "BS." Likewise for the "Adult Education" class, the "Degree" attribute is always "Continuing Ed." The inheritance hierarchy allows us to specify attributes for more and more speci c classes. Nodes lower on the hierarchy inherit **all** attributes of related nodes above. For example, the "In State" class, which represents in-state undergraduate students, would include attributes from "US Student," "Undergraduate," and "Student," in addition to attributes of its own.

The circle with an *x* indicates an exclusive relationship.* This denotes that a supertype can be at most one of the subtypes. According to Figure 3.12, for

---

*This is not standard notation. Different diagramming techniques employ different notations. Also some notations are more precise and allow you to specify precise cardinalities on the supertype-subtype relationships. For example, the cardinality (1,1) indicates that a supertype is always related to one and only one of its subtype. Another cardinality (1,2) indicates that a supertype may be related to one or two of its subtypes.

instance, a "Student" can be one of "Undergraduate," "Graduate," or "Adult Education," but not two or all three. If there is no circle with an x, the relationship is inclusive. This would signify that there is no restriction on the supertype-subtype relationship. In Figure 3.12, this would allow for the possibility that an "Undergraduate" could be, say, both a "US Student" and "Off campus."

Composition Models

Our nal example of hierarchy involves the illustration of whole-to-its-parts relationships. These hierarchies are known as composition models, because these describe a system, and what it is composed of (Figure 3.13).

In this example, we describe the components of a typical computer system. According to the diagram, it is made up of ve primary components: a motherboard, input devices, output devices, storage devices, and a power supply. These components, in turn, can be further broken down into its speci c components.

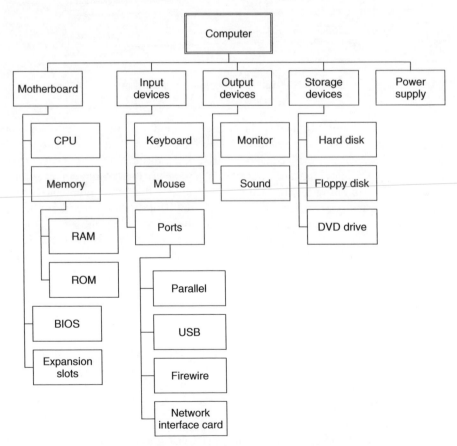

Figure 3.13. A Composition model.

For example, the motherboard is composed of a CPU, memory, BIOS, and expansion slots.

This example illustrates a form of hierarchy that is different from classi cation and inheritance, in which we are creating a top-down structure that moves from more general to more speci c. Composition models, by contrast, enable one to specify the assemblies, the sub-assemblies, the sub-sub-assemblies, and so on, of a complex system. Composition models are extremely useful especially in describing and breaking down complex physical systems, everything from man-made systems, such as an automobile or an airplane, to natural systems, such as the human body. Once again, the hierarchy emerges as a useful tool to make sense out of a lot of information by organizing it in a top-down fashion.

ASSOCIATION

Diagrams that model association show how objects, either physical objects or conceptual objects, are related to one another. One of the most common types of association diagrams is the semantic network, which is a graph of interconnected nodes—the nodes represent the objects and the links represent the relationships between the objects. In this section, we will look at a basic semantic network, as well as a more specialized association diagram called the entity-relationship diagram.

Semantic Networks

Semantic networks are used to illustrate how people organize information in their memories. Such representations have been used by cognitive psychologists to understand and theorize how one retrieves and processes information from long-term memory. In AI, semantic networks can also be used as a knowledge representation scheme that programs can use to retrieve information ef ciently just like humans do.

A basic semantic network consists of three components:

- **Units:** Words that represent the thing or subject
- **Properties:** Words that represent the features or characteristics of the units
- **Pointers:** Associations between the units, which can either be unidirectional or bidirectional

(In the previous discussion on inheritance hierarchies, we looked at properties of objects and how they can be inherited by other objects in supertype-subtype relationships; we will omit the properties in our semantic networks, but they can easily be added into our semantic networks just as they were in the inheritance hierarchies).

Figure 3.14 shows an example of a semantic network that illustrates the characters of Shakespeare's great tragedy *Hamlet*. The rectangles in the gure represent

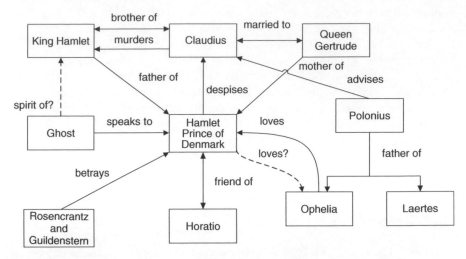

Figure 3.14. A semantic network, representing the characters in *Hamlet*.

the main characters of the play. The links, which are either unidirectional or bidirectional, denote the relationships among the characters. If a relationship is unidirectional, the subject of the relationship is on the unmarked side of the link, while the object is on the arrow side. For example, there is a link between Hamlet and Claudius (with the relationship *despises* indicated on the diagram). This indicates that Hamlet despises Claudius because Claudius is on the arrow side of the link. In other cases, the relationship is bidirectional, or symmetric, as indicated by a link with a double arrow. Examples of where this occurs in the diagram include Hamlet is a friend of Horatio, King Hamlet is a brother of Claudius, and Claudius is married to Queen Gertrude. Each of these relationships can be read in the other direction a well.

A dotted line means that the relationship is not clearly and de nitively established. For example, the ghost in the play is supposed to be the spirit of King Hamlet (who was murdered by his brother Claudius), but we do not know for sure whether this is really the case. Some have speculated that the ghost actually does not exist—that it was just imagined by Hamlet—or that the ghost represents some kind of evil end. These are some alternative interpretations. There is also a dotted line representing the relationship "Hamlet loves Ophelia." In the play, Hamlet professes his love for Ophelia, then later denounces her, so it is not really clear whether Hamlet loves Ophelia or not.

A more detailed semantic network is known as a *propositional network*.[13] These networks are used to illustrate the meaning of sentences. For example the sentence "John gave Sarah a blue car" contains two propositions:

1. John gave Sarah a car.
2. The car is blue.

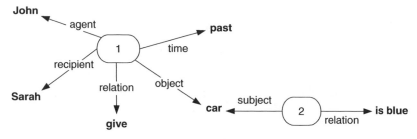

Figure 3.15. A propositional network.

We may represent the two propositions as a network as given in Figure 3.15. Each proposition in this network is represented by an ellipse, which is connected by labeled arrows that represent the arguments of the proposition. For example, the rst proposition includes the arguments agent, recipient, relation, object, and time. Propositional networks can be used to illustrate more complex relations and are commonly employed by cognitive psychologists to graphically depict the meaning of sentences.

Entity-Relationship Diagrams

An entity-relationship diagram (ERD) is a specialized type of diagram that is used by database designers to help them develop database applications. There are several variations of ERDs in use today, but the most basic variety contains three components:

- Entities, represented by rectangles, are the subjects of the database application.
- Relationships, represented by links, are how the entities are associated.
- Cardinality expresses the number of entity occurrences associated with the related entity.

Figure 3.16 shows an ERD that represents and describes a university environment. The rectangles in the diagram represent the main subjects of the university: dean, college, department, professor, student, course, etc. Two rectangles can be connected to each other to denote a relationship between two entities. Sometimes the link contains a verb (as is the case in Figure 3.16) to help the reader of the diagram understand the relationship; however, the verb is optional and can be omitted without affecting the structure of the database application. One difference between this diagram and the semantic network is that all relationships on this network are bidirectional; there is no such thing as a one-way or unidirectional relationship. Hence there are no arrows on the diagram because it is assumed that all relationships contain arrows on both sides.

A unique feature of the ERD, which does not exist on the basic semantic network, is information about cardinalities. Speci cally, cardinalities express the

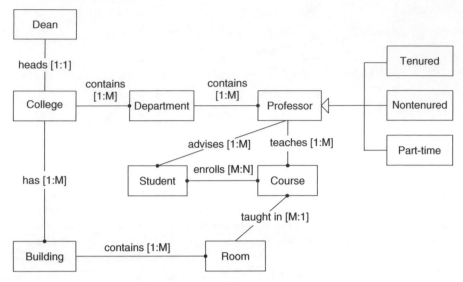

Figure 3.16. An entity-relationship diagram.

type of relationship two entities are engaged in: one-to-one, one-to-many, and many-to-many.

A one-to-one relationship means that one instance of one entity is associated with, at most, one instance of the associated entity. This means that there is often a one-to-one correspondence between the two entities. In the diagram, for example, one dean is associated with one college. Other examples of one-to-one relationships include the following:

- One capital to one country (capital to country)
- One president to one company (president to company)
- One license plate to one automobile (license plate to automobile)

One-to-many relationships are very commonplace in the ERDs. They occur when one instance on one entity is associated with multiple (i.e., two or more) occurrences on an associated entity. In the diagram, one example of a one-to-many relationship is "Professor advises student." A professor can advise multiple students (but a student will be advised by only one professor). Other examples of one-to-many relationships include:

- One painter paints many paintings (painter to painting).
- One customer places many orders (customer to order).
- One state contains many congressmen (state to congressmen).

Finally, many-to-many relationships indicate that one instance of entity A is associated with multiple instances of entity B. In addition to that, one instance of entity B is associated with multiple instances of entity A. The only example of a many-to-many relationship found in Figure 3.16 is the relationship between "Student" and "Course." One student can take multiple courses, and in addition to that, one course is taken by multiple students. Other examples of many-to-many relationships include

- Employees work on projects (one employee can work on multiple projects, and one project can have multiple employees).
- Doctors to patients (one doctor will have multiple patients, and one patient can have many doctors).

The notation used in Figure 3.16 to signify the cardinalities,* as expressed by the relationship type, is as follows:

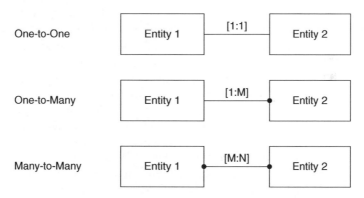

Note that a lled circle at the end of a link signi es a "many side" of the relationship. In the second example, Entity 2 is on the many side of the one-to-many relationship. In the third example, there is a circle on both ends of the link, hence indicating a many-to-many relationship.

The other notation used in the diagram describes supertype-subtype relationships of the kind described in the previous section on inheritance hierarchies. This type of relationship is represented by an arrow that points to the supertype. In the diagram the supertype professor has three subtypes—namely, tenured, nontenured, and part-time.

When developing and implementing relational database application, the database designer will rst turn each of the rectangles on the ERD into a separate table of its own.† In addition, specifying the cardinalities is important because it determines how the tables of the database application are linked together. Thus the ERD serves not only the purpose of documenting a database

---

*There are several different notations used to express cardinalities; the notation introduced here is not the standard or most common way of representing relationship type.
†In a many-to-many relationship, an additional table called the intersection table is also created. The subject of database design using entity-relationship diagrams is covered in many standard database textbooks and is beyond the scope of this discussion.

application but is used as a blueprint for building the application. It is a very important tool for a database designer and remains one of the most popular diagramming tools in use among the software engineering community today.

CAUSALITY

Building causal models is a basic human response to understanding and interacting with the real world. It is hard to imagine anyone who does not regularly build causal models of the world. Whether you are trying to understand the high cost of oil prices or trying to gure out why a friend of yours has slighted you or trying to assess what effect demanding a higher salary will have on your boss and your prospects for promotion, in all cases you are engaged in some form of causal reasoning. This section will address methods to represent causality diagrammatically, and thereby render it more explicit. We will also attempt a de nition of causality, and touch on the dif culties of determining causation—a long-standing problem that has confounded philosophers and scientists for centuries. We will, of course, not resolve all the dif culties and thorny issues in determining causation, but in the end we will have an understanding of some of the techniques that can be employed to structure and explain complex phenomena in the world.

In the realm of AI, causal knowledge can be used to develop intelligent systems that can solve problems on its own. For example, having a detailed causal model of the causes of diseases can help us develop a medical expert system that mimics the human reasoning processes of a medical doctor. Indeed, in many domains, the possession of a detailed causal model can help human experts solve dif cult problems and make recommendations to their clients. The subject of expert systems is covered in more detail in Chapter 5.

Causal utterances such as "smoking causes lung cancer" can be denoted $X \rightarrow Y$, where X is the cause (smoking) and Y is the effect (lung cancer). One commonsense notion of causality is that the cause—which can be a person, an event, an action, a state of affairs, a condition, or an attribute—is responsible for its effect. In other words, the cause in some way produces the effect. Another assumption one can make is that cause precedes its effect in time. Temporal precedence not only helps us distinguish causes from effects but also helps distinguish causation from other types of relationships, such as mere association in which temporal precedence does not hold. At the same time, we need to be careful about establishing causation based on temporal precedence alone because it can lead to spurious, sometimes ridiculous, causal associations. For example, if we know that the rooster crows before the sun rises (and the two events co-occur regularly), we cannot interpret this to mean that the rooster's crow causes the sun to rise. We will address some of the common fallacies of causal reasoning at the end of this section.

Another common conception of causation focuses on the manipulability of the cause. Under this notion, we say that X causes Y if we can change Y by manipulating X. This notion of manipulation is appealing because it suggests that we can use our understanding of causation to effect changes on the world.

For example, if we know that regular exercise leads to lower incidence of heart disease, we can implement a regular exercise regimen to prevent the occurrence of heart disease. One criticism of this perspective is that it emphasizes a human interventionist perspective—it is overly human centered, neglecting to consider causes that cannot be manipulated, such as naturally occurring events (e.g., the earthquake caused the building to collapse), causes that represent xed attributes of an object (her fair skin caused her to burn easily) or causes that represent environmental or external conditions beyond the control of humans (increased consumer con dence led to a rally in the stock market). Perhaps one way to resolve this issue is to view causal statements in the context of a counterfactual statement instead, rather than as causes to be manipulated. For example, the causal statement, "the earthquake caused the building to collapse" can be viewed as the counterfactual statement "if the earthquake hadn't occurred, the building wouldn't have collapsed."

Let us now explore some examples of causal diagrams. We will look speci - cally at three types of diagrams that model causal relationships: directed graphs, shbone diagrams, and fault trees.

Directed Graphs

The most standard and common way of representing causal structure is as a directed graph. This type of diagram contains nodes that are interconnected to one another via links or edges. In a directed graph, all the links are directed, as represented by a single arrowhead on one side of the link. The node on the unmarked side represents the cause, while the node on the arrowhead side represents the effect:

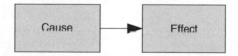

While we most often speak of cause–effect associations as being pairs of events, an effect is seldom the result of just a single cause but rather is the sum total of a number of causes. Moreover, these causes, in turn, may be determined by other causes, or may be the effect of other causes. Causal structure, then, is more likely to look like a tangled web of cause–effect associations. The directed graph enables us to represent these multiple causes and effects visually.

Directed graphs may also include directed cycles, representing mutual causation or some kind of feedback loop—e.g., $X \rightarrow Y$ and $Y \rightarrow X$. A directed graph that contains no directed cycles is called a directed acyclic graph (DAG).

Example: A Causal Model of Unemployment. Unemployment in the U.S. (speci cally the unemployment rate) is affected by a number of factors.[14] Economists classify the factors that affect unemployment into three types (Figure 3.17). *Frictional unemployment* refers to workers who are voluntarily

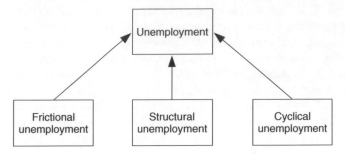

Figure 3.17. A top-level causal model of unemployment.

changing jobs and looking for work. It also includes temporary layoffs and others who are seeking reemployment. Such workers do not gain employment immediately after they leave their jobs, but there is a period of time in which the search for a new job takes place. Hence the term *frictional* suggests that placement of job seekers to jobs does not happen instantaneously or without friction.

Structural unemployment refers to unemployment that is caused by structural changes in the labor market. For example, changes over time in consumer demand and technology may alter the types of jobs that are demanded in the marketplace. One example is that the mechanization of the farms has resulted in fewer jobs in the agricultural sector. On the other hand, the demand for skills in computer programming and technology has intensi ed due to the increased computerization of the workplace. Structural unemployment can also occur when the demand for labor shifts from one geographic area to another. For example, Sun Belt states such as Nevada and Arizona witnessed a huge increase in demand for jobs due to explosive population growth in those areas, while the industrial Midwest lost a number of jobs due to a downturn in the manufacturing and the automotive industries.

Cyclical unemployment is caused by a decline in total spending in the U.S. economy and is likely to occur during the recession phase of the business cycle. Figure 3.18* illustrates a more detailed causal model of cyclical unemployment. The four components of spending that make up the U.S. economy are represented as bold boxes: (1) consumer spending, (2) business investment spending, (3) government spending, and (4) net exports.

We can use this causal model to ask questions about the factors that in uence cyclical unemployment. For example, we may want to know: What effect does high in ation have on unemployment? Our rst step is to isolate and identify the paths that the "In ation" node takes to reach the "Cyclical unemployment" node. In Figure 3.19, the "In ation" node and its interconnected nodes to "Cyclical unemployment" are extracted from Figure 3.18. In the latter diagram, we have

---

*The causal model represented in Figure 3.18, of course, is a simpli ed model that does not account for many factors. It is intended for illustrative purposes to demonstrate how we can conduct causal reasoning using causal models. Macroeconomics is an excellent domain to illustrate how multiple forces interact to produce different effects on the economy.

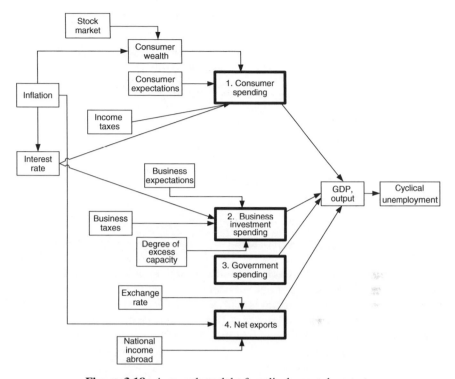

Figure 3.18. A causal model of cyclical unemployment.

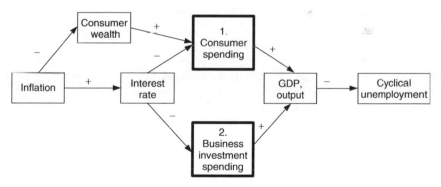

Figure 3.19. A sign diagram illustrating the influence of inflation on cyclical unemployment.

added signs to signify the direction of the causal relationship. If the sign is positive (+), then this means that the cause and the effect move in the same direction: As the value of the cause increases, the value of its effect increases. Likewise, if the value of the cause decreases, the value of its effect decreases. A negative (−) sign denotes an inverse relationship: When the cause increases the effect decreases, and vice versa.

Let us now trace the paths through the directed graph, as given in Figure 3.19. There are three possible paths. The rst path is given by:

in ation → consumer wealth → consumer spending →

GDP, output → cyclical unemployment.

We may reason as follows: High in ation will lead to a reduction in consumer wealth (because in ation reduces the purchasing power of money); this will, in turn lead to lower consumer spending, lower output, and higher unemployment.

The second path is given by:

in ation → interest rate → consumer spending →

GDP, output → cyclical unemployment

Our reasoning, in this case, proceeds as follows: high in ation will lead to a higher interest rate (to decrease in ation, the Federal Reserve will increase interest rates to slow the growth of the money supply). A higher interest rate, in turn, will lead to lower consumer spending (with higher interest rates, consumers are less likely to take out loans), lower output, and nally, higher unemployment.

The third path is given by:

in ation → interest rate → business investment spending →

GDP, output → cyclical unemployment

This path is identical to the second path, except that consumer spending is replaced by business investment spending. The chain of causal reasoning, therefore, is the same except that in this instance business investment spending is decreased (with higher interest rates, businesses are less likely to take out loans), leading to lower output and higher unemployment. Hence, in all three cases, we have argued that high in ation will lead to higher cyclical unemployment. In other cases, the different paths leading to the variable in question, representing the effect, may lead to different conclusions, so that we may also need to assess the strengths of the different causal paths. The overall strength or size of the effect, therefore, can be viewed as the sum total of the strengths of the causes, as represented by the causal paths on the diagram.

Other Notations

Although the directed graph is the most common way of representing causality, because of its exibility in rendering a great many types of causal structures, there are other notations used for causal modeling. We will discuss two additional techniques, the shbone diagram and fault tree analysis. These two alternative techniques are presented to open up our minds to considering other ways of representing causal structure.

Fishbone Diagram. Figure 3.20 shows an example of a shbone diagram. This diagram is given its name because it looks like a shbone (it is also known as an Ishikawa diagram, in honor of its originator). To draw this diagram, you begin with a problem that needs to be addressed. In our example, we wish to represent the factors that in uence whether a business defaults on a loan or not. Next, we identify "categories" of causes, which will be referred to as "primary" causes. In the diagram, there are four primary causes, as labeled in the boxes: management character, nancial strength, collateral, and competitive strength. Each of these primary causes is represented by an arrow that points to the spine of the sh. These primary causes, in turn, can have secondary causes assigned to them. These secondary causes have arrows that point to the arrows representing the primary causes. In "Management Character," for example, there are secondary causes such as trade references, management continuity, and employee morale. These causes, in turn, can have a third set of causes. For example, late payment of bills and excessive borrowing are two causes that point to the bank references arrow. In this way we can create a hierarchic structure of causal elements.

The shbone diagram is a qualitative tool that can be used to capture, in one picture, all aspects of a particular problem. It provides a structured, hierarchic approach to looking at causality. It is not as commonly used as a directed graph because it can easily become cumbersome to add additional causes and subcauses to the diagram. Moreover, some causal models do not easily lend themselves to a hierarchic rendering of causes, sub-causes, and sub-sub-causes.

Fault Tree Analysis. Fault trees were rst used by Bell Telephone Laboratories and the Boeing Corporation during the 1960s to analyze problems with the Minuteman launch control system.[15] In general, they are used to graphically show what combination of events will cause an undesirable event, or a fault to occur. Based on logic and Boolean algebra, these diagrams can help identify causes of a fault in a more visual, and hierarchic way (Figures 3.22 and 3.23).

The rst step to constructing a fault tree is de ning a top event. The top event represents the fault that you are trying to analyze and becomes the top node of the fault tree. In our example, the fault that we are trying to analyze is faulty printing—we are trying to determine the event or combination of events that causes this to occur. The next step is to actually build the fault tree. You build the tree in a top-down fashion, starting with the top event, and continue to add nodes, which represent events that may lead to the fault, as well as gates, that illustrate logical processing of the nodes. The three types of gates are illustrated in Figure 3.21. An OR gate is true if one or more of the inputs to the OR gate is true; an AND gate is true if all the inputs are true; and a Voting gate is true if at least m out of n inputs are true. In Figure 3.21, the numbers on the voting gate indicate that it has three inputs, and at least two of them must be true.

Figure 3.22 contains examples that illustrate each type of gate. For example, "faint printing" occurs when the following condition is true:

Adverse weather conditions OR Toner cartridge low OR Faulty drum unit

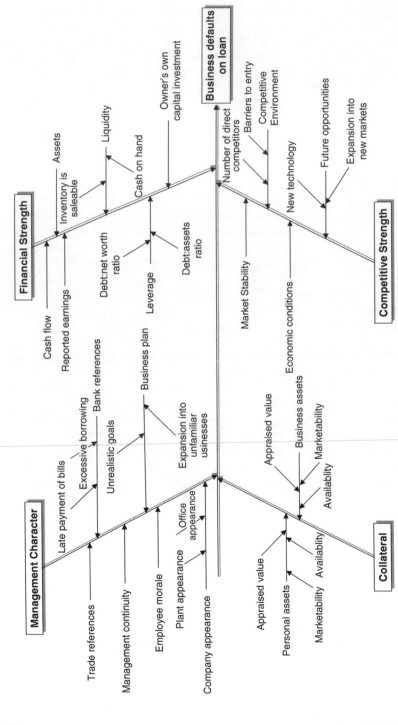

Figure 3.20. A fishbone diagram: factors influencing whether a business defaults on a loan.

Figure 3.21. Three types of gates.

"Adverse weather conditions" is true when the following condition holds:

High temperature AND High humidity

And nally, the voting gate attached to "gray background prints" is true when any two of the following conditions is true:

(1) dirty corona wire, (2) dirty drum unit, (3) dirty laser scanning window

Events with a circle attached below the rectangle represent a base event. These are stand-alone events that will not be developed any further in the fault tree. Examples of base events in Figure 3.22 include "high temperature," "high humidity," and "dirty drum unit."

Large fault trees can easily be split up into two or more pages. In the printing problem example given, the fault tree is displayed on two pages, because the entire fault tree will not easily t on a single page. The "page print skewed" node contains a reference to page 2 to show that this node is further developed on page 2 (Figure 3.23). Similarly, on page 2, there are references to page 1 on the three nodes: "faint printing," "gray background prints," and "toner specks on page."

Fault trees are fairly easy to construct and understand. Their primary bene t, in terms of representing causal structure is that they enable one to represent more complex causal relations using the Boolean operators OR, AND, and the voting gate. You cannot represent such logic using a standard directed graph.

Fallacies of Causal Reasoning

We conclude our discussion on causality by considering some of the dif cul-ties in establishing causation between two events. In general, you must think very carefully when concluding that one event causes another—you may not be observing causation at all, but rather mere correlation between the two events.

Let us suppose that we observe a relationship between two variables A and B. In the language of probability and statistics we say that the two variables are cor-related when there is a linear relationship between the two variables. This means that the two variables tend to move together or covary: If there is a positive corre-lation, larger values of A tend to be associated with larger values of B, and smaller values of A tend to be associated with smaller values of B. If there is a negative correlation, larger values of A tend to be associated with smaller values of B (and vice versa). If A and B are discrete variables, this would mean that the presence or absence of A would tend to be correlated with the presence or absence of B.

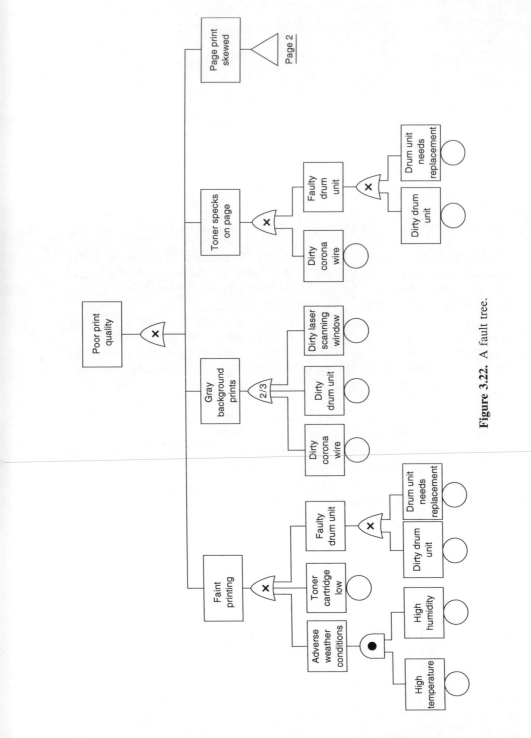

Figure 3.22. A fault tree.

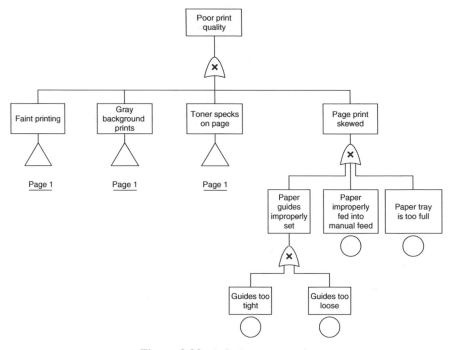

Figure 3.23. A fault tree, page 2.

When we have established correlation between A and B, however, this does not necessarily imply causation—that is $A \rightarrow B$. (Correlation is a necessary but insuf cient condition for establishing causation between two events.) There are at least four possible alternative scenarios, other than $A \rightarrow B$, that could explain the correlation between A and B.

Case 1. The direction of the relationship may not be in the hypothesized direction.

The principle of temporal precedence, described earlier, can help us determine which of two events, A or B, is the cause and which is the effect. This principle tells us that the cause always precedes the effect in time. Sometimes it is obvious which of two events occurs rst. For example: A poor diet causes vitamin de ciency. The poor diet occurs before a person develops a vitamin de ciency, and so the poor diet is undoubtedly the cause. Sometimes it may not be so clear what came rst: the cause and effect occur nearly simultaneously, as far as you can tell, so that it is dif cult to determine which is the cause and which is the effect. For example: Favorable business conditions led to the industrialization of Great Britain in the late 1800s. Did the favorable business conditions occur rst, or did the industrialization of the country? It may not always be so clear-cut, and so you end up trying to disentangle chicken-or-egg type conundrums.

Case 2. The relationship may be self-reinforcing.

It may be the case that $A \rightarrow B$ and $B \rightarrow A$. When it is dif cult to determine the direction of causality, you may, in fact, be witnessing two separate causal relationships that operate in different directions between two events. For example, suppose that you want to discover a causal relationship between studying and good grades. It may be that more studying causes good grades, but it may also be the case that getting good grades may be the cause of studying more (students who get good grades become more motivated to maintain their grade point averages, and this in turn, causes them to study more).

Case 3. There may be a hidden cause.

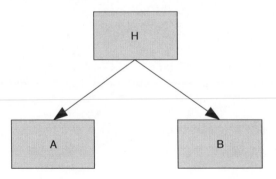

Some third unknown factor (the "hidden" cause) may be the cause of both A and B. This may explain the correlation between A and B. For example, suppose that we observe that both the sales of air-conditioners and ice cream are increasing during the summer months. We further observe that the air-conditioner sales spiked upward earlier than the ice cream sales, therefore establishing temporal precedence (owners of homes decided that they wanted to purchase air-conditioners at the very beginning of the summer season in preparation for the hot and humid days ahead). We may therefore erroneously conclude: Increased air-conditioner sales caused increased ice cream sales. In fact, the warm weather was the cause of both the increased air-conditioner sales and the ice cream sales, but there is no causal association between the two.

Case 4. The correlation may be merely coincidental. It may be that we are witnessing two events that occur simultaneously for no good reason; their co-occurrence is merely coincidental. For example: The concentration of CO_2 (carbon dioxide) gases in the earth's atmosphere has caused the life expectancy in the United States to increase. This, of course, is a spurious association, but it might be made based on the fact that in modern industrial times, the emission of greenhouse gases, such as CO_2, has increased due to the burning of fossil fuels, deforestation, and other human activities; at the same time, during this period of industrialization, we have also witnessed an unprecedented increase in human life expectancy of the U.S. population due to better nutrition, advances in medicine, and the rise of a prosperous middle class that can afford to take better care of itself. The two events, CO_2 concentrations and life expectancy in the United States, are in no way causally related.

In the end, it may very well be impossible to de nitively and rmly establish causation between two events. While we may not be 100% certain that one event *A* causes another event *B* to occur, we can at least gather three types of evidence that would increase the likelihood that *A* is the cause of *B*:

1. Establish temporal precedence. If *A* is the cause of *B*, then *A* must precede *B* in time.
2. Establish covariation between *A* and *B*. The cause *A* must covary with the effect *B*. If the potential cause and effect are unrelated, the one could not have been a cause of the other. Statistics—for example, the calculation of the correlation coef cient—can be used to determine whether there is covariation in the data or not.
3. Eliminate other possible causes of *B*. This may be the toughest condition to meet and will generally require you to search for alternative causes, such as hidden causes, and rule them out one by one, by showing that they do not covary with the effect.

At times, creating a good causal model will require you to dig deeper and deeper to discover the underlying variables, the hidden causes, and deeper explanations. The failure to dig deeper could result in an incomplete and worse, incorrect causal model. A good example (and a nice way to end this section on fallacies of causal reasoning) is illustrated in the University of California at Berkeley's study of sex bias in graduate admissions.[16] A super cial read of the data showed that male applicants were more likely to be admitted to Berkeley's graduate schools than were female applicants. Hence this simple causal model is given by:

Gender → Admissions

A closer inspection of the data, however, tells a completely different story. When the admissions data are broken down by department, it reveals that female applicants are more likely to be admitted than male applicants![17] The explanation to this is that female applicants tended to apply to Berkeley's more competitive departments, for which the admissions rates were lower. A more accurate causal model, then, would include a department node:

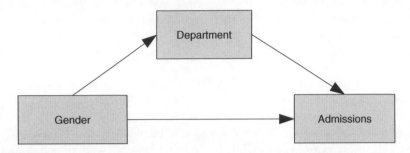

Hence the path gender → department → admissions would be interpreted: Your gender will in uence your choice of department; the department you choose to apply to, in turn, will determine you likelihood of being admitted. When department was controlled for, there was only a very weak relationship between gender and admissions (and it was opposite to what was hypothesized). The "department" node in this example is known as a *mediator* (it mediates the relationship between gender and admissions).

The search for mediators and other variables can indeed lead us to a more complete understanding of complex phenomena. We will have more to say about causal modeling when we discuss Bayesian networks in Chapter 8.

DECISION DIAGRAMS

Decision making involves a choice among two or more alternatives. If we are fortunate enough, it comes easily and naturally to us. At times, it may suf ce to rely on our own intuition, or a simple hunch, to arrive at a good decision. At other times, decision making is dif cult and may require a more thoughtful and deliberate consideration of the different issues involved. (Unfortunately, sometimes we are forced to make a quick decision, which precludes us from performing a careful analysis of a situation.) In this section, we discuss how decision makers can employ diagrams to aid in the decision-making task, especially when the decision is dif cult and complex.

Why is decision making sometimes so hard? There are a number of reasons why it may be dif cult to come to the right decision. First, a decision may be so complex that it is dif cult to keep all the issues straight at one time. We may not have a clear understanding of the myriad issues involved: the alternative courses of action, the possible outcomes of the decision, the values and objectives of the different stakeholders who may be affected by the decision, and the long-term

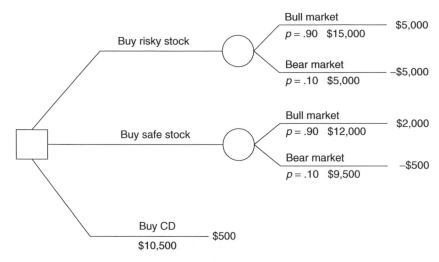

Figure 3.24. A simple decision tree.

consequences of the decision, to name some of the most important issues. Second, oftentimes we must deal with imperfect information. The real world is full of uncertainty, and we often lack good and reliable information. Moreover, we may simply not have the time or the resources to collect and gather all the information, even if it exists. For example, if we are a company that must decide which of several technology projects to invest in, we must deal with a host of issues for which we do not have complete information: Will the new technology work? Will the marketplace embrace the technology? What are the research and development costs involved? Are my competitors developing a similar technology? Third, sometimes we may have multiple objectives to satisfy, and sometimes these objectives may con ict with one another so that we need to make dif cult and carefully calibrated trade-offs.

Decision analysis is used to provide structure to the decision-making process and help us think more systematically about the issues when faced with a thorny and dif cult problem. With decision analysis, a decision maker can acquire a clearer picture of what the important issues are and how they are related to one's decision-making objectives. Equipped with this understanding, the decision maker can make decisions with more con dence. In this section, we explore two important diagramming techniques that decision makers often employ to illustrate a decision-making scenario: decision trees and in uence diagrams.

Decision Trees

In a decision tree, there are two types of nodes: squares represent decision points, and circles represent chance events (Figure 3.24). The branches coming out of the square denote the alternatives available to the decision maker, and the branches coming out of the circle denote the possible outcomes of a chance event. Figure 3.24 is a decision tree that represents the following investment decision:

> Suppose you have $10,000 to invest. You can invest in one of the following: a risky stock, a safe stock, or a CD (certi cate of deposit). If you invest in the risky stock, the stock will either increase by 50% to $15,000 if there is a bull market, or decrease by 50% to $5,000 if there is a bear market. On the other hand, if you invest in the safe stock, the stock will increase to $12,000 if there is a bull market and decrease to $9,500 if there is a bear market. Finally, you can also purchase a CD, which will guarantee that you earn 5% interest or $500. If we assume that there is a 90% chance of a bull market and a 10% chance of a bull market, which investment do you choose?

In Figure 3.24 there are three alternatives—buy risky stock, buy safe stock, or buy CD—emanating from the investment decision node, and two chance outcomes—bull market or bear market—emanating from each of the two chance nodes. Note that there are also probabilities assigned to each outcome, and that they must always add up to 1 for each chance node. This is because we assume that outcomes are mutually exclusive and collectively exhaustive (this means that there are no other outcomes possible). Finally we have included the return on investment for each outcome at the far right.

One way to solve the decision tree is to calculate the expected value of the return on investment for each of the three alternatives:

$$E(\text{return on risky stock}) = 0.9(5000) + 0.10(-5000) = 4,000$$

$$E(\text{return on safe stock}) = 0.9(2000) + 0.10(-500) = 1,750$$

$$E(\text{return on CD}) = 500$$

If you are an *expected value maximizer*, a decision maker who chooses the alternative with the highest expected value, then you would select the risky stock. This would be a reasonable choice to make if the amount of money you are investing is small relative to your total wealth. However, if you were a more risk-averse investor, you might not choose the investment with the highest expected return if the alternative posed an unacceptable level of risk to you. In this case, you might select the safe stock instead, in which case your potential losses are lower, or the CD, safest of the three alternatives because you are guaranteed to receive $500 no matter what.

Is there a way to measure and quantify risk? One approach is to use what is known as a utility function. By utility, we are referring to what a decision maker values, which may or may not be dollar amount. In our example, an appropriate utility function would map the dollar amount (in our case the return on investment) to another value (economists refer to this value as **utils**) that assesses risk. One such utility function is given by:[18]

$$U_R(x) = 1 - e^{-x/R}$$

In this function, R is called the risk tolerance, which determines how risk averse the decision maker is: Smaller values of R would model highly risk-averse decision makers; larger values of R would model more risk-seeking ones. For example, let us assume $R = 1000$, so that we can calculate the expected utility of the three alternatives as follows:

$$EU(\text{risky stock}) = 0.9 * U_{1000}(5,000) + 0.1 * U_{1000}(-5,000)$$
$$= 0.9\left(1 - e^{-5000/1000}\right) + 0.1\left(1 - e^{5000/1000}\right)$$
$$= -13.85$$

$$EU(\text{safe stock}) = 0.9 * U_{1000}(2,000) + 0.1 * U_{1000}(-500)$$
$$= 0.9\left(1 - e^{-2000/1000}\right) + 0.1\left(1 - e^{500/1000}\right)$$
$$= 0.6063$$

$$EU(\text{CD}) = 1.0 * U_{1000}(500)$$
$$= 1.0\left(1 - e^{-500/1000}\right)$$
$$= 0.3935$$

Hence the expected utility for the safe stock is the highest when $R = 1000$. When $R = 300$, you would choose the CD alternative instead because its expected utility is highest ($-1,730,777.00$, -1.804, and 0.8111 for the risky stock, safe stock, and CD, respectively).

Influence Diagrams

An influence diagram is another way of structuring a decision situation. Like a decision tree, an influence diagram uses rectangles to represent decision points and circles to represent chance events. In addition, a diamond is used to represent a consequence node. This type of node typically represents some kind of outcome variable that can be measured or calculated. The shapes on the influence diagrams are linked together with arrows to represent influence (what node influences or affects another node?). The influence diagram for the investment decision just described is illustrated in Figure 3.25.

There are three nodes in the figure. The rectangle represents the decision (which investment to choose?), the circle represents the chance event of whether a bull market or bear market will occur, and the diamond represents the outcome, the return on investment. From the influence diagram, we see that both "Investment?" and "Market" influence "Return." That is to say, the value of the "Return" node is dependent on both the "Investment?" decision node and the "Market" chance node.

Figure 3.25 is annotated to show what each node's possible values are. For example, there are two possible values for the market node: M1 (bull market) or M2 (bear market), and three possible values for the investment node: I1 (buy

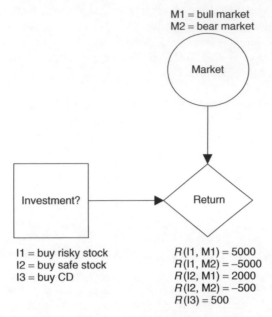

Figure 3.25. An influence diagram for the investment decision.

risky stock), I2 (buy safe stock) and I3 (buy CD). Because the return node's value depends on these two nodes, it is really a function of the values of these two nodes. Hence we specify all the relevant combinations of investment decision and market and what value the return node will assume in each case:

$$R(\text{I1, M1}) = 5000$$

$$R(\text{I1, M2}) = -5000$$

$$R(\text{I2, M1}) = 2000$$

$$R(\text{I2, M2}) = -500$$

$$R(\text{I3}) = 500$$

Sequential Decisions

A more complicated example involves a sequential decision situation in which there are a series of two or more decision points. Figure 3.26 is the decision tree represented by the following sequential decision situation, involving two decision points:

> Suppose you are a prospector who must decide whether a site is suitable for drilling oil or not. From past experience, you have determined that there is a 60% chance of there being oil at the site you have chosen. You can run a seismic survey

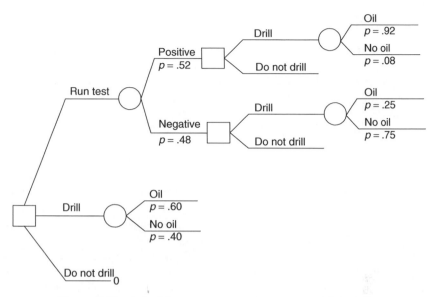

Figure 3.26. A decision tree representing a sequential decision.

test to improve your chances of knowing whether there is oil or not at the site. Unfortunately the seismic survey test is not 100% accurate because it can generate either false positives (it will detect the presence of oil when there is none) or false negatives (it will report the absence of oil when in fact there is oil). If the test turns out positive, there is a 92% chance of there actually being oil at the site (and an 8% chance of there being no oil). If the test is negative, there is a 25% chance of there being oil (and a 75% of there being no oil). You estimate that there is a 52% chance of a positive test, and a 48% chance of a negative test.*

The cost of the test is $100,000, so you must decide whether you want to run the test or not. You have estimated that the cost of drilling oil at the site is $600,000. You have also estimated that if you do decide to drill and oil is found, you will be rewarded with a $2,000,000 oil lease. If no oil is found, the site will be worthless.

In the decision tree, we start from the left with thc rst decision node and work our way to the right. Here, the prospector is faced with three alternatives: (1) run the test, (2) drill oil, and (3) do not drill oil. Alternatives 2 and 3 are straightforward. If the prospector decides to drill oil, and oil is found, the payoff is $1,400,000 ($2 million minus the $600,000 drilling costs) and if oil is not found the payoff is −$600,000 to cover the drilling costs.

If the prospector chooses to run the test instead, the second decision point occurs after the test results are known. The tree branches off into two sections at this point, signifying that the prospector can make a different decision, depending

---

*These probabilities can be calculated using Bayes theorem, a subject we address in Chapter 7, when we look at conditional probabilities.

on whether the seismic test returns a positive or negative result. The payoffs in this section of the tree are $1,300,000 if oil is found ($2,000,000 minus the drilling and seismic test costs) and −$700,000 (the costs of the drilling and seismic test).

To solve the decision tree, you would proceed in reverse: You would start at the right side of the decision tree and proceed to the left. You would calculate expected values on each of the chance nodes and pass the maximum expected values to the decision nodes. You would continue to do this until the leftmost root node is reached. See Figure 3.27 for the complete solution.

Based on expected payoff alone, the prospector would drill (without running the test). The expected payoff for this alternative is $600,000, versus $544,800, which is the expected payoff of the next-best alternative (run the test). Although running the test has a lower expected payoff, it would involve less risk: with a negative test result, you would decide not to drill, and this would result in an expected loss of only $100,000. On the other hand, there would be a signi cant probability (0.40) of losing $600,000 if you decide not to run the test.

The in uence diagram for the oil exploration decision is depicted in Figure 3.28. This diagram contains two decision nodes ("Run Test?" and "Drill?") to represent the sequential nature of the decision situation, two chance nodes ("Test" and "Oil"), and the consequence node ("Payoff"), which represents the net dollar amount that the prospector will gain or lose. Like the previous example, as given in Figure 3.25, the in uence diagram has been annotated to show what each node's possible values are.

Figure 3.28 shows that the "Payoff" node is in uenced by three other nodes, "Run Test?," "Drill?," and "Oil." If you are having trouble understanding why this is so, consider the payoff values, as given in the diagram. The value of "Payoff"

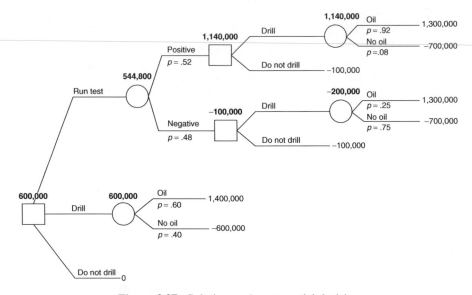

Figure 3.27. Solution to the sequential decision.

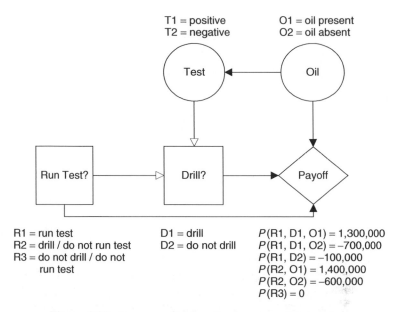

R1 = run test
R2 = drill / do not run test
R3 = do not drill / do not
    run test

D1 = drill
D2 = do not drill

$P(\text{R1, D1, O1}) = 1{,}300{,}000$
$P(\text{R1, D1, O2}) = -700{,}000$
$P(\text{R1, D2}) = -100{,}000$
$P(\text{R2, O1}) = 1{,}400{,}000$
$P(\text{R2, O2}) = -600{,}000$
$P(\text{R3}) = 0$

Figure 3.28. In uence diagram for the sequential decision.

is determined by the values of these three nodes. For example, $P(\text{R1, D1, O1}) =$ 1,300,000. As has been done in the diagram in Figure 3.25, it is useful to write out the payoff values for all relevant combinations of "Run Test?," "Drill?," and "Oil" to understand how they affect the payoff. Finally, there is an arrow from "Oil" to "Test." This arrow represents the in uence that the presence or absence of oil will have on the test result (you are much more likely to get a positive test result if there is oil, and likewise you are much more likely to get a negative test result if there is no oil).

We also introduce a new notation to the in uence diagram in Figure 3.28:

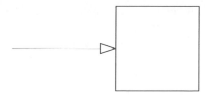

This connection, which is a line with a un lled arrowhead on the right side, represents **sequence**, not in uence (as represented by a lled arrowhead).* In Figure 3.28, there are two connections that represent sequence. The line from "Run Test?" to "Drill?" represents the fact that the "Run Test?" decision is made before the "Drill?" decision.

---

*In most in uence diagrams, the arrow represents both sequence and in uence. The notation introduced here distinguishes between the two types of relationships and eliminates ambiguity in notation.

One may get confused as to why "Test" to "Drill?" represents sequence rather than in uence. This is because the decision to drill is made knowing the outcome of the seismic test. From the decision maker's point of view, the chance event "Test" is resolved, and there is no more uncertainty associated with it. Hence the decision follows the seismic test in sequence. In general, a predecessor node (whether a decision node or a chance event) linked to another decision node will always represent sequence. Under the notation introduced for representing sequence and in uence, the following are never allowed in a properly constructed in uence diagram:

Now that we have an understanding of both decision trees and in uence diagrams, how do the two diagramming techniques compare, and which one is preferable to the other for a given decision-making situation. The examples given show that a decision tree displays more details than does the in uence diagram. This means that decision trees tend to get more unmanageable as a problem-solving situation grows more complex. Hence if your goal is to communicate just the gist of a decision situation, the in uence diagram might be more appropriate.

On the other hand, a decision tree can illustrate the twists and turns of a decision situation with more clarity and detail. In particular, it is helpful in visualizing how a sequence of decision nodes and chance events can in uence your outcomes. In this regard, it is useful to think of the nodes as occurring in a time sequence from left to right—hence we can trace a path through a decision tree to understand how a series of decisions and chance events produced a particular outcome. In terms of explanatory power, then, a decision tree can be superior to an in uence diagram.

Rather than viewing one technique as preferable to the other, perhaps a better stance to adopt is to view the two techniques as complementary to one another. According to this viewpoint, using both approaches may be better than using one alone. In fact, we can always generate a decision tree from an in uence diagram and vice versa—the two techniques can provide a different perspective on the same decision situation. One technique can reinforce the other, and the two together can provide more clarity to the decision maker who struggles to understand what the most important issues are, amid a decision-making environment that can be very dif cult to make sense of.

DISCUSSION

This chapter was about classifying the great variety of diagrams in use today. Our classi cation scheme looked at ve categories of diagrams according to their function:

1. System topology
2. Sequence and ow
3. Hierarchy and classi cation
4. Association
5. Cause and effect

Throughout this chapter, we investigated diagrams in a wide range of application areas: everything from network diagrams that show how the hardware components in a computer network are interconnected to one another, to owcharts that help doctors classify heart attack patients, to causal models used by economists to help them understand the forces that in uence unemployment, to entity-relationship diagrams that software engineers use to help them design database systems. Even with such tremendous diversity in usage, the ve categories cut across all these types of diagrams and can serve as a unifying framework for understanding and organizing a great variety of diagramming notations.

We also provided examples of decision diagrams, which is not really a separate category or new functional area of diagramming. Although we introduced two new diagrams related to decision making—namely the decision tree and the in uence diagram—these diagrams do not represent new functional categories of diagramming at all: The decision tree is about understanding the sequence of decision points and chance events involved a decision-making task; an in uence diagram is really a form of a cause and effect diagram that illustrates what variables in uence a decision outcome. Hence both of these decision diagrams are variations on sequence and ow and cause and effect diagrams. The sixth category, logic reasoning, will be discussed in the next chapter.

At the beginning of this chapter we de ned a diagram as an information graphic that is made up of geometric shapes that are typically interconnected by lines and arrows to show how things, people, ideas, activities, etc. interrelate and interconnect. The geometric shapes, whether they are squares, circles, diamonds, or any other shape represent different types of objects, and their meaning varies according to the diagramming notation chosen. For example, a diamond in a basic owchart represents a decision point, but it represents a consequence node in an in uence diagram. A simple line is used to link two objects (or shapes) together to show that they are interrelated in some way. Alternatively, an arrow may be used to denote a directed relationship between two objects. Figure 3.29 shows that the linkage between two objects has a different meaning depending on its functional category (topology, sequence and ow, classi cation, composition, association, cause and effect). Note how hierarchy has been separated into two categories: classi cation and composition. With the exception of system topology and association, all linkages are directed, as indicated by the arrows. System topology and association diagrams may also employ directed linkages, but they frequently do not. See Figures 3.3 and 3.16 for examples of

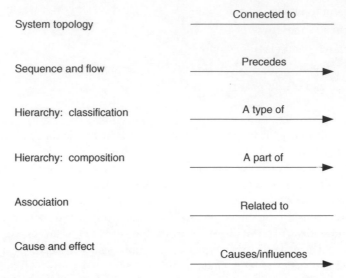

Figure 3.29. Meanings of linkages for the different types of diagrams.

diagrams with linkages that are undirected. On the other hand, see Figure 3.14 for an example of an association network with directed linkages.*

Sometimes the arrowheads are omitted but are implied in the diagram. For example, the decision trees in Figures 3.24 and 3.26 omit the arrowheads (to show sequence of decision points and chance events). Decision trees are almost always read from left to right so it is not necessary to add arrowheads to the linkages. In a similar fashion, organization charts (Figure 3.11) and composition models (Figure 3.13) will typically omit the upward pointing arrows, because by convention, we read them from top to bottom. The arrowheads should not be omitted if they will create ambiguity in the diagram. A good example of this is the entity-relationship diagram (Figure 3.16). Here, there is an arrowhead pointing to the "Professor" supertype, from its three subtypes. Because this diagram displays both association and classi cation, it is a good idea to make explicit the supertype-subtype classi cation linkage with an arrowhead, otherwise it will not be clear whether this is a regular association link on the diagram.

ENDNOTES

1. Robert Spence, *Information Visualization*. New York: Addison-Wesley, 2001.
2. Jill H. Larkin and Herbert A. Simon, "Why a Diagram Is (Sometimes) Worth Ten Thousand Words," *Cognitive Science* 8 (1987), 66.

---

*A system topology diagram may also use directed linkages. For example, a diagram that illustrates a hydraulic system may use directed linkages to show how water ows through a hydraulic system.

3. See Robert L. Harris, *Information Graphics: A Comprehensive Illustrated Reference*. Atlanta, GA: Management Graphics, 1966, for a discussion of the different types of information graphics. His classi cation is similar to the one presented in this chapter, with a few modi cations.

4. There are many references on UML. For an introduction and overview, see Martin Fowler, *UML Distilled: A Brief Guide to the Standard Object Modeling Language*, 3rd ed.. Boston: Addision-Wesley, 2004.

5. Ibid., p. 35.

6. Ibid., p. 117.

7. The Cook County Hospital case is based on the discussion from Malcolm Gladwell, *Blink*. New York: Little, Brown, 2005, pp. 125–136.

8. Ibid, pp. 131–132.

9. Lee Goldman et al., "Prediction of the Need for Intensive Care in Patients Who Come to Emergency Departments with Acute Chest Pain," *New England Journal of Medicine*, 334, no. 23 (1996), 1498–1504.

10. See, for example, Herbert A. Simon, *The Sciences of the Artificial*. Cambridge, MA: MIT Press, 1996; and Gordon H. Bower, "Organizational Factors in Memory," *Cognitive Psychology* 1 (1970), 18–46.

11. Bower, p. 41.

12. Simon, p. 185.

13. For more information on propositional networks see John R. Anderson, *Cognitive Psychology and Its Implications*, 3rd ed. New York: WH Freeman, 1990, pp. 126–133. See also M. Ross Quillian, "The Teachable Language Comprehender," *Communications of the ACM* 12 (1969), 459–476; and David E. Rumelhart, Peter H. Lindsay, and Donald E. Norman, A Process Model for Long-Term Memory, in *Organization of Memory*, New York: Academic Press, 1972; among others.

14. Causal models of unemployment can be found in many standard texts on economics. The discussion is from Campbell R. McConnell and Stanley L. Brue, *Economics: Principles, Problems, and Policies*, 16th ed. New York: McGraw-Hill, 2005.

15. Sutton, Ian, See *Fault Tree Analysis*, Sutton Technical Books, 2007.

16. P. J. Bickel, E. A. Hammond, and J. W. O'Connell, "Sex Bias in Graduate Admissions," *Science* 187 (1975), 398–404.

17. See Judea Pearl, *Causality*. Cambridge; New York: Cambridge Univ. Press, 2000. Pearl discusses the sex discrimination study and illustrates it as an example of Simpson's paradox (pp. 128–130). Simpson's paradox refers to the observation that a statistical relationship between two variables can be reversed by including additional factors in the analysis (p. 78).

18. See Richard E. Neopolitan, *Learning Bayesian Networks*. Upper Saddle River, NJ: Pearson Prentice Hall, 2004, pp. 237–239, for a discussion of utility functions that map dollar amounts to utilities. See also Robert T. Clemen, *Making Hard Decisions: An Introduction to Decision Analysis*. Belmont, CA: Duxbury Press, 1997, for a more detailed discussion of modeling risk attitudes.

CHAPTER 4

LOGIC REASONING WITH DIAGRAMS

The study of logic reasoning has had a long and storied history in AI that dates back to the very beginnings of the field. Alan Newell and Herbert Simon's *Logic Theorist*, a program that was designed to prove the basic equations of logic, was developed in 1955 and is regarded by many as the first AI program. (The program is able to prove most of the theorems in Chapter 2 of Russell and Whitehead's *Principia Mathematica*, a book that revolutionized the study of formal logic.) Another researcher, Herbert Gelertner, in 1958 developed an AI program that could prove geometry theorems. Later in 1972, PROLOG was developed as an AI programming language that had its roots in formal logic. Logic is also of great importance in the development of expert systems, in which an inference engine reasons from facts (or premises) to conclusions. Hence an understanding of logic reasoning is important in developing many kinds of AI systems today. We will look more closely at rule-based expert systems in Chapter 5.

Logic is about the study of arguments. In a typical argument, we are given premises that are intended to prove a conclusion. Here is a simple example:

All penguins are birds.
All penguins do not fly.
∴ Some birds do not fly.

The first two statements represent the premises, while the third represents the conclusion. The conclusion is preceded by ∴ (the therefore symbol). Each line contains a declarative statement (as opposed to a question, a command, or an exclamation), which is an assertion that is either true or false. An argument in which a conclusion follows from two premises, as in this example, is also known as a *syllogism*. We call an argument valid when the conclusion follows from the premises.

Formal logic is the study of argument forms or argument patterns that are common to many types of arguments. We can transform the syllogism about birds and penguins into a more generic argument form by replacing the specific words with variables:

All A are B.

All A are not C.

∴ Some B are not C.

A replaces the set of penguins, B replaces the set of birds, and C replaces the set of things that fly. By studying general forms of arguments, we can make important generalizations that apply to a whole class of arguments. Here is another example of an argument form, which is always true:

If P, then Q

Not Q

∴ Not P

This chapter is about the use of diagrams in formal logic reasoning. This is a topic that has generated great interest in recent years due to the need to visualize logic reasoning and the realization that complex logic can be made more understandable with a diagram of some sort. The study of formal logic has traditionally involved the use of linguistic representations using first order logic. This approach will be covered in brief at the end of the chapter when we compare and contrast the linguistic representation systems to the diagrammatic ones. Indeed, there remains a deep distrust toward diagrams among many logicians today. For the most part, they consider diagramming a heuristic tool only and not a serious technique for the construction of valid proofs. We will show how diagramming techniques, specifically the use of Venn diagrams, can be used in very dynamic ways to construct logic proofs for a subset of logic problems.

We begin this chapter with a discussion of two basic diagramming techniques that are used in the study of logic: argument diagrams, and Euler graphs. We then describe Venn diagrams, and discuss a formalism that renders them more dynamic, capable of solving a class of logic proofs.

ARGUMENT DIAGRAMS

A simple diagramming technique is the argument diagram, a diagram that is used to represent the structure of an argument—how premises and conclusions are interlinked and how to represent conjunctive and convergent arguments. In more complex arguments, an argument diagram can help us understand multistep argument structures in which chains of statements are interlinked to one another.

The technique is a simple one to follow. You first label each statement with a number. You then draw arrows from the statements that represent the premises to statement that represents the conclusion. For example, $1 \rightarrow 2$, means that 1 is intended as evidence for 2. If two or more statements function together as a premises (i.e., both must be true for the conclusion to hold), then you write their statement numbers together, joined by a plus sign. These statements will be referred to as *conjunctive premises*.

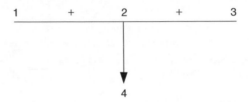

In the diagram each statement requires completion by the others in order for the argument to make sense. The above is equivalent to *If (1) and (2) and (3) Then (4)*.

On the other hand, if the premises stand on their own—that is, function as independent reasons for the conclusions, then you do not include the plus sign, but they must be linked separately to the conclusion. These arguments are called *convergent arguments*.

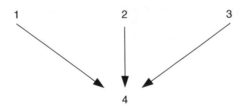

In this diagram, statements 1, 2, and 3 function as independent reasons for 4. Each statement supports 4 independently and is therefore linked by a separate arrow of its own. The diagram is equivalent to *If (1) or (2) or (3) Then (4)*. Examples of conjunctive premises and convergent arguments follow.

Example 1: Conjunctive Premises. (1) The victim died from a gunshot wound. (2) John was found in possession of a gun shortly after the crime occurred. (3) The bullets of the gun in John's possession matched the bullet found on the victim. Therefore, (4) John likely murdered the victim.

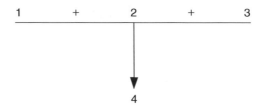

In this example, the three statements together are required in order for the conclusion to follow. One statement alone (1, 2, or 3) does not provide enough evidence for the conclusion that John murdered the victim.

Example 2: Convergent Argument. (1) You should not smoke because (2) it is a costly habit. (3) It also the leading cause of lung cancer, emphysema, and other respiratory diseases. (4) And finally, it is harmful to others because secondhand smoke can be inhaled by those around you.

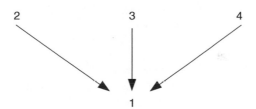

In this example, statements 2, 3, and 4 function as separate and independent reasons why you should not smoke.

Example 3: A Complex, Multi-Step Argument. (1) You are not likely to be admitted into a top law school for three reasons: (2) first, your LSAT scores are low; (3) second, your undergraduate GPA is too low; (4) third, you are not a minority student; and (5) only special considerations are granted to minority applicants. (6) The top law firms will hire you only if you graduate from a top law school. (7) Therefore, you are unlikely to be hired by a top law firm. (8) If your goal is to find a job in a top law firm, I recommend that you consider another career path.

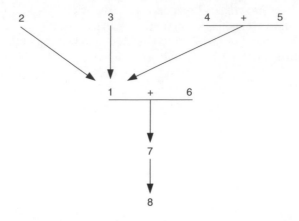

This diagram illustrates a complex argument structure, containing a multistep chain of reasoning as well as convergent premises and conjunctive premises.

LOGIC REASONING WITH DYNAMIC VENN DIAGRAMS

Leonhard Euler (born in 1707), an 18th-century Swiss mathematician, is generally credited with being the first to use circles to illustrate relations between classes. His Euler graph, while useful in visualizing these relations, was extremely limited in terms of helping one to solve logic problems. In the 19th century the British logician John Venn (born in 1834) developed a diagramming technique that was much more powerful and capable of illustrating a wider class of logic problems. This well-known technique, Venn diagramming, is widely used in set theory and logic today and is the best-known example of logic diagrams. A third figure of importance is Charles Peirce (born in 1839), whose works in logic reasoning and logic graphs were largely ignored during his lifetime. Peirce's ideas overcame many limitations of Venn diagramming and paved the way for more dynamic uses of diagramming in logic reasoning. The discussion in this chapter owes much to the work and revolutionary ideas of Peirce as well as to those of Sun-Joo Shin, who developed a diagramming technique known as Venn-I,[1] which can be used to prove logic theorems. We will explore the techniques of Venn-I and how they can be used to create more dynamic and interactive uses of Venn diagrams. Hereafter, the Venn-I techniques that Shin developed or simply referred to as Venn diagrams.

We begin our discussion with Euler graphs. Euler represented the four types of categorical statements with circles:

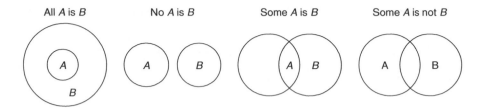

The two universal statements *All A is B*, and *No A is B* are represented in a straightforward and intuitive way. In the first diagram, the circle with the letter A is completely contained within the circle with the letter B, representing the fact that *All A is B*. The second diagram illustrates that there is no overlap between the circle with the letter A and the circle with the letter B, representing the fact that *No A is B*. Less clear and intuitive, at first glance, are the diagrams representing the two existential statements: *Some A is B* and *Some A is not B*. In the third diagram, an A is placed in the intersecting region (A∩B), and in the fourth diagram, the A is placed in the region inside A, but outside B (A∩¬B). Both these diagrams indicate that something exists where the letter A is placed.

The Euler representation system is limited in a number of ways. For one, it does not enable one to represent a great number of relations between two sets. For example, you cannot represent, among others relations, such statements as:

- Everything is either A or B.
- Everything is neither A nor B.
- There exists something in A, but not in B.
- Nothing is both A and B.

Euler graphs can represent only the four categorical statements as given earlier. To perform a wider range of logic reasoning tasks, we need a more powerful representation system that, at the very least, can represent a broader range of relations between two or more sets.

A second serious drawback of the Euler system is its inability to combine two or more pieces of information in one diagram. This is especially needed in syllogistic reasoning, because we need to combine the information from two premises to determine the validity of its conclusion. For example:

All P are Q.
Some P are R.
∴ Some Q are R.

The following are the two Euler graphs that illustrate the premises of this syllogism:

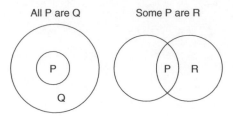

To determine the validity of this syllogism, we need to combine these two diagrams. Unfortunately, there is no easy and intuitive way to combine the two diagrams into one. In general, it is difficult to transform two or more Euler graphs into a valid Euler graph. We will see, later on, that an important capability of Venn diagrams is that they can easily be combined via rules of transformation. These rules specify what the valid or permissible transformations are. Without this ability to perform incremental transformation, we are severely limited in handling syllogistic reasoning and other types of logic reasoning tasks.

An Introduction to Venn Diagrams

We are all familiar with the Venn diagram to represent relations between sets. Suppose we want to illustrate the relations between the set of plants and the set of green things. We begin by drawing two overlapping circles:

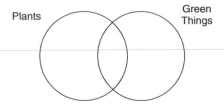

Further, we sometimes enclose the overlapping circles with a rectangle to represent the background set. In this example, the background set is the set of all things.

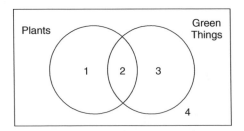

Each compartment (as numbered in the above Venn diagram) represents a possible combination of the two sets: Compartment 1 is the set of plants that are not green; Compartment 2 is the set of plants that are green; and Compartment 3 is the set of green things that are not plants. Finally, Compartment 4, as given in this diagram, is the set of non-plants and non-green things.

Venn further adopts of the convention of shading those compartments that represent nothing, or the empty set. For example:

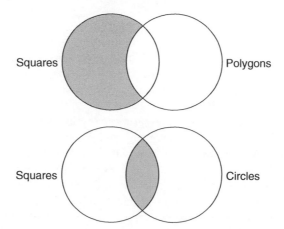

Because all squares are polygons, we shade out the compartment that represents squares that are not polygons. In a similar fashion, because no squares are circles, we shade out the compartment that represents the intersection between squares and circles. In general we can represent the two universal statements, *All A is B* and *No A is B*, as follows:

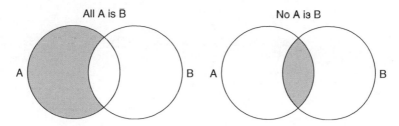

But how do we represent the two existential statements, *Some A is B* and *Some A is not B*? It is clear that we need a new syntactic device to represent the fact that something exists in a particular compartment on a Venn diagram—that is, we require notation to denote a non-empty compartment. For this, we add a ⊗ to the compartment where there exists at least one occurrence. Doing so yields the following two Venn diagrams:

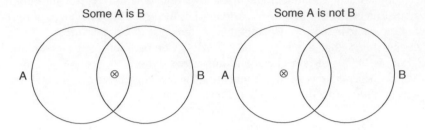

In the first diagram, we add an ⊗ to the compartment that represents the existence of at least one thing that is both A and B (A∩B). In the second diagram, we add an ⊗ to the compartment that represents the existence of at least one thing that is A and not B (A∩¬B).

We now have a technique for representing many kinds of propositions on our Venn diagrams, both categorical statements and existential statements. To make our representation system even more expressive, we also need a way to represent disjunctive information. That is to say, we would like to express the fact that either one of two existential statements (or both) is true. The syntactic device that Peirce adopts, one that we adopt in this chapter, is a line that connects the ⊗ symbols. For example, suppose we wish to represent the statement:

(Some A is not B) OR (Some B is not A)

We can do this by connecting the two ⊗ symbols as the following diagram illustrates:

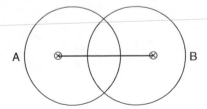

To summarize, the problem of representing the relations between sets really boils down to determining the emptiness or nonemptiness of the compartments on a Venn diagram. If a compartment is empty, we shade the compartment; and if a compartment is nonempty, we place an ⊗ in the compartment. If the set is represented by more than one compartment, we place an ⊗ in each compartment, and connect them by lines. We refer to a series of interconnected ⊗ symbols linked to one another like a chain as an *x*-**sequence**.

We can also construct three-set Venn diagrams using the same notation. The template for the three-class Venn diagram is given by:

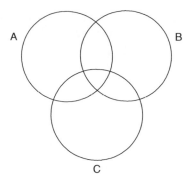

Before proceeding any further, let us define a few terms and notations that will aid in our discussion. We will refer to any enclosed area of a Venn diagram as a **region**. For example, in the last diagram we may refer to Region A, Region B, and Region C, as the circles representing the three sets. We may also refer to regions using the four set operators: union (Region A+B), difference (Region A−C), intersection (Region A∩B or simply Region AB) and negation (Region ¬C). The shadings in the next diagram represent each of these regions.

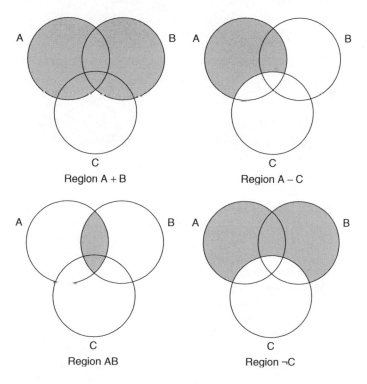

Region A + B

Region A − C

Region AB

Region ¬C

We refer to a minimal region as a **compartment**. By minimal, we mean a region that contains no other region. In the three-set Venn diagram, there are eight such compartments. We have enclosed the three-overlapping circles with a rectangle to represent the background set. (Note that in the examples that follow, the background set, or the rectangle, is omitted.)

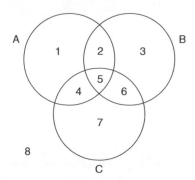

We have labeled the compartments one through eight on the diagram. Each of these compartments corresponds to the following set notations:

Compartment 1: A¬B¬C
Compartment 2: AB¬C
Compartment 3: ¬AB¬C
Compartment 4: A¬BC
Compartment 5: ABC
Compartment 6: ¬ABC
Compartment 7: ¬A¬BC
Compartment 8: ¬A¬B¬C

We may refer to a compartment by its label, Compartment 4, or by its set notation, Compartment A¬BC. The advantage of using a label is that it is easier to see and understand on a diagram, whereas the advantage of referring to its set notation is that we do not need to create additional labels on our Venn diagram.

Now that we have defined what a compartment is, we are ready to define how to create Venn diagrams for $n > 3$ classes. Although it would be impossible to graphically illustrate Venn diagrams for these higher-order Venn diagrams, one could easily construct a program that could enumerate all possible compartments for Venn diagrams containing more than three classes. To create these diagrams we will state the following rule:

A new class (or circle) introduced onto a Venn diagram must overlap each and every compartment of that diagram once and only once. This rule is referred to as the **partial overlapping rule**.[2] In general, a Venn diagram with n classes will contain 2^n compartments. For a four-class Venn diagram there would be 16 compartments, for a five-class Venn diagram, 32 compartments, and so on.

Like in the two-class Venn diagram case, we use shading to denote the empty set and an $\otimes$ to denote a nonempty set. The following three-class Venn diagrams represent the universal statements (1) *All B is C* (diagram on the left) and (2) *No B is C* (diagram on the right).

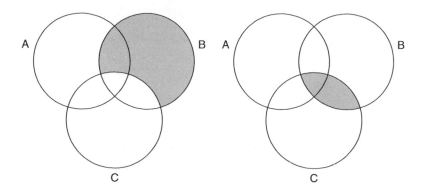

To represent the existential statement *Some B is not C* requires that we specify a disjunction of $\otimes$ symbols in two compartments.

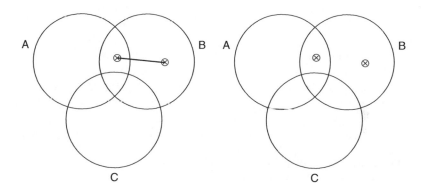

The correct specification of this statement is given by the left diagram. This diagram represents the fact that there could exist an occurrence in either one of the two compartments or in both in order for *Some B is not C* to be true. The diagram on the right does not accurately represent this statement because it represents the fact that there is at least one occurrence in each of the two compartments.

To represent the statement *There exists some A* would also require a disjunction of $\otimes$ symbols. This time it would span four compartments in our three-class Venn diagram. Again the correct specification is to join the $\otimes$ symbols so that they are all connected in one sequence. In this instance, we need to create an x-sequence of length 4.

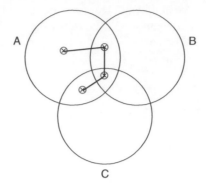

Syllogistic Reasoning with Venn Diagrams: A First Pass

Venn diagramming, it turns out, is a very effective technique for performing syllogistic reasoning. Its chief advantage (over the Euler graph in particular as we noted earlier) is the ability to incrementally add knowledge to the diagram. While an Euler graph has visual power in terms of representing the relations between sets very intuitively, it is impossible to combine more than one piece of information onto a Euler graph. A Venn diagram, on the other hand, easily lends itself to the representation of partial knowledge and can be manipulated to add successively more knowledge to the diagram. This means that when our knowledge of the relations between sets increases, we simply put in more ⊗ symbols and shadings into the appropriate compartments of the Venn diagram. Thus we are able to accumulate knowledge in a Venn diagram. This capability turns out to be a powerful feature, one that endows Venn diagrams with a more dynamic quality that is sorely lacking in the Euler system.

We begin with a formal procedure for testing the validity of a syllogism:[3]

1. Draw a diagram that represents the facts that the premises of a syllogism conveys. We will call this diagram D_P.
2. Draw a diagram that represents the facts that the conclusion of a syllogism conveys. We will call this diagram D_C.
3. Check if we can read off diagram D_C from D_P. If we can, the syllogism is valid; if we cannot, the syllogism is invalid.

What do we mean by *reading off* one diagram from another diagram, as is suggested in step 3 of this procedure? This is a difficult question to answer, but as a first pass we will state the following:

We can read off diagram D_C from D_P if D_C is *completely contained* within D_P.

As a simple example, suppose we are given the following diagram D_P, which represents the premises of a syllogism.

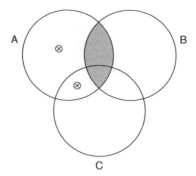

We wish to test the validity of two possible conclusions, as represented by C_1 and C_2. First, we represent each of these conclusion by a Venn diagram, as given next.

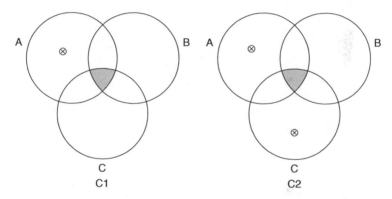

C_1 is completely contained within D_P (every $\otimes$ and shading in C_1 is also in D_P), so conclusion C_1 is valid. However, C_2 is not completely contained within D_P (the $\otimes$ in the Region C of Diagram C_2 in not included in D_P), so C_2 is invalid. We will have more to say about reading off one diagram from another in the next two examples and when we discuss rules of transformation in the next section.

Let's explore two examples of syllogistic reasoning using Venn diagrams.

Example 1. Earlier we were given the following syllogism and noted that it is impossible to combine the two premises into one Euler graph.

P_1: All P are Q.
P_2: Some P are R.
$\therefore$ Some Q are R.

The syllogism's premises are labeled P_1 and P_2 to facilitate the discussion. We can create Venn diagrams for each premise as well as a combination of the two premises as given next.

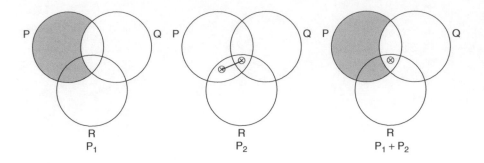

To facilitate the discussion of this example, let's label the compartments of the Venn diagram as follows:

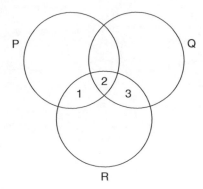

Compartment 1 represents (P¬QR), Compartment 2 represents (PQR), and Compartment 3 represents (¬PQR).

The first two Venn diagrams represent, separately, each of the two premises. The third diagram represents a combination of the two premises, $P_1 + P_2$. To combine the two diagrams, we need to reconcile the fact that Compartment 1 contains a shading in Premise P_1, while it is part of an x-sequence in Premise P_2. To reconcile this difference, we replace the ⊗ with a shading, thus resulting in the third diagram. In general, we may erase any part of an x-sequence if it is in a shaded compartment (more about nodes of transformation later).

Please note that we cannot combine the two diagrams in this way if there is a standalone ⊗ in one diagram and a shading in another. If this is the case, this situation represents a contradiction: A compartment cannot be empty and nonempty at the same time. In this case, to combine the two diagrams, we would need to reformulate our premises so that they do not contradict one another.

The conclusion of the syllogism is represented by the following Venn diagram:

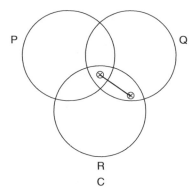

P

Q

R

C

To prove the validity of the syllogism, we need to determine whether we can read off Diagram C from the Diagram $P_1 + P_2$. In Diagram $P_1 + P_2$ there is an $\otimes$ in Compartment 2 meaning that there exists something in that compartment. Diagram C represents the conclusion that there exists something in either Compartment 2 or Compartment 3. If there exists something in Compartment 2, as given by Diagram $P_1 + P_2$, then certainly it is always true that there exists something in either Compartment 2 or Compartment 3, as given in Diagram C. Hence this syllogism is valid.

Example 2. Suppose we are given the following syllogism:

P_1: Some P are not Q.
P_2: No Q are R.
$\therefore$ Some P are R.

Like in the previous example, we first represent each premise separately and then combine them into one Venn diagram.

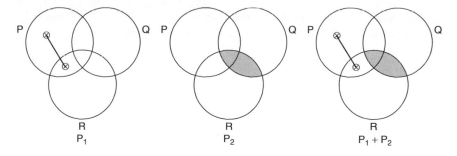

P   Q   P   Q   P   Q

R   R   R
P_1 P_2 $P_1 + P_2$

The first two Venn diagrams represent, separately, each of the two premises. It is a simple matter to combine P1 and P2 to generate $P_1 + P_2$. We simply carry over the $\otimes$ symbols and the shadings and place them into their appropriate compartments (unlike in Example 1, there is no need to reconcile differences between the two diagrams).

The conclusion is represented by the following Venn diagram:

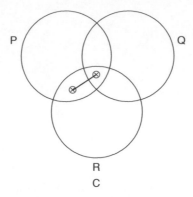

C

Can we read off Diagram C from Diagram $P_1 + P_2$? To facilitate the discussion let's label the compartments under discussion 1, 2, and 3, as given by the next diagram:

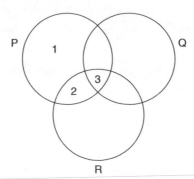

Compartment 1 represents (P¬Q¬R), Compartment 2 represents (P¬QR), and Compartment 3 represents (PQR). Diagram $P_1 + P_2$ tells us that there exists something in either Compartment 1 or Compartment 2, while Diagram C conveys that there is something in either Compartment 2 or Compartment 3. Therefore, as given by $P_1 + P_2$, there is a possibility that something exists in Compartment 1 but nothing exists in Compartment 2. If that were true, there is a possibility that Compartment 2 and Compartment 3 are *both* empty (Compartment 3 is shaded in $P_1 + P_2$). Hence it does not necessarily follow that either Compartment 2 or Compartment 3 is nonempty, as represented by Diagram C. Therefore, this syllogism is invalid.

Rules of Transformation

To make the examples of the last section more precise, we need to specify rules of transformation on Venn diagrams. That is, what are the rules for combining information and manipulating the information represented on a Venn diagram?

Our rules of transformation should correctly guide us on how to manipulate our diagrams so that we can transform one diagram into another equivalent diagram.

An apt analogy is the rules of algebra that allow us to perform transformations on algebraic equations. For example:

$$A^*(B + C) = A^*B + A^*C \quad \text{(by the law of distributivity)}$$
$$= A^*C + A^*B \quad \text{(by the law of additive commutativity)}$$
$$= C^*A + B^*A \quad \text{(by the law of multiplicative commutativity)}$$

Just like the rules of algebra, the rules of transformation will tell us what the permissible transformations are—how we can transform one diagram into another diagram, step by step.

We discussed earlier the notion of reading off one diagram from another. We need to make these ideas more rigorous and complete. Our rules of transformation will allow us to determine, with more precision, how we can transform one diagram, say D_1, into another diagram, say D_2. If we are able to transform D_1 into D_2 by using these rules of transformation, then we can read off D_2 from D_1; and if we can read off D_2 from D_1, where D_1 represents the premises, and D_2 represents the conclusion, then we have a valid syllogism. Hence our rules of transformation should enable us to formulate a procedure for determining the validity of a syllogism. Moreover, if we have precise rules of transformation, we can develop algorithms and computer programs to perform syllogistic reasoning for us.

To organize the discussion, the rules of transformation are classified into three categories of manipulations:[4]

   I. Erasure of an object
  II. Addition of an object
 III. Unification of two diagrams

By *object* we are referring specifically to one of the three types of objects on a Venn diagram: (1) circles (sets), (2) x-sequences (nonemptiness), and (3) shadings (emptiness).

I. Erasure of an object. We first consider three valid erasures: an entire shading in a compartment, a whole x-sequence, and a partial x-sequence when part of it is in a shaded region. We next consider the erasure of an entire circle on a Venn diagram.

Rule I.1: Erasure of Shading in a Compartment. We may erase a shading in a compartment.

Rule I.2: Erasure of a Whole x-Sequence. We may erase a whole x-sequence.

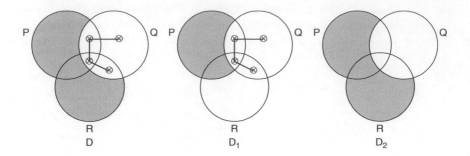

D_1 is a valid transformation of D because it erases the shading in an entire compartment (Rule I.1); D_2 is a valid transformation of D because it erases an entire x-sequence (Rule I.2).

Rule I.3: Erasure of Part of an x-Sequence in a Shaded Compartment. We may erase any $\otimes$ of an x-sequence if that $\otimes$ is in a shaded region. If the $\otimes$ is in the middle of the x-sequence, then after we erase the $\otimes$, we must connect both of the remaining parts so that we have one x-sequence. The number of x-sequences in a diagram does not change.

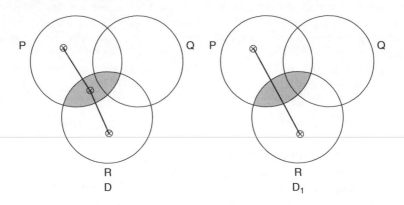

The transformation from D to D_1 is legitimate in this diagram. We first erase the $\otimes$ in the shaded region; then we connect the two remaining $\otimes$ symbols.

Rule I.4: Erasure of a Circle. We may erase an entire circle. By doing so, one of two situations may arise: (1) The resulting Venn diagram may contain a partial shading in a compartment or (2) the resulting Venn diagram may contain an x-sequence with more than one $\otimes$ in a compartment.

Rule I.4.a: A Partial Shading in a Compartment. When a circle is erased and the resulting Venn diagram contains a partial shading in a compartment, then the shading in that compartment should be erased.

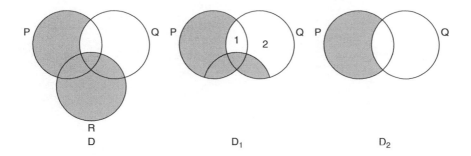

In D we may erase circle R, resulting in Diagram D_1. Compartments 1 and 2 contain partial shadings that must be erased. The correct transformation is given in D_2.

Rule I.4.b: An x-Sequence with More Than One ⊗ in a Compartment. When a circle is erased, and the resulting Venn diagram contains an x-sequence in which there is more than one ⊗ in a compartment, then that part of the x-sequence should be replaced by one ⊗ and should be connected to the rest of the x-sequence.

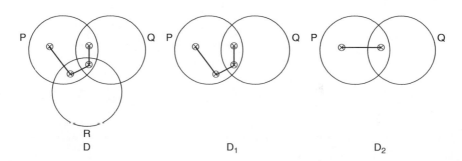

In D, we erase circle R, and the resulting Venn diagram D_1 contains two compartments with two ⊗ symbols. By applying this rule twice (once for each compartment), we obtain D_2, which is a legitimate transformation of D.

II. Addition of an object. Two types of objects may be added to a diagram: Any number of ⊗ symbols may be added to an exisiting x-sequence and a circle may be added to a diagram. Adding shadings or a new x-sequence are *not* legitimate transformations.

Rule II.1: Lengthening an x-Sequence. We may add any number of ⊗ symbols to an existing x-sequence. The number of x-sequences in a diagram will not change.

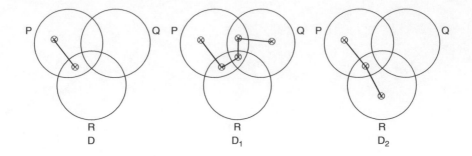

By this rule, both D_1 and D_2 are valid transformations of D.

Rule II.2: Addition of a Circle. We may add a circle to the Venn diagram. It must satisfy the **partial overlapping rule**. As stated previously, a new circle introduced onto a Venn diagram must overlap each and every compartment of that diagram once and only once. For example, suppose that we have a two-set Venn diagram, with P and Q, represented by two overlapping circles:

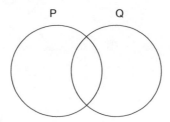

The following diagrams are invalid transformations when adding a third circle R:

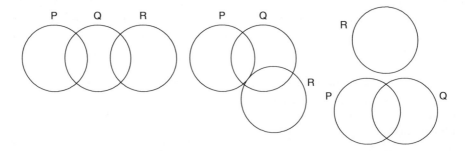

In all these cases, the circle representing R is introduced into the Venn diagram such that its does not overlap every compartment. The following Venn diagrams illustrate the correct addition of a third circle:

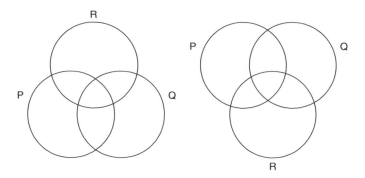

Rule II.2.a: Inclusion of All Compartments of a Region in an x-Sequence.
When a circle is added to a Venn diagram, it will create compartments that
previously did not exist. If there is an x-sequence in the original diagram, an
$\otimes$ must be added to each new compartment that is created, which is part of the
region containing the $\otimes$ in the original diagram. These $\otimes$ symbols must be joined
to form a single x-sequence. The number of x-sequences in the diagram does
not change.

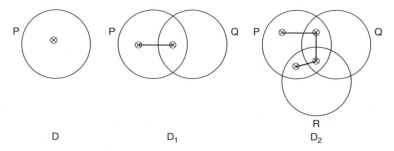

In this example, Diagrams D_1 and D_2 are two valid transformations of D. D_1
results when the Circle Q is added to the diagram. In this case, Region P now
contains two compartments, and hence there are two connected $\otimes$ symbols. D_2
results when the Circle R is added to D_1. Four compartments now make up the
Region P, and therefore the four connected $\otimes$ symbols form an x-sequence to
represent that something exists in Region P.

III. Unification of Two Diagrams. We may unify two diagrams, D_1 and D_2,
into one diagram. In syllogistic reasoning, for example, we need to combine
two premises before we are able to determine if a conclusion follows from the
premises. We need rules to guide us on how to correctly combine two diagrams
into one. We will call the unified diagram $D_1 + D_2$.

Rule III.1: Copying Circles to the Unified Diagram. We first copy the circles
from Diagram D_1. If there are circles on Diagram D_2 that do not exist in D_1,

we must copy these circles as well, observing the **partial overlapping rule** (as discussed in Rule II.2).

Rule III.2: Copying Corresponding Shadings to the Unified Diagram. For any region shaded in D_1 or D_2, the corresponding region in $D_1 + D_2$ should be shaded.

Rule III.3: Copying Corresponding x-Sequences to the Unified Diagram. For any region with an x-sequence in either D_1 or D_2, an x-sequence should be drawn in the corresponding compartments of $D_1 + D_2$, satisfying the rules for adding x-sequences, as specified earlier (see Rule II.2.a).

We will illustrate these unification rules with a few specific examples.

Example 1

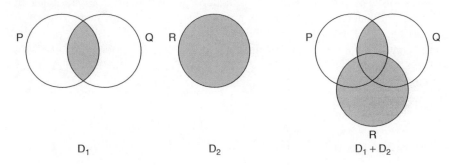

D_1 D_2 $D_1 + D_2$

By Rule III.1, we copy all the circles that are contained in D_1 and D_2—namely P, Q, and R. We draw the circles so that they satisfy the partial overlapping rule. By Rule III.2, we then shade the corresponding regions in $D_1 + D_2$ that are shaded in D_1 and D_2.

Example 2

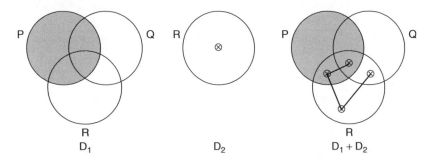

D_1 D_2 $D_1 + D_2$

By Rule III.1, we first copy all circles from D_1 to $D_1 + D_2$—namely, Circles P, Q, and R. We then copy all circles from D_2. Because Circle R is already on the diagram, we do not need to add any additional circles. By Rule III.2, we copy the shadings onto the unified diagram. By Rule III.3, we copy the x-sequence from R. Because Circle R contains four compartments in the unified diagram, we need to include four $\otimes$ symbols joined together as one x-sequence (Rule II.2.a). Finally by Rule I.3, we can erase any part of an x-sequence that is in a shaded compartment. Hence the final transformation is given by:

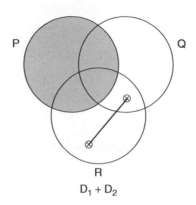

$D_1 + D_2$

Example 3

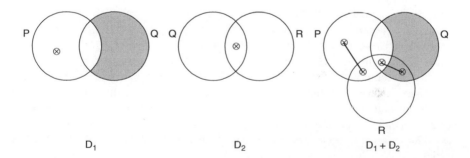

D_1 $\qquad\qquad\qquad$ D_2 $\qquad\qquad\qquad$ $D_1 + D_2$

By Rule III.1, we copy Circles P, Q, and R to the unified diagram in concordance with the partial overlapping rule. By Rule III.2, we copy over all the corresponding shadings, in this example, the shading in Diagram D_1. By Rule III.3, we then copy over all the corresponding x-sequences, one from D_1, and the one from D_2. Rule II.2.a tells us that we need to include all relevant compartments in the x-sequence, hence we need to include two $\otimes$ symbols in our first x-sequence and two $\otimes$ symbols in our second x-sequence. Finally, by Rule I.3, we can eliminate the $\otimes$ in the shaded compartment. Our final unified diagram, $D_1 + D_2$, is given by:

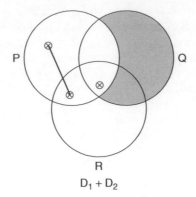

R

$D_1 + D_2$

The rules of transformation are summarized in Table 4.1.

Syllogistic Reasoning Revisited

Earlier, we discussed how to use Venn diagramming to aid in syllogistic reasoning. We discussed how we would represent the premises with one Venn diagram—namely D_P, and the conclusion with a second Venn diagram—namely D_C. We then introduced the idea of reading off D_C from D_P. If we are able to read off D_C from D_P, then the syllogism is valid; if we cannot it is invalid. Our initial ideas about reading off one diagram from another diagram were rather tentative and vague and did not suggest a specific procedure for proving the validity of a syllogism. Now that we have specified rules of transformation, we are in a better position to formulate a procedure for proving the validity of a syllogism. It turns out that the rules of transformation are just what we need to determine if we can read off one diagram from another. The first step is to create separate Venn diagrams for each of the premises and then combine the two diagrams using the unification rules (Rules III.1, III.2, and III.3) discussed earlier. While the basic structure of a syllogism consists of two premises only, the unification rules enable us to reason with more than two premises—we may incrementally add more information to the unified diagram with each additional premise. There is nothing in the rules of transformation that would limit us to two-premise syllogisms.

The next step is to create the Venn diagram that represents the conclusion. We are now ready to determine whether we can read off D_C from D_P. We will do the following:

1. Begin with D_P (the unified diagram that represents all the premises).
2. Using the rules of transformation, attempt to transform D_P to D_C.

Table 4.1. Rules of Transformation

___

I. Erasure of an object

I.1: Erasure of shading in a compartment	We may erase a shading in a compartment.
I.2: Erasure of a whole x-sequence	We may erase a whole x-sequence.
I.3: Erasure of part of an x-sequence in a shaded compartment	We may erase any $\otimes$ of an x-sequence if that $\otimes$ is in a shaded region.
I.4: Erasure of a circle	We may erase an entire circle.
I.4.a: A partial shading in a compartment	When a circle is erased, and the resulting Venn diagram contains a partial shading in a compartment, then the shading in that compartment should be erased.
I.4.b: An x-sequence with more than one $\otimes$ in a compartment	When a circle is erased, and the resulting Venn diagram contains an x-sequence in which there is more than one $\otimes$ in a compartment, then that part of the x-sequence should be replaced by one $\otimes$ and should be connected to the rest of the x-sequence.

II. Addition of an object

II.1: Lengthening an x-sequence	We may add any number of $\otimes$ symbols to an existing x-sequence.
II.2: Addition of a circle	We may add a circle to the Venn diagram, observing the partial overlapping rule.
Partial overlapping rule	A new circle introduced onto a Venn diagram must overlap each and every compartment of that diagram once and only once.
II.2.a: Inclusion of all compartments of a region in an x-sequence	If there is an x-sequence in the original diagram, an $\otimes$ must be added to each new compartment that is created, which is part of the region containing the $\otimes$ in the original diagram.

III. Unification of two diagrams (D_1 and D_2)

III.1: Copying circles to the unified diagram	We first copy the circles from Diagram D_1. If there are circles on Diagram D_2 that do not exist in D_1, we must copy these circles as well, observing the partial overlapping rule.
III.2: Copying corresponding shadings to the unified diagram	For any region shaded in D_1 or D_2, the corresponding region in D_1+D_2 should be shaded.
III.3: Copying corresponding x-sequences to the unified diagram	For any region with an x-sequence in either D_1 or D_2, an x-sequence should be drawn in the corresponding compartments of D_1+D_2, satisfying the rules for adding x-sequences.

3. If it is possible to transform D_P to D_C, then the syllogism is correct; if it is not possible to perform the transformation, the syllogism is incorrect.

Let's revisit the two syllogisms discussed earlier in the chapter to illustrate the procedure. The syllogisms are copied here and some of the discussion is repeated so that the reader need not refer back to the earlier discussion.

Example 1

P_1: All P are Q.
P_2: Some P are R.
∴ Some Q are R.

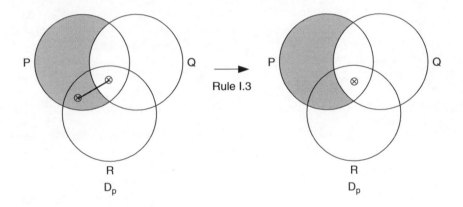

Diagram D_P, on the left, represents the unified diagram of the two premises P_1 and P_2. By Rule I.3, we can erase an ⊗ in an x-sequence if the ⊗ is in a shaded compartment, resulting in D_P on the right.

The creation of Diagram D_c is straightforward and is given next:

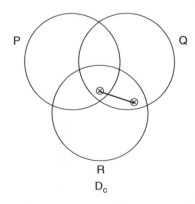

Can we transform D_P into D_C? We can easily accomplish this transformation by using the rules of transformation.

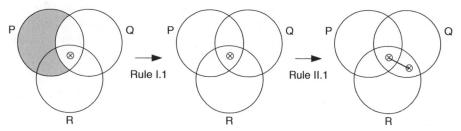

By applying Rule I.1, we can transform D_P into the second diagram by eliminating the shading. By Rule II.1 we can lengthen an x-sequence, so that we obtain the third diagram, which is precisely D_C. Hence we have proven the validity of the syllogism.

Example 2

P_1: Some P are not Q.
P_2: No Q are R.
$\therefore$ Some P are R.

As discussed and presented earlier, we can create Diagram D_P to represent the two premises, and Diagram D_C to represent the conclusion.

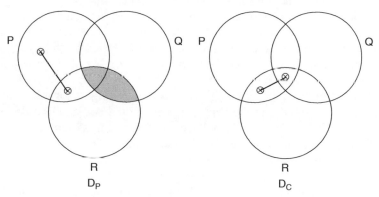

We will now attempt to transform D_P into D_C.

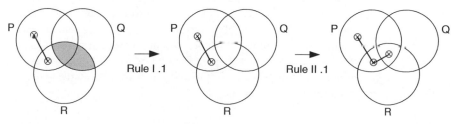

First, we eliminate (by Rule I.1) the shading in D_P to obtain the second diagram, and then lengthen the x-sequence by adding another $\otimes$ (by Rule II.1). We cannot transform this diagram any further to match D_C because that would entail eliminating the first $\otimes$ in the x-sequence. This transformation is not permitted—remember we can eliminate an $\otimes$ only if it is in a shaded compartment. Therefore, this syllogism is invalid.

Proof by Two Representation Systems: Linguistic (First Order Logic) vs. Nonlinguistic (Venn Diagrams)

We demonstrated in the previous section how Venn diagrams can be employed in a novel way to construct logic proofs. The technique involves the use of rules of transformation that specify what the allowable manipulations are. We illustrated the diagramming technique with one narrow type of deductive reasoning—namely, syllogistic reasoning in which the premises and conclusion are limited to categorical statements. But even in this limited domain, logicians have largely resisted the use of diagrams as valid proof. Indeed, a negative attitude toward diagramming persists to this day, despite their widespread use and their acknowledged usefulness in solving problems in mathematics and logic. The prevailing sentiment among logicians is that diagramming is a heuristic tool only, not to be used to perform rigorous logic proofs. Moreover, many believe that diagrams are prone to mislead us and therefore cannot and should not function as a real proof.[5] For the construction of a valid logic proof, the logician is more likely to turn toward first order logic.

One purpose of this chapter is to show that Venn diagrams, in fact, can be presented as a standard representation system, one that can be used to construct valid logic proofs, albeit in a limited domain. It is beyond the scope of this book to prove the validity of the Venn diagramming system, but Shin[6] proves that the Venn diagramming system described in this chapter is both sound and complete. The soundness of the Venn system guarantees that as long as we follow the rules of transformation, the use of the Venn diagrams should not lead us astray toward invalid proofs. In addition, the completeness of the Venn system means that the rules of transformation can generate all valid argument forms.

A side-by-side comparison of a linguistic representation system and the Venn representation system will serve to highlight the differences between the two approaches to proving logic theorems. First, we will look in brief at **first order logic**, the conventional approach to proving logic theorems. This section will merely introduce the reader to the syntax of first order logic to give a flavor for how a linguistic representation system can be used to construct logic proofs. (For the reader who does not wish to delve into this topic, this section can easily be skipped without loss of continuity.) A more comprehensive treatment of first order logic is beyond the scope of this chapter, but can be found in many standard texts on logic. Second, we will prove a simple syllogism by first using first order logic, and then by using Venn diagrams.

First Order Logic: A Brief Introduction. Earlier in the chapter, we discussed four types of categorical statements:

1. All A is B
2. No A is B
3. Some A is B
4. Some A is not B

As a first step to constructing a logic proof, we will need notation to represent these four statements. Using the letter x as a variable standing for any object, we may express the first categorical statement as:

For all x, if x is A, then x is B.

Similarly, the second categorical statement can be expressed as:

For all x, if x is A, then x is not B.

Under the syntax adopted by first order logic, a $\forall$ means "for all." This symbol is called the *universal quantifier*. In addition, instead of writing "x is A" we will write instead Ax. In a similar fashion, "x is B" becomes Bx. Hence the first two categorical statements are written:

1. $\forall x(Ax \rightarrow Bx)$
2. $\forall x(Ax \rightarrow \neg Bx)$

The third categorical statement is expressed as:

For some x, x is A and x is B.

The fourth categorical statement is expressed as:

For some x, x is A and x is not B.

Instead of writing "for some x," we will adopt the symbol $\exists$. This symbol is called the *existential quantifier* and it means "for some," or more precisely, "for at least one." Hence the third and fourth categorical statements are written:

3. $\exists x(Ax \& Bx)$
4. $\exists x(Ax \& \neg Bx)$

Note that it is wrong to formulate the first two statements (the universal statements) with conjunctions. For example, it is wrong to formulate the statement

All A is B with:

$$\forall x (Ax\&Bx)$$

This formulation would mean "for all x, x is both A and B." The statement "All penguins are birds" is clearly not the same as "for all x, x is both a penguin and a bird," which means that everything is both a penguin and a bird.

Likewise, it would be incorrect to formulate the third and fourth statements (the existential statements) with conditionals. The third statement, *Some A is B* cannot be formulated as:

$$\exists x (Ax\rightarrow Bx)$$

This formulation would mean that there exists at least one x such that if x is A then x is B. However, "some unicorns are red" is not equivalent to "for some x, if x is a unicorn then x is red." The argument here is a little more subtle and difficult to understand. The latter statement is true even though there are no unicorns. (For example, if x is an elephant, this statement is true). On the other hand, it is false that "some unicorns are red" because there is no such thing as a unicorn.

Now that we have a basic understanding of how to formulate the four categorical statements using the syntax of first order logic, let's attempt to prove the following syllogism:

All dogs are mammals.
All mammals have hair.
∴ All dogs have hair.

We will replace M with the set of all mammals, H with the set of all things with hair, and D with the set of all dogs to arrive at the following syllogism:

All D is M.
All M is H.
∴ All D is H.

To construct a logic proof using first order logic, we will need inference rules that will allow us to transform our statements into other statements (much like the rules of transformation that allow us to transform Venn diagrams into other equivalent Venn diagrams).

Example 1: Proof by First Order Logic. A first-order logic proof of the above syllogism would look something like the following:

1. $\forall x (Dx\rightarrow Mx)$ Premise 1
2. $\forall x (Mx\rightarrow Hx)$ Premise 2

3. Da→Ma   1 Universal instantiation

4. Ma→Ha   2 Universal instantiation

5. Da→Ha   3, 4 Hypothetical syllogism

6. $\forall x(Dx \to Hx)$ 5 Universal generalization

Explanation. The steps of the proof are labeled 1 through 6. Steps 1 and 2 simply formulate the two premises of the syllogism into first order logic notation, as discussed earlier. Steps 3 and 4 use the inference rule known as universal instantiation. This means that we can replace x (which represent all individuals) with a specific occurrence—namely a. Step 5 uses the inference rule known as hypothetical syllogism. This means that given three categorical statements,[7] α, φ, and ω, whenever $\alpha \to \varphi$, and $\varphi \to \omega$, then we can infer $\alpha \to \omega$ (this inference rule functions as a kind of transitivity between three categorical statements). Finally Step 6 uses the inference rule known as universal generalization. It does not matter whether we are talking about individual a, b, c, etc. Because we have made no assumption about individual a, our proof is perfectly general. Hence in Step 6 we are able to state the formula in Step 5 more generally—namely, $\forall x(Dx \to Hx)$. But this is precisely equivalent to *All D is H*. Hence we have proven that the conclusion, *All D is H* or "all dogs have hair" from the two premises using the language and conventions of first order logic.

Example 2: Proof by Venn Diagrams. We now look at proofing the exact same syllogism using Venn diagrams. It is an easy matter to draw the Venn diagrams that represent the premises $P_1 + P_2$:

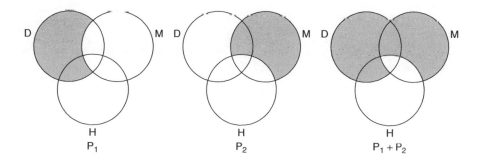

We first create, separately the Venn diagrams for P_1 and P_2, and then combine the two diagrams by copying over the shadings from both diagrams into the corresponding compartments.

The Venn diagram for the conclusion is given by:

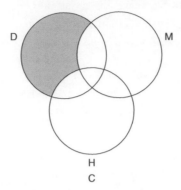

Can we transform Diagram $P_1 + P_2$ into Diagram C? By Rule I.1, we can eliminate the shading in two compartments to arrive at Diagram C. See the next diagram.

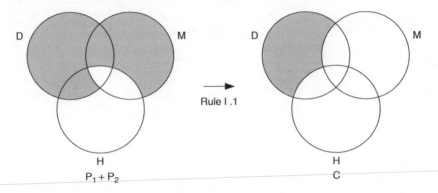

We have established the validity of the syllogism through two different representation systems, one linguistic and one nonlinguistic.

Our discussion of Venn diagrams has taken us, step by step, through a procedure that enables one to construct logic proofs in a graphical and visual way. The Venn diagrams described in this chapter go far beyond the conventional Venn diagram used in mathematics and set theory: They are not merely static diagrams that depict the relations between two or three sets; rather, they are meant to be modified, updated, and combined in many different ways. The technique uses a small number of notations: overlapping circles to denote sets and how they intersect (the traditional notation that we already knew) and, in addition, shadings to represent emptiness and ⊗ symbols to represent nonemptiness. A further convention adopted in this chapter is the interconnected ⊗ symbols, joined by lines (referred to as an *x*-sequence) that enable us to depict disjunctive information. These conventions are fairly easy to learn and apply in logic reasoning, unlike first-order logic whose syntax requires much more practice and skill to master.

The rules of transformation are a central feature of these dynamic Venn diagrams. They enable us to manipulate Venn diagrams in myriad ways: we can subtract objects, add objects, and combine objects. The rules of transformation tell us what the permissible transformations are—they allow us to transform one Venn diagram into another equivalent Venn diagram. These rules are important because they provide us with a procedure for proving the validity of a syllogism. First, the unification rules tell us how to combine two or more premises onto one Venn diagram. Second, the addition and subtraction rules are used to prove whether a conclusion follows from the premises: If we can transform the Venn diagram representing the premises into the Venn diagram representing the conclusion, then the syllogism is valid.

We concluded this section by looking at how a linguistic representation system, first order logic, differs from a nonlinguistic representation system, Venn diagramming. In the case of the linguistic system, relations are represented by linguistic symbols and other syntactic devices. These symbols and devices employ their own conventions, which need to be learned to construct valid logic proofs. One problem with first order logic is that it is very difficult to learn and not at all intuitive and obvious how to construct a proof. Indeed, it may well be the case that just because we cannot construct a proof does not mean that the syllogism is invalid—rather, it may be that we are not skillful enough to produce the proof! On the other hand, diagrammatic representation systems represent relations in terms of spatial arrangement of objects. Although their conventions must also be learned, they are far easier to master and understand. This is because they are highly visual and allow us to see relationships in a perceptually more obvious way. This is their primary advantage over first order logic.

While the Venn diagramming technique illustrated in this chapter shows great promise in solving logic problems, it is important to reiterate that they can solve only one narrow class of problems—syllogistic reasoning in which the premises and conclusions are limited to categorical statements. First order logic is a system that can solve a much wider variety of logic problems—it has more expressive power, despite its steep learning curve—and this in great part would explain why it is the logicians' first choice in proving logic theorems. Of course, it is possible to extend the capabilities of the Venn diagramming technique to account for more logic tasks, but we cannot represent everything we want through Venn diagrams or diagrams in general. For example, there is no general way of representing disjunctive or negative information on a single Venn diagram (it is very difficult to represent this information visually and perceptually). In the end, the logician must employ a number of techniques, be they linguistic or diagrammatic, to tackle some of the most thorny and challenging logic problems that he or she might encounter.

ENDNOTES

1. Sun-Joo Shin, *The Logical Status of Diagrams*. Cambridge; New York: Cambridge Univ. Press, 1994. The discussion of Venn diagramming in this chapter is based on Shin's diagrammatic method Venn-I, which is discussed in Chapter 3.

2. Ibid., pp. 57–60. Shin discusses a set of rules that describe a well-formed diagram (wfd), or a valid diagram. One of these rules she refers to as the partial overlapping rule.

3. Ibid. pp. 41–42. This procedure is suggested as a way of testing the validity of a syllogism.

4. The discussion of rules of transformation has been reorganized for the sake of clarity. Shin provides a different organization but the rules are the same. One of her rules, the rule of conflicting information, has been omitted from the discussion.

5. For a discussion of the mistrust of Venn diagrams see the discussion in ibid., pp. 1–5.

6. Ibid., pp. 93–110. Shin shows that Venn-I is both sound and complete.

7. Logicians refer to α, φ, and ω as wff's (well-formed formulas) as defined by the formation rules of the language. For example "$\forall x \ (Ax \ \&(Bx \cup Cx))$" is a wff, but "$Tx \ \&\exists \ x \ (xA\neg)$" is not because the latter is an invalid expression according to the formation rules of predicate logic.

CHAPTER 5

RULE-BASED EXPERT SYSTEMS

In the early years of AI there was great hope that universal problem solvers would be capable of solving a wide array of problems by employing general problem-solving methods, much like the human mind does. A good example is General Problem Solver (GPS),[1] a computer program created in 1957 by famed AI researchers Alan Newell and Herbert Simon. GPS was intended to provide a generic set of rules and processes that could handle many different types of problems, everything from solving puzzles, to proving logic theorems, to playing chess. Although these programs were introduced to the AI community with great fanfare and excitement, GPS and other universal problem solvers were unable to solve anything but simple puzzles and problems, the so-called toy problems. In other areas of AI as well, generalized solutions in areas such as natural language translation, speech recognition, and vision still elude us today. Such AI problems have been addressed more successfully only when the problem domain is severely restricted—for example, speech recognition systems are much more useful when the input is restricted to limited vocabularies.

Until the mid-1960s the AI research community continued to focus on systems that relied on general methods of reasoning rather than on knowledge in speci c domain areas. By the 1970s, the focus shifted with the realization that domain knowledge was the key to producing systems that could solve more complex and realistic problems. One prominent example was the expert systems, developed as a special type of AI program to deal with complex problems in domains such as medical disease diagnosis (MYCIN), computer con guration design (XCON), and the analysis of geologic data for mineral exploration (PROSPECTOR). The success and track record of these applications has been much more fruitful and enduring. In this chapter we introduce the topic of expert systems and describe one of its most common forms, rule-based expert systems. In the next chapter, we continue the discussion when we investigate ways in which diagrams can be used to create expert systems that are more transparent to the end user.

An expert system is an AI program that emulates the decision-making ability of a human expert, a person who has expertise in a certain area, such as a doctor, lawyer, or nancial planner.[2] In contrast to the general problem solvers, these programs are intended to function only in restrictive domains, making the use of the specialized knowledge of domain experts. There was never a pretense to use these systems in any other way than that for which they were preprogrammed to do. In the knowledge domain that it knows about, the expert system would reason and make inferences (just as a human expert would) about some problem. That is, given some input data, a conclusion (or recommendation) is inferred.

To this day, expert systems can be viewed as a veritable success story* amid the many failures and overhyped applications in AI. Before the 1980s, expert systems were largely con ned to the research laboratory, a time when its ideas were still being tested out, and the idea of a computer program performing expert functions was not widely accepted in the marketplace. However, the rate of application to the larger commercial world was dramatic in the 1980s: During this time period, one estimate[3] is that over two thirds of the Fortune 1000 companies applied expert systems technology to their daily business operations. This was due, in large part, to the introduction of easy-to-use expert system shells, which made developing the complex systems less cumbersome and quicker to implement. Moreover, companies took the time to learn how to embed the technology in current business processes. Another survey[4] looked at publications on operational expert systems from 1980 to 1993 and found that many expert systems have had a profound impact on organizations, in some cases shrinking the time for tasks from days to hours or from minutes or seconds. In addition, this same survey found that there were many nonquanti able bene ts such as improved customer satisfaction, improved quality of products and service, and more consistent decision making.

Although the study of Expert Systems is no longer the high-pro le research area that it once was (notably in the 1970s and 1980s), there have been several noteworthy achievements and landmark systems that have contributed to our understanding of decision making and human expertise. MYCIN, perhaps the most famous expert system of them all, was developed at Stanford University in the 1970s to diagnose bacterial infections.[5] In a typical consultation with MYCIN, an end user (typically a physician) would answer questions about patient data such as symptoms, test results, and patient characteristics. Based on these responses, MYCIN would reach a diagnosis on what the infection might be. While MYCIN was a system that never achieved commercial success, it introduced

---

*Some would argue that expert systems have not been all that successful and that we have not yet accomplished the goal of creating programs that can solve problems as well as human experts can. To understand this viewpoint, we will explore some of the problems and limitations of expert systems at the end of the chapter.

several features that have become hallmarks of expert system technology. Perhaps it is best known for its rule-based approach. That is, it organizes its knowledge into a collection of IF–THEN rules.

Before we delve more deeply into the topic of rule-based expert systems, it would be useful at the outset to re ect on the nature of human expertise. In particular: What makes an expert an expert? How do human experts reason? Answers to these questions can help us understand what an expert system is trying to accomplish and what we can expect from them, in terms of performance and capabilities. Further, understanding the nature of human expertise can help us design expert systems. For example, if we have an understanding of the reasoning process of a human expert, perhaps we can use such information to mimic this in a computer program. That is precisely the approach that AI researchers have taken over the years to design systems that come closer and closer to acting like human experts and making decisions for us.

Let us re ect for a moment on people whom we consider experts: auto mechanics, doctors, accountants, plumbers, electricians, lawyers, and chess masters, to name a few. All these individuals are considered experts because they can solve problems that the general lay population cannot or they can solve them much more ef ciently at least. (Expert reasoning, in this respect, is different from commonsense reasoning, a type of reasoning that almost everyone can perform quite easily.) Experts can solve problems because they possess specialized knowledge, typically acquired through years of formal schooling and training. However, expertise is not merely about possessing knowledge—it is not only about learning in the classroom, or possessing textbook knowledge, or graduating with a PhD. Experts must also be able to *directly solve problems* in their speci c area of expertise. This type of knowledge can be acquired only through practice and experience. (This is why a newly minted medical doctor will typically undergo a residency to gain more hands-on training in a speci c area of medicine.) Through such practice and training, often acquired in a painstaking manner, a highly pro cient expert ends up with a ne-tuned understanding of different types of problems and situations. This quality is really the hallmark of expertise: Expertise is fundamentally about applying knowledge to solve different types of problems in a speci c domain.

How do human experts reason? That is, how do they arrive at their expert judgments, and how do they solve problems in their domain? Here are six possibilities:

1. They use rules of thumb, also known as heuristics, to solve problems and to reduce the time necessary to reach a solution.
2. They use past experiences as a guide to solving a current problem. They may look at a current situation and compare it to an identical or similar situation they have experienced in the past.
3. They create elaborate classi cations of knowledge in their domains. That is, they build sophisticated hierarchies that categorize the objects in their domains.

4. They create "models" of their domain—for example, causal models. They are able to run their models in their heads to help them solve problems.
5. They are good at recognizing patterns in their data.
6. They use judgment, intuition, and creativity to solve some problems they have not seen before.

The first approach is the basis for rule-based Expert Systems in which knowledge is represented as a collection of IF–THEN rules. This has been the most traditional way of representing knowledge in an expert system and is the subject of this chapter. We will look at a number of examples, in this chapter and the next, on how rules can be used to capture an expert's knowledge and how we can process these rules in a systematic way to solve real-world problems.

The second approach, the use of experiential knowledge, is the basis for an AI method known as case-based reasoning (CBR). This method for building expert systems is based on the principle that a current or new problem can be solved by looking at similar problems, termed *cases*, that have occurred in the past. Obviously, for this approach to work, a number of cases, together with their solutions, need to be entered into a CBR database. A CBR system would retrieve cases from this database, by matching a current case to a past case. The solution to the current problem is inferred by taking into account any differences between the current problem and the previous cases. The CBR approach is especially useful in supporting technicians in a help desk application who must troubleshoot technical problems that have been most likely experienced by other customers.

The third approach involves the creation of classification hierarchies, a technique that is especially useful in organizing a lot of information. We have already explored the classification hierarchy and one of its forms, the inheritance hierarchy (Chapter 3). These diagrams can be used to represent a taxonomy of items in a domain. A medical expert system, for example, may use such a diagram to illustrate a classification of diseases. Because expertise is associated with having a large quantity of knowledge, such a hierarchy can help an expert retrieve knowledge more efficiently. Moreover, knowing a particular disease in the hierarchy may enable an expert to infer its characteristics from its position in the hierarchy. For example, if we know that meningitis is a type of bacterial infection, we may infer that it can be treated with antibiotics. Experts typically possess well-developed classification schemes, honed and fine-tuned after many years of training and practice in their fields.

With respect to the fourth approach, the creation and running of models, we have previously explored (Chapter 3) a number of different ways of creating models, and representing them diagrammatically. These include diagrams that illustrate topology, flow and sequence, association, causality, and decision making. In addition, we explored mental models in Chapter 2. Not only do experts create static models of their domain, but they actively run them in their heads. A good example is a causal model that an expert may use to predict the behavior of a complex system. (For a review of this topic see the discussion of how an electromechanical thermostat works in Chapter 2.) We will continue the discussion of dynamic models when we describe model-based reasoning in Chapter 7. This approach is an alternative to rule-based reasoning, and addresses some of its problems and limitations.

The fth approach recognizes that experts are adept at pattern recognition. A good example is a master chess player, who must develop this skill through lots of practice to become pro cient in chess. Chess experts, when presented with chess board con gurations, are able to recognize patterns, or meaningful chunks, in chess board arrangements.[6] They see not only random pieces on a chessboard but can discern larger patterns and chunks of information. A novice chess player, by contrast, may understand how to move the pieces, possessing only a super cial understanding of the rules of the game, but has no deeper understanding of chess board con gurations. The ability to perceive patterns that the lay person would otherwise miss is another hallmark of any kind of expertise.

It is possible to emulate pattern recognition in a computer program. For one, patterns can be preprogrammed as a collection of rules, as in a rule-based expert system. The problem with this approach is that all the patterns must be thought out in advance, with all possible con gurations and scenarios accounted for. This may be possible to accomplish in well-restricted domains, but in more complex applications it is very dif cult to consider each and every possibility. A human expert is better able to learn patterns acquired through years and years of practice and experience (indeed, the acquisition of patterns for many experts is a lifelong pursuit), and possesses more exibility in terms of processing these patterns. Another AI technology, neural networks, was developed for the express purpose of learning to recognize patterns. The most well known application of neural networks is voice recognition and handwriting recognition systems. Another interesting application is the identi cation of normal and abnormal electrocardiograms (ECGs), which are graphical charts that illustrate the electrical activity of the heart. A neural network can be "trained" to learn how to distinguish a normal ECG from an abnormal one. Many of these neural networks, in fact, have attained a level of performance equal to or exceeding that of a trained human cardiologist.

Of course, we cannot emulate all the reasoning processes of a human expert no matter how hard we tried. The last and sixth point—the use of judgment, intuition, and creativity to solve novel problems—was included in this discussion to underscore the idea that the human expert should not be entirely replaced by a computer program. The ingenuity and the extraordinary ability of human mind to arrive at original and innovative solutions places the human expert in a league all its own, capable of solving very complex problems that are not possible by a computer.*

---

*There are a few notable exceptions. The program Deep Blue beat the reigning chess champion, Gary Kasparov, and is often cited as an example of a computer program that exceeded the performance of even the best human expert in the world. In general, however, expert systems remain incapable of solving many complex and dif cult tasks.

RULE-BASED REASONING

One way to represent knowledge in an Expert System is as a collection of rules of the form:

```
IF (condition) THEN (action)
```

The condition part of the rule is also referred to as the antecedent, the LHS (left-hand side) or the premise. The action is sometime referred to as, respectively, the consequent, the RHS (right-hand side) or the conclusion.

To get a general sense of how a rule-based representation would encode a human expert's knowledge, consider the following six rules that a driver of a car might possess and process when he or she approaches a traf c light at an intersection.

```
1. IF light is green
      THEN action is go

2. IF light is red
      THEN action is stop

3. IF light is yellow AND there is enough time to go through
   intersection
      THEN  action is go

4. IF light is yellow AND there is not enough time to go through
   intersection
      THEN  action is stop

5. IF action is go
      THEN  press on the gas pedal

6. IF action is stop
      THEN press on the brake
```

Each of the rules is expressed in understandable English so as to make clear to the reader the meaning of the rule. It is often more convenient, and parsimonious, to express each clause as an object-value pair instead so that there are only two parts to each clause. Moreover, a more structured notation will help us translate the rules to an expert system language later on. Later on in this chapter, we will discuss the syntax of CLIPS, a software tool used for building expert systems.

Under the notation of object-value pairs, Rules 3 though 6 would be expressed more succinctly as:

```
1. IF (light green)
      THEN  (action go)
```

2. IF (light red)
       THEN   (action stop)

3. IF (light yellow) AND (enough-time true)
       THEN   (action go)

4. IF (light yellow) AND (enough-time false)
       THEN   (action stop)

5. IF (action go)
       THEN   (gas-pedal press)

6. IF (action stop)
       THEN   (brake press)

The rst part of the clause, the object, can represent a physical object (as in light), an attribute (as in enough-time, an attribute that signi es whether or not there is enough time to go through the intersection), or a state or condition (as in action). A convention adopted in this chapter is to represent the object as a single symbol so that two or more words are joined together as one symbol by a hyphen—for example, "enough time" is expressed as enough-time. The second part of the clause, the value, represents the speci c value that the object takes on.

An object may also represent a relation between two or more entities. For example, we might represent the fact that Bill is the father of Sarah by the clause:

(father-of Bill Sarah)

In this object-value example father-of represents a relation object, and there are two values assigned to this object—namely the father and the child.

Here is another example of a relation object that has three values assigned to it:

(gives John Mary car)

The rst value is the agent, the second is the recipient, and the third is the object that is given. Hence the notation represents the fact that John gives Mary a car.

The following rule could be used to determine whether two individuals y and z are siblings:

 IF (father-of ?x ?y) AND (father-of ?x ?z)
      THEN (siblings ?y ?z)

This rule uses variables $?x$, $?y$, and $?z$. The syntax for variables is adopted and borrowed from CLIPS. To distinguish a regular symbol from a variable, CLIPS place a question mark (?) before the name of the variable. This rule states that if ?*x* is father of ?*y* and ?*x* is father of ?*z*, then ?*y* and ?*z* are siblings. The use of variables to encode this rule allows us to state it generically so that it applies to all values of ?*x*,?*y*, and ?*z*.

The condition part of the rule must always evaluate to either true or false, and as such, a complex Boolean expression may be formed to represent the condition. Such expressions may contain any number of relational operators and/or logical operators.

Relational operators include the following:

= equal to
< less than
> greater than
<= less than or equal to
>= greater than or equal to
<> not equal to*

For example the following rule would classify a person as middle-aged if he or she is between 45 and 65 years of age:

```
IF (age >= 45) AND (age <= 65)
    THEN (person middle-aged)
```

Whenever the conditional operator is =, it is frequently omitted under the notation of object-value pairs, For example:

```
age 45
```

```
sex male
```

```
height 5'7"
```

The logical operators AND, OR, and NOT may also be used to create more complex expressions. For example, the following rule, which uses the logical operator OR, determines whether two individuals, ?*y* and ?*z*, are siblings:

```
IF ((father-of ?f ?y) AND (father-of ?f ?z)) OR
   ((mother-of ?m ?y) AND (mother-of ?m ?z))
     THEN (siblings ?y ?z)
```

The condition in this rule would evaluate to true if either (1) ?*y* and ?*z* have the same father ?*f* or (2) ?*y* and ?*z* have the same mother ?*m*.

Up to this point, the rules in this section have been rather simplistic and uninteresting in terms of encoding real expertise. A more realistic expert system

*This is the CLIPS syntax for not equal to. Other languages, such as C++ and Java, use != instead.

can contain hundred, or even thousands of rules, some of them quite complex. To give you a avor of a more sophisticated rule, here is one from the aforementioned MYCIN, an expert system that was designed to determine the cause of a bacterial infection:

```
IF the infection that requires therapy is meningitis AND
    the patient has evidence of serious skin or soft tissue
    infection AND
    organisms were not seen on the stain of the culture AND
    the type of infection is bacterial
        THEN there is evidence that the organism that might be
            causing the infection is Staphylococcus (0.75) OR
            Streptococcus (0.25)
```

The rule is expressed in sentence form so that it is easier to understand, but each clause can easily be expressed in the object-value notation described above. MYCIN contained about 500 such rules. An interesting feature of MYCIN is that it can process uncertain conclusions. The two probabilities in the action part of the rule represent the *certainty factors*, or how likely it is that the infection is caused by *Staphylococcus* and *Streptococcus*. This is an important point to note, as much of expertise is based on subjective judgments, not on hard-and-fast conclusions. We will explore the topic of uncertainty and inexact reasoning in more detail in Chapter 8.

Components of a Rule-Based Expert System

Figure 5.1 illustrates the four main components of a basic rule-based expert sys-tem. In this gure, the user is the person who interacts with the expert system, through the user interface. He or she will enter facts about the problem-solving

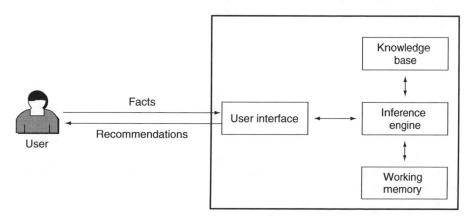

Figure 5.1. Components of a basic expert system.

situation; based on these inputs the expert system will render an expert recommendation or conclusion.

The two main components of the expert system are the knowledge base and the inference engine. The knowledge base contains the knowledge about the domain, as represented by the rules. Hence the knowledge base is really a database, or collection of IF–THEN rules. The knowledge base, in and of itself, cannot do anything for the user. The second main component, the inference engine, is what endows the expert system with the ability to process the rules and make expert recommendations. The inference engine is really the central processing unit of the expert system, and it is important to understand this component to understand how an expert systems works. In the next section we will discuss how the inference engine uses the problem facts, as entered by the user, together with the rules, as contained in the knowledge base, to make recommendations.

The third component illustrated in the diagram is working memory. This component represents the short-term memory of an expert system. It contains all the facts, as initially entered by the user, as well as the new facts that have been inferred by the inference engine.

The nal component is the user interface. This component is the means by which the user interacts with the expert system. In the early days of the technology, the user interface was a simple text-based interface that represented a back-and-forth dialogue between user and system. In a typical consultation, the expert system would ask the user to enter facts about the problem, and the expert system would output the recommendation in text form. Today, of course, graphical, high-resolution displays are the norm (most typically displayed on a PC), and so a wider variety of user interfaces are possible. For example, an expert system that runs a nuclear power plant might contain a graphical control panel that contains dials, switches, alerts, graphs, and various other displays to help an operator run and monitor the nuclear power plant. Another option, which we will explore more fully in the next chapter, is the creation of diagrammatic representations that a user can interactively explore and manipulate. We look at some varieties of diagrammatic user interfaces that can make expert systems more transparent and exible to use.

There is an optional fth component, known as the explanation module, which is sometimes included in discussions on the components of expert systems. The explanation module's purpose is to provide users with explanations and justi - cations as to why an expert system made the recommendation that it did. This component traditionally has provided a user with the ability to inquire on how a particular conclusion is reached. For example, the user may request a rule trace, or the sequence of rules that were executed, to reach a given recommendation. This component is omitted because we treat it as part of the user interface itself. Indeed a central tenet of the next chapter is that a diagram, which can be a central part of the user interface itself, can be used to provide an expert system with more explanatory power. We will have more to say about user interfaces and explanatory power in the next chapter.

The Inference Engine

The inference engine is perhaps the most interesting feature of rule-based expert systems. It is the part of the expert system that processes the problem facts and searches for rules in the knowledge base to reach a nal recommendation for a user. For this reason, it is sometimes referred to as the rule interpreter. It is what endows the expert system with its dynamic qualities, and without it, an expert system would be incapable of making its recommendations.

There are two basic types of rule-based inferencing. **Forward chaining** is a data-driven approach in which you start with the initial problem facts and then try to draw conclusions from them using the rules of the knowledge base. **Backward chaining**, on the other hand, is a goal-driven approach in which you start with some kind of expectation of what is to occur, or hypothesis, and then nd rules that either support or contradict your hypothesis. The best way to understand these two forms of inferencing is to look at speci c examples on how these two approaches work. We will rst look at a very simple example of six rules, and then work through a more detailed second example.

A Simple Example. Let us suppose that we are given the following six rules that encode expertise on the cause and effect relationship between currency uctuation and the decision to buy bonds:

```
R1.  IF the dollar rises*
          THEN interest rate decreases

R2.  IF the dollar falls
          THEN interest rate increases

R3.  IF interest rate increases
          THEN bond prices decrease

R4.  IF interest rate decreases
          THEN bond prices increase

R5.  IF bond prices increase
          THEN sell bonds

R6.  IF bond prices decrease
          THEN buy bonds
```

In forward chaining, we begin with our problem facts. Let us suppose that our client observes that the dollar is falling in value against the other major currencies (fact = dollar falls). Our client, based on this information, wants to know whether

---

*That is, the dollar's value against the other major currencies increases, or its foreign exchange rate increases.

it is a good idea to buy bonds or not. The following sequence of rules are   red
to reach a recommendation:

- From the initial problem fact that the dollar falls, R2 infers that interest rate
  increases.
- Because the interest rate increases, R3 infers that bond prices decrease.
- From the bond price decline, R6 infers that we should buy bonds.

Hence the sequence of rule   rings that leads us to the recommendation is R2 →
R3 → R6. Working memory, as noted earlier, would keep track of both the initial
facts, as well as all new facts that are inferred from the rules, in the process of
forward chaining through the rules.

The process of backward chaining is a little more dif cult to understand. In
this case, we work in reverse. We start with an expectation or a hypothesis, and
seek evidence to support or refute the hypothesis. Let us suppose that our initial
hypothesis is that we should buy bonds. Again, we are initially given the fact
the the *dollar falls*.

In Step 1, we look for a rule containing our initial hypothesis *buy bonds* in the
THEN part of the rule. The only such rule is R6. In order to prove R6, we need
to establish that *bond prices decrease*. Because we have not proven the condition
yet, R6 is placed on our stack of rules.

In Step 2, we look for a rule containing *bond prices decrease* in the THEN
part of the rule. The relevant rule is R3, and in order to prove this rule we need
to prove *interest rate increases*. We therefore place R3 on the stack.

In Step 3, we look for a rule containing *interest rate increases* in the THEN
part of the rule. R2 is the correct rule to use and we therefore need to establish
the fact *dollar rises* to prove this rule. Because we already know that the dollar
has fallen, as given by our initial facts, we have hence proven that we should buy
bonds. The sequence of rules that are stacked is R6 → R3 → R2, just the reverse
of the order of the rules   red in the forward chaining example. Although in this
simple example the order is simply reversed, this is frequently not the case.

Another Example: Stock Selection Expert System. Let us look at another
slightly more elaborate example. The following 23 rules are used to help us
pick stocks. To facilitate the discussion, the rules are clustered into four different
headings.

I. General Rules

```
R1. If market is up and sector ?x is strong
        THEN buy in sector ?x
R2. IF market is down and sector ?x is weak
        THEN short in sector ?x
R3. IF market is sideways
        THEN stay-out
```

II. Rules Determining Market Trend

R4. IF S&P500 is up AND NASDAQ is up
            THEN market is up
R5. IF S&P500 is down AND NASDAQ is down
            THEN market is down
R6. IF S&P500 is little-changed OR NASDAQ is little-changed
            THEN market is sideways

III. Rules Pertaining to Oil Price Hikes

R7. IF increase in oil prices > 20%
            THEN oil prices are high
R8. IF oil prices are high
            THEN sector energy is strong
R9. IF oil prices are high
            THEN sector transportation is weak
R10. IF sector energy is strong
            THEN buy in sector energy
R11. IF buy in sector energy
            THEN buy ExxonMobil
R12. IF buy in sector energy
            THEN buy BP
R13. IF oil prices are high
            THEN short in sector transportation
R14. IF short in sector transportation
            THEN short United Airlines
R15. IF short in sector transportation
            THEN short American Airlines

IV. Rules Pertaining to Interest Rates

R16. IF interest rate > 9%
            THEN interest rate is high
R17. IF interest rate < 6%
            THEN interest rate is low
R18. IF interest rate is high
            THEN sector financial is weak
R19. IF interest rate is low
            THEN sector financial is strong
R20. IF buy in sector financial
            THEN buy Countrywide Financial
R21. IF buy in sector financial
            THEN buy Bank of America
R22. IF short in sector financial
            THEN short Countrywide Financial
R23. IF short in sector financial
            THEN short Bank of America

The three general rules, the rst cluster, are based on three fundamental principles of investing:[7]

1. Buy stocks in strong sectors in an upward-trending market.
2. Short weak stocks in weak sectors in a downward-trending market.
3. Stay out of the market and in cash when there is no discernable trend.

The rst two rules state that the decision to buy or short-sell stocks is based on two factors, general market conditions and sector trends. A sector refers to a subdivision in the economy, such as transportation, energy, nancial, or utilities. Short-selling, also known as shorting, refers to the practice of selling stocks that the investor actually does not own (short sellers "borrow" the stock), in the hope of buying them back later at a lower price. The investor adopts a bearish stance and expects that the price of the stock will decrease—hence the use of short-selling when the market is trending downward and a particular sector is weak.

R1 and R2 are stated generically so that they work for any sector. As noted previously, you need to use variables to create generic rules—in this case, the variable $?x$ represents a particular sector. We also could have created a separate rule for each sector. For example:

```
If market is upward and sector transportation is strong
        THEN buy in sector transportation

If market is upward and sector technology is strong
        THEN buy in sector technology
```

By using variables, we are able to encode expertise in our knowledge base much more ef ciently and succinctly.

The second cluster of rules determines whether the general market is moving upward, downward, or sideways (i.e., no de nable trend). The determination is based on trends in the S&P500 and NASDAQ, two stock market indices. The third cluster of rules looks at what happens when there is a spike in oil prices, speci cally what happens to the energy and transportation sectors. Finally, the fourth cluster of rules describes the effect of interest rates on the nancial sector.

Let us rst look at a forward chaining example to see how the stock-picking expert system works. We will assume the following initial facts:

```
S&P500 is up
NASDAQ is up
Interest rate = 5.5%
```

The following sequence of rules is red, based on these initial facts:

1. R4 infers the fact *market is upward*.
2. R17 infers the fact *interest rates are low*.

Facts in Working Memory	Inferred From
(A) S&P500 is up	Initial fact
(B) NASDAQ is up	Initial fact
(C) Interest rate = 5.5%	Initial Fact
(D) Market is upward	R4, from A and B
(E) Interest rates are low	R17, from C
(F) Sector financial is strong	R19, from E
(G) Buy in sector financial	R1, from D and F
(H) Buy Countrywide Financial	R20 from G
(I) Buy Bank of America	R20 from G

Figure 5.2. Working memory of forward chaining example.

3. R19 infers the fact *sector financial is strong*.
4. R1 infers *buy in sector financial*.
5. R20 infers the recommendation *buy Countrywide Financial*.
6. R20 infers the recommendation *buy Bank of America*.

See Figure 5.2 for the facts in working memory and how they are inferred using forward chaining. In the end, the expert system recommends that the user buy Countrywide Financial and Bank of America stock.

Let us now look at a backward chaining example. We will rst state our hypothesis: *short American Airlines*. In backward chaining, we nd evidence to either support or refute this hypothesis. In addition, we will assume the following initial facts:

```
Increase in oil prices = 40%
S&P500 is down
NASDAQ is down
```

In Step 1, we look for a rule that contains our hypothesis *short American Airlines* in the THEN part of the rule. The only rule is R15 and it tells us that we need to establish *short in sector transportation* to prove R15. We place R15 on the stack.

In Step 2, we use R2 to prove *short in sector transportation*. To prove R2, we need to establish two facts: *market is downward* and *sector transportation is weak*. We place R2 on the stack.

In Step 3, we use R5 to prove *market is downward*. We know this is true because of two initial facts: *S&P500 is down* and *NASDAQ is down*. We may add *market is downward* to our working memory.

In Step 4, therefore, we need to establish that *sector transportation is weak*. We can do this by using R9. To prove this fact, we need to establish that *oil prices are high*.

In Step 5, we use R7 to prove that *oil prices are high*. We know that this is true because of the initial fact that states *Increase in oil prices* = 40%.

Hence we have used the following sequence of rules R15 →R2 →R5 →R9 → R7 to prove our hypothesis. The expert system will recommend that the user should short American Airlines.

The backward chaining method may have proceeded differently in this same example. It is possible that the goal *short American Airlines* could have been proven by taking a different path through the knowledge base. The following sequence of rules could also have been activated to prove the same thing:

In Step 1, we use R15 (like before). To prove *short American Airlines*, we need to establish *short in sector transportation*.

Now, however, we go to R13 instead. To prove *short in sector transportation*, we need to establish *oil prices are high*.

To prove that *oil prices are high*, we need to use R7. We know that this is true because *Increase in oil prices* = 40%, as given by initial fact.

Hence, in this case, we have used only three rules R15 →R13 →R7 to prove our hypothesis.

Which is the better approach to take, forward chaining or backward chaining? Forward chaining is certainly simpler to understand—you simply enter a number of facts into the system and let the expert system make a recommendation, whatever it may be. Many experts, in fact, gather information and data rst before they make their recommendation. To many, forward chaining seems a natural way for expert reasoning to occur. Moreover, forward chaining allows for the greatest amount of exibility in terms of enabling an expert system to determine how it will make a recommendation.

However, backward chaining has a number of advantages to offer as well. If the human experts in a domain typically start out with some kind of initial hypotheses and want to nd evidence to either support or refute the hypothesis, then a backward chaining approach may be more appropriate. Diagnostic expertise (i.e., determining what is wrong with someone or something), for example, frequently begins with an initial hypothesis that needs to be proven or refuted. In medical diagnosis, as one example, a doctor will typically begin with a hunch as to what is wrong with a patient. The doctor will typically perform tests and other diagnostics to determine whether the patient has a particular disease or not. Backward chaining, it turns out, is a more natural way to process this type of expert reasoning.

Another advantage of backward chaining is that it is oftentimes a more focused and directed search through a knowledge base. A complex knowledge base may contain hundreds of rules, and a backward chaining approach can limit and focus the search through a vast knowledge base to only those rules relevant to the initial hypothesis. In contrast, a forward chaining approach will execute whatever rules it nds related to the initial facts and may derive new facts that can be unrelated to the task at hand. The forward chaining method, therefore, may be less ef cient in reaching a recommendation.

Conflict Resolution. It is quite possible, especially in a large and complex knowledge base containing hundreds of rules and many different interactions among the rules (oftentimes unforeseen by the designer), for an expert system to arrive at two conflicting recommendations. In our stock-picking example, the expert system could make two conflicting recommendations based on the following two initial facts:

```
S&P500 is little-changed
Increase in oil prices = 25%
```

When forward chaining, one pathway that the expert system might take is the following sequence of rules:

1. R6 would infer the fact *market is sideways* from the initial fact *S&P500 is little-changed*.
2. R3 would infer *stay-out* from the fact *market is sideways*.

Hence the expert system would recommend that the user stay out of the market (and stay in cash).

Another possible pathway through the knowledge base, again via forward chaining, is firing the following sequence of rules:

1. R7 would infer the fact *oil prices are high* from the initial fact *Increase in oil price = 25%*
2. R8 would infer the fact that *sector energy is strong* from the fact *oil prices are high*.
3. R9 would infer the fact that *sector transportation is weak* from the fact *oil prices are high*.
4. R10 would infer *buy in sector energy* from the fact *sector energy is strong*.
5. R13 would infer *short in sector transportation* from the fact *sector transportation is weak*.
6. R11 would infer the recommendation *buy ExxonMobil* from the fact *buy in sector energy*.
7. R12 would infer the recommendation *buy BP* from the fact *buy in sector energy*.
8. R14 would infer the recommendation *short United Airlines* from the fact *short in sector transportation*.
9. R15 would infer the recommendation *short American Airlines* from the fact *short in sector transportation*.

Under this chain of reasoning a total of nine rules are fired, and the expert system makes not one, but four final recommendations: (1) buy ExxonMobil, (2) buy BP, (3) short United Airlines, and (4) short American Airlines. These four recommendations are not conflicting because it is possible for an investor to buy multiple stocks and short multiple stocks. In fact, it is good thing that the expert system is able to make multiple stock recommendations (after all, a human expert would do the same for us). However, these four recommendations contradict the recommendation made earlier: that is, stay out of the market.

How do we resolve this problem of con icting recommendations? There are at least four distinct possibilities:

1. Fine-tune the rules so that you eliminate the possibility of con icting recommendations.
2. Assign priority values to the rules so that rules with higher priority are executed over those with lower priority.
3. Implement a control strategy that dictates to the inference engine when and how the rules are executed.
4. Make the determination of which rules are executed rst based on *characteristics of the rules themselves*.

It is possible to ne-tune the rules of an expert system so that con icting recommendations are not made. For example, we may change R3 as follows:

```
R3.   IF market is sideways AND oil prices are not high
            THEN stay-out
```

By ne-tuning this rule, the expert system will never make the recommendation to stay out of the market and, at the same time, make the con icting recommendations to buy the energy stocks and short the transportation stocks. The advantage of this approach is that it ensures that con icting recommendations are not made. The disadvantage of this approach is that it is extremely dif cult to foresee every possible con ict and ne-tune the rules appropriately. Moreover, the rules can become very complex and cumbersome when you add condition upon condition to ensure that they do not make con icting resolutions. In a very large knowledge base, another approach may be more desirable.

A second approach is to assign a priority level each rule. Hence rules with a higher priority are red rst, and if a recommendation is still not reached, rules with lower priority considered. For instance, we may assign all the rules pertaining to oil price hikes (cluster III above) with a higher priority than the three general rules (cluster I above), or vice versa. This approach has a lot to offer it, and should be seriously considered when creating a complex knowledge base. Indeed, human experts frequently prioritize factors and information when making their recommendations: In some cases, they may completely ignore one factor in the presence of another more important factor. The problem with this approach is that there in fact may not exist a natural prioritization of the rules, and so one is left to guess. One may guess wrong, and incorrect decisions can be made by the expert system. Another disadvantage with this approach is that it is not as precise as a ne-tuning of individual rules.

A third approach is to implement a control strategy that tells the inference engine how the rules in the knowledge base are executed. Without some kind of higher-level strategy, the inference engine treats every rule uniformly, so there is no strong sense how the expert system is processing the rules. A control strategy can be used to impose a plan or approach for problem solving. For example, one type of strategy might be to cluster the rules in some way and create a plan for how the clusters are ordered. In our example, we might enforce the following rule:

```
If oil prices are high
     Execute the Cluster II Rules before the Cluster I Rules
```

Such a rule is referred to as a **metarule**, a type of rule that speci es a strategy, or a high-level approach for solving a problem.

Here is a more realistic example of a metarule from an expert system called Neomycin,[8] an offspring of MYCIN:

```
IF (1) the infection is pelvic-abscess, and
   (2) there are rules which mention in their premise
       enterobacteriaceae, and
   (3) there are rules which mention in their premise gram-pos-rods,
       THEN there is suggestive evidence (.4) that the former should
       be done before the latter
```

This metarule will cause one goal (2) to be pursued before another goal (3). Such meta-rules make the expert system's problem-solving strategy more explicit and therefore help prevent con icts from occurring.

The use of control strategies is a very effective way, in general, for organizing a very complex knowledge base. It is strongly recommended for all but the simplest of knowledge bases because it can provides an organizational structure for an expert system that may seem to making decisions in a rather haphazard way. We will further consider the issue of strategic knowledge in the next chapter, when we explore ways to make the reasoning process more visible through diagrams.

The fourth approach to resolving con icts is to prioritize rules based on the charactcristics of the rules themselves. One way is to execute rules that are more speci c rst. For instance, suppose we are given two rules with the following conditions:

R1: (A and B and C and D)

R2: (A and D)

The more speci c rule is R1, so that it may be given a higher priority. Given two rules R1 and R2, whenever a condition in R1 is a superset of a condition in R2 (as in this case), then R1 is deemed more speci c and hence should be executed rst. Some inference engines will also judge speci city of a rule by simply counting the number of conditions in a rule: Rules with more conditions get executed rst. Still other inference engines will look at the data themselves so that data (or facts) have priority values assigned to them. Rules that have conditions that use data with a higher priority will be executed rst.

CLIPS

CLIPS is a tool that is used to develop expert systems. It stands for C Language Integrated Production System. It was created in 1986 by NASA/Lyndon B. Johnson Space Center. Although it was originally written in C, its syntax more closely resembles that of the AI programming language LISP. CLIPS is now in the public domain, which means that you may download a free copy on the web to develop your own expert system applications.[9] Moreover the software's documentation is also freely available for download. Because it is free, ef cient, and easy to learn, CLIPS has become the most widely used expert system tool today. It is a very good choice for creating many different types of expert system applications in a relatively short amount of time.

Like most expert system shells, CLIPS contains three basic components:

1. Fact list: working memory for data
2. Knowledge base: the collection of rules
3. Inference engine: controls the execution of the rules

In this section, we look at how these three components work as well as the basic syntax of the CLIPS language. A more in-depth look at CLIPS, can be found in the literature.[10] To acquire a basic understanding of CLIPS language requires an understanding of two items in the CLIPS language: (1) facts (working memory) and (2) IF–THEN rules (the knowledge base). We rst describe the syntax of these two items. Next, we code two short examples, using the traf c light example and the stock selection problem that were described earlier in this chapter, to illustrate how an expert system is created from facts and rules. The inference engine is used to process the facts and rules and to make recommendations. The CLIPS inference engine is designed to perform forward chaining only, although there are ways to emulate backward chaining.[11] We illustrate how the forward chaining process works when we discuss basic input/output functions, and a simple question-and-answer user interface. By the end of this discussion, you should have a basic understanding of how the four components (working memory, knowledge base, inference engine, and user interface) work together in an expert system.

Facts. Facts are used to represent information in CLIPS. A fact may consist of a single eld, or multiple elds. Some examples of facts follow:

1. `(animal)`
2. `(San-Francisco)`
3. `(age 27)`

4. (weight 154.4 kilograms)
5. (name "Robbie T. Nakatsu")
6. (place-of-birth Austin Texas USA)
7. (place-of-birth "Austin, TX USA")
8. (sex male)
9. (gives Bob Harry apple)
10. (grocery-list apples cereal eggs chicken ketchup)

Facts, and all commands in CLIPS for that matter, are always delimited by parentheses (this notation is a carry-over from the programming language LISP). The facts listed contain three types of elds: (1) symbols, (2) strings, and (3) numbers. Before we proceed any further in our discussion, let us rst describe the differences among these three eld types.*

A **symbol** is a eld that starts with a printable ASCII character and is followed by zero or more characters. Symbols cannot contain delimiters such as the following characters:

spaces tabs & | ,   ~   " (   )

Also, ? and $? cannot be placed at the beginning of a symbol because they are used to represent variables (see discussion on variables later in this section). Valid symbols include the following:

cat cat-2 cat2 set-off-alarm 567-87-9000   !A alert?

Invalid symbols, on the other hand, include:

A&P   "house"   boy|girl   ?why   house,100   car~

The second eld type is a **string**, which must begin and end with a double quotation mark. Strings are used, rather than symbols, when you wish to capture and represent descriptive information, especially sequences of characters containing embedded spaces. Examples include proper names, titles of books, addresses, instructions, and descriptive sentences:

"Mr. & Mrs. Smith"
"The House of the Seven Gables"
"132 Orchard Drive. Baltimore, MD"
"Turn on the faucet."

For the most part, you should use symbols, rather than strings, when you are encoding the rules of your knowledge base. Strings tend to be longer and are

---

*There are really eight eld types in CLIPS: oat, integer, symbol, string, external address, fact address, instance name, and instance address. We consider only the four most basic forms (symbol, string, integer, and oat). Number is a composite type that includes both oats and integers.

more likely to be mistyped; hence they are less suitable for the pattern matching operations that an inference engine performs. Strings are most appropriate for displaying output messages containing literal strings of information.

Finally, **numbers** may be represented as integers as in the following:

3   +5   106   0   -65

Alternatively, numbers may be expressed as oats:

1.2   -3.4   4.976   -14.5   4.67e10

Facts may be **ordered** or **unordered**. A fact is ordered when the order of the elds is signi cant. For example, the fact

(gives Bob Harry apples)

is ordered because the rst eld represents the relation *gives*, the second eld is the agent *Bob*, the third is the recipient *Harry*, and the fourth is the item given *apples*. On the other hand, a fact such as

(grocery-list apples cereal eggs chicken ketchup)

is unordered because it does not matter in what order the grocery items are listed. (However, the rst eld, *grocery-list*, is most de nitely ordered because it represents the relation and must occur rst in the list).

It is considered good practice to encode a fact as an object-value pair, as opposed to a single eld. We described earlier in the chapter the use of object-value pairs to represent IF–THEN rules. For example:

IF light is green
    THEN action is go

may be expressed as:

(A) IF (light green)
      THEN (action go)

(B) IF (green)
      THEN (go)

Both A and B are acceptable ways of expressing facts in CLIPS; however A is preferable to B because it is clearer what the fact means. We adopt the convention of always stating a fact as an object-value pair in this book.

Facts are placed onto a **fact-list** in CLIPS. The fact-list is a collection of all active facts about a current problem that have been either entered by the user as an initial fact or inferred by the inference engine. Facts are added to the fact-list by issuing the assert command:

```
(assert (age 27))
(assert (weight 154.4 kilograms))
```

Facts may also be removed from the fact-list by issuing the retract command:

```
(retract (age 45))
(retract (weight 154.4 kilograms))
```

Notice how the fact itself must be enclosed in a set of parentheses, and the entire command itself must also be enclosed in a set of parentheses; thus one set of parentheses is embedded within another set of parentheses.

One must also be careful, when expressing facts, about the use of capitals and lowercase letters, because CLIPS is a **case-sensitive** language. Hence CLIPS will not recognize the two facts as representing the same thing:

```
(city Los-Angeles)
(city los-angeles)
```

To CLIPS, the two facts represent two different cities.

Rules. The general syntax for a rule is given in Figure 5.3. A rule is divided into two parts: the LHS, or condition, part of the rule and the RHS, or action, part of the rule. The LHS side of the rule can contain any number of patterns or facts. CLIPS will attempt to match these facts against the facts found in the fact list—in this respect, an important function of an inference engine is to match patterns found on the LHS of a rule. If it nds all the facts in the LIIS of the rule in the fact list, the rule is said to be red, or activated. The RHS side of the rule speci es the actions that will take place when the rule is activated. Any number of actions can be placed on the RHS of the rule.

Let us now look at how the traf c light example would be coded in CLIPS. The six rules follow:

```
(defrule green-light "Go when green."
     (light green)
=>
     (assert (action go))
     (printout t "Go." crlf))

(defrule red-light "Stop when red."
     (light red)
=>
     (assert (action stop))
```

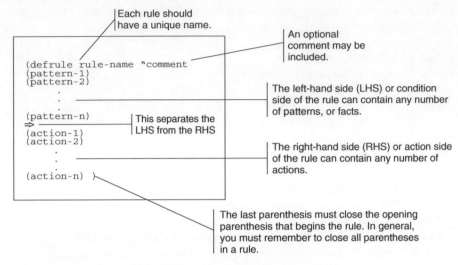

Figure 5.3. The syntax of a rule in CLIPS.

```
        (printout t "Stop." crlf))


(defrule yellow-light1 "Yellow Light:  enough time"
        (light yellow)
        (enough-time true)
=>

        (assert (action go))
        (printout t "Proceed with caution." crlf))


(defrule yellow-light2 "Yellow Light:  not enough time"
        (light yellow)
        (enough-time false)
=>

        (assert (action stop))
        (printout t "Stop." crlf))


(defrule press-gas-pedal "Press on gas pedal."
        (action go)
=>

        (assert (gas-pedal press))
        (printout t "Press on gas pedal." crlf))


(defrule press-brake "Press on brake."
        (action stop)
=>

        (assert (brake press))
        (printout t "Press on brake." crlf))
```

Each of these six rules contains one or two patterns that indicate when the rule is to be activated. The yellow light rules (*yellow-light1* and *yellow-light2*) contain two patterns. Whenever there is more than one pattern in a rule, there is an implicit AND that indicates that both patterns must be true in order for the rule to re. For example, rule *yellow-light1* indicates that (light yellow) AND (enough-time true) must both be true in order for it to re.

Each of the rules contains an assert action, which means that a new fact is established and added to the fact list. For example, rule *green-light* will assert (action go), which means that this fact is placed on the fact list. This action, in turn, will re rule *press-gas-pedal*, because (action go) is a pattern that is found in the LHS of this rule. This rule will assert (gas-pedal press). This simple sequence of rule rings illustrates a simple example of forward chaining in CLIPS: One rule res, which asserts a new fact, and that leads to another rule ring. Forward chaining will often result in a sequence, or chain, of rule rings, as new facts are established and added to the fact list, until eventually a nal recommendation is reached.

Input/Output. Another type of action that is included in each of the six traf c light rules is an output action. The **printout** function is used to display a message to the user on the computer screen. The syntax for this function is:

```
(printout t "text" crlf)
```

The *t* in this function refers to the standard output device of a computer, which is typically the user's computer screen. The printout function is a very basic way of communicating text messages to a user. It can be used to display an expert system's recommendation and other informative messages to the user.

One function that is missing in these six rules is a way for a user to enter input data, or initial facts. In this particular cxamplc, thcrc is no way for a uscr to tell the system what the color of the traf c light is. We will need at least two additional rules that will allow users to enter inputs so the expert system has enough data to make a recommendation:

```
;get input from user on the color of the traffic light
(defrule get-light-color
=>
    (printout t "What is the color of the traffic light?" crlf)
    (bind ?color(read))
    (assert (light ?color)))

;get input from user if yellow light.
(defrule get-enough-time
    (light yellow)
=>
    (printout t "There is enough time to go through the
```

```
intersection.   Enter true or false." crlf)
(bind ?truefalse(read))
(assert (enough-time ?truefalse)))
```

The rst of these two rules, *get-light-color* will prompt the user: What is the color of the traf c light? The user can enter the input at this point. The rule will then read the input and bind it (or store its value) to the variable ?color. Finally, the rule will assert the fact (light ?color), the value of ?color being the value entered by the user. The symbol *crlf* refers to a carriage return-linefeed. It is used to start a new line on the screen and can be used to improve the appearance of lines displayed on a computer screen.

This rule, it should be noted, does not contain any patterns in the LHS of the rule. This is a perfectly valid way of coding a rule—it means that the rule will always re, unconditionally. Any number of comments may also be added to document the rules. In the rst rule, there is a comment describing the function of the rule:

```
;get input from user on the color of the traffic light
```

Comments may be added anywhere in a knowledge base by preceding the text with a semicolon. The inference engine, in effect, ignores all text following a semicolon up until the end of the line.

The second rule, *get-enough-time*, will ask the user whether there is enough time to go through the intersection and will assert the fact (enough-time true) if true or (enough-time false) if false. This rule will execute only when the traf c light is yellow; hence the pattern (light yellow) on the LHS of the rule. (It certainly does not make sense to ask this question when the light is green or red). This example illustrates how an expert system can direct the question-and-answer session through the knowledge base. It is usually not the case that a user needs to enter every input imaginable to the expert system. Through the use of rules, the inference engine will request information only as it is needed. This is considered good practice in the design of knowledge bases.

The printout and bind actions together form a very simple input/output expert system user interface. These actions alone can create a text-based question-and-answer dialogue that takes place between the user and the expert system. Although very basic, this user interface can be used to create a great variety of interactions. See Figure 5.4 for a sample consultation taking placing in CLIPS when the traf c light knowledge base is loaded into the system.

The user rst enters the command (reset) at the CLIPS> command prompt. This command resets the working memory—that is, it clears the fact list and begins a new a session with the expert system. The next command (run) will run the expert system, at which point the system asks its rst question: What is the color of the traf c light? Figure 5.4 shows three different sessions, each initiated by a separate (reset) and (run); the questions that the expert system poses; the user's answers; and nally the recommendations.

```
CLIPS> (reset)
CLIPS> (run)
What is the color of the traffic light?
green
Go.
Press on gas pedal.
CLIPS> (reset)
CLIPS> (run)
What is the color of the traffic light?
yellow
There is enough time to go through the intersection. Enter true or
false.
true
Proceed with caution.
Press on gas pedal.
CLIPS> (reset)
CLIPS> (run)
What is the color of the traffic light?
yellow
There is enough time to go through the intersection. Enter true or
false.
false
Stop.
Press on brake.
```

Figure 5.4. An interactive question-and-answer dialogue with CLIPS.

This question-and-answer dialogue is obviously very limited in what it can do. We will need to do better than this rigid dialogue. The subject of enhanced user interfaces, which are more graphical and diagrammatic in nature, is addressed more fully in the next chapter. In the next chapter we also consider myriad approaches to developing more effective user interfaces that are more transparent, exible, and user-friendly.

Stock Selection Expert System Revisited. We will now look at our second example, the stock selection expert system, which was described earlier in this chapter. We now have enough knowledge of the syntax of CLIPS so that we are able to code most of its rules. However, there are still some more advanced features that we have not yet addressed. In this section, we look at more complex examples of rules, so that, in the end, we will be able to complete the knowledge base. (The completed CLIPS code of the stock selection expert system is given in the appendix to this chapter.) In particular, we need to address the following questions to complete our discussion:

- How do we use variables to create more generic rules?
- How do we create more complex Boolean expressions that include conditional elements AND, OR, and NOT?
- How do we create rules that can process and compare numeric information?
- How do we implement a control strategy so that the inference engine cannot make con icting recommendations?

In the discussion that follows, we look, one by one, at each of these questions.

The rst question asks how we will use variables to code more generic rules. In the stock selection knowledge base, we will need to use CLIPS variables to code the rst two rules:

```
R1.  If market is up and sector ?x is strong
          THEN buy in sector ?x
R2.  IF market is down and sector ?x is weak
          THEN short in sector ?x
```

The use of variables in CLIPS was illustrated earlier when we described how input values are read into variables. Like in other programming languages, variables are used to store values. The syntax that CLIPS uses to represent a variable is a question mark followed by a symbolic name (there should be no space between the question mark and the symbolic name). The symbolic name must follow the rules of forming valid symbols discussed earlier, with the additional constraint that they must also begin with a character. It is also considered good programming practice to use a meaningful variable name, one that re ects its function in the code.

Variables are very useful for specifying generic rules. Here, R1 and R2 are coded in CLIPS so that they will work for any sector:

```
;If market is up and sector is strong, then buy in sector
(defrule R1-market-up
      (market up)
      (sector ?name strong)
=>
      (assert (buy sector ?name)))

;If market is down and sector is weak, then short in sector
(defrule R2-market-down
      (market down)
      (sector ?name weak)
=>
      (assert (short sector ?name)))
```

In general, a variable with the same name can be used in multiple places within a single rule. The rst time a variable is referenced in the LHS side of the rule, it is bound (or assigned) to a value. The variable retains its value within the rule, so that it may be used again in the RHS. For example, in the following rule, the ?name and ?age variables may be used again in the RHS:

```
(defrule Print-Name-and-Age
      (person ?name)
      (person ?age)
=>
      (printout t ?name " is " ?age " years old."))
```

If two facts (name "John Doe") and (age 57) are asserted, this rule will print out: "John Doe is 57 years old." Without the power of variables, our expert system would be far less exible and far less capable of accomplishing many types of expert reasoning.

The second question that needs to addressed is how to create more complex rules containing the conditional elements AND, OR and NOT. In the stock selection knowledge base is the following rule that requires an OR:

```
R6.  IF S&P500 is little-changed OR NASDAQ is little-changed
            THEN market is sideways
```

In this rule, it is necessary only to establish that one or the other fact is true. Up to this point, all the rules that we have seen assume that *all* facts on the LHS must match—that is to say, there is an implicit AND between the facts. CLIPS also allows one to specify an OR conditional element between the facts. R6 would be coded as:

```
;If either S&P500 or NASDAQ is little changed, the market is
sideways
(defrule R6-market-sideways
      (or (SP500 little-changed)
          (NASDAQ little-changed))
=>
      (assert (market sideways)))
```

The syntax of an OR conditional element uses a type of syntax known as **prefix form**. This means that an operator, the logical operator OR in this case, precedes its arguments, which are the patterns or facts. In general, an OR conditional element with *n* arguments, or facts, is coded as:

```
(or (fact1) (fact2) (fact3). . .(factn) )
```

In accordance with CLIPS notation, the entire expression must be enclosed within parentheses. An **infix form**, which most of us are accustomed to, would code the rule as:

```
(fact1) or (fact2) or (fact3) . . . or (factn)
```

The in x form is the syntax that is adopted by most procedural languages, but not by CLIPS.

You may use a combination of AND, OR, and NOT to create more complex Boolean expressions. The following two rules encode the expertise representing the conditions under which one would stop at a traf c light.

```
;The following two rules demonstrate more complicated conditional
```

```
;processing using conditional elements AND, OR, and NOT.

;
(defrule stop-at-traffic-light1
     (or (light red)
         (and (light yellow)
              (enough-time false)))
=>
     (assert (action stop))
     (printout t "Stop." crlf))

(defrule stop-at-traffic-light2
     (or (light red)
         (and (light yellow)
              (not (enough-time true))))
=>
     (assert (action stop))
     (printout t "Stop." crlf))
```

The rst rule, *stop-at-traffic-light1*, will re when either (light red) or (light yellow) AND (enough-time false). Notice how the use of indentation can greatly aid in understanding the logic of this rule. This rule encodes the exact same expertise as the traf c light rules described earlier, except that in this case only one rule is used. As a general principle, you may avoid using the OR conditional element by creating two separate rules instead. By doing so, the rules that you create are much less complex and easier to understand.

The second rule, *stop-at-traffic-light2*, is equivalent to the rst rule; in this rule a **not** conditional element is also used. Rather than use (enough-time false), this rule uses (not (enough-time true)), which are two equivalent facts. There is no good reason to code the rule this way, as it creates a rule that is unnecessarily complex. Four parentheses are now needed to close off all the levels of logic contained in this complex rule.

The third question we will address is how to process numeric data and infor-mation. Speci cally, there are three rules in the stock selection knowledge base that involve quantitative data:

```
R7.  IF increase in oil prices > 20%
          THEN  oil prices are high
R16.  IF interest rate > 9%
          THEN  interest rate is high
R17.  IF interest rate < 6%
          THEN  interest rate is low
```

CLIPS uses what is called the **test conditional element** to compare numbers and variables on the LHS of a rule. The three rules are coded as follows:

```
;Oil prices are high when increase > 20%
(defrule R7-classify-oil-prices
      (oil-increase ?percent)
      (test (> ?percent 20) )
=>
      (assert (oil-prices high)))

;Interest rate is high when > 9%
(defrule R16-classify-high-interest-rate
      (interest-rate ?percent)
      (test (> ?percent 9.0) )
=>
      (assert (interest-rate-class high)))

;Interest rate is low when < 6%
(defrule R17-classify-low-interest-rate
      (interest-rate ?percent)
      (test (< ?percent 6.0) )
=>
      (assert (interest-rate-class low)))
```

The test conditional element provides a way to make numeric comparisons on the LHS of a rule. In addition to > (greater than) and < (less than), you may also use the following relational operators to compare two numeric values:

```
=   (equal to)
<>  (not equal to)
>=  (greater than or equal to)
<=  (less than or equal to)
```

The logical operators AND, OR, and NOT may also be used in the test conditional element. For example, the following rule will classify a person as middle-aged if he or she is between the ages of 45 and 65, inclusive:

```
(defrule classify-middle-aged
      (person ?age)
      (test (and (>= ?age 45)
                 (<= ?age 65)))
=>
      (assert (age-class middle-aged)))
```

The fourth and nal question is the need for a control strategy to process the rules. Earlier, we observed that the stock selection expert system would reach two con icting recommendations when two facts are asserted:

```
S&P500 is little-changed
Increase in oil prices = 25%
```

The ﬁrst fact would be used to infer that the market is sideways and, therefore, that one should stay out of the market. The second fact would be used to infer that oil prices are high and, therefore, that the energy sector is strong. It would then be inferred that one should buy stocks in the energy sector.

One way to prevent these conﬂicting recommendations from occurring is to control what inputs the system will request from the user. For example, let us suppose that we wanted the expert system to make the recommendation that an investor should stay out of the market, and do nothing else, when the market is sideways. To prevent the conﬂicting recommendation from occurring, the following rule might be added to the knowledge base:

```
;Get oil price increase; request this input only when market is up
 or down
(defrule get-oil-price-increase "Oil price increase"
       (or (market up)
           (market down))
  =>
       (printout t "Enter oil price increase (in %)." crlf)
       (bind ?percent(read))
       (assert (oil-increase ?percent)))
```

The inclusion of this rule would force the system never to request information on oil price increases if the market is sideways; it would not even bother to ask. It would ask the user only when the market is either up or down. In this manner, the expert system is prevented from reaching conﬂicting recommendations by controlling what information is allowed to enter the system and when.

This is not the only way to prevent conﬂicting recommendations from occurring. As discussed earlier, another technique is to prioritize the rules so that the most important ones are forced to execute ﬁrst. In CLIPS, this is possible by declaring a **salience** value. Salience is set by assigning a numeric value, from -10,000 to 10,000 (when no salience value is entered it is assumed to be 0). Higher values represent higher priorities. Accordingly, it is possible to control the execution of the rules through the assignment of salience values. Here is an example:

```
(defrule high-priority-rule
       (declare (salience 50))
       (rule high-priority)
  =>
       (printout t "This will print first."))

(defrule low-priority-rule
       (declare (salience -50))
       (rule low-priority)
  =>
       (printout t "This will print second."))
```

BENEFITS AND LIMITATIONS

The success of expert systems in the computer age is unmistakable. Successful examples of their applications range from medical expert systems that can diagnose human diseases to expert systems that can con gure and design complex objects such as computer systems to expert systems that can plan sequences of actions that might be performed by a robot. Increasingly today, expert systems are not standalone systems but are embedded as intelligent modules within larger applications so that the untrained observer would not even notice that they are working on our behalf.

Many companies have discovered the great potential of expert systems. Shrewd organizations may see opportunities for their deployment whenever there is an activity where human experts are overburdened, undersupplied, or expensive to obtain. A commercial bank, for instance, may decide that its commercial loan of cers are overworked and that a commercial loan assistant, in the form of an expert system, can help them make better, quicker, and more consistent decisions when processing loan applications. Although there may be some unease about replacing human experts with a computer program, as well as ethical arguments that these systems can depersonalize and dehumanize a company that values the human touch and interaction that a human expert offers, in most cases the expert system will not completely replace the human decision maker. Indeed, the expert system's role is usually one of assistant rather than outright replacement. The expert system's function may be to eliminate the mundane tasks and grunt work associated with making a decision, and therefore, free the human expert to focus more on the trickier aspects of a problem. Or perhaps the expert system will suggest a number of candidate solutions, which the human decision maker ultimately has the nal say on. Many prefer the gentler term *expert support system*, because it implies that the human decision maker is supported in some kind of task, but not completely eliminated.

What speci c bene ts might an organization expect to reap from a successful expert system implementation? A number of case studies of real-world applications and the literature on expert systems offer the following possibilities:

- Increased output and productivity
- Reduced costs, including decreased personnel required
- Reduced errors
- Better customer service
- Better, quicker, and more consistent decision-making
- Knowledge transfer to remote locations
- Formalization of organizational knowledge

To understand how these bene ts might actually materialize, let's look at the expert system XCON, developed by Digital Equipment Corporation in 1978.[12] XCON is frequently cited as the rst expert system to achieve real commercial success, and its example demonstrates, in a concrete way, how one company grasped the potential of the technology, committed enormous resources to building a fully actualized expert system, and took the time to learn how to embed the system within its organizational processes.

Digital was a company that was well known for its minicomputers, including most famously the VAX and PDP minicomputers that were popular in the 1970s and 1980s. Digital's business strategy at the time was to build a highly customized computer tailored to t each customer's speci c needs—that is, a built-to-order, a la carte approach to the design and con guration of computers. (In later years this approach would be upended by the PCs industry's strategy of producing computers in super-ef cient, high-volume assembly lines at the lowest cost possible).

Before XCON, the system con guration task was performed manually. Trained technical editors reviewed all customer orders for technical correctness and order completeness. This was a very dif cult and time-consuming task, sometimes involving the expertise of many different people. Sometimes the same parts were assembled inconsistently and this was sometimes a source of quality issues and complaints from customers.

XCON was a rule-based expert system that was developed to automate and improve upon the computer con guration task. XCON took as its input a customer's order and produced as its output a set of speci cations and diagrams, which were used by the technical editors as a guide to building the system. The development of XCON spanned over nearly 10 years and resulted in very complex expert system. To give one a sense of its complexity, the XCON knowledge base itself contained over 10,000 rules (other related knowledge bases added another 8,000 rules).[13] Rule count alone, however, did not account for the broad scope of the system. Another dimension was the complexity of the rules themselves:

- An average rule contained about six patterns in the LHS of the rule.
- Each pattern, in turn, contained about ve attributes.
- The average number of actions speci ed in the RHS of the rule was four.

Thus, on average, the number of tests that each rule performed during each cycle or run was about 6×5 or 30 tests.

In addition to the knowledge base, XCON contained databases to store information about the computer parts themselves. The component database contained con guration information on over 30,000 parts, and there were from 25 to 125 attributes per part. There were over 40 types of parts, including, CPUs, cables, cabinets, controllers, disks, and tapes. This was indeed a quite extensive and complex expert system.

How did XCON perform? How can we evaluate the performance of XCON, in terms of how it enhanced the organizational performance of Digital? When XCON was rst installed, the system had limited capability and knowledge and required extensive interaction with the technical editors to acquire its expertise and build up its knowledge base. Digital also realized early on that building a successful expert system was not simply about adding more and more rules into a knowledge base. Digital realized that, aside from resolving technical issues, it also needed to integrate the technology into the fabric of its business and attend to the organizational and human resource issues. Only then would Digital begin to realize actual improvements in its performance.

Over time, XCON proved to be a huge bene t for Digital. Its results were astonishing by almost all standard benchmarks. First, XCON signi cantly increased the technical accuracy of the customer orders. Before XCON, a large percentage of customer orders had con guration errors and/or lacked completeness. By one estimate, before XCON 35% of orders had inaccurate con gurations, whereas after XCON the error rate was reduced dramatically to 2% of orders. The error rate was a critical measure of XCON's success because straightening out problem orders was a costly process that consumed a large portion of Digital's time and was highly disruptive to the normal customer order cycle. Therefore, XCON ultimately resulted in a shorter customer cycle time, a lower number of personnel needed for a given volume of orders, and a much smoother running organization in general. Moreover, in terms of time spent on the orders alone, it was estimated that without XCON, technical editors spent 20 to 30 min on each order, but after XCON even very complicated orders could be handled in less than 1 min. It is not at all surprising, then, that customer satisfaction and sales volume increased.

Another bene t that Digital witnessed was that system con guration information was delivered consistently throughout the organization. The use of XCON ensured that computers were con gured to optimize system performance, and this was done on a consistent basis. Before XCON, Digital would sometimes ship systems containing the same parts that were con gured differently—there are multiple ways of con guring the same set of components. Just imagine what challenges the technical support staff faced when dealing with components that were inconsistently con gured. Moreover, the existence of a consistent set of con guration information meant that it was much easier to shift manufacturing from one plant to the next without costly training and disruptions in staf ng. This led to a much more exible manufacturing environment.

In the end, the introduction of XCON was an all-out winner for Digital. It led to increased productivity, lower costs, increased ef ciency in ful lling customer orders, and better customer service. In the history of AI, too, XCON is a watershed system because it represents a huge departure from the universal problem solvers that AI researchers were initially hoping to create. These programs were capable of solving only toy problems and playing games, but XCON demonstrated in a spectacular way that it was possible for AI to solve realistic and complex problems. It is a testament to Digital that it possessed the foresight and con dence to commit to an AI technology during a time when AI technologies were not widely accepted and adopted in the commercial world.* XCON was more than a research vehicle for Digital; it was a system that supported its core

---

*Unfortunately, Digital's success in the computer industry was short lived. In a few years, Digital would witness the rapid growth of PCs, and would eventually be overtaken by companies like Dell

business strategy and in many ways undergirded the operations of the entire company.

We would be remiss if we neglected to include a discussion of problems and limitations of expert systems as well. It has been almost four decades since they were rst introduced to us by the AI community, and yet many weaknesses and limitations that were identi ed at the very outset are very much unresolved and remain with us today. Here are some of the main problems and limitations of expert systems:

- Expertise is hard to extract.
- Not all knowledge can be captured.
- Expert systems cannot learn.
- Expert systems are in exible.
- Lack of trust
- Expert systems have limited capability in explaining a solution.
- Expert systems are dif cult to verify and validate.

Let's address each of these problem areas one by one.

Expertise Is Hard to Extract

In many domains, it is very dif cult to capture expertise and encode it as IF–THEN rules. Oftentimes, human experts are unable to articulate just how they make decisions in their domains. At times, expert decision making may be dif cult to capture and express because it involves subjective judgments or the consideration of many different factors and variables; at other times, the domain requires the processing of imperfect, uncertain, or noisy data, and the rules for processing such data are vague and ad hoc. Indeed, many types of expert decision making do not involve clear-cut procedures, and black and white solutions. The unfortunate result is that rule-based approaches sometimes "force" simple solutions on dif cult and multifaceted problems. Another problem is that experts themselves often have disagreements on what the correct answers are, so the designer of the expert system, also known as the knowledge engineer, is faced with the dif cult and sometimes impossible task of reconciling these opposing viewpoints.

Not All Knowledge Can Be Captured

There are many types of expertise that cannot, and should not, be encoded as IF–THEN rules. Here are but a few examples: pattern recognition tasks*

---

whose business model and strategy were different from the customized, proprietary con gurations that Digital championed and pioneered. However, this in no way diminishes the remarkable achievements of XCON, and its ability to transform the workings of an entire organization.

*As noted previously, pattern recognition tasks can more effectively be addressed by neural networks.

(e.g, reading an electrocardiograph, detecting abnormalities on an x-ray), motor skills (e.g., operating complicated equipment and machinery), verbal skills (e.g., teaching a foreign language), interacting with and observing people (e.g., interviewing patients), making ethical judgments, and creative decision making that may involve borrowing knowledge from a wide number of disciplines. Expertise, in general, involves interacting with the physical world, and much of the knowledge must be experienced and processed through our eyes, ears, and other senses. At best, we can only hope to support such expertise in some meaningful way, but we can never completely replace the human expert.

Expert Systems Cannot Learn

Rule-based expert systems require that you preprogram all the rules that represent the knowledge in the domain. To create a realistic and complete solution, the knowledge engineer must be well versed in the domain and have a clear sense of what the decision procedures are. This understanding must take place beforehand, before the system is created; misunderstandings about the domain can be very costly later on because rule-based expert systems can be extremely dif cult to modify and extend into other areas. Even when this is possible, the new rules must be created manually—the expert system does not learn how to ne-tune the rules on its own. Case-based reasoning and neural networks are two AI approaches that are more suitable when you want to create a system that "learns" how to solve problems on its own.

Expert Systems Are Inflexible

The previous issue (the inability to learn) is certainly related to the issue of system exibility, for if an expert system could learn, it could extend its knowledge base over time as it acquired more experience with solving problems. This ability to grow and evolve over time would result in a far more exible system. The issue of in exibility, however, is not about learning alone. In addition, it refers to the idea that expert systems are extremely brittle: They are able to solve problems in one narrow domain, the one in which they were preprogrammed to function in, but are utterly ignorant outside the domain and unable to adapt even to closely related domains. In other words, they completely break down if they are pushed beyond their bounds of expertise. Human experts, of course, degrade much more gracefully and can often infer solutions to closely related areas quite well.

Lack of Trust and Limited Capability in Explaining a Solution

Many users do not trust a recommendation from an expert system because they do not understand how the system arrived at its recommendations. To the user, the expert system is a black box, one whose internal mechanism is not visible for inspection. Such users need a user interface that is more transparent, one that can "explain" why it reached the recommendation that it did. After all, we regularly expect human experts to explain their reasoning processes to us. To their credit, MYCIN and some earlier expert systems, were equipped with limited explanation capabilities, so that users could inquire what chain of rules (called a rule trace) were executed to reach a given recommendation. But as we will see in the next chapter, these forms of explanations were very limited in promoting system understanding.

Expert Systems Are Difficult to Verify and Validate

To verify an expert system's usefulness and worthiness, you must be able to show that it is able to solve problems of realistic complexity that would otherwise require a considerable amount of human expertise. (Otherwise, you have created nothing but a toy system that is of no real practical interest). It must be accurate, arriving at the correct solution, most of the time or at least as frequently as a human expert would. We observed earlier in the case of XCON that it was able to solve problems accurately 98% of the time, as opposed to 65% of the time without the aid of XCON. This was a clear demonstration of XCON's ef cacy. In general, it is dif cult to demonstrate the performance of an expert system without a full-scale implementation in the eld, in which the expert system is solving the problems that human experts ordinarily face.

Short of a full-scale implementation, the developers of an expert system may wish to conduct some kind of experimental study to evaluate its performance. In one type of evaluation, you would create a set of problems, of suf cient complexity that represent typical problems that human experts in the domain face. This set of problems is given to (1) the expert system and (2) a panel of experts. The expert system passes the performance test if it is able to arrive at solutions that are just as good as those arrived by the panel of human experts. (This evaluation resembles a kind of Turing test except that it is meant to compare an expert system to a human expert.)

Such an experimental evaluation, in fact, was conducted on MYCIN in 1979. This study demonstrated that MYCIN's performance compared favorably vis-à-vis that of physicans in treating patients with bacteremia and meningitis. Ten real cases were given to both the expert system as well as to a group of physicians at Stanford University, who were asked to provide a diagnoses as well as therapy recommendations. Eight other experts were then asked to rate the 10 therapy recommendations, not knowing which came from MYCIN and which came from the physicians. The results revealed that there were very few differences between MYCIN's performance and that of the Stanford physicians, but that MYCIN actually outperformed the nonexpert physicians (those who did not specialize in bacterial infections).[14]

In sum, in over four decades of its existence, expert systems have matured to the point that today they are solving complex problems in realistic settings.

In some cases, organizations have found ways to enhance their performance by providing quicker decisions, increased output, and better customer service, to name some of the bene ts associated with successful implementations of the technology. On the other hand, there are problems with the technology that require careful management if the system is to succeed in an organizational setting. They cannot solve all kinds of problems, nor do they usually replace the human expert in the organization. Moreover, unless they are appropriately veri ed and validated, they may fail to solve complex problems as well as human experts can.

Three weaknesses of expert systems—in exibility, lack of trust, and limited explanation capability—can be addressed through an enhanced user interface. The use of diagrams to make an expert system more transparent and exible, and therefore one that is more likely to be trusted by a user, is a tantalizing possibility, one that will be explored more thoroughly in the next chapter.

APPENDIX A: STOCK SELECTION EXPERT SYSTEM

```
;Stock Selection Knowledge Base
;CLIPS Example
;
;**********************************************************************
;Get Inputs from User
;**********************************************************************
;
;Get S&P 500 trend.
(defrule get-SP500-trend "S&P500 trend"
=>
     (printout t "What is the S&P500 trend?  Enter up, down, or
little-changed." crlf)
     (bind ?trend(read))
     (assert (SP500 ?trend)))


;Get NASDAQ trend.
(defrule get-NASDAQ-trend "NASDAQ trend"
=>
     (printout t "What is the NASDAQ trend?  Enter up, down, or
little-changed." crlf)
     (bind ?trend(read))
     (assert (NASDAQ ?trend)))


;Get oil price increase; request this input only when market is
;up or down.  Note:  this rule is specified so that the user is
;never asked to enter the oil price increase when the market
;is sideways. Otherwise, the system may make a conflicting
```

```
;recommendation:  stay out of the market.
;
(defrule get-oil-price-increase "Oil price increase"
     (or (market up)
         (market down))
=>
     (printout t "Enter oil price increase (in %)." crlf)
     (bind ?percent(read))
     (assert (oil-increase ?percent)))

;Get interest rate; request this input only when market is up
or down
(defrule get-interest-rate "Interest rate"
     (or (market up)
         (market down))
=>
     (printout t "Enter interest rate (in %)." crlf)
     (bind ?percent(read))
     (assert (interest-rate ?percent)))

;*******************************************************************
;Cluster I:  General Rules
;*******************************************************************
;
;If market is up and sector is strong, then buy in sector
(defrule R1-market-up
     (market up)
     (sector ?name strong)
=>
     (assert (buy sector ?name)))

;If market is down and sector is weak, then short in sector
(defrule R2-market-down
     (market down)
     (sector ?name weak)
=>
     (assert (short sector ?name)))

;If market is sideways, stay out of the market.
(defrule R3-market-sideways
     (market sideways)
=>
     (assert (stay-out))
     (printout t "Stay out of the market." crlf))
```

```
;**********************************************************************
;Cluster II:  Rules Determining Market Trend
;**********************************************************************
;If both S&P500 and NASDAQ are up, the market is up
(defrule R4-market-up
     (SP500 up)
     (NASDAQ up)
=>
     (assert (market up)))


;If both S&P500 and NASDAQ are down, the market is down
(defrule R5-market-down "Market is down"
     (SP500 down)
     (NASDAQ down)
=>
     (assert (market down)))


;If either S&P500 or NASDAQ is little changed, the market
is sideways
(defrule R6-market-sideways
     (or (SP500 little-changed)
         (NASDAQ little-changed))
=>
     (assert (market sideways)))


;**********************************************************************
;Cluster III:  Rules Pertaining to Oil Price Hikes
;**********************************************************************

;Oil prices are high when increase > 20%
(defrule R7-classify-oil-prices
     (oil-increase ?percent)
     (test (> ?percent 20) )
=>
     (assert (oil-prices high)))

;Sector energy is strong when oil prices are high.
(defrule R8-sector-energy-strong
     (oil-prices high)
=>
     (assert (sector energy strong)))

;Sector transportation is weak when oil prices are high.
(defrule R9-sector-transportation-weak
```

```
     (oil-prices high)
=>
     (assert (sector transportation weak)))

;Buy in sector energy when sector energy is strong
(defrule R10-buy-sector-energy
     (sector energy strong)
=>
     (assert (buy sector energy)))

;Buy ExxonMobil
(defrule R11-buy-ExxonMobil
     (buy sector energy)
=>
     (assert (buy ExxonMobil))
     (printout t "Buy ExxonMobil." crlf))

;Buy BP
(defrule R12-buy-BP
     (buy sector energy)
=>
     (assert (buy BP))
     (printout t "Buy BP." crlf))

;Short in sector transportation when oil prices are high
(defrule R13-short-sector-transportation
     (oil-prices high)
=>
     (assert (short sector transportation)))

;Short United Airlines
(defrule R14-short-United-Airlines
     (short sector transportation)
=>
     (assert (short United-Airlines))
     (printout t "Short United Airlines." crlf))

;Short American Airlines
(defrule R15-short-American-Airlines
     (short sector transportation)
=>
     (assert (short American-Airlines))
     (printout t "Short American Airlines." crlf))
```

```
;************************************************************************
;Cluster IV:   Rules Pertaining to Interest Rates
;************************************************************************

;Interest rate is high when > 9%
(defrule R16-classify-high-interest-rate
     (interest-rate ?percent)
     (test (> ?percent 9.0) )
=>
     (assert (interest-rate-class high)))

;Interest rate is low when < 6%
(defrule R17-classify-low-interest-rate
     (interest-rate ?percent)
     (test (< ?percent 6.0) )
=>
     (assert (interest-rate-class low)))

;Sector financial is weak when interest rates are high.
(defrule R18-sector-financial-weak
     (interest-rate-class high)
=>
     (assert (sector financial weak)))

;Sector financial is strong when interest rates are low.
(defrule R19-sector-financial-strong
     (interest-rate-class low)
=>
     (assert (sector financial strong)))

;Buy Countrywide Financial
(defrule R20-buy-Countrywide-Financial
     (buy sector financial)
=>
     (assert (buy Countrywide-Financial))
     (printout t "Buy Countrywide Financial." crlf))

;Buy Bank of America
(defrule R21-buy-BankofAmerica
     (buy sector financial)
=>
     (assert (buy BankofAmerica))
     (printout t "Buy Bank of America." crlf))

;Short Countrywide Financial
```

```
(defrule R22-short-Countrywide-Financial
    (short sector financial)
=>
    (assert (short Countrywide-Financial))
    (printout t "Short Countrywide Financial." crlf))

;Short Bank of America
(defrule R23-short-BankofAmerica
    (short sector financial)
=>
    (assert (short BankofAmerica))
    (printout t "Short Bank of America." crlf))
```

ENDNOTES

1. Alan Newell and Herbert A. Simon, "GPS, a Program That Simulates Human Thought," in *Lernende Automaten* (1961), 109–124.

2. See Joseph Giarratano and Gary Riley, *Expert Systems: Principles and Programming*, 4th ed. Boston: Thomson Course Technology, 2005. I am adopting their de nition of an expert system. They state that "the term emulate means that the expert system is intended to act in all respects like a human expert. An emulation is much stronger than a simulation which is required to act like the real thing in only some respects" (p. 5). Giarratano and Riley mean that expert sytems attempt to mimic the reasoning process of human experts, not just the decision outcomes.

3. John Durkin, "Expert Systems: A View of the Field," *IEEE Expert* 11, no. 2 (1996), 56–63.

4. Sean B. Eom, "A Survey of Operational Expert Systems in Business (1980–1993)," *Interfaces*, 26, no. 5 (1996), 50–70.

5. For more information on MYCIN, see Bruce G. Buchanan and Edward H. Short- liffe, *Rule Based Expert Systems: The Mycin Experiments of the Stanford Heuristic Programming Project*. Reading, MA: Addison-Wesley, 1984.

6. See the study conducted by William G. Chase and Herbert A. Simon, "Perception in Chess," *Cognitive Psychology* 4 (1973), 55–81. Chase and Simon looked at the differences between novice and expert chess players and found that expert chess players can see a large pattern of many pieces as a single meaningful chunk.

7. The three fundamental rules of investing are from nancial expert Peter Navarro, *When the Market Moves, Will You Be Ready?*. New York: McGraw-Hill, 2004, p. 15.

8. For a discussion on metarules and strategic knowledge in expert systems see the following articles: William J. Clancey, "The Epistemology of Rule-Based Expert System—A Framework for Explanation," *Artificial Intelligence* 20 (1983), 215–251; and Diane W. Hasling, William J. Clancey, and Glenn Rennels, "Strategic Explana- tions for a Diagnostic Consultation System," *International Journal of Man-Machine Studies* 20, (1984), 3–19.

9. The CLIPS website contains both software downloads and documentation. Go to http://clipsrules.sourceforge.net.

10. More information on the CLIPS language can be found on the CLIPS website, which contains basic and advanced programming guides. A good book to learn the CLIPS

language is Giarratano and Riley, which contains many examples of how to code a rule-based expert system.

11. See Giarratano and Riley, pp. 724–736, for a discussion on how backward chaining may be emulated using the forward chaining rules of CLIPS.

12. For more information on XCON, see the following articles Virginia E. Barker and Dennis E. O'Connor, "Expert Systems for Con guration at Digital: XCON and Beyond," *Communications of the ACM* 32, no. 3 (1989), 298–318; and John J. Sviokla, "An Examination of the Impact of Expert Systems for the Firm: The Case of XCON," *MIS Quarterly* 14, no. 2 (1990), 127–140.

13. Barker and O'Connor, pp. 305–306.

14. Peter Jackson, *Introduction to Expert Systems*, 3rd ed. Reading, MA: Addison-Wesley, 1999, pp. 53–54.

CHAPTER 6

RULE-BASED REASONING WITH DIAGRAMS

In recent years, many critics of expert systems have argued for more flexibility in the user interface if further progress in the field is to take place. While there have been several notable and successful commercial applications, such as XCON as discussed in the previous chapter, practitioners and researchers alike have recognized that traditional expert system user interfaces are largely rigid and intolerant of an user's need to understand the assumptions and reasoning underlying the knowledge base. The user, in effect, is forced to view the knowledge base as a black box. While some limited forms of explanation may be available, there is usually no easy and intuitive way to understand why and how a given set of inputs produced a final recommendation. Especially problematic for the user is gaining an understanding of the problem-solving strategies employed by the expert system to make its decisions.

For example, in a typical consultation with MYCIN, a user (typically a physician) would answer questions about patient data such as symptoms, test results, and patient characteristics. Based on these responses, MYCIN would reach a diagnosis on what the bacterial infection might be, and recommend an appropriate treatment. However, from the user's perspective, the system seemed to ask a series of unrelated questions, and there was no sense of coherence to what was being asked. In short, a user was unable to form an appropriate mental model of how the system produced its recommendation because the expert system is lacking in explanatory power.

In Chapter 1, we defined more precisely what explanatory power is. An intelligent system that is capable of explaining its actions is said to be one endowed with explanatory power. Two system characteristics are relevant to understanding explanatory power. One is system transparency, which refers to the ability to understand the internal mechanism of the system so that it is not merely a black box. A second characteristic is system flexibility, which refers to features of the user interface that make it more flexible and easier to use. Features of the user interface that can contribute to system flexibility include a more naturalistic interaction between user and computer, the provision of feedback, ease of recoverability when errors are made, the ability to display different levels of detail (granularity), the ability to process missing and imperfect data, and the ability to display multiple representations. (For a review, see the discussion in Chapter 1.)

Explanatory power is all too often given short shrift by system designers, but it is a very important design issue to consider because it can lead to greater trust and acceptance of an expert system's recommendation.[1] Should a user become suspicious of an expert system recommendation (not an uncommon occurrence), he or she should be able to request some kind of explanation for why and how the system arrived at its conclusions. For instance, a user, baffled by an expert system recommendation may wish to seek out the answers to any one of the following questions: What sequence of rules were fired? What methods and problem-solving strategies were employed to come to the conclusion? How robust is the recommendation—that is, would it change if one piece of data were modified just a little bit? What domain principles led to the conclusion? Indeed, a human expert regularly engages in a two-way exchange with clients; it is simply not enough to collect data and issue a recommendation, as if by fiat. We should expect the same from a computer program, whose purpose is to mimic a human expert's behaviors, one of which is to convince the user that its recommendation is a sound and correct one.

A central proposition of this chapter is that user interfaces having greater explanatory power will enable users to more readily acquire a good conceptual model of how the expert system works. As a result, users will be more effective problem solvers and will be able to use expert systems in more flexible and intelligent ways. This chapter illustrates a variety of diagrammatic user interfaces that can be used to enhance both system transparency and system flexibility.

EXPERT SYSTEM TRANSPARENCY

The importance of system transparency was recognized early on in the history of expert systems. In the 1970s, MYCIN pioneered the idea that expert systems should be able to explain their reasoning process to users.[2] At first, to aid with system debugging, MYCIN included a RULE command that, when requested, asked the inference engine which rule was currently being used. The rule was initially displayed in the AI language LISP, but was later displayed in English because it was easier to understand, especially for non-programmers who could not make sense of the computer code. However, it readily became apparent that this command alone was inadequate in assuring users that the system's reasoning was logical and that the recommendation was correct. Therefore, the developers of MYCIN later added a WHY command that meant "Why are you asking me to input these data?" In response, the system would display the rule using the input data currently being requested. In addition, a second command, HOW, was added that meant "How did you arrive at this conclusion?" In response, the system would display the chain or sequence of rules fired, what has come to be known as the **rule trace**. Ever since the early days of MYCIN, the rule trace has remained one of the most commonly used forms of explanation and is still widely used in expert systems today.

Despite their usefulness and simplicity, rule traces have a number of shortcomings that limit their effectiveness as way of increasing system transparency. First of all, the Why-How paradigm of questioning offers only a limited form of explanation. Users may want to ask other questions as well. For example, What if? questions would allow users to explore the effect of changing the values of input variables and thereby test how robust a conclusion is to a given range of values. Why not? questions or "Why did you not conclude that <such and such> is true?" might be asked by users who want to explore the possibility of alternative solutions and hypotheses. In fact, these types of questions are quite common when probing real human experts. For instance, an expert in financial decision making might recommend to a client that he or she should invest in high-growth stocks because the economy is expected to expand in the next few years. The client, not completely clear about the expert's recommendation, might want to further probe the expert to consider other possibilities. For example: Why not blue chip stocks? Why not bonds? Why not real estate? The consideration of alternative recommendations arises quite naturally in a number of expert–client interactions.

Second, rule traces are often difficult for users to process and understand. Because a rule trace is based on a display of the rules, which are reproduced directly from the knowledge base, the quality of the explanation is based on how clearly the rules are expressed. Variable names that appear in the rules should be meaningful, and the logic of the rules clear, otherwise the rule trace will be difficult to understand. To improve its clarity, rules produced directly from computer code may be replaced with easy-to-understand English, also known as pseudocode. However, even when converted to understandable English, rules sometimes contain too much detail, which a user is simply not interested in seeing. Portions of a knowledge base typically contain rules that appear only because they are intended to be implemented as an algorithm on a computer. These rules are likely to be confusing to a user who does not need to understand every implementation detail. A rule trace might be pitched at a higher level by rewriting the rules, or it might be "cleaned up" so that confusing details are left out. (The disadvantage, of course, of rewriting rules in this way is that this task needs to be maintained and updated whenever there is a change in the knowledge base, whereas computer-generated rule traces require no such maintenance because they are entirely automated.) Many, if not most, current expert system shells in use today include a feature that will generate rule traces upon request.

Another criticism leveled at traditional rule traces is that the individual rules themselves are incapable of justifying their actions; because of this, a rule is often said to be opaque (the opposite of transparent). Let us look at a simple rule to understand how rules can be opaque, and, therefore, unsatisfying to users who want to understand why a rule's conclusions follow from its premises (or conditions). In Chapter 3, we described and illustrated causal models that illustrate knowledge about macroeconomics. One piece of knowledge might be encoded as the following rule:

```
IF inflation increases
    THEN consumer spending decreases
```

This rule, in and of itself, provides no justification at all about the relationship between inflation and consumer spending. A user, not knowing anything about macroeconomics, would have to accept the rule on blind faith alone. We can, and should, do a better job of justifying such rules.

One solution would be to link rules to a deeper causal model of the domain. This is the function of the **domain model**, which is descriptive knowledge about the domain and consists of such information as taxonomic knowledge and causal relationships. The domain model may be represented diagrammatically as a classification hierarchy, in the case of taxonomic knowledge, or as a directed graph, in the case of a causal model. To illustrate the relationship between inflation and consumer spending, we might provide the causal model in Figure 6.1 (this diagram is a portion of Figure 3.19). The signs on the diagram indicate the direction of the relationship. Hence the top path on the diagram would be interpreted as follows: An increase in inflation leads to a decrease in consumer wealth, which in turn leads to lower consumer spending. The bottom path would be interpreted in a similar fashion: An increase in inflation leads to a higher interest rate, which would lead to lower consumer spending. Therefore, when inflation increases,

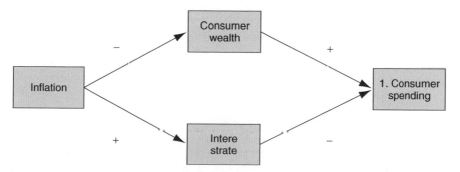

Figure 6.1. A causal model illustrating the relationship between inflation and consumer spending.

both paths leading into the consumer spending node would result in lower consumer spending. If the two paths, instead, came to conflicting conclusions, one path resulting in an increase, and the other path in a decrease, we would need to determine the strength of each conclusion, and calculate its net effect. That is a subject that will be discussed when the topic of probabilistic reasoning is addressed in Chapter 8.

The causal model in Figure 6.1 certainly provides more justification than the simple IF–THEN rule alone would. Thus we may increase system transparency by illustrating mechanisms of cause and effect in a causal model of some kind. Alternatively, we might also add more rules to the knowledge base, which would, in effect, produce a more fine-grained rendering of how inflation influences consumer spending:

```
IF inflation increases
    THEN consumer wealth decreases

IF consumer wealth decreases
    THEN consumer spending decreases

IF inflation increases
    THEN interest rate increases

IF interest rate increases
    THEN consumer spending decreases
```

We would also need to include rules that would lead to the opposite conclusion—that is, consumer spending would increase when inflation decreases:

```
IF inflation decreases
    THEN consumer wealth increases

IF consumer wealth increases
    THEN consumer spending increases

IF inflation decreases
    THEN interest rate decreases

IF interest rate decreases
    THEN consumer spending increases
```

In fact, we may not want to add these additional rules, which may have the effect of unnecessarily complicating the knowledge base. It may be quite adequate to keep the rules simple and clean; this will depend on the needs of the users and the nature of the decision-making task itself. On the other hand, by consolidating the eight just listed into a single one, all the knowledge of causal relationships is effectively lost in the knowledge base. The end result is that the knowledge is compiled into a single opaque rule. Clancey expressed this idea well when he remarked, "rules are 'compiled' in the sense that they are optimizations that leave out unnecessary steps—evolved patterns of reasoning that cope with the demands of ordinary problems."[3] When left out, these intermediate steps frequently need to be explained later to users who may not understand how an expert system reached its conclusions.

Another way of providing justifications is to add a piece of canned text to each rule that further explains it. Such a rule could take on the following form:

```
IF (condition)
      THEN (conclusion)
BECAUSE explanation
```

The explanation part of this rule would contain a textual justification, which could describe a domain principle that explains why the conclusion follows from its condition(s). For example, explanatory fragments that describe domain principles can be added to the rules as follows:

```
IF inflation increases
      THEN consumer wealth decreases
BECAUSE ''Inflation reduces the purchasing power of consumers.''

IF consumer wealth decreases
      THEN consumer spending decreases
BECAUSE ''With fewer dollars to spend, consumer
  spending decreases.''

IF inflation increases
      THEN interest rate increases
BECAUSE ''In order to decrease inflationary pressures, the Federal
Reserve is likely to increase interest rates to slow the
growth of the money supply; hence higher inflation will typically
result in a higher interest rate.''

IF interest rate increases
      THEN consumer spending decreases
BECAUSE ''With higher interest rates, consumers are less likely to
take out loans to purchase goods and services; consumer spending
will decline as a result.''
```

By including a textual justification, a rule trace could display not only the rule itself but also an English explanation. The causal diagram, together with these explanatory textual fragments, would offer even more system transparency than either one alone could.

Domain principles could be included that are even more elaborate and detailed than the short descriptions specified in the example. They could describe procedures and methods for solving problems in the domain; they could describe caveats that indicate situations under which the rule does not apply; they may define difficult terminology and taxonomic knowledge in the domain. Indeed, because they are expressed in a free-form sentence format, they can be any type of description to help a user better understand the rationales underlying the logic of IF–THEN rules.

A final criticism of rule traces is that they lack structural knowledge. One reason why it is so difficult to understand an expert system is that the structural relationships among the rules are not clear and explicit. The uniformity of standalone rules—that is, that they are largely "flat" rules having the same IF–THEN structure—means that users have no real sense of how they are organized in a knowledge base. This lack of organization is especially problematic in very large knowledge bases, which can contain hundreds of rules.

How do we create a knowledge base so that it has some kind of larger structure underlying it? We already discussed one approach in Chapter 5. It involves the creation of **strategic knowledge**.[4] By this, we are referring to a higher-order plan or approach for solving a problem. For example, one type of problem-solving strategy might be to break up a problem into subproblems, which may in turn be broken into sub-sub-problems (a kind of hierarchic ordering on how to solve the components of a problem). Without some kind of higher-level strategy operating on the knowledge base, the expert system is left to its own devices, so that, to the user, it seems to be making decisions in a rather random and haphazard way. We will be discussing strategic knowledge in more detail later on in this chapter.

A second way to provide structure is to cluster rules into larger topics so that they are organized in some fashion. For example, a knowledge base consisting of hundreds of rules can be grouped into a dozen or so broader categories, so that a knowledge base contains higher-order landmarks to help guide a user through all the rules. By doing so, the knowledge base will be easier to understand because it now contains discrete, easy-to-understand chunks. These chunks, ideally, should have some intuitional appeal for a user so that a system can use them as convenient explanatory segments. Moreover these chunks can be organized in some kind of diagram, such as a hierarchy, flowchart, or network dependency diagram. We will explore how to create diagrammatic representations of knowledge bases later in the chapter.

The use of diagrammatic structure can also help a user follow a line of reasoning through a knowledge base more effectively than a rule trace could. As noted earlier, rule traces are difficult to follow and understand. Translating them into more understandable English certainly can help, but that alone is not enough. Users will still have difficulty seeing how the rules are processed through the knowledge base. A graphical diagram can be used to visualize the line of reasoning because it can provide a larger context—for example, the alternative pathways through the knowledge base can be visualized. Context, unfortunately, is sorely lacking in a rule trace.

Table 6.1. Enhancing Expert System Transparency: Specific Recommendations

Type of Explanation	Specific Recommendations
Rule trace	• Different types of questions are allowed, such as What if? and Why not? • Rules are displayed in a natural language as opposed to computer-generated code • Rules traces are displayed at the right level of detail
Deep justification	• An explanation is linked to an underlying domain model that represents causal relationships and taxonomic knowledge in the domain • A rule is tied to underlying domain principles
Structural knowledge	• The rules are clustered into meaningful chunks or topics • Strategic knowledge or higher-level approaches to problem solving are made more explicit. • Diagrammatic representations are used to help users visualize the knowledge base and trace a line of reasoning

We summarize the recommendations for enhancing expert system transparency in Table 6.1, as discussed in this section. The specific recommendations are organized into three types: (1) rule trace, (2) deep justification, and (3) structural knowledge.

DIAGRAMMING A SIMPLE EXPERT SYSTEM

When the knowledge base is simple enough, a basic flowchart can be created to illustrate how the expert system reaches its recommendations. (In fact, if the decision-making task is so simple that it can be illustrated in a single flowchart, there may be no real need for an expert system at all.) See Figure 3.10 for a flowchart that can aid in determining the risk level of potential heart attack patients entering an emergency room.

Figure 6.2 illustrates the knowledge base of a fictitious expert system that classifies a client into one of seven risk levels, ranging from very conservative (Portfolio A) to very risky (Portfolio F).* A very conservative portfolio would consist of mostly safe investments, in which the returns are more guaranteed and less volatile; however, the average returns of this portfolio over the long term tend to be lower than average. On the other hand, a very risky portfolio would be made up of investments with high-growth potential; the downside is that these investments have a greater chance of losing value in the short term.

*I am indebted to Nathan Peranelli, my undergraduate research assistant, for this simple example.

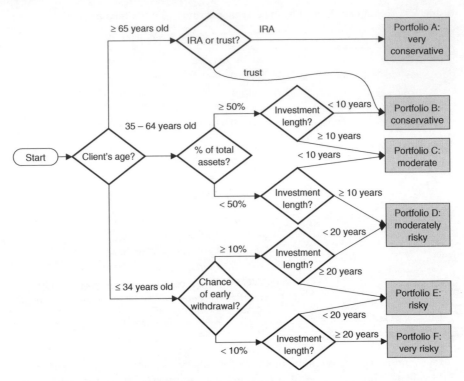

Figure 6.2. A flowchart illustrating the risk classification expert system.

The expert system begins by asking for the client's age, and then classifies him or her into one of three types: (1) 34 or younger (young adult), (2) between 35 and 64 (middle adult), and (3) 65 and older (retired). A set of questions is then posed to further characterize the client's risk propensity. Each age group, as illustrated in Figure 6.3, is asked a different set of questions. All other things being equal, clients in the older age groups are placed in more conservative portfolios, whereas younger age groups are placed in riskier ones.

For clients who are retired, the expert system asks whether funds are to be held in an IRA or a trust. If the funds are to be held in a trust, it is acceptable for the client to be placed in a riskier investment category (Portfolio B) because the money won't be used for some period of time (thus allowing for the fluctuations in a risky market). If, on the other hand, the money is to be placed in an IRA, the expert system assumes that the client will need it in a shorter amount of time; hence the client is classified in the most conservative category (Portfolio A).

For clients who are middle adults, the expert system first asks what percentage of their total assets represents the funds that are to be invested. Any percentage over 50% is considered high; any percentage below 50% is considered low. If low, this means that the client can withstand the fluctuations of a riskier portfolio because such a client has plenty of assets elsewhere that can buffer the effects of possible losses. The client is then asked for the anticipated amount of time the funds are to remain in the investment account. Obviously, a longer time frame will mean that a riskier portfolio is allowable. Hence clients who are prepared to commit to an investment timeline greater than 10 years will be recommended a riskier portfolio.

Finally, for clients who are classified as young adults, the expert system first asks what the chances of an early withdrawal are (the question concerning percent of total assets is not posed at all because it is assumed that young adults do not have many other assets to consider). Any percentage greater than or equal to 10% is considered high; any percentage below 10% is considered low. The expert system will then ask for the investment time frame. However, in this case, 20 years is the cutoff length, because younger investors have a longer time to invest. Young adult investors who are willing to commit to longer than 20 years, and have little chance of an early withdrawal (<10%) are placed into the most risky Portfolio (Portfolio F).

This simple expert system was invented to illustrate how an *entire* knowledge base could conceivably be contained entirely within a one-page diagram. This expert system is obviously artificially simple, as indeed the investment decision-making task can be made much more complex, involving many more variables and interactions among them. However, it is usually not possible, or at least very difficult, to create a single flowchart to represent the reasoning processes of a more complex knowledge base. It might be possible to partition a knowledge base into segments so that separate flowcharts can be created for each smaller segment. In addition, the off-page reference symbol

may be employed to create a multipage flowchart, if the entire process cannot fit on a single page. (See Figures 6.14, 6.15, and 6.16 for examples) When possible, flowcharting is an excellent technique for enhancing expert system transparency. In the next section we explore how these techniques might scale up in a more complex application.

The flowchart could become the user interface itself (not just a static diagram for informational purposes only), an alternative to a text-based question-and-answer dialogue. Interacting with the diagram itself would allow for a more flexible dialogue between user and expert system. The user would start from the leftmost node and proceed to the right, taking the appropriate pathways, depending on the answers given. In Figure 6.3, a line of reasoning is traced through the diagram as the user enters first the age of the client (40 years), then the percent of total assets (25%), and finally the investment length (9 years). The final recommendation is Portfolio C (moderate). The entire line of reasoning is boldfaced.

The diagram allows a user to visualize how a set of inputs resulted in a conclusion. Seeing the line of reasoning within the larger context of the entire

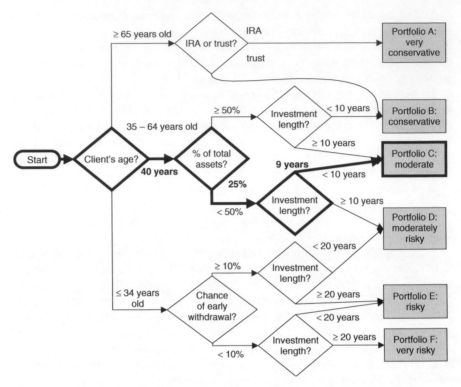

Figure 6.3. Tracing a line of reasoning through the flowchart.

knowledge base enables the user to understand why the other risk levels were not recommended. For example, in Figure 6.3, the user may want to know why a riskier portfolio was not selected instead. It can easily be gleaned from the flowchart that the investment length needs to be ≥ 10 years, or the client needs to be ≤ 34 years for a riskier portfolio to be recommended. The flowchart makes this type of reasoning very easy to perform.

A MORE COMPLEX APPLICATION: TRANSPORTATION MODE SELECTION (TRANSMODE)

An expert system whose job is to select a transportation mode was created to illustrate a more complex knowledge base. Hereafter, this expert system is referred to as **TransMode**.[5] The complete set of rules is provided in the appendix to this chapter. In this section we first illustrate a traditional text-based consultation with an expert system that has very little explanatory power. Then we consider a variety of ways of enhancing both the expert system's transparency as well as its flexibility through diagramming methods, including the use of diagrams that graphically illustrate strategic knowledge. But first, let us begin by describing the system and providing a simple example.

A transportation broker makes a determination concerning the type of transportation mode (air, trucking, rail, or small package service) to use to transport a client's shipment. The determination is made based on the following factors:

- **Shipment weight:** What is the weight of the shipment? (lb)
- **Weight of one item:** What is the weight of one item to be shipped? (oz)
- **Value of one item:** What is the dollar value of one item to be shipped?
- **Fragility rating:** How fragile is the item? (high, average, low)
- **Shipping distance:** How far is the item to be shipped? (distance in miles)
- **Transit time:** In how many days must the shipment reach its destination?
- **Special products:** Are special products to be shipped? (hazardous minerals, hazardous chemicals, agricultural, none)
- **Perishable:** Are the items to be shipped perishable? (yes no)
- **Door-to-door service:** Is door-to-door service required? (yes no)
- **Frequency of service:** How frequently is the shipment made? (daily, weekly, monthly, infrequent)

This information is obtained from the client, and these inputs are entered into TransMode. Based on these inputs, TransMode makes its recommendation.

A traditional text-based dialogue will pose a series of questions to the user. In the following dialogue, a user enters information about a client's shipment. (User's responses are in boldface.)

```
Begin TransMode Consultation.

What is the total weight of the shipment? (lb)
10000

What is the shipping distance? (miles)
2500

In how many days must the shipment reach its destination?
14

What is the value of one item? ($)?
500

What is the weight of one item? (oz)
10.0

How fragile is the shipment?
Answer one of the following:
```

```
high, average, low
high
```

Based on these inputs the system renders its final decision:

```
The recommended transportation mode is TRUCKING.
```

The user may wish to inquire how the recommendation was determined by requesting a rule trace. When the rule trace is requested, the user learns that the following sequence of rules was fired:

RULE TRACE

```
R3.   IF Shipment-Weight > 5,000 lb and <= 15,000 lb.
         THEN Load-Type = large-shipment


R37.  IF Load-Type = large-shipment
         THEN Alternatives = rail-or-trucking AND Preference =
         trucking


R12.  IF Transit-Time > 10 days
         THEN Speed-Rating = slow


R8.   IF Distance > 1000 miles
         THEN Distance-Range = long


R14.  IF Distance-Range = long and Speed-Rating = (average or slow)
         THEN Haul-Type = long-slow
```

```
R24.  IF Weight-of-one-time is not null AND Value-of-one-item is not
      null
         THEN Value-Weight-Ratio =
         Value-of-one-item / Weight-of-one-item
```

Note: Value-Weight-Ratio is calculated as 500/10 = 50.0

```
R26.  IF Value-Weight-Ratio >= $20 and < $100
         THEN Valuable-Rating = high


R30.  IF Valuable-Rating = high AND Fragility-Rating = high
         THEN Loss-and-Damage-Rating = important


R51.  IF Alternatives = rail-or-trucking AND Loss-and-Damage-
      Rating = (important or somewhat important)
         THEN Recommendation = TRUCKING
```

Hence a total of nine rules were fired to reach the recommendation that trucking should be used. In terms of system transparency, this user interface is very limited in helping us understand the reason for the recommendation. The rule trace points us to which rules are fired and in what sequence, but it is difficult to process and understand. Furthermore, it is difficult to understand the problem-solving strategies, if any, that are used by the system, and we are not provided with the underlying domain principles that are used to justify the recommendation. In short, we do not have an appropriate mental model for how the system is working. In terms of system flexibility, too, the text-based question-and-answer dialogue asks questions in a very rigid manner—in a prescribed, noninterrupted sequence. This dialogue does not allow a user to explore the system in different ways to test out assumptions and in general to seek out more information. We need to do a better job with this expert system consultation. In the sections that follow we show how this human-computer dialogue can be improved to deliver more system transparency and system flexibility.

A Hierarchic Model of the Knowledge Base

A diagram can illustrate the structure of an expert system knowledge base. Figure 6.4 shows the TransMode knowledge base rendered as a hierarchy of nodes so that users will have an easier time visualizing its structure. Hereafter, we refer to this system as **TransMode Hierarchy**, to distinguish it from a text-based question-and-answer dialogue. The hierarchy is intended to both segment the knowledge base into more manageable chunks and to create a graphical representation of the knowledge base so that the interrelationships among these chunks

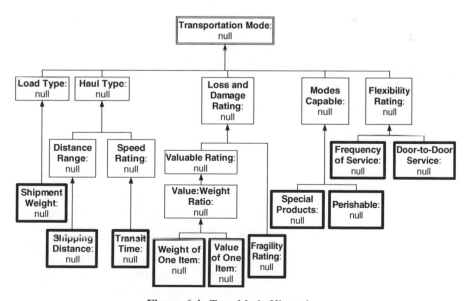

Figure 6.4. TransMode Hierarchy.

are made explicit. The use of hierarchies and other diagrams attempts to address and overcome the criticism that rules are inherently flat and lack structure, which means that the rules are treated uniformly by an expert system inference engine.

TransMode Hierarchy is composed of nodes (denoted by rectangles in Figure 6.4) and links among these nodes. There are three types of nodes in this diagram. The **root node** is the topmost node, which represents the topmost goal of the decision-making problem, in this case, the transportation mode recommendation. The root node is represented as a double-boxed rectangle. At the bottom of the hierarchy, the **leaf nodes** represent the raw or unprocessed data inputs. They are represented by boldfaced rectangles. For example, *Shipment Weight, Shipping Distance*, and *Transit Time*, are all leaf nodes. In between the root node and the leaf nodes are the **intermediate nodes**. These nodes read in values from the node(s) attached directly below it, their child node(s), and process this input to produce an output, which, in turn, is passed to the node attached directly above it, the parent node. (In this diagram, all child nodes have at most one parent node, but this need not be the case. Diagrams in which all nodes have at most one parent are formally called **trees**.) For instance, the *Load Type* node reads in the value passed to it by the *Shipment Weight*, its child node; the output from *Load Type* is then passed to the *Transportation Mode*, its parent node. In Figure 6.4, all of the values are null, signifying that no input data have yet been entered.

A user can visually track a line of reasoning through the hierarchy. The upward-pointing arrows on the hierarchy signify that information moves from bottom to top (i.e., the forward chaining inference engines moves from inputs upward toward the recommendation). For example, Figure 6.5 shows the following data inputs entered directly onto the hierarchy (the exact same data as that entered in the text-based question-and-answer dialogue described earlier):

- **Shipment weight:** 10,000 (lb)
- **Shipping distance:** 2,500 (miles)
- **Transit time:** 14 (days)
- **Weight of one item:** 10.0 (oz)
- **Value of one item:** 500 ($)
- **Fragility rating:** high

By entering 10,000 as the *Shipment Weight*, the *Load Type* is set to large-shipment. Similarly, when 10.0 is entered as the *Weight of One Item* and 500 as the *Value of One Item*, the *Value: Weight Ratio* is set to 50.0, which will, in turn, set the *Valuable Rating* to high. When the *Fragility Rating* is also set to high, the *Loss and Damage Rating* is set to important. In Figure 6.5, some of the nodes are null, signifying that some information has not been entered (and may not be needed). TransMode Hierarchy will make a recommendation as soon as there is enough information to make a determination. The three values from *Load Type, Haul Type*, and *Loss and Damage Rating* are sufficient to make a recommendation—in this case, *Trucking* is the transportation mode selected. Hence not all user inputs are required. This may at times result in a sparse hierarchy in which only a small portion of the hierarchy is actually involved in making a recommendation.

In Figure 6.5 all the nodes that have been activated are shaded and the associated links are in boldface to show the user what part of the hierarchy is activated at any given point in time.

Knowledge bases that are partitioned into object nodes reap many of the benefits associated with object-oriented design. Essentially, the nodes on the hierarchy represent self-contained objects and, as such, can be viewed as possessing many of the same beneficial properties associated with object-orientation, a design philosophy that stresses the modularity and standardization of components so that they can be mixed and matched in a wide variety of configurations. Three benefits of object-oriented design are abstraction, encapsulation, and inheritance.

First, an object node in TransMode Hierarchy embodies an abstraction that is meaningful to users. Instead of referring to lower-level details of the domain of discourse, such as the specific data, and individual rules, the object nodes represent higher-level abstractions that users are more immediately familiar with. In TransMode Hierarchy, nodes such as *Load Type, Loss and Damage Rating*, and *Flexibility Rating* are used to identify some of the higher-level factors that are involved in making a transportation mode determination. Similarly, if one were to develop an expert system whose job is to make decisions regarding the approval of commercial loans, nodes such as *financial strength* of the company, *management character, collateral*, and *competitive environment* of the industry might be used as higher-order factors used to determine the credit-worthiness of a

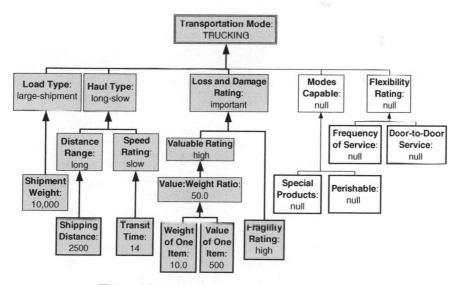

Figure 6.5. Data entered on TransMode Hierarchy.

company. The important point to remember in this regard is that a system should be developed for a nonexpert user, one who may not be interested in seeing all the implementation details of the system. A hierarchic model can provide a convenient high-level view of the knowledge base, one that is more manageable and considerably less complex for the user to deal with.

A second benefit of object orientation is known as encapsulation. This property means that the implementation details of an individual object are hidden from the other objects. Each node on the hierarchy need not know about the internal structure—that is, the specific details of the rules—of any other node. In addition, a node receives inputs only from directly attached nodes, thus further limiting interaction among the object nodes. For both the user and the developer of the expert system, this modularity in design is a great benefit in terms of understanding the system. For the developer who must periodically maintain and update the knowledge base, this means that modifying the rules of one node will not have unintended repercussions throughout the rest of the system because the rules are confined to just that one node. This benefit cannot be overstated.

Figure 6.6 shows three interconnected nodes lifted from TransMode Hierarchy, *Haul Type, Distance Range*, and *Speed Rating*. Each of these three nodes is encapsulated so that the other nodes cannot see its implementation details. (In the figure the implementation details are shown in each rectangle, which contains the rules associated with the node.) This means that *Haul Type* need not be concerned with how the *Distance Range* and *Speed Rating* nodes are assigned. Communication between the nodes is limited to the way that data are passed between them. Specifically, the *Haul Type* node reads in as input, the values assigned from the *Distance Range* and *Speed Rating* nodes, without any knowledge about how these values were assigned. Therefore, one node's interface to other nodes is clearly defined.

Finally, partitioning knowledge bases into objects facilitates their inheritance and reuse. This means that we can take any object node, copy it, and use it in a new expert system application. The new copy inherits its properties from the original, so that the nodes do not need to be created from scratch. Indeed, an entire hierarchic model, or large portion thereof, may be reused to create variations on a problem-solving situation. For example, after developing a hierarchic model for commercial loan approval decisions, we may create a modified version for personal loan approval decisions. The original hierarchy can be reused, and because we have partitioned its knowledge base, it should be an easy matter to modify only the affected nodes related to the new context. Encapsulation ensures that the modification will not have unintended affects in the rest of the knowledge base.

Expert System Flexibility

Let us now turn our attention to the increased system flexibility offered by TransMode Hierarchy. We already discussed at length ways to increase system transparency, which is focused on providing additional content in order for the user to understand an expert system recommendation. System flexibility focuses

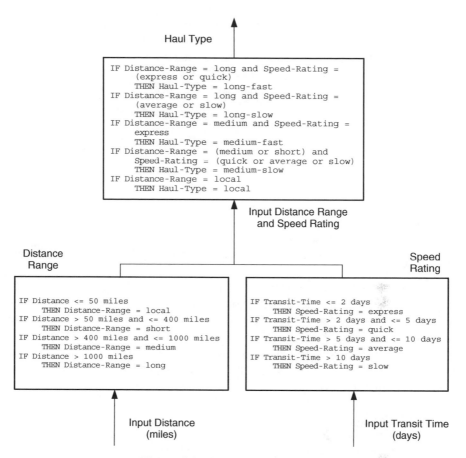

Haul Type

```
IF Distance-Range = long and Speed-Rating =
     (express or quick)
     THEN Haul-Type = long-fast
IF Distance-Range = long and Speed-Rating =
     (average or slow)
     THEN Haul-Type = long-slow
IF Distance-Range = medium and Speed-Rating =
     express
     THEN Haul-Type = medium-fast
IF Distance-Range = (medium or short) and
     Speed-Rating = (quick or average or slow)
     THEN Haul-Type = medium-slow
IF Distance-Range = local
     THEN Haul-Type = local
```

Input Distance Range
and Speed Rating

Distance
Range

Speed
Rating

```
IF Distance <= 50 miles
     THEN Distance-Range = local
IF Distance > 50 miles and <= 400 miles
     THEN Distance-Range = short
IF Distance > 400 miles and <= 1000 miles
     THEN Distance-Range = medium
IF Distance > 1000 miles
     THEN Distance-Range = long
```

```
IF Transit-Time <= 2 days
     THEN Speed-Rating = express
IF Transit-Time > 2 days and <= 5 days
     THEN Speed-Rating = quick
IF Transit-Time > 5 days and <= 10 days
     THEN Speed-Rating = average
IF Transit-Time > 10 days
     THEN Speed-Rating = slow
```

Input Distance
(miles)

Input Transit Time
(days)

Figure 6.6. Encapsulation of rules.

instead on characteristics of the user interface itself and the nature of the human interaction with the expert system.

Unlike a traditional expert system dialogue in which the system prompts the user for data inputs in a prescribed sequence, TransMode Hierarchy is intended to be as interactive and flexible as possible. The motivation behind this free-form interaction is to allow, and indeed to actively encourage, the user to inspect parts of the hierarchy to better understand why and how the system reached the conclusion that it did. Such a user, for example, may disagree with the system recommendation and may want to understand what input variable was the cause of the erroneous recommendation. Through an exploration of the components of the hierarchy, the user should be able to track how the value of the input variable propagated through the hierarchy to reach the given conclusion. The hierarchy provides a structure to make this line of reasoning more transparent, and therefore, easier to track.

How the hierarchic models are used will depend on the extent to which a user agrees with the system's recommendations and also on the level of understanding sought. Some problems are fairly routine and require no further understanding. Other problems are more complicated and it may be difficult to understand why the system made the recommendation that it did. In such cases, further probing and exploration are necessary if the user is to trust and accept a system's advice. Given how brittle experts system are, another issue is that a user may need to know when an expert system has been pushed beyond its boundaries of expertise or when system breakdown has occurred. In such situations, it may be beneficial to know how an expert system's recommendation can be modified to account for its limited expertise.

It is useful, at this point, to anticipate the types of situations in which a deeper understanding of the knowledge base is sought, as this will help us judge whether hierarchic models will actually provide users with the flexibility they need. Let us look specifically at four types of questions that may be asked: How? Why? What if? and Why-not?

As discussed earlier, the How? question is posed when a user would like to know how a certain recommendation or conclusion is reached. Typically a rule trace of the reasoning process is given. The Why? question is commonly requested when a user would like to know why a certain type of input is needed by the system. Let's look at how these two questions are answered by a traditional expert system question-and-answer dialogue and compare it to the interaction with TransMode Hierarchy.

As illustrated earlier, under a traditional expert system dialogue, the **How?** question will result in a listing of all the rules that were fired, in succession, to reach the final recommendation. In TransMode Hierarchy, by contrast, the user can exert more control over this question. A user can obtain the individual rules that were fired by clicking on the appropriate nodes of the hierarchy. A more fine-grained understanding can be obtained by descending the branches of the hierarchy and clicking on lower-level nodes, one by one, to obtain each rule that was responsible for setting that node's value. The difference between the two interactions is significant: It means that under a traditional expert system dialogue the user is bombarded with quite a lot of information, given by the rule trace dump, whereas TransMode Hierarchy allows one to filter out unnecessary rules by focusing on one node at a time. Moreover, in TransMode Hierarchy, the user can view the line of reasoning in the context of the entire hierarchic structure.

Let's look at an example. In Figure 6.7, a portion of TransMode Hierarchy, the *Loss and Damage Rating* branch, is displayed. A user can click on any node to obtain the rule that was responsible for setting its value. For example, a user can click on the *Valuable Rating* node to obtain the following rule:

```
IF Value-Weight-Ratio >= $20 and < $100
      THEN Valuable-Rating = high
```

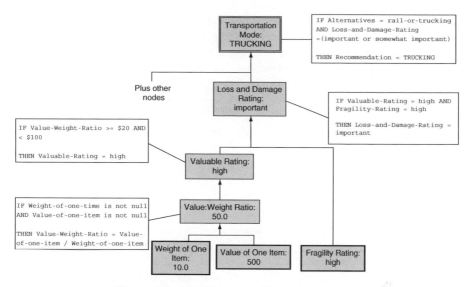

Figure 6.7. Clicking on a node to obtain a rule.

The user can further explore the rest of the hierarchy to see how this rule relates to other nodes on the hierarchy. Going down the hierarchy, we see that the *Value: Weight Ratio* is 50.0, so this rule makes sense. Going up the hierarchy, the *Valuable Rating* = high is passed to *Loss and Damage Rating* as an input to that node. It uses this value, together with the value from *Fragility Rating* to set the *Loss and Damage Rating* node's value to important. The rule fired on the *Loss and Damage Rating* node can be displayed to understand how this determination was made:

```
IF Valuable-Rating = high AND Fragility-Rating = high
    THEN Loss-and-Damage-Rating = important
```

In this way, the hierarchy provides a structure to understand a rule trace and how a recommendation is reached by the expert system. The line of reasoning can easily be followed one node at a time, up and down a branch of a hierarchy.

For the **Why?** question, a different problem arises under a traditional expert system dialogue: Too little information is offered. For example, the system might ask for the *Shipment Weight* (in lb). The user may ask Why? at this point (i.e., "Why do you need to know this?"), and the system might respond: "I need to know this so that I can determine what the *Load Type* is." The problem with this answer is that the user is provided with very limited information and is unable to see the bigger picture. On the other hand, a user interacting with TransMode Hierarchy is able to easily see that *Shipment Weight* determines *Load Type*, which, in turn determines (along with other variables) the *Transportation Mode*. The hierarchic model provides an easy way to visualize and understand the interrelationships among the nodes. In short, the hierarchic model provides a higher-level context, or a broader view, that is not possible by asking a single, isolated Why? question, or even a series of Why? questions.

What if? type questions, also known as hypothetical questions, enable one to test the effect that changing a value on a node will have on the final system recommendation. For example, what impact will changing the *Shipping Distance* from 1000 to 2000 miles have on the *Transportation Mode* recommendation? Many expert system user interfaces allow some form of hypothetical questioning, but hierarchic models are especially well suited to this kind of questioning. All the nodes on TransMode Hierarchy, leaf nodes as well as intermediate nodes, can be modified to observe what effect a change in the value on one node will have on the system recommendation. By changing a value on a node, a user can easily observe how its modification cascades through the hierarchy. In addition, users are not limited to changing one node only. They may modify two or more nodes and observe their possible interaction effects. Hence, while traditional expert system dialogues may allow for some limited forms of What if? testing, hierarchic models are superior because they allow more flexibility and power in modifying and visualizing the values of the variables used in a knowledge base.

Finally, **Why not?** type questions, or counterfactual questions, take the form "Why did you not conclude <such and such>?" For example, a user might ask the system, "Why did you not conclude that the recommendation is Air?" This type of question is usually quite difficult to answer, and yet, as we already noted, it frequently arises in expert–client dialogues. There is usually no single answer to this kind of question (it is less structured and more difficult to construct a satisfying answer than the previous three question types); however, it is an important one to consider because it may naturally arise in a user's mind, and answering it may deepen one's understanding of the expert system's reasoning process.

A satisfactory answer to Why not? questions often requires a meta-level or higher-level understanding of the expert system knowledge base. Individual rule traces will probably be inadequate in conveying a higher-level understanding of the knowledge base. The hierarchic models may provide one tool to aid the user in gaining this level of understanding because it provides a top-down view of the knowledge base. Further, it encourages users to explore and seek out what is driving the knowledge base due to its transparent and flexible graphical user interface. However, the hierarchic models, by themselves, may be insufficient in providing support to answering this type of question. Because they are so difficult to answer, Why not? questions may be supported more effectively by other types of diagrams and explanations. One possibility is a flowchart representing strategic knowledge, a subject that we approach later on in the chapter.

In sum, TransMode Hierarchy offers an alternative user interface that is highly visual, flexible, and interactive. The hierarchic model is really the user interface itself and is intended to be explored and modified by the user. Input data can be entered in any order a user chooses—there is no prescribed sequence or way for entering input data. Moreover, the system will make a recommendation as soon as it has enough information to do so; thus the system allows for missing data and imperfect information. Furthermore, the hierarchic model allows one to test out different assumptions in a very flexible manner—a number of variables can be tested at one time, and the hierarchic model updates appropriately to reflect these new values. Such feedback is immediate and provided directly on the hierarchy. All in all, TransMode Hierarchy represents a much more naturalistic interaction between human user and expert system and is a great leap forward in system flexibility.

Rule Trace Diagrams

Another type of diagram that may foster understanding of an expert system's reasoning processes is a rule trace diagram. Unlike TransMode Hierarchy, which is a diagram that displays the relationships among the segments of a knowledge base, a rule trace diagram is a dependency diagram that shows graphically how the conditions of a rule are linked to its conclusions. For example, see Figure 6.8 for a graphical rendering of the rule trace given earlier in the chapter. Included in the diagram are the references to the actual rules that are fired. See the appendix to the chapter for the actual rules that are referenced.

The rule trace diagram looks rather similar to TransMode Hierarchy, except that its orientation is reversed: It is displayed bottom-up from data inputs to system recommendation, while TransMode Hierarchy is displayed top-down from system recommendation to data inputs. In fact, when you compare the nodes on Figure 6.8 to those found on TransMode Hierarchy (Figure 6.5), they do look similar. However, there are a few notable differences between the two diagrams.

The first obvious difference is that TransMode Hierarchy contains more nodes than the rule trace diagram. Because TransMode Hierarchy is intended to model the entire knowledge base, it contains all knowledge segments in the knowledge base. In contrast, the rule trace diagram displays only nodes that are used to render a system recommendation. Hence the purpose of the two diagrams differ: One is used to represent the structure of an entire knowledge base, whereas the other is used to model only the rules that are fired. In other words, the rule trace diagram is case-specific in that it models only the current problem-solving situation.

The second difference is that the rule trace diagram models information at a lower-level of detail. In particular, all conditions and all actions contained within a rule are included in the diagram. In Figure 6.8, for example, one node is labeled *Alternatives = rail-or-trucking*. The variable *Alternatives* is set to denote the fact the system has narrowed down the choices to just rail and trucking. *Alternatives* is an implementation-level variable, one that is not included in TransMode Hierarchy because it does not represent a higher-level determinant of the transportation mode recommendation. Remember that TransMode Hierarchy was created as a kind of conceptual model of the knowledge base, so that the nodes are supposed to represent higher-level knowledge segments. Ideally, the nodes should be meaningful to users and should serve as convenient guideposts

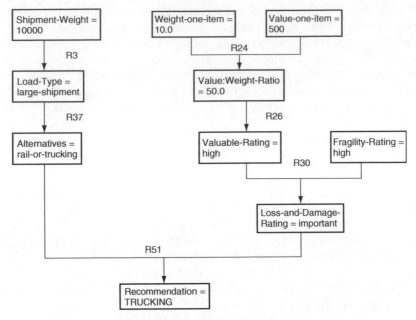

Figure 6.8. Rule trace diagram.

to understanding a complex expert system. That said, each diagram has its own benefits and uses. A hierarchic model such as TransMode Hierarchy is more appropriate when a user doesn't want to become bombarded with implementation details but would rather see the bigger picture; on the other hand, a rule trace diagram is preferable when more case-specific detail is sought after—what specific variables and actions an inference engine undertook to reach a decision, the pathway taken through the knowledge base. Together, both diagrams can be useful in revealing expert system actions.

Because rule trace diagrams are intended to represent the logic of specific rules, such diagrams may employ notation to represent more complex Boolean expressions in the condition part of the rule. First of all, special notation is needed to represent both conjunctive (AND) conditions as well as disjunctive (OR) conditions. See Figures 6.9 and 6.10 for the notation that can be used to differentiate the two types of conditional expressions. The difference in the notations is that in conjunctive conditions only one arrow points to the conclusion, whereas in disjunctive conditions separate arrows point from each of the conditions to the conclusion node. This notation is similar to that of the argument diagrams described in Chapter 4, a type of diagram used to illustrate the structure of an argument (see the discussion on the difference between conjunctive and convergent arguments on p. 113).

More complex Boolean expressions containing both ANDs and ORs can also be diagrammed using a combination of the notations. For example, see Figures 6.11 and 6.12. Figure 6.11 illustrates the conditional expression *(A and*

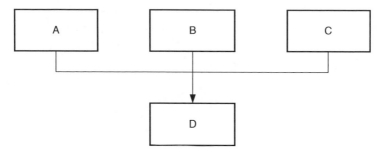

Figure 6.9. Conjunction of conditions: IF A and B and C THEN D.

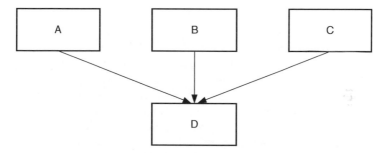

Figure 6.10. Disjunction of conditions: IF A or B or C THEN D.

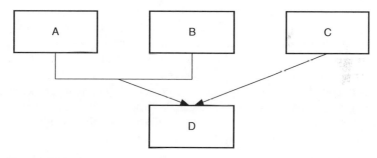

Figure 6.11. Complex Boolean expression: IF (A and B) or C THEN D.

B) or C. We must be careful when diagramming the conditional expression *A and (B or C)*. Figure 6.12 contains an oval, to hold the (temporary) value for just *B or C* alone.

Strategic Knowledge

Even with hierarchic models and rule trace diagrams, users will experience much difficulty when trying to understand the deeper rationale underlying expert

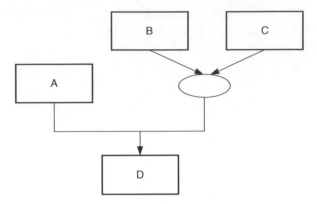

Figure 6.12. Complex Boolean expression: IF A and (B or C) THEN D.

system actions. In fact, one experimental study that we conducted on Trans-Mode Hierarchy[6] specifically demonstrated that users have a very difficult time understanding expert system strategies used for problem solving. In this study, participants were presented with a series of problems testing their understanding of how the TransMode expert system worked. One question presented the participants of the study with a situation in which TransMode Hierarchy reached the conclusion that trucking should be selected as the transportation mode. Participants were then asked to explain why it was not rail instead (a Why not? type question). Almost all participants were stumped by this question, in large part because they could not understand the problem-solving strategies that TransMode was using. Even when provided with a hierarchic model of the knowledge base, they were unable to answer this question in a satisfactory way. Hence most participants were utterly at a loss when asked to reflect on the broader issues and deeper reasons underlying the expert system.[7]

Strategic knowledge can help users acquire a deeper understanding of the expert system. As discussed in Chapter 5, strategic knowledge refers to an approach for solving a problem, a kind of high-level plan of attack. Without strategic knowledge, an expert system reacts opportunistically to input data as they come in—there is no real sense to how a system works. For all but the simplest expert systems, strategic knowledge is necessary to create a sense of order in a knowledge base that may otherwise appear random and unorganized. Strategic knowledge can be extremely beneficial in helping one understand a very complex knowledge base, possibly containing hundreds or even thousands of rules. Strategic knowledge can assume a number of forms. It can refer to the order in which data are used and prioritized by an expert system. It can refer to algorithms and methods used in the domain to winnow a set of candidate possibilities to a narrower set—for example, in a medical diagnosis expert system, it can be used to narrow down the number of disease possibilities to only a few. It may refer to methods that are triggered when failure occurs—for example, it may prevent an expert system from pursuing blind alleys and infeasible pathways through the knowledge base. (In Chapter 1, we noted that we want our intelligent systems to be possessed with "self-reflection," such as the ability to stop in midstream when something is going astray.) It may refer to how complex tasks can be subdivided into subgoals and they, in turn, subdivided into even smaller subgoals, thus resulting in a tree of goals.

The TransMode expert system provides us with a simple case study on how strategic knowledge can be graphically illustrated. Although the TransMode knowledge base is relatively simple, containing just over 50 rules, strategic knowledge can be used to organize these rules and provide one with a sense of structure to the knowledge base. TransMode's strategy consists of three main components (Figure 6.13):

1. Determine special needs.
2. Narrow down the alternatives by considering Load Type.
3. Break ties between two alternatives by considering Haul Type, Flexibility Rating, and Loss and Damage Rating, in that order of importance.

The first step of TransMode's strategy is to determine special needs. TransMode undertakes this task at the outset to ensure that it does not suggest a transportation mode that is incapable of processing the client's special needs. It begins by inquiring whether special products are to be shipped (i.e., hazardous minerals, hazardous chemicals, agricultural products) and whether the products are perishable. If the client is shipping hazardous materials, TransMode decides that rail is the transport mode because this is the only mode that can handle this type of request (*Modes-Capable* is set to *rail-only*). Another special request involves agricultural goods that are perishable. Only rail and trucking can handle this type of shipment due to the need for special refrigeration units (*Modes-Capable* is set

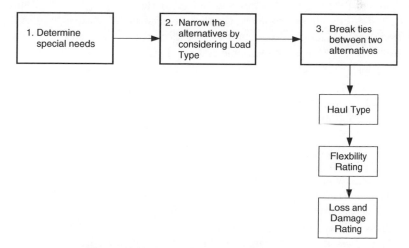

Figure 6.13. Overview of TransMode strategy.

to *rail-or-trucking*). The determination of special needs occurs before any other input data are collected because this limits the available transport modes and thus focuses TransMode's path through the knowledge base so that it collects only input data related to transport modes capable of handing a client's special requests.

The second step of TransMode's strategy is to narrow down the alternatives (if it hasn't done so in the first step) by considering the shipment's load type. *Load Type* is based on *Shipment Weight*. Because the shipment size really limits what transport modes are feasible, *Load Type* is an important variable that must be considered early on. Specifically, here are some of the underlying rationales for selecting a particular transportation mode given its *Load Type*:

- For small shipments (<100 lb), the transport mode of choice is small package service. Companies such as UPS, Federal Express, and Airborne Express are most suited to providing small package services for small shipments.
- For average shipment sizes (between 100 and 5000 lb), trucking and air are the preferred transport modes. Air service is generally restricted to average shipments because it is constrained by the physical dimensions of a cargo plane. Trucking is the most versatile of the transport modes, handling average, large, and even very large loads. Rail, however, tends to move large and very large shipment of at least full carload size ($>15,000$ lb) and is generally not competitive for smaller shipment sizes.
- For large shipments (between 5,000 and 15,000 lb), RAIL and TRUCKING are the best transport mode choices. However, trucking has a slight advantage over rail for large shipments (all other things being equal). For large shipments $<15,000$ lb, trucking is generally (but not always) more suitable.
- Finally, for very large shipments ($>15,000$ lb), RAIL and TRUCKING are the candidate transport modes. However, rail has a slight advantage over trucking for very large shipments (all other things being equal). Rail tends to move very large shipment sizes of at least a full carload ($>15,000$ lb) owing to the heavy load capability of railroads and their cost structure (i.e., high fixed costs and low variable costs). Therefore, rail is a cheaper mode of transport. This makes rail good for bulk commodities (e.g., coal and lumber) and low-valued manufactured goods.

Figure 6.14 displays a flowchart that shows how the system narrows down its choices, based on, first, the determination of special needs, and, second, the load type. Off-page references are used to show how processing continues when there is a tie between two alternatives. Off-page reference A indicates that TransMode needs to break a tie between trucking and air, and off-page reference B indicates the same for trucking and rail. When a final recommendation is made and no further input data are required, the system exits. The flowchart also shows paths where a system recommendation is made based on limited data. For example, when *Load Type* is large-shipment and no other input data are entered (all other values on TransMode Hierarchy are null), then the system will select trucking.

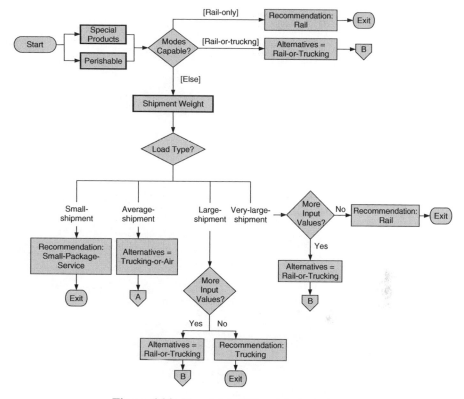

Figure 6.14. Flowchart of TransMode strategy.

Similarly, when *Load Type* is very-large-shipment and all other values are null, the system selects rail. This processing reflects how TransMode Hierarchy will make a system recommendation based on incomplete information—that is, it will make the best determination based on the limited data that have been entered. (Later on, if more data are entered, the system may amend its recommendation.)

The third step of TransMode's strategy is to break a tie when the alternatives have been narrowed down to two transport modes. TransMode will look at *Haul Type, Flexibility Rating*, and *Loss and Damage Rating*, in that order of importance. Figure 6.15 is the flowchart that illustrates how TransMode breaks a tie between air and trucking.

Haul Type is considered first. This variable is set based on both *Shipping Distance* and *Shipping Time* (Figure 6.4). When *Haul Type* is long-fast (long distance, fast transit time) or medium-fast (medium distance, fast transit time), AIR is the only viable transport mode. That is, air is the only feasible transport mode for speedy hauls greater than 400 miles. Trucking, while capable of handling longer hauls, is a slower mode of transportation and, therefore, cannot handle this haul type. On the other hand, when the *Haul Type* is long-slow or medium-slow, trucking is selected instead. This is because trucking is a cheaper

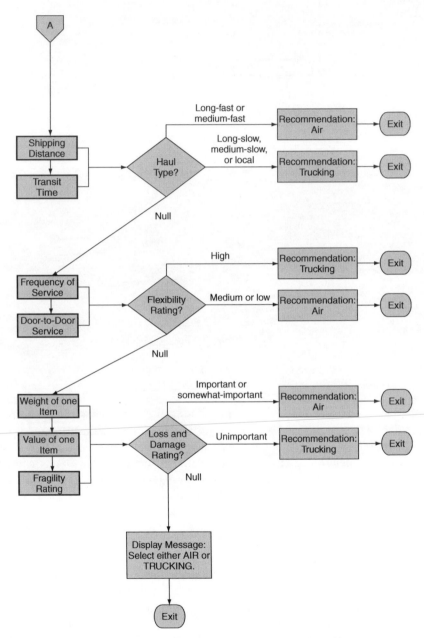

Figure 6.15. Breaking the tie between air and trucking.

form of transportation than air; therefore, when a speedy delivery is not required, trucking is the mode of choice. Finally, trucking is always selected for *local* hauls because obviously air is not used when trucking is within the same city.

Next, TransMode considers *Flexibility Rating*. This variable is assigned a value of high when *Frequency of Service* is daily and *Door-to-Door Service* is required. When this is the case, trucking is selected over air because trucking offers the most extensive service over a wide geographic area, providing door-to-door service almost anywhere. In addition, trucking is the most convenient transport mode in terms of its frequency and availability of service.

Finally, if a transportation mode determination is still not made, TransMode considers *Loss and Damage Rating*. This variable is assigned a value based on how valuable and how fragile a shipment is. The *Valuability Rating* of a shipment is based on its *Value: Weight Ratio*, which equals the dollar value of one item divided by the weight of one item. Highly valuable items, such as precious gems and expensive jewelry, will have a very high *Value: Weight Ratio*, whereas bulk commodity items will tend to have a lower value. When the *Loss and Damage Rating* is important or somewhat-important, as determined by its *Value: Weight Ratio* and *Fragility Rating*, AIR is selected as the transport mode. This is because air, as compared to trucking, is generally a more secure way of transporting goods. When *Loss and Damage Rating* is unimportant, trucking is selected instead. It is possible that a final system recommendation will not have been determined. Figure 6.15 shows that it if the user did not enter enough information on Trans-Mode Hierarchy, the system will make the ambiguous recommendation: "Select either air or trucking" (see bottom of the flowchart).

Figure 6.16 is the flowchart that shows how TransMode breaks a tie, this time between trucking and rail. Like in Figure 6.15, it considers the three variables, *Haul Type, Flexibility Rating*, and *Loss and Damage Rating*. The processing and logic is very similar. When considering *Haul Type* first, TransMode will recommend TRUCKING for local hauls (rail is for longer hauls only) as well as for medium-fast hauls because trucking is a faster transport mode than rail. For long-fast hauls, no transport mode is possible because neither trucking nor rail can handle a speedy long-distance hauls. (The speediest transport mode is air, but air cannot handle large and very large shipments). Therefore, the system will display the message: "It is not possible to send the shipment via any of the transport modes." When considering *Flexibility Rating*, once again trucking is selected when a high level of flexibility is required because, as noted before, trucking is the most flexible transport mode in terms frequency and availability of service. Third, when *Loss and Damage Rating* is important or somewhat-important, trucking is selected because it is a more secure way of transporting goods than is rail.

Diagrams depicting strategic knowledge can be further enhanced with deep justifications that explain system actions. Earlier, we discussed how explanatory fragments of text can be attached to IF–THEN rules to provide some kind of domain principle that explains why the conclusion follows from its condition(s). Rather than attaching the explanatory fragments to individual rules, we might

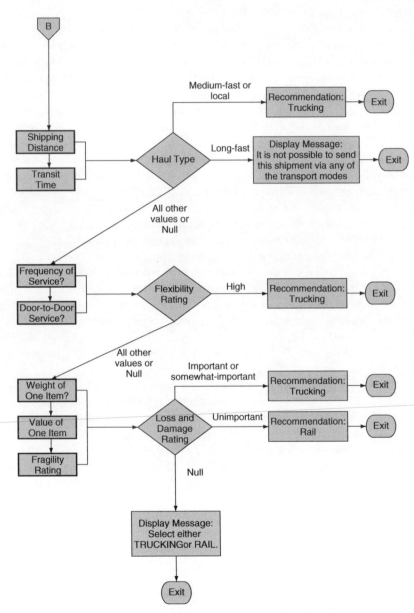

Figure 6.16. Breaking the tie between trucking and rail.

instead include them on the strategic diagrams themselves. For example, let us suppose that we enter the following four data inputs onto TransMode Hierarchy:

```
Shipment Weight:  10,000
Value of one item:  500
Weight of one item:  10.0
Fragility Rating:  high
```

First of all, *Shipment Weight* would set *Load Type* to large-shipment. Based on the strategic diagram (Figure 6.14), TransMode would first use the value of *Load Type* to narrow down the choices to RAIL and TRUCKING. An explanatory fragment can be attached to the appropriate node in the diagram that contains a justification for this action:

```
For (large) to (very large) load types, RAIL and TRUCKING are the
preferred transport modes.  RAIL tends to move (large) and (very
large) shipment sizes of at least a full carload (>15,000 lb)
due to the heavy load capability of railroads as well as their
associated cost structure (i.e., high fixed costs and low variable
costs). AIR service, on the other hand, is generally restricted to
(average) and (small) load types because it is more constrained by
the physical dimensions of a cargo plane.
```

Once the choices have been narrowed down to just rail and trucking, TransMode is now in a position to look at the other data inputs to make the final determination. Based on the *Value of One Item, Weight of One Item*, and *Fragility Rating*, TransMode would set the value of *Loss and Damage Rating* to important. This action, in turn, would make the final recommendation to select trucking. The following explanatory fragment can then be attached to the appropriate node on the diagram (i.e., the *Loss and Damage Rating* node in Figure 6.16):

```
In choosing between RAIL and TRUCKING, trucking is a more secure way
of transporting goods than rail is.  This is due in part to the
longer transit times involved in shipping goods by rail as well as
the greater handling involved in rail transport. In this particular
case, because the loss and damage rating is important, trucking is
selected as the transportation mode.
```

DISCUSSION

This chapter explored some of the techniques that may be employed to increase the explanatory power of rule-based expert systems. We considered a number of ways not only to enhance system transparency but also to provide more system flexibility by creating a more interactive graphical user interface. Specifically, we looked at a number of diagrams that can serve as the central component of the user interface itself:

- Flowchart diagrams that allow one to visually trace the line of reasoning through the knowledge base, taking the user step by step through the reasoning process (Figures 6.2 and 6.3).
- Diagrams in which a complex knowledge base is partitioned into meaningful segments that can be organized in a hierarchic way (Figures 6.4 and 6.5).
- Rule trace diagrams that graphically show the interrelationships between the conditions and actions in a rule trace (Figure 6.8).
- Diagrams that model strategic knowledge and the methods and approaches used for problem solving so that users have a high-level sense of how the expert systems is reaching its conclusions (Figures 6.13–6.16).

Table 6.2 provides a comparison of two interface types in terms of transparency and flexibility. On the one hand, a traditional text-based user interface lacks explanatory power because there is no way to understand how and why the system reached the recommendation that it did. Moreover, the dialogue is a rigid question-and-answer session in which inputs are entered in a predefined order, so there is no way to backtrack and test assumptions without having to start all over again. On the other hand, a diagrammatic interface provides a high degree of explanatory power because the user is provided with a graphical model of how the system is reaching a recommendation. This interface enables a user to visualize how the system is working, thereby enabling a deeper understanding of the system's internal mechanism. Moreover, the system is highly flexible as the user is encouraged to explore and test out different scenarios and assumptions.

Although the diagrammatic representations described in this chapter are a very powerful way of improving an expert system user interface, there are weaknesses

Table 6.2. A Side-by-Side Comparison of the Traditional Interface vs. the Diagrammatic Interface

	Traditional Interface	Diagrammatic Interface
Transparency	Black box: no system understanding	More transparency: enables visualization of the system's reasoning process
Flexibility	Rigid dialogue: questions are asked in a predefined order; no way to modify inputs and test assumptions	Free-form dialogue: can input information in any order; can modify inputs, test assumptions, and backtrack

and limitations of the TransMode expert system that we should be careful to note. First of all, TransMode is a toy system that illustrates a very simple problem. Although it was created based on actual domain principles derived from transportation logistics, it is a fictitious system whose purpose is to demonstrate the principles of explanatory power described in this chapter. Therefore, a very natural question to ask is whether these diagrammatic user interfaces can scale up to more complex domains. For example, a designer who must create hierarchies for larger and more complex applications must consider the problem of fitting a large hierarchy on a single screen. One alternative is to create the hierarchy for one screen and have the user scroll (either up/down or left/right) to get to the relevant portion of the hierarchy. Another option is to let the user zoom in/out—zooming out to get the larger picture, and zooming in to focus in on the relevant portion of the diagram. However, scrolling and zooming are clearly limited in terms of providing an easy-to-use interface. One can easily imagine how frustrating it could become to scroll through pages of a hierarchy to get to the relevant information.

Another approach would be to subdivide a large diagram into separate screens of information. For example, one could place only the top level of a large hierarchy on one screen, and require that the user click on these nodes to obtain more detail. Such a solution would allow for embedded descriptions of hierarchic models as well as a user interface that allows for granularity, or multiple levels of detail. This is the approach that we strongly advocate when creating diagrams for more complex applications. In fact, the flowcharts illustrated in Figures 6.14–6.16 really do represent a larger single flowchart that has been split into three separate components. The use of off-page references can show how the flowchart continues onto another flowchart.

A second problem is that not all problem-solving situations can be described using simple hierarchies or flowcharts. The transportation mode problem is a relatively easy one to represent (and indeed an artificial one expressly constructed so that it would be amenable to a tree structure) because it can be decomposed into subcomponents. The root node (the transport mode recommendation) is decomposed into subcomponents, which are further decomposed into more sub-subcomponents, so that a multileveled structure of the problem-solving situation can be constructed. However, many problem-solving domains do not fit into neat and tidy hierarchic descriptions. We do not mean to suggest that all knowledge bases can be represented as a hierarchy. However, most complex knowledge bases can and should be segmented into meaningful chunks. Other graphical representations, besides hierarchies and tree structures, may be more appropriate in tying together these chunks, whether they are semantic networks, causal diagrams, decision flowcharts, or some other kind of knowledge structure.

A third issue is that the free form nature of the user interaction with the diagrammatic interface (such as with TransMode Hierarchy) means that a user may enter data inputs in any order, or may choose not to enter any data at all in some cases. While this can promote system flexibility, this feature is a double-edged sword that may come at a cost: The user may get lost or may not know what data need to be entered when interacting with the diagram. In contrast, a very structured question-and-answer dialogue can direct the request for data inputs—the user is told what to enter and when, thus eliminating the guesswork out of what data are required. There is, however, a diagrammatic alternative that may resolve this problem. A flowchart may be used to show what data need to be entered and when, step by step, until the expert system reaches its recommendation. See Figure 6.3 for a simple example of a diagrammatic interface that shows the line of reasoning taken, as well as the data inputs that are required. (See also the flowcharts representing the strategic knowledge of TransMode in Figures 6.14–6.16.).

Finally, it is often said that an advantage of rule-based expert systems is that its problem-solving methods do not need to be exact, nor do they need to occur in the same sequence of steps. By contrast, a conventional program, such as one developed by a conventional programming language such as C++ or Java, follows a very structured sequence of steps. The use of flowcharts and other diagramming techniques suggest that an expert system is proceeding in a more structured and orderly step-by-step manner—in a very algorithmic way—and is, therefore, losing some of its more dynamic and opportunistic qualities. We do not disagree with this point. However, without structure and order, a knowledge base can very easily become unwieldy and difficult to manage and maintain. Even the TransMode knowledge base, which contains all of 52 rules, would be difficult to modify and maintain without some kind of higher-order structure underlying it. We do not advocate the use of flowcharts to model strategic knowledge in all cases, and in some cases a lack of structure may allow for more emergent and dynamic forms of expert decision making. However, in most cases, some kind of structure is needed. At the very least, some kind of segmentation or modularization of the knowledge base should take place to manage its complexity. Otherwise, the user of the expert system will easily become lost, and the developer will have a very difficult time updating and maintaining a disordered knowledge base.

APPENDIX A: TRANSMODE KNOWLEDGE BASE

I. Rules That Categorize:

Load Type (input Shipment-Weight):

R1.   IF Shipment-Weight <= 100 lbs.
          THEN Load-Type = small-shipment
R2.   IF Shipment-Weight > 100 lbs. And <= 5,000 lbs.
          THEN Load-Type = average-shipment
R3.   IF Shipment-Weight > 5,000 lbs and <= 15,000 lbs.
          THEN Load-Type = large-shipment

```
R4.   IF Shipment-Weight > 15,000 lbs.
          THEN Load-Type = very-large-shipment
```

Distance Range (input Distance):

```
R5.   IF Distance <= 50 miles
          THEN Distance-Range = local
R6.   IF Distance > 50 miles and <= 400 miles
          THEN Distance-Range = short
R7.   IF Distance > 400 miles and <= 1000 miles
          THEN Distance-Range = medium
R8.   IF Distance > 1000 miles
          THEN Distance-Range = long
```

Speed Rating (input Transit-Time):

```
R9.   IF Transit-Time <= 2 days
          THEN Speed-Rating = express
R10.  IF Transit-Time > 2 days and <= 5 days
          THEN Speed-Rating = quick
R11.  IF Transit-Time > 5 days and <= 10 days
          THEN Speed-Rating = average
R12.  IF Transit-Time > 10 days
          THEN Speed-Rating = slow
```

Haul Type (inputs Distance-Range and Speed-Rating):

```
R13.  IF Distance-Range = long and Speed-Rating = (express or quick)
          THEN Haul-Type = long-fast
R14.  IF Distance-Range = long and Speed-Rating = (average or slow)
          THEN Haul-Type = long-slow
R15.  IF Distance-Range = medium and Speed-Rating = express
          THEN Haul-Type = medium-fast
R16.  IF Distance-Range = (medium or short) and Speed-Rating =
             (quick or average or slow)
          THEN Haul-Type = medium-slow
R17.  IF Distance-Range = local
          THEN Haul-Type = local
```

Modes Capable (inputs Special-Products and Perishable):

```
R18.  IF Special-Products = (hazardous-minerals or
             hazardous-chemicals)
          THEN Modes-Capable = rail-only
```

R19.   IF Special-Products = agricultural AND Perishable = yes
          THEN Modes-Capable = rail-or-trucking

Flexibility Rating (inputs Frequency-of-Service and Door-to-
Door-Service):

R20.   IF Frequency-of-Service = daily AND Door-to-Door-Service = yes
          THEN Flexibility-Rating = high
R21.   IF Frequency-of-Service = daily AND Door-to-Door-Service = no
          THEN Flexibility-Rating = medium
R22.   IF Frequency-of-Service is not daily AND Door-to-Door-
       Service = yes
          THEN Flexibility-Rating = medium
R23.   IF Frequency-of-Service is not daily AND Door-to-Door-
       Service = no
          THEN Flexibility-Rating = low

Value-Weight-Ratio (inputs Weight-of-one-item and Value-of-
one-item):

R24.   IF Weight-of-one-time is not null AND Value-of-one-item is not
       null
          THEN Value-Weight-Ratio =
          Value-of-one-item / Weight-of-one-item

Valuable-Rating (input Value-Weight-Ratio):

R25.   IF Value-Weight-Ratio >= $100
          THEN Valuable-Rating = very-high
R26.   IF Value-Weight-Ratio >= $20 and < $100
          THEN Valuable-Rating = high
R27.   IF Value-Weight-Ratio >= $1 and < $20
          THEN Valuable-Rating = average
R28.   IF Value-Weight-Ratio < $1
          THEN Valuable-Rating = low

Loss-and-Damage-Rating (inputs Valuable-Rating and
       Fragility-Rating):

R29.   IF Valuable-Rating = very-high
          THEN Loss-and-Damage-Rating = important
R30.   IF Valuable-Rating = high AND Fragility-Rating = high
          THEN Loss-and-Damage-Rating = important
R31.   IF Valuable-Rating = high AND Fragility-Rating = not high
          THEN Loss-and-Damage-Rating = somewhat-important

R32.   IF Valuable-Rating = average AND Fragility-Rating = high
         THEN Loss-and-Damage-Rating = somewhat-important

Note: all other values of Loss-and-Damage-Rating are unimportant

II. Rules Using Modes-Capable

R33.   IF Modes-Capable = rail-only
         THEN Recommendation = RAIL
R34.   IF Modes-Capable = rail-or-trucking
         THEN Alternatives = rail-or-trucking

III. Rules Using Load-Type

R35.   IF Load-Type = small-shipment
         THEN Recommendation = SMALL-PACKAGE-SERVICE
R36.   IF Load-Type = average-shipment
         THEN Alternatives = trucking-or-air
R37.   IF Load-Type = large-shipment
         THEN Alternatives = rail-or-trucking AND Preference =
         trucking
R38.   IF Load-Type = very-large-shipment
         THEN Alternatives = rail-or-trucking AND Preference =
         rail

If all other values on the tree are null:

R39.   IF Alternatives = rail-or-trucking and Preference = trucking
       AND all other values are null
         THEN Recommendation = TRUCKING
R40.   IF Alternatives = rail-or-trucking and Preference = rail
       AND all other values are null
         THEN Recommendation = RAIL

IV. Rules for Deciding between Trucking or Air:

A.   Using Haul Type to narrow down the choices:

R41.   IF Alternatives = trucking-or-air AND Haul-Type = (long-fast
       or medium-fast)
         THEN Recommendation = AIR
R42.   IF Alternatives = trucking-or-air AND Haul-Type = (long-slow
       or medium-slow or local)
         THEN Recommendation = Trucking

B. Using Flexibility-Rating to narrow down the choices:

R43. IF Alternatives = trucking-or-air AND Flexibility-Rating =
       high
            THEN Recommendation = Trucking
R44. IF Alternatives = trucking-or-air AND Flexibility-Rating =
       (medium or low)
            THEN Recommendation = AIR

C. Using Loss-and-Damage-Rating to narrow down the choices:

R45. IF Alternatives = trucking-or-air AND Loss-and-Damage-Rating =
       (important or somewhat important)
            THEN Recommendation = AIR
R46. IF Alternatives = trucking-or-air AND Loss-and-Damage-Rating =
       (unimportant)
            THEN Recommendation = TRUCKING

V. Rules for Deciding between Rail or Trucking:

A. Using Haul Type to narrow down the choices:

R47. IF Alternatives = rail-or-trucking AND Haul-Type = medium-fast
            THEN Recommendation = TRUCKING
R48. IF Alternatives = rail-or-trucking AND Haul-Type = long-fast
            THEN Display ''It is not possible to send this
            shipment via any of the transport modes. Please try
            another set of parameters.''
R49. IF Alternatives = rail-or-trucking AND Haul-Type = local
            THEN Recommendation = TRUCKING

B. Using Flexibility-Rating to narrow down the choices:

R50. IF Alternatives = rail-or-trucking AND Flexibility-Rating =
       high
            THEN Recommendation = Trucking

C. Using Loss-and-Damage-Rating to narrow down the choices:

R51. IF Alternatives = rail-or-trucking AND Loss-and-Damage-
       Rating = (important or somewhat important)
            THEN Recommendation = TRUCKING
R52. IF Alternatives = rail-or-trucking AND Loss-and-Damage-
       Rating = (unimportant)
            THEN Recommendation = RAIL

ENDNOTES

1. There are a number of articles that deal with the subject of explanations in expert systems. For an overview of the topic see the following: Richard W. Southwick, Explaining Reasoning: An Overview of Explanation in Knowledge-Based Systems, *The Knowledge Engineering Review* 6, no. 1 (1991), 1–19; B. Chandrasekeran, Michael C. Tanner, and John R. Josephson, "Explanation: The Role of Control Strategies and Deep Models," in *Expert Systems, The User Interface*. Norwood, NJ: Ablex Pub, 1988. pp. 219–247; and Charlie Ellis, "Explanation in Intelligent Systems," in *Expert Knowledge and Explanation: The Knowledge-Language Interface*. Chichester, England: E. Horwood, 1989, pp. 108–126.

2. For more information on MYCIN, see Bruce G. Buchanan and Edward. H. Shortliffe, *Rule-Based Expert Systems: The Mycin Experiments of the Stanford Heuristic Programming Project*. Reading, MA: Addison-Wesley, 1984.

3. William J. Clancey, "The Epistemology of Rule-Based Expert System—A Framework for Explanation," *Artificial Intelligence* 20 (1983), 225.

4. For more information on strategic knowledge in expert systems, see Clancey. See also William R. Swartout, "XPLAIN: A System for Creating and Explaining Expert Consulting Programs," *Artificial Intelligence* 21 (1983), 285–325.

5. **TransMode** is a variation of **expert strategy**, an expert system that is described in Robbie T. Nakatsu and Izak Benbasat, "Improving the Explanatory Power of Knowledge-Based Systems: An Investigation of Content and Interface-Based Enhancements," *IEEE Transactions on Systems, Man, and Cybernetics, Part A* 33, no. 3 (2003), 344–357.

6. For more information on the experimental study, see ibid.

7. Half the participants in this experimental study were provided with a hierarchic model, and the other half were not. The hierarchic models were *not* found to significantly affect problem-solving performance. In fact, almost all subjects performed poorly on this task. Of the 80 study participants, only 3 were able to come to a perfect or near-perfect solution to the problem. See ibid., pp. 350–351.

CHAPTER 7

MODEL-BASED REASONING

Models are an important form of knowledge representation because expertise often lies in one's ability to reason about how the objects, or components, of a system are interconnected—whether physically, causally, relationally, or otherwise—in a domain of discourse. In Chapter 2, we described how human problem solvers will sometimes build mental models to help them solve complex problems. This notion underlies model-based reasoning, a class of AI techniques used to solve problems by analyzing the structure of a system, as speci ed by some kind of model. In many ways, this chapter is a continuation of the discussion on mental models. It is also a continuation on expert systems, because model-based reasoning can be used to extend and enhance the power of expert systems. To limit the design of expert systems to logic IF–THEN rules would be to seriously ignore a powerful way of representing knowledge; such an expert system would be far less intelligent than it might otherwise be capable of being.

Indeed, model-based reasoning, in large part, came into being as an area of promise to address the void created by systems employing only rule-based reasoning and other limited forms of reasoning (e.g., owcharts, fault dictionaries, and decision trees). For example, a rule-based expert system that troubleshoots a malfunctioning device might employ rules that associate symptoms to their underlying faults. Such a system can account for only empirical associations that have been acquired to date (often in a haphazard or happenstance way) and is likely to miss some faults. By contrast, model-based reasoning would try to determine what is wrong based on the *underlying structure* of the device. A system employing model-based reasoning, if constructed correctly, can provide

Diagrammatic Reasoning in AI, by Robbie Nakatsu
Copyright © 2010 John Wiley & Sons, Inc.

for more systematic and comprehensive coverage of a domain. This means that model-based reasoning may be able to detect novel faults and solve problems that have not been encountered before. Moreover, systems employing model-based reasoning tend to be *device-independent*.* A model may be specified in such a generic way that it is supposed to work for many different device configurations. Rule-based approaches are not as likely to be so flexible but highly device-specific, meaning that a different set of rules is required to specify the behavior of each new device.

In a very complex system, possibly consisting of thousands of components and many more interactions among these components, model-based reasoning provides a way to cope with cognitive complexity. The user of a very complex device or system may have to contend with hundreds of operating procedures. Such an individual is unlikely to memorize all these procedures. Model-based reasoning may be employed so that a user can generate these procedures from a relatively small set of models.[1] Embeddedness is one way to accomplish this. By this, we mean that models are specified at different levels of detail. One component of a complex system, for example, may be described by a more detailed and fine-grained model (called an embedded model) composed of many other subcomponents and their interconnections. Embeddedness, in effect, allows one to define hierarchic organizations of a complex system.

Before we proceed any further in our discussion, let us define more precisely what model-based reasoning is: Model-based reasoning involves the analysis of both the structure and behavior of a system.

Structure is the way that the individual components of a system are interconnected (as given by a system's topology); **Behavior** refers to what each of these components is supposed to do. From this definition, we may distinguish three levels of system description. First, *diagrams* are models, graphical in nature, that are used to illustrate structure (e.g., how components are physically interconnected); they do not capture functional behavior of a system. Second, *heuristics* describe relationships between inputs and outputs, based on the way that experts describe how inputs are transformed into outputs. (Heuristics may be represented as IF-THEN rules). Heuristic knowledge, however, does not attempt to create an explicit representation of system structure. Model-based reasoning is a more complete representation system in the sense that it describes both structure and behavior. From this, three levels of system description can be distinguished, based on whether they describe structure, behavior, or both:[2]

	Describes Structure?	Describes Behavior?
Diagrams	Yes	No
Heuristics	No	Yes
Model-Based Reasoning	Yes	Yes

---

*Many of the applications of model-based reasoning involve the troubleshooting of malfunctioning devices, such as electronic circuits.

Table 7.1. Terminology Used in Model-Based Reasoning

Describing Object Models	
Structure	How components of a system are interconnected; typically, speci ed by the topological model
Behavior	What the components of the system do; how they interact (e.g., may be speci ed by a causal model)

Constituents of Object Models	
Materials	What passes through the system
Components	Nodes; they can process and change the materials or they transform inputs into outputs
Conduits or connections	Links between nodes; they transport materials from one node to the next but perform no actual processing

To describe structure and behavior, we also need to distinguish three types of constituents that are part of a system model: *materials, components*, and *conduits* (or *connections*).[3] **Materials** is what passes through a system. In a physical system, this may be an actual physical element such as water, air, or electricity. In a manufacturing system, this may be a product (e.g., an automobile), which moves through the different processes of a manufacturing plant. In a service-oriented system, this may be an abstract thing such as a purchase order or a customer service request, which is moved through the different departments of an organization. **Components** are the constituents that can act on and change the form of the materials. A component can have both inputs and outputs (inputs are transformed into outputs). **Conduits**, or **connections**, are the simple constituents that transport materials from one component to another. Unlike components, they do no actual processing on the materials. See Table 7.1 for a summary of the terminology used in model-based reasoning.

In model-based reasoning, behavior is determined from structure. One way to describe system behavior is to specify how individual components of a system *causally interact* to produce an observable behavior. In Chapter 2, the device behavior of the electromechanical thermostat was described as a cascading series of events in which one component of the device affects its neighboring component, which in turn, affects its neighboring component, and so on, until the nal behavior of the device can be explained in a coherent way (for a review see pp. 31–40). Hence explanatory power arises quite naturally in systems employing model-based reasoning.

The principle of *adjacency* speci es that a component can act on another component only if it is directly connected to it. In Figure 7.1, only neighboring components can act on each other. (For example, A can act directly on B but cannot act directly on C, D, or E). A system model may also be directional: information (or materials) in a system can move in only a speci ed direction, as is the case in Figure 7.1. Several formalisms have been developed on how to produce causal models to explain the behaviors of devices and systems.[4]

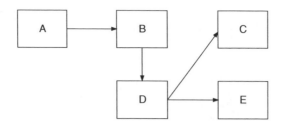

Figure 7.1. Diagram illustrating structure.

We must be very careful with the concept of adjacency. The components of a device may be "adjacent" in different ways: They may be physically wired to one another, they may be electromagnetically adjacent, or they may be thermally adjacent, to illustrate three different notions of adjacency. If a system de nition of adjacency is not modeled appropriately, model-based reasoning may render inappropriate and incorrect recommendations.

Model-based reasoning is sometimes known by other names, the most notable of which is *reasoning from first principles*, a term used to signify that reasoning is based on basic principles of causality, and *deep reasoning*, a term intended to distinguish model-based reasoning from more surface-oriented forms of reasoning such as rule-based, associational reasoning.[5] Other related terms include *qualitative reasoning* and *commonsense reasoning*, terms that have been closely associated in the arti cial intelligence world with qualitative physics, or reasoning about the physical world.

Let us now look more closely at how we may apply these principles to solving problems. We will rst look at model-based diagnosis, or determining which component of a system is responsible for a system malfunction. Then we will explore how model-based reasoning can be used to help us design network models.

MODEL-BASED DIAGNOSIS

Much of the prior work on model-based reasoning has focused on fault diagnosis and troubleshooting, in particular, of simple devices such as electronic circuits.[6] Model-based diagnosis starts with an observed malfunction of a device (a symptom that something is wrong) and works backward to determine which underlying component(s) might be the cause.

The driving force behind model-based diagnosis is that we wish to understand the difference between an *observed* behavior (what a device actually does) and a *predicted* behavior (what a device is supposed to do when working correctly). This difference is referred to as a **discrepancy**. A discrepancy is an outward sign that the device is not working properly, so diagnosis involves the determination of which component is responsible for the discrepant behavior. As is common in the eld (and to simplify the discussion in this section) we assume single point failure, meaning that there is a single source of error—one component alone is the cause of the malfunctioning behavior.

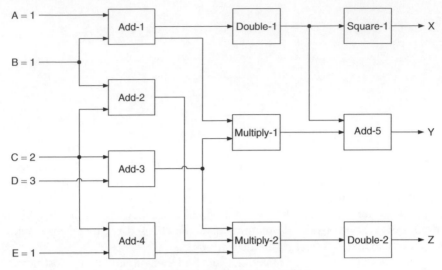

Figure 7.2. A simple device topology.

Joined   Not Joined

Figure 7.3. Notation for crossed wires that are joined and not joined.

Troubleshooting a Simple Device

To illustrate the principles of model-based diagnosis, let us look at a simple device whose structure is illustrated in Figure 7.2. The device contains ten components: ve adders (Add-1 through Add-5); two doublers (Double-1 and Double-2), two multipliers (Multiply-1 and Multiply-2), and a squarer (Square-1). This device topology shows how the components are interconnected to one another. Furthermore, the connections are directional, as indicated by the arrows, signifying that they either lead into a component, as an input, or lead out from a component, as an output. Note in the diagram how the intersection of two wires can be either joined or not joined. Figure 7.3 illustrates notation used to distinguish between joined wires and nonjoined wires. Joined wires are indicated by a blob where the lines cross; nonjoined wires are indicated by the bridge symbol to show that two wires cross, but are not connected.

In addition to device structure, we also require a description of component behavior. Behavior can be represented by a mathematical expression or equation that indicates how the inputs into a component are transformed into outputs. The components in Figure 7.2 will do one of the following: add the inputs (components Add-1 through Add-5), multiply the inputs (components Multiply-1 and Multiply-2), double the input (component Double-1), or take the square of the input (component Square-1).

Figure 7.2 also indicates that the device contains ve inputs, labeled A through E, and three observable outputs labeled X, Y, and Z.

Let us suppose that we detect a discrepancy at Y (see Figure 7.4 for a diagram of this situation). This diagram indicates that when we run the device model, we predict Y = 14; instead we observe Y = 9.

Our rst step in model-based diagnosis is to identify which of the components could account for the device's discrepant behavior. We call this rst step **hypothesis generation** because we are hypothesizing, based on a device's structure and behavior, which of the components could plausibly account for the discrepancy. We de ne a **suspect** as being a component that is identi ed as a possible cause of the discrepancy. Our objective is to eliminate or exonerate as many suspects as possible so that only a few remain, or in the best case, only one suspect remains. To do this, a number of rules may be employed to identify and constrain the set of suspects.

Rule 1.

A suspect must be connected to the discrepancy.

Based on the device topology, a component can be implicated only if it is connected to the discrepancy. In Figure 7.4, all 10 components are connected to the discrepancy that occurs at Y, so that this rule, in this case, has not eliminated any component from the suspect set.

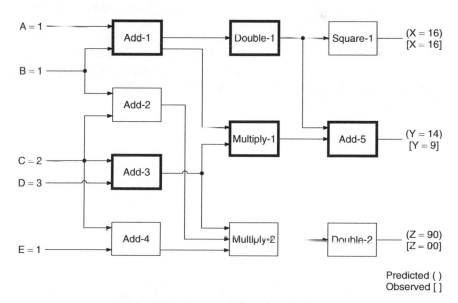

Figure 7.4. An observed malfunction at Y.

Rule 2.

A suspect must be upstream from the discrepancy.

What do we mean by upstream? Components that are upstream refer to those that are attached on the input side of the discrepancy. To identify which components are upstream, we require device topology with directed connections, speci ed by arrows, that indicate a component's inputs and outputs. Five components are upstream from discrepancy Y in Figure 7.4: Add-1, Add-3, Double-1, Multiply-1, and Add-5. (These ve components are boldface in the gure). Hence Rule 2 has eliminated the ve other components from the set of suspects.

Rule 3.

We may exonerate a suspect if it is upstream from an output that is conforming; however, we must be careful not to exonerate a suspect if fault masking is involved.

Outputs are conforming when the predicted value is the same as the observed value. Hence, X and Z are conforming outputs. By Rule 3, we may exonerate Add-1 and Double-1 because they are upstream from X as well as Add-3 because it is upstream from Z. Hence we are left with only two suspects, Multiply-1 and Add-5.

Unfortunately, Rule 3 can result in a spurious exoneration of a suspect if fault masking is involved. Fault masking occurs when a device receives incorrect inputs, yet produces a conforming output. Figure 7.5 is an example of how fault masking might occur. The output at Z is conforming, where both the predicted and observed values are 90. However, two upstream components, Add-2 and Add-4, are discrepant so that the incorrect inputs are read into Multiply-2. Despite this, a conforming output is produced at Multiply-2 (9*5*1 is 45) and at Z. Further testing of components may be required to ensure that fault masking does not occur (we discuss this later on in the hypothesis testing stage).

In Figure 7.5, a multipoint failure occurs—two components Add-2 and Add-4 are broken. However, fault masking can certainly occur with single point failure, and it is easy to construct an example of fault masking when only one component is broken. Figure 7.6 shows a simple example of fault masking when only one component is broken (Add-2). The component Min reads in two inputs and outputs the minimum of the two. The output Z is conforming, because Min in insensitive to observed inputs and predicted inputs (Min(10, 45) is the same as Min(10, 30)—both are 10.

Rule 4.

We may use information from more than one discrepancy to further constrain the set of suspects. In particular, assuming single-point failure, we may generate a set of suspects for each discrepancy and take the intersection of the sets.

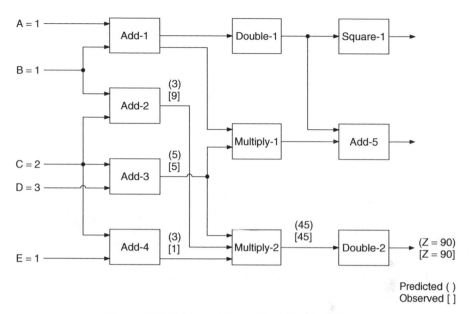

Figure 7.5. Fault masking at Z, multipoint failure.

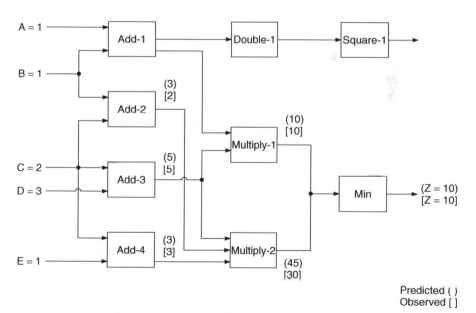

Figure 7.6. Fault masking at Z, single-point failure.

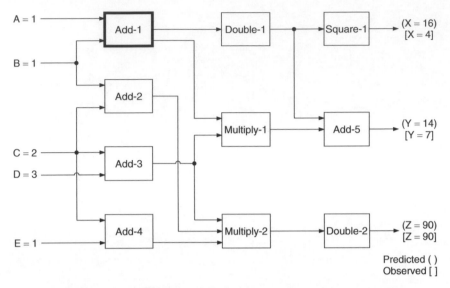

Figure 7.7. Intersecting the upstream set X and the upstream set Y.

In Figure 7.7, two discrepancies occur, one at output X, and one at output Y. Upstream components to X are (Add-1, Double-1, and Square-2); upstream components to Y are (Add-1, Add-3, Multiply-1, and Add-5). The intersection of the two sets is the component Add-1. Hence, by applying this rule, Add-1 is the component responsible for the malfunction.

Rule 5.

We may use knowledge of the output to constrain the suspect set.

Sometimes the nature of the output implies that particular components in a device are at fault. For example, let us assume the device topology in Figure 7.8. The Add component adds the inputs, the Double component doubles the input, and the Subtract-one component subtracts 1 from the input. We know that if we double an integer, it always even, and that if we subtract 1 from it, it is odd; hence we expect the output to be odd. If it is even instead, as is the case above, we conclude that (Double and Subtract-one) is the suspect set; we do not even need to consider the Add component as a possible suspect, even though it is upstream from the discrepancy.

In a similar fashion, in the simple Device topology given in Figure 7.2, X must be a perfect square (4, 16, 25, 36, etc.) because the component Square-1

Figure 7.8. A simple device illustrating how the output affects the suspect set.

Table 7.2. Model-Based Diagnosis Procedure

Step 1: Hypothesis generation: Generate suspects

Rule 1: All components connected to the discrepancy are part of the suspect set.

Rule 2: Exonerate suspects that are not connected to the discrepancy on the upstream side.

Rule 3: Exonerate suspects if they are connected to conforming outputs on the upstream side.

Rule 4: When there is more than one discrepancy, intersect the sets of suspects resulting from each discrepancy and exonerate all suspects that not part of the intersected set.

Rule 5: Look at the nature of special outputs to further constrain the suspect set.

Step 2: Hypothesis testing and discrimination: Choose the most likely suspect If there is more than one suspect remaining after Step 1, collect additional information by doing one of the following:

1. Probe inputs and outputs of each suspect; if the suspect output is discrepant from the inputs, then the component is malfunctioning.
2. Test the device with different inputs. (May want to perform this step to ensure that fault masking is not occurring.)

takes an integer as its input and outputs the square of the input. If it is not a perfect square, then Square-1 is the only logical suspect. Likewise, Z must be an even number, and if it is not, then Double-2 is the likely suspect.

Even when we have used the ve rules to eliminate suspects, we may still be left with more than one suspect. In a second phase of diagnosis, **hypothesis testing and discrimination,**[7] we need to collect additional data by (1) making additional observations (probing inputs and outputs of the device components) or (2) modifying the inputs of the device and making observations in the new situation (testing with different inputs). Our goal is to choose the most likely suspect that is the cause of the discrepancy

Let us return to the device given by Figure 7.4. Here, we have exonerated most of the device components, so that only two suspects remain, Multiply-1 and Add-5. (We hope that after applying the ve rules only a few components remain in the suspect set so that we may focus our testing on just those components.) To eliminate one of the suspects, we need to collect additional data. For example, we might probe the inputs of Multiply-1 (2 and 5), and discover that its output is 5 instead of the expected 10. This would indicate that Multiply-1 is the faulty component and, assuming single-point failure, imply that Add 5 is working ne. Finally, if fault masking is suspected, it is a good idea to modify the inputs of the device and make additional observations to ensure that the outputs conform. Table 7.2 summarizes the model-based diagnosis procedure outlined in this section.

Table 7.3. Logic Gates

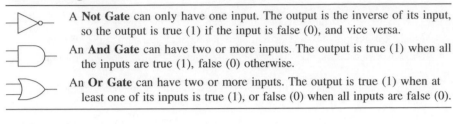

	A **Not Gate** can only have one input. The output is the inverse of its input, so the output is true (1) if the input is false (0), and vice versa.
	An **And Gate** can have two or more inputs. The output is true (1) when all the inputs are true (1), false (0) otherwise.
	An **Or Gate** can have two or more inputs. The output is true (1) when at least one of its inputs is true (1), or false (0) when all inputs are false (0).

Another Example: Troubleshooting a Device of Logic Gates

Logic gates process signals that represent one of two values: true (1) or false (0). Table 7.3 describes three types of logic gates that are used in this example.

Figure 7.9 shows the device topology of interconnected logic gates. The device has eight inputs labeled A through H. In addition, the device has three outputs labeled X, Y, and Z. All signals ow from left to right, so arrows, or directed connections, are not shown but implied in the diagram. As noted in the diagram, there are two discrepancies, one at X and one at Y. X expects a (1) but receives a [0] instead. In addition, Y expects a (1) but receives a [0].

How do we determine which component is faulty? First, Rule 2 tells us to include only components upstream from the discrepancies in the suspect set. Unfortunately, this includes all the logic gates in the device, so this rule adds no further understanding. Rule 3, however, allows us to exonerate Not-4, And-4, and Or-3, because they are all upstream from a conforming output. Finally, Rule 4 lets us intersect the two suspect sets, X (Not-1, Or-1, Not-2, And-1, Or-2) and Y (Not-2, Not-3, And-2, And-3). The only component that is part of both suspect sets is Not-2.

To con rm that Not-2 is, in fact, the faulty component, we may wish to probe its input and output. (In addition, this may con rm that fault masking has not occurred.) Because its input is false (0), its expected output should be true (1). By probing that it is returning an output that is false, we will have established that Not-2 is the component responsible for the malfunctioning behavior.

In sum, the important point to remember about model-based diagnosis is that there is a model that predicts what the device is supposed to do. When there is a discrepancy between this prediction and what the device actually does, the model-based reasoning technique works backwards to nd the faulty component. In the examples given, because we are reasoning from the structure of the device to determine which component is malfunctioning, we are using model-based reasoning. We could have used a heuristic-based approach instead, as a traditional rule-base expert system would, and encode our diagnostic procedures as a series of IF–THEN associational rules, in which observable discrepant behaviors are

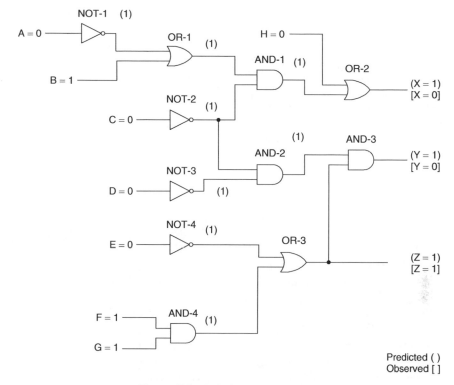

Figure 7.9. A device of logic gates.

related to speci c system states. Such an approach would need to anticipate all the possible ways in which a particular component can fail and associate it to a particular discrepancy. Even in the simple devices illustrated in this section, this would be a time-consuming and laborious undertaking. As these examples demonstrate, the model-based approach is far more effective in providing more comprehensive and systematic coverage of the troubleshooting task.

DESIGNING BUSINESS LOGISTICS NETWORKS

Much of the previous work in model-based reasoning has focused on fault diagnosis of physical devices and systems (e.g., the diagnosis of industrial gas turbines used for power generation). In more recent years, there has been a proliferation of applications in other areas, everything from diagnosing diseases in medicine, to locating software bugs in programs, to diagnosing learner behaviors in an automated tutoring system. In all these cases, the focus has been on a diagnostic task of some kind.

In this section and the next, we discuss a novel use of model-based reasoning to solve a class of network design problems in business logistics management. The Council of Logistics Management de nes business logistics management as:

> . . . the process of planning, implementing and controlling the ef cient, cost-effective ow and storage of raw materials, in-process inventory, nished goods, and related information from point-of-origin to point-of-consumption for the purpose of con- forming to customer requirements.[8]

The coverage of this area is broad, encompassing business problems that con- cern customer service, traf c and transportation, warehousing and storage, plant and warehouse site selection, inventory control, order processing, procurement, material handling, and demand forecasting, to name some of the major areas of study within the eld.[9] The selection of business logistics network design as a model-based reasoning application is a logical choice because there are many problems in logistics strategy planning that could bene t from a diagrammatic visualization of some kind.

The intelligent system described in this section is called LogNet.[10] LogNet employs model-based reasoning to design the most cost-effective network satisfy- ing a certain customer service level. It speci cally addresses the facility location problem: How many warehouses are needed in a logistics network? Where should these warehouses be located, and to which customer market(s) should they be assigned? Also, which factory should supply each warehouse? Unlike a diagno- sis problem that typically works backwards from a symptom to determine what component might be responsible for the faulty behavior, LogNet instead works in a forward direction and looks at a variety of network designs, evaluating each one to recommend which among them is the most cost effective.

Description of LogNet

At the heart of LogNet is the network model. One way to view and model a logis- tics environment is as a network of nodes interconnected by transportation links. The problem of specifying the model would be one of specifying the network structure through which manufactured goods ow. To model this environment, three types of nodes* are considered: rst, the **factories**, where the products are manufactured; second, the **warehouses**, which receive the nished products from the factories for storage and possibly for further processing; and third, the **customer zones** (or markets), which place orders and receive the desired products from the assigned warehouse(s). Product moves through the logistics network via different transportation options (e.g., rail, trucking, shipping, air), which are represented by the connections or links between the nodes. There are two types of transportation links: **inbound links** move products from factories to

---

*Limiting the logistics network to only three types of nodes is a simpli cation of the problem. For example, this network does not consider the suppliers who source the factories. In addition, there may be two types of warehousing, such as regional warehousing and local warehousing, or products may be moved rst to distributors before they actually reach customer markets.

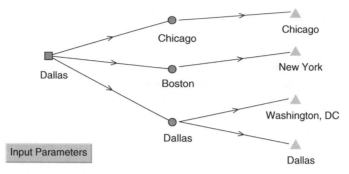

Figure 7.10. A network model in LogNet.

Table 7.4. Road Mileage between Selected U.S. Cities

	Atlanta	Chicago	Dallas	Denver	Seattle
Atlanta		674	795	1398	2618
Chicago	674		917	996	2013
Dallas	795	917		781	2078
Denver	1398	996	781		1307
Seattle	2618	2013	2078	1307	

warehouses, and **outbound links** move products from warehouses to customers. See Figure 7.10 for a simple example of a logistics network model created using LogNet. In this diagram, squares represent factories, circles represent warehouses, and triangles represent customer zones.

Spatial reasoning on the network model is possible to the extent that LogNet contains information about distances between two nodes for all transportation links. See Table 7.4 for a sample of a ve-node system of selected U.S. cities. Distances are road miles between two cities. Whenever a user connects two nodes, the system will automatically update the distance-between-nodes attribute for that transportation link, via a look-up from a table containing road mileage between two cities.

LogNet enables users to build, directly manipulate, and inspect components of the network model. Different network con gurations can be created, and such benchmarks as network costs and customer service level can be obtained. In addition, users may modify different input assumptions (such as inventory rates and transportation rates) and see how these modi cations will affect the network benchmarks

Network Benchmarks

LogNet calculates benchmarks in order to evaluate different network models and provide intelligent advice on which network designs perform best on these benchmarks. Two main benchmarks are considered: network costs and customer service level.

Network Costs. The total cost of a given network con guration consists of three components: *transportation costs, warehousing costs*, and *inventory carrying costs*.

Transportation costs depend on the volume transported between the two nodes and the distance between the nodes. There are two types of transportation costs: inbound (factory to warehouse) and outbound (warehouse to customer zone). Transportation costs for a given transportation link are given by the following functions:

```
If inbound:
  Inbound Rate * no. of units in 1000's * distance between nodes
If outbound:
  Outbound Rate * no. of units in 1000's * distance between nodes
```

Inbound Rate and Outbound Rate are input parameters that can be set by the user. They are expressed as the dollar rate per 1000 units per mile. Total transportation cost is the sum of the inbound costs and outbound costs.

Warehousing costs are a combination of xed costs (a cost that is set by the user) and variable costs (e.g., handling costs per unit). Warehousing costs for a single warehouse, are calcualted by the following function:

$$\text{Warehouse } \text{ xed cost} + (\text{no units stored} * \text{Warehouse handling rate})$$

Fixed costs and variable handling rates are input parameters that are set by the user.

Inventory carrying costs depend on the average inventory maintained at a warehouse (in-transit inventories are not considered). LogNet considers only the cost of the money tied up in inventory, or the capital cost of inventory. Other inventory costs such as stock-out costs, inventory service costs, and risk are not considered. In LogNet, inventory carrying costs are estimated, based on the *square root rule*. (The square root rule simpli es inventory consolidation, but is a useful principle nevertheless. More accurate functions may be used to estimate the cost savings achieved by consolidating inventories.) This rule can be used to estimate the cost of inventory when consolidating n stocking points, or warehouses. It states the following:

$$\text{Consolidated inventory} = \frac{\text{Decentralized inventory}}{\sqrt{n}}$$

For example, if previously a network used three warehouses at a cost of $500,000 each, for a total inventory investment of $1,500,000, after consolidation inventory carrying costs are calculated as follows:

$$\frac{1,500,000}{\sqrt{3}} = \$866,025$$

Inventory carrying costs, therefore, are decreased by \$633,975 (1,500,000 − 866,025). This is because the more consolidated the logistics network becomes (i.e., the fewer warehouses used), the greater the inventory per warehouse. As a result, economies of scale are achieved, resulting in lower inventory carrying costs. Based on this principle, LogNet calculates inventory carrying costs using the following function:

$$\text{Inventory carrying cost} = \sqrt{\frac{\text{Monthly demand}}{1000}} * \text{Inventory rate}$$

For example, if the monthly demand of a warehouse is 5000 units per month, and the inventory rate is \$10,000, then the inventory carrying costs are given by:

$$\sqrt{5} * 10,000 = \$22,361$$

Inventory rate is an input parameter that may be set by the user.

Table 7.5 summarizes the input parameters, set by the user, that determine the total network cost.

Customer Service Level. In the real world, customer service is a complex and multifaceted benchmark. To simplify matters, LogNet assumes that the logistics decision maker would like to locate a warehouse stocking point as close to customers as possible to improve customer service. (One may think of customer service in terms of having speedier deliveries to a customer; hence local warehousing might allow for same-day deliveries.) LogNet calculates the customer service in terms of how close the customer zones are to the warehouses. LogNet calculates the average customer-to-warehouse distance over each customer zone i:

$$\frac{\sum_i (\text{Monthly demand})i * (\text{Distance between customer zone and warehouse})i}{\sum_i (\text{Monthly demand})i}$$

Table 7.5. Input Parameters That Affect Total Network Cost

Network Costs	Input Parameters
1. Inbound transportation cost	1. Inbound rate per 1000 units
2. Outbound transportation cost	2. Outbound rate per 1000 units
3. Warehousing cost: xed	3. Warehouse xed cost
4. Warehousing cost: variable	4. Warehouse handling rate
5. Inventory carrying cost	5. Inventory rate for 1000 units

For example, let us suppose that there are three customer zones, Dallas, Denver, and Atlanta with monthly customer demand of 5,000, 6,000, and 10,000 units, respectively. There is one warehouse that provides customers with products for each of these three customer zones, and it is located in Dallas. Average customer service is the weighted customer-to-warehouse distance:

$$\frac{(5,000) * (0 \text{ miles}) + (6,000) * (781 \text{ miles}) + (10,000) * (795 \text{ miles})}{5,000 + 6,000 + 10,000}$$

$$= 601.7 \text{ miles}$$

According to this de nition of customer service, if a warehouse is located in every city in which there are customers, then perfect customer service is attained—that is, the average distance between customer and warehouse is 0.

There is one obvious trade-off between inventory carrying cost and customer service level that a logistics network designer will need to weigh and balance. On the one hand, consolidation will result in lower inventory carrying costs due to economies of scale; on the other hand, consolidation will result in a lower customer service level because average customer-to-warehouse distance is increased when all customers are served by a consolidated warehouse. Therefore, the logistics network designer will want to create a logistics network that provides adequate customer service while not adding too much to overall inventory carrying costs.

Visual Interactive Modeling with a Diagrammatic User Interface

LogNet was designed so that users can directly interact with a business logistics network via a direct manipulation, graphical user interface. The LogNet user interface allows a user to to modify a network diagram by adding a node, deleting a node, connecting two nodes, or disconnecting two nodes to create a new network design. The advantage of visual interactive modeling is that it enables one to incrementally build and test a new network design, step by step. Upon request, LogNet will evaluate the new network design by calculating the benchmarks. Hence users can iteratively test a network design until they are satis ed that (1) the network design meets a suitable cost and/or (2) the network design satis es a given customer service level.

An example of a logistics network design problem follows. Figure 7.11 depicts a completely decentralized logistics network: All customer zones are assigned to a warehouse located in the same city. In this example, ve customer zones are assigned to ve warehouses. These warehouses, in turn, are sourced by a single factory (located in Dallas). The numbers above the nodes represent the number of units that ow through that node. Because the network is completely decentralized, the customer service level (or average customer-to-warehouse distance) is a perfect 0.

Network benchmarks can be requested at any point during the formulation of a network design. This enables the user to modify a network design and

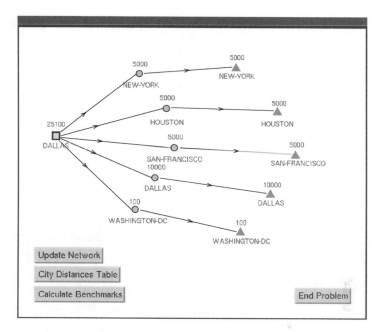

Figure 7.11. A decentralized network.

immediately observe the effect of the modi cation on the network benchmarks. Figure 7.12 displays the benchmarks for the network model speci ed by Figure 7.11. We assume that the following input parameter assumptions are in effect:

```
Inbound Rate(per 1000 units per mile)          10
Outbound Rate(per 1000 units per mile)         20
Warehousing Fixed Cost(per warehouse)      50,000
Warehousing (Variable) Handling Rate(per unit)  5
Inventory Rate(per 1000 units)              1,000
```

This screen contains information about network costs as well as customer service levels. Outbound transportation costs are zero—because the network is perfectly decentralized. Warehousing xed costs are $250,000, because there are ve active warehouses at $50,000 each. As expected, average customer-to-warehouse distance is 0 miles.

Visual interactive modeling, then, allows the user to create many different network designs easily and obtain network benchmarks to judge which of several network designs is most desirable. A user may directly compare two network designs by performing the following sequence of steps: (1) create the rst network design, (2) request benchmarks, (3) create a second network design (which might entail a number of changes to the rst network design), and (4) request the network benchmarks a second time. By performing these steps, the third column

	Benchmarks	percent (%)	Difference
Transportation Costs:			
Inbound—Factory to Warehouse	178719.0	27.2	0.0
Outbound—Warehouse to Customer	0.0	0.0	0.0
Total Transportation Costs	178719.0	27.2	
Warehousing Costs:			
Fixed Costs	250000.0	38.1	0.0
Variable Handling Costs	125500.0	19.1	0.0
Total Warehousing Costs	375500.0	57.2	
Inventory Carrying Costs	101868.0	15.5	0.0
Total Network Costs	656087.0		0.0
CUSTOMER SERVICE LEVEL BENCHMARKS			
Average Distance (Customer-to-Warehouse)	0.0		0.0
% Customers Less than 500 Miles Away	100.0		0.0
% Customers Less than 1,000 Miles Away	100.0		0.0

OK

Figure 7.12. Network benchmarks.

of Figure 7.12 would display how the **before** and **after** network designs are different for each of the benchmarks.

MODEL-BASED REASONING: GUIDANCE TOWARD A BETTER NETWORK DESIGN

Up to this point, the speci cation of LogNet, as described in the previous section, does not contain the intelligence necessary to guide a user toward better network designs. The decision maker engaged in visual interactive modeling is limited to trial-and-error and eyeballing techniques to test different network con gurations and to inspect the costs and customer service levels that result from each. Such techniques may work reasonably well for simple problems, but model-based reasoning reasoning—reasoning from structure—can be employed to create a system capable of solving more complex problems, both more consistently and more systematically. For purposes of this discussion, we break down the network design problem into two basic types of actions: **consolidation** (combining two or more warehouses into one) and **decentralization** (adding a warehouse to a network design). We consider the tradeoff between cost and customer service involved in consolidating and decentralizing a network. The goal of the logistics decision maker is really to balance this tradeoff: We wish to design a network so that *network costs are minimized, while maintaining a certain customer service level*.

Network Consolidation

Why would a network need to be consolidated? It may be the case that the current network is too decentralized (i.e., the network contains too many warehouses) leading to excessive inventory carrying costs, and greater warehousing costs. If this is the case, the user will want to eliminate a warehouse and reassign all of its customers to another existing warehouse. By doing so, consolidation will lead to reduced inventory carrying costs because economies of scale are gained as several locations' inventories are combined into one. In addition, warehouse xed costs are decreased with the elimination of each warehouse. On the negative side, consolidation will lead to increased outbound transportation costs (because the customers, formerly assigned to the eliminated warehouse, are now farther away from the newly assigned warehouse) and may lead to increased inbound transportation costs as well. Furthermore, customer service levels are decreased because average distance between warehouse and customer is increased. If deterioration of customer service level is of no concern to the logistics decision maker, LogNet will assess these cost tradeoffs and recommend the consolidation that will result in the greatest cost savings.

LogNet employs model-based reasoning to analyze the structure of the current logistics network, and evaluates all possible consolidation opportunities between two warehouses. The model-based algorithm considers consolidations for each active warehouse in the network (an active warehouse is de ned as a warehouse having customers assigned to it, or a warehouse that has at least one customer zone connected to it).

For any two active warehouse W_i and W_j:
  1) Merge warehouse W_i into warehouse W_j.
     (1a) Disconnect all customers zones currently connected to warehouse W_i
     (1b) Connect all customer zones formerly assigned to warehouse W_i to warehouse W_j
  2) Assess the new benchmarks (transportation costs, inventory costs, and warehousing costs, and customer service level) for the proposed consolidation candidate W_i into W_j.

LogNet will consider all possible mergers between two active warehouses on the network. For example, if there are three active warehouses in the current network model—W_1, W_2, and W_3—the following six consolidation candidates are considered:

W_1 into W_2 W_1 into W_3

W_2 into W_1 W_2 into W_3
W_3 into W_1 W_3 into W_2

A total of six possible mergers are considered, taken two at a time (to simplify the discussion, we do not consider consolidations taken three at a time and, more generally, n at a time). For the consolidation W_1 into W_2, for instance, all customer zones connected to W_1 are disconnected and reconnected to W_2, so that W_1 is shut down and becomes an inactive warehouse. In general if there are n active warehouses, $n * (n - 1)$ consolidations are considered.

If the user's only goal is to reduce network costs, then LogNet will look at each consolidation candidate and suggest the one that will result in the largest cost savings. A reduction in network costs occurs when the costs savings (inventory carrying costs + warehousing xed costs) is greater than the increase in transportation costs (outbound in inbound) resulting from the consolidation of two warehouses.* In addition, LogNet can rank order the consolidation candidates in terms of the cost savings that results from each. The consolidation rule that LogNet uses to make a consolidation recommendation follows:

Consolidation 1.

Suggest the consolidation candidate that will result in the greatest reduction in network costs.

The real dif culty facing the logistics decision maker is that a number of trade-offs must be considered in deciding which of several network designs is most suitable. The consolidation problem would be much easier if the only goal was to reduce network costs. If this were the case, we could more easily automate the network design task using Consolidation 1 alone. However, the lowest-cost network design is frequently not the one we seek because it results in an unacceptable deterioration of customer service level.

Therefore, we require a procedure that recommends a consolidation candidate that does not degrade customer service level too much. The second consolidation approach was expressly created for this purpose. It suggests the consolidation candidate that results in a network cost savings, but does so with the least damage to customer service level.

Consolidation 2.

Suggest the consolidation candidate that results in a network cost savings and is achieved with the least damage to customer service level.

For example, suppose that LogNet generates three consolidation candidates for a given network design: Candidate 1 results in network cost savings of $120,000 achieved at a deterioration in customer service levels of 20 miles, Candidate 2

---

*A consolidation of two warehouses into one does not necessarily result in a cost savings. This occurs when the costs savings (inventory carrying costs + warehousing xed costs) are **less than** the increase in transportation costs. If this is the case, LogNet will not suggest any consolidation.

results in network cost savings of $750,000 achieved at a deterioration of 100 miles, and Candidate 3 results in network cost savings $5,000 achieved at a deterioration of 1 mile. Consolidation 2 will recommend the third consolidation candidate because it results in the least damage to customer service levels.

The problem with Consolidation 2, however, is that LogNet may recommend a consolidation candidate that has minimal impact on reducing network costs. In fact, the logistics network designer may want to balance costs savings with customer service deterioration levels. Therefore, a more germane question to ask is, Which network consolidation will give me the biggest bang for the buck? One way to approach this question is to calculate the ratio **cost savings per mile of deterioration:**

$$\frac{\text{Cost savings}}{\text{Deterioration in customer service}}$$

The third consolidation rule would recommend the consolidation candidate that results in the highest cost savings per mile of deterioration.

Consolidation 3.

Suggest the consolidation candidate having the highest **cost savings per mile of deterioration** *(cost savings/deterioration).*

If this criterion were used instead, LogNet would recommend Candidate 2 because it has the largest cost savings per mile of deterioration. Here are the relevant calculations:

$$\text{Candidate 1: } 120,000/20 = 6,000$$

$$\text{Candidate 2: } 750,000/100 = 7,500$$

$$\text{Candidate 3: } 5,000/1 = 5,000$$

Network Decentralization

Whereas consolidation involves the elimination of a warehouse, decentralization involves the addition of a warehouse to the network and reassigning all customer zones that are closer to the new warehouse than they are to their current warehouse assignment. In this manner, the goal of network decentralization is usually (but not always) to improve the customer service level (or decrease average warehouse-to-customer distance). A secondary goal is to reduce transportation costs. Which warehouse location will LogNet suggest? The user can provide LogNet with a number of candidate warehouse locations (e.g., Seattle, Dallas, Atlanta), and LogNet will suggest the location that results in the greatest improvement in customer service level, *regardless of cost*. In addition, LogNet can rank-order the candidate decentralization opportunities in terms of the customer service levels that result from each. Hence one decentralization rule that LogNet can use to make a decentralization recommendation is as follows.

Decentralization 1.

Suggest the decentralization candidate that will result in the greatest improvement in customer service level (average warehouse-to-customer distance).

Like the consolidation problem, the decentralization problem involves a trade-off between customer service level and network costs. Decentralization 1 will suggest the decentralization candidate that results in the largest improvement in customer service level. However, the logistics decision maker may wish to balance customer service level against network costs, because the best decentralization candidate (in terms of customer service level) may turn out to be excessively costly. Hence the second decentralization approach will suggest the decentralization candidate that offers an improvement to customer service level, but accomplishes this at the lowest possible additional cost:

Decentralization 2.

Suggest the decentralization candidate that results in an improvement to customer service level (average customer-to-warehouse distance) and is achieved at the lowest possible additional cost.

Suppose that a network design will result in three candidate decentralizations: Candidate 1 improves customer service level by 10 miles and is achieved at an additional network cost of $10,000, Candidate 2 improves in customer service level by 20 miles and is achieved at an additional network cost of $40,000, and Candidate 3 improves customer service level by 5 miles and is achieved at an additional network cost of $7,500. Decentralization 2 will recommend the third candidate because it costs the least.

Unfortunately, Decentralization 2 may recommend a decentralization candidate that has minimal impact on customer service level because it is focused on network costs alone. In fact, the logistics network designer may want to balance network costs with customer service levels. Therefore, a better question to address is; Which network decentralization will cost the least per mile of customer service level improvement (like Consolidation 3, this question addresses which candidate will give me the biggest bang for the buck). To answer this question, we will calculate the ratio **additional network cost per mile of improvement:**

$$\frac{\text{Additional network cost}}{\text{Improvement in customer service level}}$$

Decentralization 3 will recommend the decentralization candidate that results in the lowest additional network cost per mile of improvement.

Decentralization 3.

*Suggest the decentralization candidate having the lowest **additional network cost per mile of improvement** (additional network cost/improvement in customer service level).*

If this criterion were used instead, LogNet would recommend the Candidate 1 because it has the lowest additional network cost per mile of improvement. Here are the relevant calculations:

$$\text{Candidate 1: } 10{,}000/10 = 1{,}000$$

$$\text{Candidate 2: } 40{,}000/20 = 2{,}000$$

$$\text{Candidate 3: } 7{,}500/5 = 2{,}500$$

Finally, another reason for network decentralization, besides improving customer service level, is that total network costs can be reduced. Adding another warehouse may be bene cial to the extent that the outbound transportation cost savings resulting from an additional warehouse (i.e., customers are now located closer to the new warehouse) exceeds the increase in inventory carrying costs (because inventory becomes more distributed) and the additional warehousing xed costs. Hence a fourth decentralization procedure looks at the possibility of reducing network costs.

Decentralization 4.

Suggest the decentralization candidate that will result in the greatest network cost savings.

In fact, it is often be the case that *no* decentralization candidate will reduce total network costs. If this is true, Decentralization 4 will not suggest any decentralization candidate.

Table 7.6 summarizes the three consolidation and four decentralization procedures described in this section. The seven procedures may be invoked at any point during the creation of a network design. In general, a user will request one of the consolidation procedures to reduce total network costs. After all, consolidation results in shutting down a warehouse (thereby eliminating the xed costs associated with a warehouse), as well as lower inventory carrying costs. Consolidation 1 is the most aggressive consolidation procedure in terms of reducing network costs. Consolidation 2 and Consolidation 3 are more balanced approaches, both of which consider deterioration to customer service level as well. If a network designer is especially concerned about customer service level, Consolidation 2 recommends the candidate that is least damaging. If a network designer instead wants to create a network that makes best use of a company's money, then Consolidation 3 should be used instead.

In general, the decentralization procedures are invoked when a network designer wishes to improve customer service level. Decentralization 1, in particular, is the most aggressive procedure in this respect because it suggests

Table 7.6. A Summary of the Seven Model-Based Reasoning Procedures

Consolidation Procedures
will suggest the consolidation candidate that results in:

Consolidation 1
Greatest reduction in network costs

Consolidation 2
A reduction in network costs achieved with the least damage to customer service level

Consolidation 3*
Highest cost savings per mile of deterioration

Decentralization Procedures
will suggest the decentralization candidate that results in:

Decentralization 1
Greatest improvement in customer service level

Decentralization 2
An improvement in customer service level achieved at the lowest possible additional cost

Decentralization 3*
Lowest additional network cost per mile of improvement

Decentralization 4
Greatest reduction in network costs

the candidate that will most improve customer service level, regardless of cost. Decentralization 2 and Decentralization 3 (like Consolidation 2 and Consolidation 3) balance customer service level with network cost. If increasing network cost is a big concern, then Decentralization 2 will suggest the candidate that improves customer service at the lowest possible additional cost. If the network designer wants to make the most effective use of the company's money, then Decentralization 3 is the appropriate procedure to request.

It is possible for a decentralization to reduce network costs (although in most cases this is not likely because decentralization results in higher warehousing costs as well as higher inventory carrying costs). This will happen when the reduction in transportation costs (both inbound and outbound) is more than enough to offset the increase in these costs. This is the reason for Decentralization 4.

Problem-Solving Using LogNet: Two Scenarios

How do all the pieces t together? What are some of the steps that a user would take to seek out advice by the system? To demonstrate how to use LogNet, we

---

*Consolidation 3 and Decentralization 3 were never added to the actual implementation of LogNet as described in the original article. R. Nakatsu, "Designing Business Logistics Networks Using Model-Based Reasoning and Heuristic-Based Searching," *Expert Systems with Applications* 29, no. 4 (2005), 735–745.

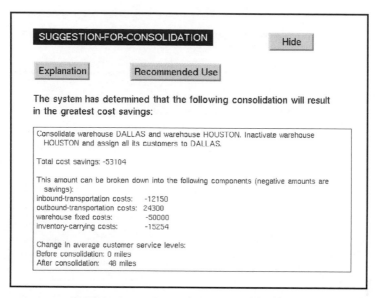

Figure 7.13. Consolidation 1 recommendation.

will look at two simple problems: rst, a consolidation problem and, second, a decentralization problem.

A Consolidation Problem. First, let us return to Figure 7.11, which represents a completely decentralized network: All ve customer zones are assigned a warehouse located in the same city; hence the customer service level (average customer-to-warehouse distance) is 0.

Suppose we are given the following goal for redesigning this network:

Design the logistics network such that the customer service level can deteriorate to 20 miles. Your goal is to design the network at the lowest possible cost.

LogNet allows us to re-design the network and calculate new benchmarks (see Figure 7.12 for the network benchmarks). The **Consolidation 1** procedure is rst requested, and its recommendation is displayed in Figure 7.13. It suggests that warehouses Dallas and Houston be consolidated into one warehouse Dallas. A total cost savings of $53,104 results from this consolidation. LogNet also provides a breakdown of the cost savings by network cost type. For example, while warehouse xed costs decrease by $50,000, outbound transportation increase by $24,300

In addition, LogNet also shows that the customer service level deteriorates from 0 miles to 48 miles. However, our customer service goal is 20 miles, so this consolidation results in an unacceptable deterioration in customer service level. Therefore, we will request **Consolidation 2**. Remember that Consolidation 2, unlike Consolidation 1, will request the consolidation that results in a

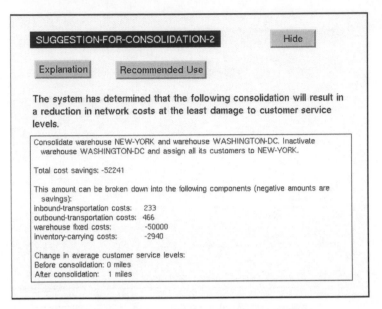

Figure 7.14. Consolidation 1 recommendation.

cost savings but at the lowest level of deterioration to customer service level. The recommendation of Consolidation 2 is shown in Figure 7.14. It suggests that warehouses New York and Washington, DC be consolidated into warehouse New York. A total cost savings of $52,241 results from this consolidation. The customer service level deteriorates only to 1 mile, so this is much better alternative. The solution to this problem is given in Figure 7.15. We may continue to request one of the consolidation procedures because we are allowed to deteriorate customer service level to 20 miles.

A Decentralization Problem. Figure 7.16 represents the converse of the previous problem: The logistics network in this case is completely consolidated. All customers are assigned to a single warehouse. In this example, the four customer zones are assigned to the warehouse located in Dallas. Two other warehouses, Memphis and New York, are candidate warehouses for decentralizing the network. The network benchmarks for this network are displayed in Figure 7.17.

Suppose we must re-design the network so that it satis es the following goal:

Design the logistics network such that you achieve the best customer service level, regardless of the additional network costs.

Because we are not concerned with network costs, **Decentralization 1** should be requested. Remember that Decentralization 1 displays the decentralization opportunity that results in the greatest improvement to your customer service levels.

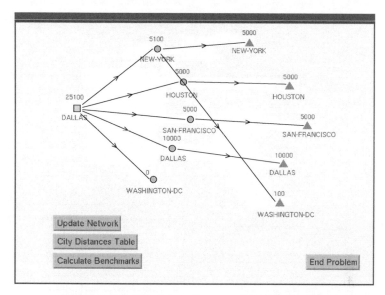

Figure 7.15. Solution to the consolidation problem.

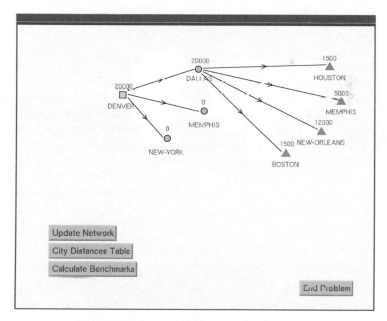

Figure 7.16. A decentralization problem.

	Benchmarks	percent (%)	Difference
Transportation Costs:			
Inbound--Factory to Warehouse	156200.0	27.2	0.0
Outbound--Warehouse to Customer	223970.0	39.0	0.0
Total Transportation Costs	380170.0	66.1	
Warehousing Costs:			
Fixed Costs	50000.0	8.7	0.0
Variable Handling Costs	100000.0	17.4	0.0
Total Warehousing Costs	150000.0	26.1	
Inventory Carrying Costs	44721.0	7.8	0.0
Total Network Costs	574891.0		0.0
CUSTOMER SERVICE LEVEL BENCHMARKS			
Average Distance (Customer-to-Warehouse)	559.9		0.0
% Customers Less than 500 Miles Away	92.5		0.0
% Customers Less than 1,000 Miles Away	92.5		0.0

OK

Figure 7.17. Network benchmarks for the decentralization problem.

The recommendation is displayed in Figure 7.18. As it turns out the recommendation for **Decentralization 1** is the same as that given by **Decentralization 2**. After we add warehouse New York to the network and attach factory Denver and customer zone Boston, we can request the decentralization procedure once again. The second time we request Decentralization 1, the system advises us to add warehouse Memphis and attach customer zone Memphis to this warehouse. Finally, we should attach customer zone New Orleans to warehouse Memphis, because it is closer to Memphis (390 miles) than its current assignment to warehouse Dallas (496 miles). The nal solution to the decentralization problem is given in Figure 7.19.

Fine-Tuning with Heuristic-Based Searching

The astute reader may have noticed a problem with the model-based procedures discussed earlier: For a network design with many nodes, the problem could easily become computationally infeasible, because there are so many network design possibilities to consider. Such combinatorial problems are well known in AI. In Chapter 1, we identi ed one well-known example, the traveling salesman

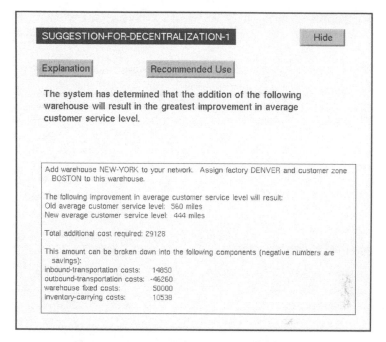

Figure 7.18. Decentralization 1 recommendation.

problem, a problem that quickly becomes computationally intractable. Here is a summary of the problem: Given a set of cities, nd the route that will take a salesperson to each of the cities with the shortest mileage. One possibility is to try all the possible routes and pick the shortest (an exhaustive search through all the possibilities). However, for n cities the number of routes is $n!$, a number that quickly becomes very large, as the number of cities increases.

We noted earlier that LogNet considers $n * (n - 1)$ consolidations for a network design containing n warehouses. However, we also pointed out that this number represents only two warehouses taken at a time. It does not consider three warehouses at a time, four warehouses at a time, and, more generally, n warehouses at a time. Obviously the number of possibilities grows very large with network designs containing many warehouses, especially when we consider all possible mergers of warehouses taken n at a time.

If LogNet is to be able to scale up to problems of increasing size and complexity, it must employ means other than exhaustive searching. One possibility is to use heuristic-based searching to cut down on the number of possibilities that LogNet considers. Heuristics are short-cut procedures that search for satisfactory, but not necessarily optimal solutions to a problem. A heuristic reduces the time spent in the search for the solution of the problem, by employing a rule or computational procedure that limits the number of alternative solutions to a

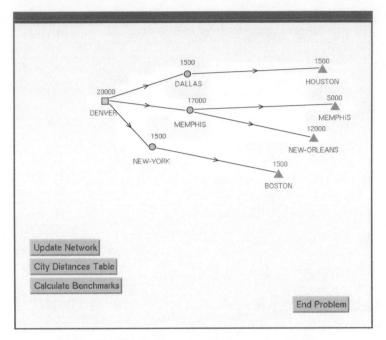

Figure 7.19. Solution to the decentralization problem.

problem. There are a number of possible heuristics that we may use to limit the possible consolidations and decentralizations that LogNet will consider.

One heuristic is to consider consolidations of only warehouses that are close to one another. In fact, a human logistics decision maker will often eyeball a network design and merge the warehouses that seem close to one another. We might implement this heuristic by considering only consolidation candidates that are within n miles of each other (n could be an input parameter set by the user). For example, we might allow only consolidations of warehouses that are within 400 miles of each other. If we return to the logistics network as given by Figure 7.11 (where $5 * 4 = 20$ consolidations, taken two at a time, are possible) LogNet would then consider only consolidations between Houston and Dallas and between New York and Washington, DC. Along these same lines, another technique we might use is to regionalize a network. That is, we might divide a logistics network into separate regions, such as warehouses in the Northeast, the South, the West, and the Midwest. (A warehouse's region would be speci ed as an attribute of the warehouse.) LogNet would consider only consolidations of warehouses within the same region.

Let us consider another heuristic used by logistics decision makers: The most likely sites for warehouses are those that are in or around centers of greatest demand.[11] To implement this heuristic, we could scan our network design for "high-demand" customer zones that are served by a "distant" warehouse. Again we could let the user de ne what high-demand and distant mean. If, for example, high-demand is de ned as greater than 10,000 and distant is de ned as greater than 500 miles, then LogNet would search for high-demand customer zones that are connected to a warehouse located more than 500 miles away and would suggest a decentralization—that is, adding a warehouse that is closer to the high-demand customer zone.

A third heuristic is given by the following: The most expensive customers from a distribution standpoint are those that purchase in small quantities (i.e., low-demand customer zones) and are located at the end of transportation lanes.[12] If the goal is to reduce network costs, LogNet will scan the network to search for low-demand customers zones (lower than, say, 1000—again, an input parameter set by an end user) that contain a warehouse in the same city or a nearby city. LogNet would then suggest that this warehouse be shut down and its inventory consolidated with the closest warehouse.

These are but a few possibilities for cutting down on searching through a very large design space. There are many more possibilities, and they will enable us to employ model-based reasoning techniques to solve a wide class of problems in logistics network design, despite the inherent combinatorial nature of the design task.

Alternatively, the warehouse location problem in business logistics management can be tackled using a variety of optimization techniques well known in the management sciences. Such quantitative methods as linear programming, integer programming, and dynamic programming have been successfully employed to nd the optimal solutions to many types of network design problems. For example, optimization techniques can nd the minimum network cost satisfying a variety of constraints (e.g., customer service level must be at least a certain level).

However, these methods, which use precise analytical methods to evaluate alternatives, frequently compromise too much in terms of exibility and realism of the problem solving situation. Because they impose a strong mathematical structure on the problem, they hardly lend themselves to the visual interactive modeling approach of LogNet. On the other hand, heuristic-based searching, together with visual interactive modeling, are better suited to more open-ended design tasks, because they provide guidelines to reason about a business logistic networks in a more intuitive way. This approach offers an alternative to optimization methods if one wishes to have more exibility in terms of problem formulation and the incremental testing and design of different network design. Their major disadvantage, however, is that they do not guarantee optimal solutions.

DISCUSSION

Our discussion of model-based reasoning has taken us systematically through two types of applications. On the one hand, a diagnostic application employs diagrams to nd out which of several components is responsible for a malfunctioning device or system. This type of system works backwards in the sense that it rst starts out with a discrepancy between predicted and actual system behavior and then looks systematically through the system components to nd which one is the culprit for the discrepancy. On the other hand, a network design application is more dynamic in the sense that new diagrams can be generated and model-based reasoning can evaluate these new diagrams according to a set of benchmarks. In LogNet the benchmarks are network cost and customer service level. This type of application is forward moving in the sense that it searches "the design space" for better network designs (in the case of LogNet it searches for candidate consolidations and decentralizations). Unfortunately, without the use of heuristics, these applications quickly become computationally intractable because the design space grows very large as the size of the network increases.

While diagnostic and network design applications are different in nature, what underlies the two domains is that they both employ model-based reasoning to implement their capabilities. Both start out with a diagram of some kind, and both reason with the structure as represented by the diagram. The diagrams, in this respect, are not merely descriptive of system structure but are also used to infer solutions to dif cult problems. This is really the raison d'être of model-based reasoning: Diagrams that represent system structure are employed to help us solve problems.

We noted at the outset of this chapter that model-based reasoning represents a departure from rule-based expert systems. For certain classes of problems it would be very dif cult to enumerate a collection of IF–THEN rules to capture the knowledge and expertise of the domain. For example, the designer of a rule-based diagnostic expert system is quite likely to miss every possibility in the domain—that is, every possible symptom–fault combination must be thought out in advance and encoded as an IF–THEN rule. An important bene t of model-based reasoning is the ability to provide more comprehensive coverage of a domain *without having to enumerate every possibility beforehand*. Indeed, many model-based reasoning systems are able to detect novel faults and come up with novel solutions to problems that a system designer had failed to anticipate beforehand.

Here is a summary of the main bene ts of model-based reasoning:

- **More coherence in the system**. Model-based reasoning may serve as a unifying foundation for a complex expert system. By structuring an expert system around an underlying domain model, as represented by a diagram, a system can be developed with more organization and coherence. Such coherence can be used to integrate several related problems into one common framework.

- **Generic power of model-based reasoning**. Model-based reasoning can apply to an entire class of structures and behaviors. This means that separate rules do not need to be speci ed for each speci c case in the problem-solving domain. Rather, they can be speci ed for large classes of structures and behaviors. This may, in part, address the problem of brittle expert systems that break down when you try to extend its capabilities, even to problems closely related to the original problem.

- **Support for graphical user interfaces**. Model-based reasoning systems typically exploit the capabilities of powerful graphical user interfaces that allow for multileveled descriptions of complex domains. Users, for example, may be able to click on components of a graphical model to obtain a more ne-grained description of a component. Conversely, users may seek a higher-level system description by moving up a level. In this respect, model-based reasoning can provide a more naturalistic human-computer interaction with an intelligent system.

One might be tempted to conclude that model-based reasoning is always a superior form of reasoning and represents an evolutionary step forward from its predecessor, rule-based reasoning. However, such an easy conclusion belies the fact that model-based reasoning is not suitable for all types of problems and domains and may actually be detrimental in certain cases. It is certainly not a panacea that can solve all classes of problems requiring expertise.

In fact, certain classes of problems will not work well with model-based reasoning techniques.[13] First of all, the system may simply be too dif cult to model: There may be very subtle interaction effects among a variety of components, and predicting system behavior from a model structure would be impossible to do. In such situations, it would be much easier to capture the knowledge in the form of IF–THEN rules. On the other end of the spectrum, the problem-solving domain may be so simple, that the use of a model may be overkill. It would be much easier to simply enumerate the rules, which can much more easily and succinctly capture the expertise required to solve problems in the domain.

Throughout our discussion, and in the examples presented in this chapter and the previous ones, we have presented model-based reasoning and rule-based expert systems as two separate and distinct techniques used to capture and represent expert knowledge. In fact, one could create an expert system that integrates model-based reasoning with rule-based reasoning—the development of one type need not preclude the other. For example, the designer of an intelligent system may use model-based reasoning for base cases in a problem-solving domain, and ne-tune these cases with the addition of rules. Thus it is possible to integrate model-based reasoning with rule-based reasoning, which would result in a more powerful system than a system developed using only one of the techniques alone could. Indeed, this is very much the trend in arti cial intelligence today: A number of AI techniques can be embedded within a single program to create a more powerful application.

There is a vast array of possibilities of model-based reasoning that we have not considered in this chapter. In recent years, applications have been developed to perform problem-solving tasks in a wide variety of domains. For example, intelligent systems employing model-based reasoning have been developed to perform fault diagnosis of industrial gas turbines, to help manage type 1 diabetes, to locate software bugs in VHDL programs and to monitor and diagnose learner behaviors for an automated tutoring system, to name but a few examples.[14] In many of these cases, these systems incorporate a variety of techniques, not only model-based reasoning but also case-based reasoning, temporal reasoning, and probabilistic reasoning, suggesting, once again, that model-based reasoning techniques are frequently embedded within larger intelligent systems.

One tantalizing possibility is to employ model-based reasoning techniques for the diagnosis of diseases in medicine.[15] Such medical applications might allow a doctor to better understand the underlying causal mechanisms of disease processes. Graphical user interfaces employing causal diagrams and models might be created that explain a patient's illness. For example, using model-based reasoning, a program might be developed to reason about the details of the disease process, to recognize how one disease can alter another, to understand the effects of treatments and medications on the patient, and to sort out what is responsible for the disease itself. The possibilities of model-based reasoning are endless and promising: They could potentially result in the development and proliferation of many innovative AI applications.

ENDNOTES

1. Michael D. Williams, James D. Hollan, and Albert L. Stevens, "An Overview of STEAMER: An Advanced Computer-Assisted Instruction System for Propulsion Engineering," *Behavior Research Methods & Instrumentation* 13 (1981), 85–90.
2. John C. Kunz, "Model Based Reasoning in CIM," in *Proceedings from the First International Conference on Expert Systems and the Leading Edge in Production Planning and Control* (1987), pp. 93–112.
3. This terminology is from Johan De Kleer and John S. Brown, "A Qualitative Physics Based on Con uences," in *Formal Theories of the Commonsense World*. Norwood, NJ: Ablex Pub, 1985, pp. 109–183
4. See for example, Johan de Kleer and John S. Brown, "Assumptions and Ambiguities in Mechanistic Mental Models," in *Mental Models*. Hillsdale, NJ: L. Erlbaum Associates, 1983, pp. 155–190. Johan de Kleer, "How Circuits Work," *Artificial Intelligence* 24 (1984), 205–280; and Kenneth D. Forbus, "Qualitative Physics: Past, Present, and Future," in *Exploring Artificial Intelligence*. San Mateo, CA: Morgan Kaufmann, 1988, pp. 297–346.
5. Randall Davis and Walter Hamscher, "Model-based Reasoning: Troubleshooting," in *Exploring Artificial Intelligence*. San Mateo, CA: Morgan Kaufmann, 1988, p. 299.
6. The discussion on model-based diagnosis presented in this chapter is based on David and Hamscher, pp. 297–346 and Randall Davis, "Diagnostic Reasoning Based on Structure and Behavior," *Artificial Intelligence* 24 (1984), 347–410.
7. Davis and Hamscher propose a slightly different framework for model-based diagnosis. Under their scheme, hypothesis testing addresses the question: Given a set of suspects implicated during hypothesis generation, which of them could have failed so as to account for all available observations of behavior? The technique they propose is referred to as **constraint suspension**. This technique involves retracting all assumptions about the component's behavior ("suspending its constraints") or removing it from the network temporarily. If the network is still inconsistent even with the

suspect's constraint suspension, the suspect is exonerated; otherwise the component is still a part of the suspect set.

8. This quote is in Ronald H. Ballou, *Business Logistics Management*, *3rd ed.*. Englewood Cliffs, NJ: Prentice-Hall, 1992, p. 4.

9. Douglas M. Lambert and James R. Stock, *Strategic Logistics Management*, 3rd ed. Homewood, IL: Irwin, 1993.

10. The discussion on LogNet is from Robbie T. Nakatsu, "Designing Business Logistics Networks Using Model-Based Reasoning and Heuristic-Based Searching," *Expert Systems with Applications* 29, no. 4 (2005), 735–745.

11. Ronald H. Ballou, "Heuristics: Rules of Thumb for Logistics Decision Making," *Journal of Business Logistics* 10, no. 1 (1989), 122–132.

12. Ibid.

13. See Davis and Hamscher, p. 305, for a discussion on the limitations of model-based reasoning.

14. There are numerous examples of model-based diagnosis in the literature. For example, R. Milne, C. Nicol, and L. Trave-Massuyes, "TIGER with Model-Based Diagnosis: Initial Deployment," *Knowledge-Based Systems* 14, no. 3–4, (2001), 213–222. S. Montani et al., "Integrating Model-Based Decision Support in a Multi-Modal Reasoning System for Managing Type 1 Diabetic Patients," *Artificial Intelligence in Medicine* 29, no. 1–2 (2003), 131–151. F. Wotawa, "Debugging VHDL Designs Using Model-Based Reasoning," *Artificial Intelligence in Engineering* 14, no. 4 (2000), 331–351.

15. See, for example, Ramesh S. Patil, "Arti cial Intelligence Techniques for Diagnostic Reasoning in Medicine," in *Exploring Artificial Intelligence*. San Mateo, CA: Morgan Kaufmann, 1988, pp. 347–380. He explores the arti cial intelligence techniques used for diagnosing diseases in medicine. Of particular relevance is their experimental program called ABEL. ABEL's knowledge base attempts to capture the underlying causal mechanisms of disease processes.

CHAPTER 8

INEXACT REASONING WITH CERTAINTY FACTORS AND BAYESIAN NETWORKS

Human decision makers face uncertainty on a daily basis. At times, we don't possess enough knowledge to solve a problem at hand, and therefore struggle to nd ways to ll the gaps of our own knowledge and expertise. At other times, the data we are given are noisy and imprecise, or worse, we have no data at all on which to base a decision. On the other hand, there may be situations in which all the data are at our disposal, but precise and exact methods do not exist that tell us how to process and analyze the data. Somehow, though, human decision makers—through intuition, creativity, leaps of imagination, or sheer will and perseverance—often manage to cope with uncertainty and arrive at pretty good decisions.

In fact, much of human expertise is really about the ability to render reasonably good decisions despite the complexity and uncertainty of a problem-solving task. A doctor, for example, may have to deal with lab test results that are imprecise or symptoms that may indicate the presence of a disease with varying degrees of certainty. Despite this, the doctor must come to a conclusion as to what is ailing a patient in order to prescribe an appropriate treatment. Similarly, an expert system, or any other kind of intelligent system for that matter, should be able to represent and process uncertain data, otherwise the system will be far less capable of coping with an array of real-world problems where data are often incomplete, inconsistent, noisy, or altogether missing.

Indeed, uncertainty pervades the real world and is present in every area of expertise. Its sources can be classi ed into two types: imperfect domain knowledge and imperfect case data.[1] In the rst case, the theory of the domain may be incomplete. Therefore, experts, by necessity must employ heuristics or rules of thumb to arrive at satisfactory, but not necessarily optimal solutions. In a rule-based expert system, in which expertise is captured as a collection of IF–THEN rules, a knowledge engineer* is forced to establish concrete correlations between a rule's premise and its conclusions. Unfortunately, in many domains, these correlations are weak and not clearly understood. (Indeed, science is forever progressing so that new and stronger empirical associations are continually being discovered and ne-tuned). Moreover, in many domains, there are contradictory opinions as to what the solutions to the problems are. Combining the views of multiple experts into a "consensus" knowledge base can be a huge challenge.

In the second case, the actual case data may be imprecise or unreliable. Reasons for imprecision might include any of the following: the unreliability of sensors such that precise measurements are not possible, lab test results that are only approximate, reports that are subjective and ambiguous, evidence that may be contradictory, and an assortment of human errors and biases that can stymie even the most exacting and meticulous of experts. Even when it is possible to collect more precise data, it may not be practical or reasonable to do so. One case in point: It may be possible for a doctor to obtain better patient data by means of some type of invasive surgery, but such procedures could be costly and risky to the patient's health. Another limitation is that collecting more data takes time, and quick decisions sometimes need to be made. In a moment of crisis, for example, a decision maker must rely on incomplete information to come to a quick decision, and there is simply not enough time to gather all the data and perform a rigorous and painstaking analysis on the collected data.

Because of the presence of uncertainty in almost every interesting domain, a good expert system must be able to handle uncertainty. For this reason, a number of formalisms have been developed for handling inexact reasoning, among them: fuzzy logic, the theory of belief functions (also known as Dempster-Shafer theory of evidence), subjective probability theory (including Bayesian reasoning), and certainty factors.[2] This chapter focuses on two of the more popular inexact reasoning paradigms: certainty factors and Bayesian reasoning. A theme that emerges in this discussion is that inexact reasoning can be aided by a diagrammatic representation. This chapter will show how the certainty factors approach and Bayesian networks can employ in uence and causal diagrams to illustrate their reasoning process, and shed light on how uncertainty propagates in a system.

CERTAINTY FACTORS

We begin our discussion with certainty factors, because it is the easier of the two approaches to understand. Indeed, it was ically invented by the developers of MYCIN in the 1970s as a convenient, albeit not mathematically correct approach to dealing with processing of uncertain data and conclusions.[3] MYCIN, as you

---

*The knowledge engineer is the person who designs and implements the expert system.

may recall from Chapter 5, was a rule-based expert system that was developed to diagnose (and recommend treatments for) bacterial infections. It allowed for the representation of IF–THEN rules in the following form:

```
IF (condition₁ holds with certainty x₁ AND condition₂ holds with
      certainty x₂ . . . AND conditionₙ holds with certainty xₙ)
THEN (conclusion₁ holds with certainty y₁ AND conclusion₂ holds with
      certainty y₂ . . . AND conclusionₙ holds with certainty yₙ)
```

In MYCIN the conditions typically represent evidence, such as lab test results and patient symptoms; the conclusions represent the hypothesis (e.g., the disease that the patient has) given the evidence. The values of x represent the degree to which the evidence was thought to be true; it is a value in the range $(0, 1)$. The values of y represent the degree to which the conclusion follows from the evidence. MYCIN allowed a value to be assigned in the range $(-1, +1)$. A value of 1 means that the conclusion is certain to be true whenever all the conditions are met, while a value of -1 means that the conclusion is certain to be false under the same conditions. Table 8.1 provides one way of assigning these values to a rule, obtained by interviewing a domain expert. For example, a cardiologist, a specialist in the diseases of the heart, might state: "I am almost certain (but not 100% certain) that given the patient's cholesterol readings (both HDL and LDL readings), as well as other patient risk factors, that the patient would bene t from a treatment of cholesterol-lowering drugs." Based on this information, the knowledge engineer might assign a certainty factor of $+0.8$ to a rule that recommended cholesterol-lowering drugs.

How would an expert system process certainty factors when the evidence is imprecise or the data are noisy? Here is a rule from MYCIN[4] with (ctitious) certainty factors assigned:

```
IF (1) the stain of the organism is gramneg (0.9) AND
   (2) the morphology of the organism is rod (0.7) AND
   (3) the aerobicity of the organism is aerobic (0.4)
THEN there is strongly suggestive evidence (0.8) that the class of
organism is enterobacteriaceae
```

Table 8.1. An Interpretation of Certainty Factors

De nitely not	-1.0
Almost certainly not	-0.8
Probably not	-0.6
Maybe not	-0.4
Unknown (neutral)	-0.2 to $+0.2$
Maybe	$+0.4$
Probably	$+0.6$
Almost certainly	$+0.8$
De nitely	$+1.0$

One convention is to take the *minimum* of the certainty factors whenever a conjunction (AND) of conditions is involved. In this example we take the minimum of (0.9, 0.7, 0.4), which is 0.4. The reason for using the minimum of the certainty factors is that we are con dent in a conjunction of conditions only to the extent that we are con dent it is weakest element. This is rather like saying that a chain is only as strong as its weakest link.[5]

To calculate the overall certainty of the conclusion, taking the uncertainty of the premises into account, we would apply the simple calculation:

```
CF (action of the rule) = CF (premise) X CF (conclusion)
```

Hence, by this formula, we may calculate the certainty factor:

```
CF (organism is enterobacteriaceae) = 0.4 * 0.8 = 0.32
```

Suppose instead of a conjunction of conditions, the rule is encoded as a disjunction (OR) of conditions as in the following:

```
IF (1) the stain of the organism is gramneg (0.9) OR
   (2) the morphology of the organism is rod (0.7) OR
   (3) the aerobicity of the organism is aerobic (0.4)
THEN there is strongly suggestive evidence (0.8) that the class
   of organism is enterobacteriaceae
```

In this case, we would instead use the maximum of (0.9, 0.7., 0.4). The argument here is that we are con dent of a disjunction of conditions to the extent that we are con dent in its strongest element. Hence, for the disjunctive rule, the certainty factor is calculated as follows:

```
CF (organism is enterobacteriacease) = 0.9 * 0.8 = 0.72
```

Sometimes two or more rules can affect the same hypothesis. How would an expert system propagate certainty factors when this occurred? Suppose, for example, that we are given the following three rules, which all affect the hypothesis H:

```
Rule 1:   IF A and B and C
          THEN H (CF 0.8)

Rule 2:   IF D or E
          THEN H (CF 0.9)

Rule 3:   IF F
          THEN H (CF −1.0)*
```

*Rule 3 expresses disbelief in hypothesis H; hence certainty factor −1.0.

How do we propagate certainty factors if we observe all the evidence in the above three rules? That is, A, B, C, D, E, and F are all observed with varying degrees of certainty. To calculate a combined certainty factor involving cf_1 (the certainty factor established by one rule) and cf_2 (the certainty factor established by a second rule) we would use one of the following equations.[6]

Propagation Eq. 1. Belief in hypothesis increases ($cf_1 > 0$ and $cf_2 > 0$)

$$cf(cf_1, cf_2) = cf_1 + cf_2(1 - cf_1)$$

Propagation Eq. 2. Disbelief in hypothesis increases ($cf_1 < 0$ and $cf_2 < 0$)

$$cf(cf_1, cf_2) = cf_1 + cf_2(1 + cf_1)$$

Propagation Eq. 3. Contradictory conclusions (certainty factors have opposite signs):

$$(cf_1 > 0 \text{ and } cf_2 < 0) \text{ or } (cf_1 < 0 \text{ and } cf_2 > 0)$$

$$cf(cf_1, cf_2) = \frac{cf_1 + cf_2}{1 - \min(|cf_1\|cf_2|)}$$

where $|cf_1|$ and $|cf_2|$ are absolute magnitudes of cf_1 and cf_2, respectively.

Let us suppose that we rst observe A (cf 0.8), B (cf 0.4), and C (cf 0.6). Based on this evidence, Rule 1 executes and the cf (H) is calculated as:

```
min(0.8,0.4,0.6) * 0.8 = 0.4 * 0.8 = 0.32
```

Next we observe D (cf 0.8) and E (cf 0.9). Based on this evidence Rule 2 is red and the cf is calculated as:

```
max(0.8,0.9) * 0.9 = 0.9 * 0.9 = 0.81
```

By Propagation Eq. 1 (because cf_1 and cf_2 are both positive), we can calculate the combined certainty factor as:

```
0.32 + 0.81 (1 - 0.32) = 0.87
```

This example shows that the two rules together result in an incremental increase of belief in the hypothesis H resulting in a certainty factor $= 0.87$.

Finally, when we observe F (cf 0.6), Rule 3 is executed and the cf is calculated as:

```
0.6 * -1.0 = -0.6
```

Because this results in a contradictory conclusion (i.e., cf_1 and cf_2 have opposite signs), we apply Propagation Eq. 3 to obtain the nal certainty factor:

$$\frac{0.87 + -0.6}{1 - \min(|0.87\| - 0.6|)} = 0.675$$

In accordance with our expectation, the certainty factor of H has decreased (from 0.87 to 0.675).

Belief Networks

Belief networks are diagrams that show how the beliefs (or disbeliefs) in hypotheses are updated, as new evidence is introduced. They provide a convenient way to display how certainty factors are propagated in a rule-based reasoning system. We will use the notation adopted in Chapter 6, when we introduced the notion of Rule Trace Diagrams. These diagrams show graphically how the conditions of a rule are linked to its conclusions. If you recall, two different notations are used to represent the conjunction of conditions and the disjunction of conditions (Figure 8.1). The main difference between the two notations is that only one arrow points to the conclusion when representing conjunctive conditions, whereas separate arrows point from each of the conditions to the conclusion node when representing disjunctive conditions.

Using this notation, Rule 1, Rule 2, and Rule 3 can be represented as in Figure 8.2. Unfortunately, this representation is ambiguous because it does not

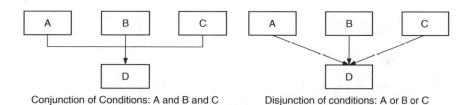

Conjunction of Conditions: A and B and C   Disjunction of conditions: A or B or C

Figure 8.1. Notation used to represent dependencies in rules.

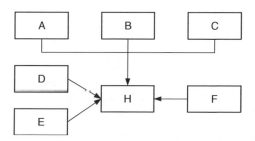

Figure 8.2. Representing dependencies of Rule 1, Rule 2, and Rule 3: rst pass.

show that three separate rules are used to determine H. As it reads now, it could just as well represent the single rule:

```
If (A and B and C) or D or E or F
Then H
```

Therefore, to disambiguate the diagram, we will introduce a third symbol, the circle, to indicate the rule that the condition(s) belong to (Figure 8.3). This diagram explicitly indicates which conditions belong to which rule. Moreover, the certainty factors are indicated on the diagram: The numbers in the squares represent the certainty factors for each of the conditions, A through H, while the calculated certainty factors are indicated on the appropriate part of the diagram.

Malware Detection System. Let us now look at a more detailed example of how certainty factors can be propagated on a belief network. In this example, a rule-based expert system determines the likelihood that a computer is infected with malware. It bases its determination on three factors: (1) whether the computer is safe or not, (2) the riskiness of the user's behaviors, and (3) the reliability of the system.

The ﬁrst three rules determine whether a computer is safe or not:

```
R1:  IF (no firewall AND computer is not connected to router) OR
         (user is admin)
     THEN computer is unprotected (CF 1.0)

R2:  IF (operating system is not updated OR browser is not updated)
     THEN software is not updated (CF 1.0)
```

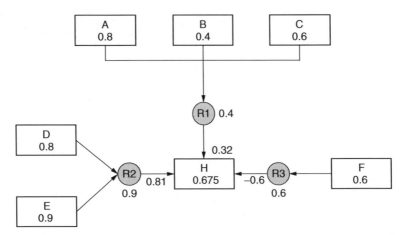

Figure 8.3. Belief network of Rule 1, Rule 2, and Rule 3 with certainty factors.

```
R3:  IF (computer hardware is unprotected OR software is not
         updated OR no antivirus software)
     THEN computer is unsafe (cf 1.0)
```

R1 determines whether a computer is unprotected or not. The rst clause states that a computer is unprotected when both (1) there is no rewall and (2) a computer is connected to a router. A router can serve as a security device that lters inbound and outbound traf c; therefore both a rewall and a router are not needed—one or the other alone should suf ce. Second, a computer can be deemed unsafe simply because a user logs on as administrator—an administrator has too many privileges (e.g., the ability to update system les) that malicious code can take advantage of. It is more secure to run as a limited user.

To simplify these rules, they are stated in terms of characteristics that contribute to a system's vulnerability. For example the conclusion of R1 is "computer is unprotected." R1 could also have been expressed as "computer is protected" with $+1.0$ representing the fact that the computer is de nitely protected and -1.0 representing the fact that the computer is de nitely unprotected.

All three rules above have certainty factors of 1.0; hence there is no uncertainty associated with the conclusion when the conditions of the rules are satis ed. Moreover, all variables used in the conditions are yes/no variables, so that if the condition is true, the variable has a certainty factor of 1.0, and 0.0 otherwise.

R2 determines whether the computer software is updated or not. If either the operating system is not updated or the browser software is not updated (i.e., the most current version is not being used), then the R2 reaches the conclusion that the software in not updated (cf = 1.0). Finally, R3 looks at both conclusions reached by R1 (computer unprotected) and R2 (software not updated), together with whether the user has antivirus software installed. If even one of these three conditions is true, the computer is deemed unsafe.

Let's suppose that a user enters the following values in a consultation with the system (user responses are in boldface, and system cf assignments are in italics):

1. Is the rewall turned on? **No** (*No firewall*, $cf = 1.0$)
2. Is the computer connected to a router? **Yes** (*No router*, $cf = 0.0$)
3. Does the user log on as an administrator? **No** (*User admin*, $cf = 0.0$)
4. Is the operating system up-to-date? **No** (*OS not up to date*, $cf = 1.0$)
5. Is the browser up-to-date? **Yes** (*Browser not up to date*, $cf = 0.0$)
6. Is antivirus software installed? **Yes** (*No antivirus software*, $cf = 0.0$)

See Figure 8.4 for the belief network and how the certainty factors are propagated in the network. Based on these user responses, the system calculates the certainty factors for each of the rules—that is, cf(rule) = cf(premise) * cf(conclusion):

```
CF(R1) = max(min(1.0,0.0),0.0)) * 1.0 = 0.0
CF(R2) = max(1.0,0.0) * 1.0 = 1.0
CF(R3) = max(0.0,1.0,0.0) * 1.0 = 1.0
```

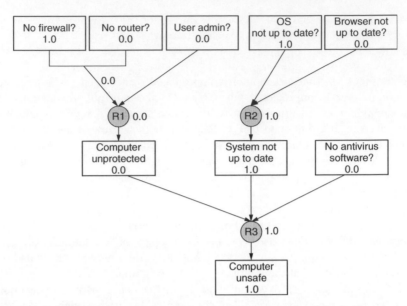

Figure 8.4. Belief network determining *computer unsafe* (certainty factors shown).

The belief network shows that while the computer is protected (*Computer unprotected*, $cf = 0.0$), and antivirus software is installed (*No antivirus software*, $cf = 0.0$), the system is not up to date (*System not up to date*, $cf = 1.0$). Therefore, in the end, it is concluded that the computer is unsafe (*Computer unsafe*, $cf = 1.0$).

The second factor that the system considers is the riskiness of the user's behaviors. The next three rules are used to gauge these risky activities:

```
R4:  IF user downloads files from risky sites
     THEN user behavior is risky (cf 0.7)


R5:  IF user clicks links on emails
     THEN user behavior is risky (cf 0.2)


R6:  IF user clicks file attachments on emails
     THEN user behavior is risky (cf 0.7)
```

R4 looks at whether the user downloads les from sites that are considered risky. File-sharing sites such as BitTorrent, Kazaa, Morpheus, Grokster, and Limewire are notorious for having spyware, Trojan horses, and other malware embedded in the les. R5 asks whether a user clicks links on e-mails. It is considered bad practice to click on links because this can lead to drive-by downloads, or malicious code installed on your computer simply by visiting a site. Finally, R6 considers whether a user clicks on le attachments in e-mails because these attachments may be infected with malware.

R4, R5, and R6 use certainty factors less than 1.0, which indicates that their conclusions are less than de nitive. This makes sense because "risky behavior" is an imprecise and unmeasurable user characteristic. File downloads and clicking on le attachments are considered riskier behaviors than clicking links in e-mails; hence, R4 and R6 are assigned higher certainty factors than R5. Furthermore, the conditions themselves are stated with varying degrees of certainty, because these risky behaviors are not black and white but involve varying degrees of involvement. For sake of argument, let us suppose that the system assigns the following values based on how frequently the user engages in the risky behavior:

All the time	1.0
Frequently	0.8
Sometimes	0.6
Occasionally	0.4
Rarely	0.2
Never	0.0

Once again, here are the user responses to the questions asked by the system (user responses are in boldface and system cf assignments are italics):

1. Do you download les from lesharing and other risky sites?
   Frequently (*Download risky files*, $cf = 0.8$)
2. Do you click links in e-mails?
   Sometimes (*Click email links*, $cf = 0.6$)
3. Do you click on le attachments in e-mails, even when you not expecting the le attachment?
   Rarely (*Click file attachments*, $cf = 0.2$)

Based on these responses, the system calculates the certainty factors for each of the rules:

```
CF(R4) = 0.7 * 0.8 = 0.56
CF(R5) = 0.2 * 0.6 = 0.12
CF(R6) = 0.7 * 0.2 = 0.14
```

Because these three rules all affect the same hypothesis and all are positive, the system calculates the combined certainty factor based on Propagation Eq. 1:

```
cf(cf_R4, cf_R5) = 0.56 + 0.12 * (1 - 0.56) = 0.6128
```

```
cf(cf_R4 + R5, cf_R6) = 0.6128 + 0.14 * (1 - 0.6128) = 0.667
```

Hence the certainty factor of the hypothesis that the user behavior is risky is **0.667**. See Figure 8.5 for the belief network and the associated certainty factors assigned to the appropriate nodes.

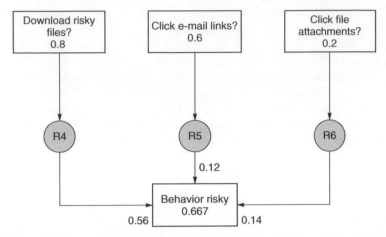

Figure 8.5. Belief network determining *behavior risky* (certainty factors shown).

The third and final factor is system reliability. A system infected with malware is often plagued with poor performance and unreliability. R7 through R10 will assess the system unreliability:

```
R7:   IF computer freezes
      THEN system is unreliable (cf 0.8)

R8:   IF computer crashes
      THEN system is unreliable (cf 1.0)

R9:   IF system is slow and there is sufficient RAM
      THEN system is unreliable (cf 0.4)
```

```
R10:  IF system is slow and there is not enough RAM
      THEN system is unreliable (cf -0.5)
```

R7 and R8 base system reliability on whether a system freezes or crashes. Because a system crash is more serious than a system freeze, the certainty factor is higher in R8 than in R7 (1.0 vs. 0.8). A third determinant of system reliability is whether the system is slow or not. A slow system, however, is not necessarily a symptom of system reliability; rather, it may be caused by insufficient RAM. Hence R10 assigns a negative certainty factor to reflect disbelief in the hypothesis that a system slowdown means that a system is unreliable.

The system consultation will involve the following questions and certainty factor assignments, based on the following user responses (user responses are in boldface, system assignments are in italics):

1. How often does your computer freeze?
   Weekly (*Computer freezes, cf* = 0.5)

2. How often does your computer crash?
   Monthly (*Computer crashes*, $cf = 0.2$)

For questions 1 and 2, the possible responses are (certainty factors are in parentheses): Constantly (1.0), Daily (0.8), Weekly (0.5), Monthly (0.2), Rarely (0.0)

3. How slow is your system?
   Annoyingly slow (*System slow*, $cf = 0.8$)

For question 3, the possible responses are Unresponsive (1.0), Annoyingly slow (0.8), Tolerably slow (0.5), Occasionally slow (0.2), Not slow (0.0)

4. How much RAM does your system have?
   512 MB (*RAM insufficient*, $cf = 0.6$) and (*RAM sufficient*, $cf = 0.0$)

Presumably, for question 4, the system will inquire what operating system the user has installed, together with other user requirements, and determine the sufficiency of the RAM based on what the user needs. We will assume that the RAM is insuf cient with certainty factor 0.6. Moreover, the system will also assign $cf = 0.0$ to the variable *RAM sufficient*. (Suf cient RAM, let us assume, is 2 GB).

Now that the system has gathered all certainty factors for the input conditions, it can now calculate and propagate the certainty factors to the other nodes of the belief network. First, it will calculate the certainty factors for each of the rules.

```
CF(R7)  = 0.5 * 0.8 = 0.40
CF(R8)  = 0.2 * 1.0 = 0.2
CF(R9)  = min(0.0,0.8) * 0.8 = 0.0
CF(R10) = min(0.8,0.6) * -0.5 = -0.30
```

Next, the system will calculate the combined certainty factor of the four rules, which all affect the hypothesis *System unreliable* (we can ignore R9 because it has a 0.0 certainty factor).

$$cf(cf_{R7}, cf_{R8}) = 0.4 + 0.2 * (1 - 0.4) = 0.52$$

$$cf(cf_{R7+R8}, cf_{R10}) = \frac{0.52 + -0.3}{1 - \min(|0.52||-0.3|)} - 0.314$$

Note that we use Propagation Eq. 3 because the certainty factors have opposite signs. The nal certainty factor of the hypothesis that the system is unreliable is **0.314**. See Figure 8.6 for the belief network diagram and the associated certainty factors.

The nal portion of the belief network involves the determination of whether the computer is infected with malware. It makes this determination based on the three factors calculated above. The belief network culminates in the node

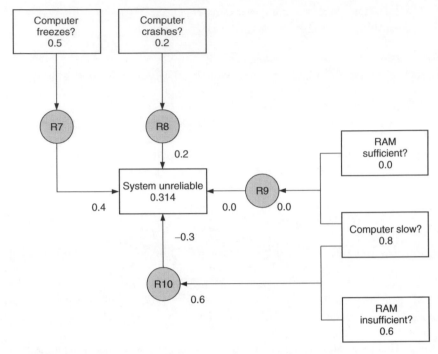

Figure 8.6. Belief network determining *system unreliable* (certainty factors shown).

Computer infected, in which all other nodes lead into. The nal two rules are used to update the certainty factor of this node:

```
R11:  IF computer is unsafe AND system is unreliable
      THEN computer is infected (cf 0.4)
R12:  IF user behavior is risky AND system is unreliable
      THEN computer is infected (cf 0.95)
```

All conditions in the IF part of the rules R11 and R12 have been determined previously. In particular, *Computer unsafe, Behavior risky*, and *System unreliable* and have already been discussed. The certainty factors of these three variables serve as inputs for R11 and R12. Observe further that both R11 and R12 do not execute unless the system deems the system to be unreliable. The reason for this is that neither risky behavior alone nor an unsafe computer alone indicates the presence of a malware infection. A system must also show some outward signs of infection, such as system slowdown, system crashes, system freezes, and the like, in order for one to believe that a system is infected. Finally, note that R12 has a signi cantly higher certainty factor than R11. This re ects the idea that risky behaviors are more likely to be the cause for a system infection, rather than an unsafe computer. No amount of computer protection (e.g., rewalls and antivirus software) will prevent a system infection from occurring if a user engages in risky behaviors.

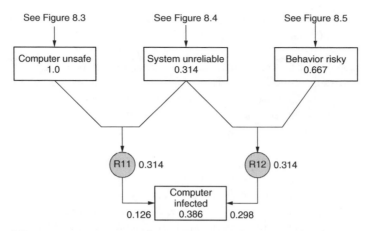

Figure 8.7. Belief network determining *computer infected* (certainty factors shown).

The system will proceed as before to propagate the certainty factors. The relevant calculations are:

```
CF(R11) = min(1.0,0.314) * 0.4 = 0.126
```

```
CF(R12) = min(0.667,0.314) * 0.95 = 0.298
```

cf(cf_R11, cf_R12) = 0.126 + 0.298*(1 − 0.126) = 0.386

Figure 8.7 shows the   nal piece of the malware detection belief network. It is really a continuation and culmination of the previous three diagrams. The   nal calculations indicate that the computer is infected with cf = 0.386. This is a moderate-to-weak degree of belief that the computer is infected. Figure 8.7 shows that a stronger belief (a higher cf) in the hypothesis did not occur because the system was deemed to be only moderately unreliable (cf = 0.314), despite a computer that was believed to be unsafe (cf = 1.0) and a user who engaged in risky behaviors (cf = 0.667).

One criticism of this   nal calculation is that it is fairly insensitive to the variable *Behavior risky*. The belief in *Computer infected*, in effect, will not change whenever *Behavior risky* is in the range 0.314 to 1.0 (this result occurs because the conjunctive condition of R12 takes the minimum of *Behavior risky* and *System unreliable*, which is always 0.314 for all values in this range). If this is an unsuitable side effect of R12, then one solution is to eliminate the *System is unreliable* condition from the rule. On the other hand, this might not be a good solution because, as was stated earlier, there needs to be some kind of evidence of system unreliability in order for malware infection to be suspected.*

---

*There are workaround solutions to this problem. One could code a number of rules such that higher values of risky behavior are assigned a higher certainty factor. For example, IF (system is unreliable) AND (Behavior risky) > 0.5 Then computer infected (cf = 1.0). This rule would increase the cf from 0.95 to 1.0 whenever *Behavior risky* > 0.5.

We have thus demonstrated the certainty factors approach for the processing of uncertain data and information. Ever since certainty factors were adopted by MYCIN in the 1970s, they have become a popular way of processing uncertainty in rule-based expert systems. Their major advantages are their simplicity in computation and their ability especially to combine multiple sources of evidence in a single composite number. However, certainty factors are awed because they were developed as an ad hoc approach to dealing with the dif cult subject of processing uncertainty, and they lack a rm mathematical basis in probability theory.

A more mathematically correct approach, therefore, is desirable. One approach that has garnered much attention by the AI community in recent years is Bayesian networks. During the last two decades especially, the practice and research on Bayesian networks has increased dramatically. The remainder of this chapter provides an overview of this dynamic and burgeoning area. But before we begin the discussion, it is necessary to discuss some basic concepts of probability theory to understand the power of this technique for representing uncertainty.

BASICS OF PROBABILITY THEORY

The notion of probability enters our everyday life and permeates our language. We frequently employ probabilistic notions when we communicate with others: "It is very likely to rain in November in Seattle, Washington." "My chances of getting the promotion are about one in two." "It is very rare that he comes to visit us." Each of these sentences expresses a probabilistic notion, or likelihood that some event will occur.

Although probabilistic notions have been around with us since time immemorial, the study of the mathematics of probability is relatively recent in the history of humankind. When the French mathematician Blaise Pascal devised methods for calculating the exact probabilities for gambling problems in the 17th century, probability theory was just beginning to be understood as a eld of study. Over the years since, the eld has steadily grown in importance and prominence. Today, probability theory is an important tool in many diverse elds—in areas such as business, medicine, and engineering—and helps solve a host of problems; quality control, risk assessment, and forecasting are a few application areas that have bene ted from the mathematics of probability theory.

One very important development in the history of probability theory is Bayes' theorem, formulated by the 18th-century British mathematician the Reverend. Thomas Bayes (1702–1761) to calculate conditional probabilities—the probability that an event A occurs, given that another event B has occurred. This theorem provides the theoretical underpinnings for Bayesian networks, so a basic understanding of probability theory is essential to understanding how Bayesian networks work. This section provides a basic review of probability theory,[7] especially as it relates to Bayes' theorem, so that the reader may learn to grasp the meaning behind probabilities, in particular, conditional probabilities, and learn to how to apply these concepts to calculate some basic probabilities. Later, these concepts will be important for understanding how probabilities are propagated in Bayesian networks.

Two different interpretations of probability are useful to de ne and distinguish at the outset: objective vs. subjective. The objective view of probability holds that probability measures the frequency with which an outcome would be obtained, if repeated a large number of times. For example, if I were to roll a fair die a large number of times, the probability that I would roll a 3 would be 1/6. On the other hand, the subjective viewpoint maintains that probability represent an individual's opinion of the likelihood of an event occurring, based on the person's beliefs and best judgment. For example, an economist might say "there is a good chance (more than 50%) that the economy will improve over the next year." Subjectivists believe that there is not one "true" probability. It turns out that both types of interpretations are important to the development of expert systems and Bayesian networks, as we will see later on in the chapter.

Basic Concepts

It is useful to envision probability as the likelihood of an outcome occurring when some kind of experiment is performed. The term *experiment* is used in probability theory to refer to any "process whose outcome is not known in advance with certainty."[8] For example:

- In an experiment in which a fair coin is tossed, an experimenter wishes to know the probability that there will be six or more heads when the coin is tossed 10 times.
- When 2 cards are selected from a well-shuf ed 52-card deck, an experimenter wishes to determine the probability of a blackjack (a blackjack occurs when two cards are dealt and their total equals 21: an ace and a 10-value card).
- Two different boxes contain different proportions of red balls. In Box 1, 8 out of 10 balls are red (80% red) and in Box 2, 2 out of 10 are red (20% red). An experimenter would like to determine the probability that Box 1 was selected when a red ball is selected.

In these three examples, an actual experiment, in the traditional sense of the word, is never involved. The beauty and power of probability theory, in fact, is that these probabilities can all be calculated without actually conducting the experiment.

The collection of all possible outcomes of an experiment is called the *sample space*. We will denote the sample space S. The sample space is the **set** of all possible outcomes, while each outcome is an element of the set. Because of this convention, the language and concepts of set theory provide a convenient framework for understanding probability theory.

For example, when a fair die is rolled, we may denote the sample space as $S = \{1, 2, 3, 4, 5, 6\}$. We call the sample space a *simple sample space* if each outcome is equally probable. Further, let A be any event, which de nes a subset of S, expressed in set notation as $A \subseteq S$. The probability of an event is denoted by P(A). For example, in the die example, if A is the event that an even number is thrown, then $A = \{2, 4, 6\}$. Given that the event A contains m outcomes, and the sample space contains n outcomes, then

$$P(A) = \frac{m}{n} \tag{8.1}$$

Hence

$$P(A) = \frac{3}{6} \text{ or } 0.5$$

Example. Suppose a fair coin is tossed three times. Calculate the probability that (1) exactly two heads are obtained and (2) at least two heads are obtained.

We may denote the sample space of this experiment as follows:

$$S = \{\text{HHH, THH, HTH, HHT, TTH, THT, HTT, TTT}\}$$

If A is the event that exactly two heads are obtained, then $A = \{\text{THH, HTH, HHT}\}$. There are three equi-probable outcomes in A, and eight equi-probable outcomes in S; therefore, $P(A) = \frac{3}{8}$. Likewise, if B is the event that at least two heads are obtained, then $B = \{\text{HHH, THH, HTH, HHT}\}$ and

$$P(B) = \frac{4}{8}$$

Mathematicians formally de ne probabilities by specifying three axioms that all interpretations of probability must satisfy. The rst axiom states that a probability must always be nonnegative.

Axiom 1: For any event $A, P(A) \geq 0$

The second axiom states that if an event is certain to occur, its probability must be 1.

Axiom 2: $P(S) = 1$

Axioms 1 and 2 combine to produce the following result:

$$0 \leq P(A) \leq 1 \tag{8.2}$$

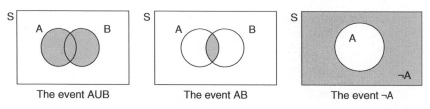

Figure 8.8. Set operations.

Eq. 8.2 de nes the range of probabilities to be the real numbers from 0 to 1. An impossible event is assigned a probability of 0, while a certain event is assigned probability 1. All other probabilities between these two extremes represent varying degrees of uncertainty in the outcome.

Before stating Axiom 3, we will discuss three set operations useful to know when calculating probabilities. As already noted, the language of set theory is convenient for expressing probabilities. The rst set operation is **union:** for any two events A and B, the **union** of A and B is de ned to be the event containing outcomes that belong to A alone, B alone, or to both A and B. The union is denoted by $A \cup B$. Second, the **intersection** of A and B is de ned as the event containing all outcomes that belong to both A and B. The intersection is denoted by $A \cap B$, or simply AB. Finally, the **complement** of an event A refers to outcomes in the sample space that do not belong to A. Sometimes the complement is referred to as "not A." We denote it $\neg A$. See Figure 8.8 for the Venn diagrams representing these set operations.

Example. Suppose a card is randomly drawn from a standard deck of playing cards* containing 52 cards. The sample space S contains the 52 possible outcomes. Further suppose the following three events:

1. A is the event that a face card—king, queen, or jacks—is drawn
2. B is the event that a queen of hearts is drawn
3. C is the event that a two is drawn

The relevant probabilities for these three events are $P(A) = \frac{3}{13}, P(B) = \frac{1}{52}$, and $P(C) = \frac{1}{13}$. We may calculate the following probabilities:

$P(A \cup B) = P(\text{a face card OR a queen of hearts}) = P(\text{a face card}) = \frac{3}{13}$

$P(A \cup C) = P(\text{a face card OR a two}) = \frac{3}{13} + \frac{1}{13} = \frac{4}{13}$

$P(AB) = P(\text{a face card AND a queen of hearts}) = P(\text{a queen of hearts}) = \frac{1}{52}$

$P(AC) = P(\text{a face card AND a two}) = P(\emptyset) = 0$

---

*A standard deck of 52 playing cards contains 13 ranks—2 through 10, jack, queen, king, and ace. Each rank in turn will have one of four suits—hearts, diamonds, clubs, and spades.

To calculate the probability of the complement of an event, we can simply calculate the probability of the event and subtract it from one:

$$P(\neg A) = 1 - P(A) \qquad (8.3)$$

For example, to calculate the $P(\neg A) = P$(a face card is not drawn):

$$P(\text{a face card is not drawn}) = 1 - P(\text{a face card is drawn}) = 1 - \frac{3}{13} = \frac{10}{13}.$$

Two events A_1 and A_2 are said to be mutually exclusive, or disjoint, when A_1 and A_2 have no common outcomes, that is $A_1 A_2 = \emptyset$. For any two such disjoint events A_1 and A_2,

$$P(A_1 \cup A_2) = P(A_1) + P(A_2)$$

Now we are ready to state Axiom 3, which is the general case for k disjoint events.

Axiom 3: Given k mutually exclusive events $A_1, A_2, A_3, \ldots, A_k$, the probability that at least one of the events occurring (i.e., the probability of the union of the k events) is equal to the sum of the individual probabilities: $P(A_1 \cup A_2 \cup A_3 \ldots \cup A_k) = \sum_{i=1}^{k} P(A_i)$

On the other hand, when two events A_1 and A_2 are not mutually exclusive,[*] (i.e., $A_1 A_2 \neq \emptyset$), then we must use the following formula when calculating the union of the two events:

$$P(A_1 \cup A_2) = P(A_1) + P(A_2) - P(A_1 A_2) \qquad (8.4)$$

Example. In the last example, when calculating $P(A \cup C)$, we may calculate $P(A) + P(C)$ because the event A (a face card is drawn) and the event C (a two is drawn) are mutually exclusive. It is never possible to draw a face card and a two at the same time. On the other hand, events A (a face card is drawn) and B (a queen of hearts is drawn) are not mutually exclusive because it is possible to draw the queen of hearts, which is also a face card. Hence

$$P(A \cup B) \neq P(A) + P(B)$$

By Eq. 8.4, P(a face card is drawn or a queen of hearts is drawn) $= \frac{3}{13} + \frac{1}{52} - \frac{1}{52} = \frac{3}{13}$.

As another example, let us suppose that A is the event that a face card is drawn, and B is the event that a card with spades is drawn. By Eq. (8.4) and using the fact that $P(AB) = \frac{3}{52}$, we may calculate the following:

$$P(A \cup B) = \frac{3}{13} + \frac{1}{4} - \frac{3}{52} = \frac{22}{52}$$

---

[*]The formula for calculating the probability of the union of three events is more complicated:
$P(A_1 \cup A_2 \cup A_3) = P(A_1) + P(A_2) + P(A_3) - [P(A_1 A_2) + P(A_2 A_3) + P(A_1 A_3)] + P(A_1 A_2 A_3)$

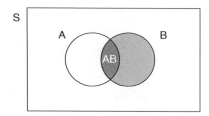

Figure 8.9. P($A|B$) is the proportion AB to B.

Conditional Probability and Bayes Theorem

A conditional probability refers to the notion that the probability of an event changes when it is known that another event has occurred. The notation for it is P($A|B$), which is read "the probability of A given B." To calculate the conditional probability for any two events A and B, we use the following formula:

$$P(A|B) = \frac{P(AB)}{P(B)} \qquad (8.5)$$

where $P(B) > 0$.

This formula can be more clearly understood by viewing Figure 8.9. If we know that event B has occurred, then to evaluate the probability that A has occurred, we merely take the proportion of AB to B.

Example. Let us suppose that two dice are rolled and we wish to determine the probability that the sum of the two dice ≥ 11. We may represent the sample space S of the two dice roll as the set containing the following 36 equally probable outcomes:

$$
\begin{array}{cccccc}
(1, 1) & (1, 2) & (1, 3) & (1, 4) & (1, 5) & (1, 6) \\
(2, 1) & (2, 2) & (2, 3) & (2, 4) & (2, 5) & (2, 6) \\
(3, 1) & (3, 2) & (3, 3) & (3, 4) & (3, 5) & (3, 6) \\
(4, 1) & (4, 2) & (4, 3) & (4, 4) & (4, 5) & (4, 6) \\
(5, 1) & (5, 2) & (5, 3) & (5, 4) & (5, 5) & (5, 6) \\
(6, 1) & (6, 2) & (6, 3) & (6, 4) & (6, 5) & (6, 6)
\end{array}
$$

If A is the event that the sum of the dice ≥ 11, then to calculate P(A), we rst note that there are three possible outcomes in which A occurs: $A = \{(5, 6), (6,5), A = (6, 6)\}$. Hence, by Eq. 8.1

$$P(A) = \frac{3}{36} \text{ or } \frac{1}{12}$$

Let us further suppose that we have observed event B, in which the rst die thrown is observed to be a 6. How does $P(A)$ change in light of this observation?

Our intuition tells us that the probability should increase in light of this new information. To see if this is true we need to calculate $P(A|B)$, where B is the event that a 6 is the rst die.

By Eq. 8.5, we need to calculate $\frac{P_{(AB)}}{P_{(B)}}$. If AB represents the event that the sum of the two dice ≥ 11 and the rst throw is 6, then $AB = \{(6, 5), (6, 6)\}$, while $B = \{(6, 1), (6, 2), (6, 3), (6, 4), (6, 5), (6, 6)\}$. Hence

$$P(A|B) = \frac{2/36}{6/36} = \frac{2}{6} = \frac{1}{3}$$

In accordance with our expectation, the probability increases from $\frac{1}{12}$ to $\frac{1}{3}$ when we learn that 6 is the rst die thrown.

We are now ready to derive Bayes's theorem from Eq. 8.5:

1. $P(B|A) = \frac{P_{(BA)}}{P_{(A)}}$ A and B are reversed from Eq. 8.5.

2. $P(BA) = P(B|A) * P(A)$ Rearrangement of terms

3. $P(AB) = P(B|A) * P(A)$ By commutativity of joint probabilities, $P(BA) = P(AB)$

4. $P(A|B) * P(B) = P(B|A) * P(A)$ From Eq. 8.5 replace $P(AB)$ with $P(A|B) * P(B)$

5. $P(A|B) = \frac{P_{(B|A)} * P_{(A)}}{P_{(B)}}$ Divide both sides by $P(B)$

The nal equation is the simple form of Bayes' theorem. It is restated as follows:

$$P(A|B) = \frac{P(B|A) * P(A)}{P(B)} \tag{8.6}$$

where $P(B) > 0$.

Disease Detection Tests. Suppose that there is a disease detection test that has been found to be 95% accurate. That is, when the test is administered on patients who actually have the disease, 95% of them test positive for the disease (the other 5% receive a false-negative result). Likewise, when the test is administered to patients who actually do not have the disease, 95% of them test negative (the other 5% receive a false-positive result). Suppose further that the prevalence of the disease in the population is 1/1000. What is the chance that a person found to have a positive test result will actually have the disease?

We may formulate this problem as a conditional probability and use Eq. (8.6) (Bayes's theorem). Let A be the event that a person has the disease and B be the event that a person tests positive. We therefore need to solve and calculate $P(A|B)$. First we know that $P(B|A) = 0.95$, which is given. Second, we also know that $P(A) = 1/1000$ (the prevalence of the disease in the population).

But what about $P(B)$? To calculate $P(B)$ we will use the following formula:

$$P(B) = P(B|A) * P(A) + P(B|\neg A) * P(\neg A) \tag{8.7}$$

The calculation of $P(B)$ involves partitioning the event B into two mutually exclusive, and exhaustive events: The person has the disease (the event A), and the person does not have the disease (the event $\neg A$). (We will have more to say about partitioning a sample space later on). Substituting Eq. (8.7) into Eq. (8.6) yields a very useful form of Bayes's theorem:

$$P(A|B) = \frac{P(B|A) * P(A)}{P(B|A) * P(A) + P(B|\neg A) * P(\neg A)} \tag{8.8}$$

To solve the equation we need $P(B|\neg A)$ and $P(\neg A)$. $P(B|\neg A)$ is the probability that a person tests positive given that he does not have the disease. This is $1-0.95$ or 0.05. $P(\neg A)$ is the probability that a person does not have the disease. This is $1-1/1000$, which is 999/1000. Substituting the values into Eq. (8.8) yields the following calculation:

$$P(A|B) = \frac{0.95 * 1/1000}{(0.95 * 1/1000) + (0.05 * 999/1000)} = 0.0187 \approx 2\%$$

Hence the probability that a person has the disease, when it has been discovered that he tested positive, is about 2%. This result often surprises people who expect that a reliable test (95% accurate) will produce a much higher result. (In fact, in a well-known study, this problem was posed to students and staff at Harvard Medical School, and over half of them thought that you would have a 95% chance of having the disease, given a positive test result). Contrary to intuition, you only have a very slight 2% chance of actually having the disease even when you do test positive for it. In fact, this human bias is so well known and documented that it is given the name "base-rate fallacy" in the decision sciences literature. It refers to the phenomenon that when human problem solvers rely on intuition alone they will ignore the base rate data, when determining such probabilities. In this example, the base rate information is the rarity (1 out of 1000) of the disease in the population.

General Form of Bayes's Theorem. The general form of Bayes's theorem requires an understanding of partitions. See Figure 8.10 for an example. A partition on the sample space S is formed on k events $A_1, A_2, \ldots, A_k$ when they are mutually exclusive (i.e., they do not intersect) and exhaustive on S (i.e. $A_1 \cup A_2 \cup \ldots \cup A_k = S$). Furthermore, the events of $A_1 B, A_2 B, \ldots, A_k B$ form a partition on B such that:

$$B = (A_1 B) \cup (A_2 B) \cup \ldots \cup (A_k B)$$

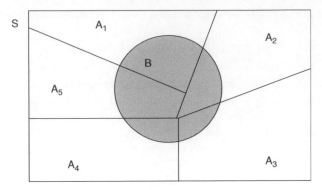

Figure 8.10. A_1 through A_5 form a partition on S.

In addition, because $A_1B, A_2B, \ldots, A_kB$ are mutually exclusive, from Axiom 3, we may write:

$$P(B) = \sum_{j=1}^{k} P(A_jB)$$

Finally, from Eq. (8.5), $P(A_jB) = P(A_j) * P(B|A_j)$. Therefore:

$$P(B) = \sum_{j=1}^{k} P(A_j) * P(B|A_j) \tag{8.9}$$

We are now ready to state the general form of Bayes's theorem:

Suppose that k events $A_1, A_2, \ldots, A_k$ form a partition on S (the k events are mutually exclusive and exhaustive on S), such that $P(A_i) > 0$ for all i and let B be any event such that $P(B) > 0$. Then for all $i = 1, \ldots, k$:

$$P(A_i|B) = \frac{P(A_i) * P(B|A_i)}{\sum_{j=1}^{k} P(A_j) * P(B|A_j)} \tag{8.10}$$

Proof. From Eq. 8.5:

$$P(A_i|B) = \frac{P(A_iB)}{P(B)}$$

The numerator of the right side of Eq. (8.10) is equal to $P(A_iB)$, while the denominator is equal to $P(B)$ from Eq. 8.9.

Example. A manufacturer of hard drives sells three types of hard drives: Brand 1, Brand 2, and Brand 3. After one year of use, the three different brands have different rates of failure: Brand 1 fails at a rate of 20%, Brand 2 fails at a rate of 10%, and Brand 3 fails at a rate of 5%. The manufacturer produces the three brands in the following proportions: 30% Brand 1, 50% Brand 2, and 20% Brand 3.

Suppose that a hard drive, which has been under operation for exactly one year, is randomly selected from the population of hard drives. It is discovered to have failed after one year. What is the probability that a Brand 1 hard drive was selected? What is the probability that Brand 2 was selected? What is the probability that Brand 3 was selected?

Let A_i be the event that a Brand i hard drive was selected, where $i = 1, 2, 3$, and let B be the event that the hard drive fails after one year. We will need to calculate the conditional probability $P(A_i|B)$. From Bayes's theorem, Eq. 8.10:

$$P(A_i|B) = \frac{P(A_i) * P(B|A_i)}{\sum_{j=1}^{3} P(A_j) * P(B|A_j)}$$

From the above we are given the following probabilities:

Brand 1: $P(A_1) = 0.3$ $P(B|A_1) = 0.2$
Brand 2: $P(A_2) = 0.5$ $P(B|A_2) = 0.1$
Brand 3: $P(A_3) = 0.2$ $P(B|A_3) = 0.05$

Hence the relevant calculations are

$$P(A_1|B) = \frac{0.3 * 0.2}{0.3 * 0.2 + 0.5 * 0.1 + 0.2 * 0.05} = 0.50$$

$$P(A_2|B) = \frac{0.5 * 0.1}{0.3 * 0.2 + 0.5 * 0.1 + 0.2 * 0.05} = 0.42$$

$$P(A_3|B) = \frac{0.2 * 0.05}{0.3 * 0.2 + 0.5 * 0.1 + 0.2 * 0.05} = 0.08$$

Note that the use of the general form of Bayes's Theorem, Eq. 8.10, is possible because the events A_1, A_2, and A_3 form a partition on S: They are both mutually exclusive and exhaustive on S.

BAYESIAN NETWORKS

In recent years, Bayesian networks have become very popular in the AI community as a method for processing uncertain information. The term was originally coined by Judea Pearl in 1985[9] to reflect both the subjective nature of the input information as well as the use of Bayes' theorem to update probabilities in light of actual observations of events.

The ideas and techniques underlying Bayesian networks are not that easy to understand, for they require a sophisticated understanding of probability theory and mathematics. This section will attempt to make some of the basic ideas accessible to someone with a limited understanding of probability theory (if you understood the last section, which reviews conditional probabilities and the calculation of basic probabilities, then you should be able to grasp the concepts in this section). The reader who seeks a deeper and more thorough treatment of Bayesian networks should consult one of a number of books that provide a more rigorous treatment of the subject.[10]

A Bayesian network may be envisioned as a causal diagram that represents a web of cause and effect relationships (alternatively, a Bayesian network may represent a belief network that shows the factors that in uence the degree of belief in a hypothesis). See Figure 8.11 for a simple Bayesian network example. The nodes, indicated by the rectangles, represent variables. In the gure all variables are discrete, having only two possible values, yes and no. In a more complex application, the variables can assume more than two discrete values—for example, *bad weather* can assume values (1) extremely bad, (2) bad, (3) slightly bad, and (4) not bad—or can be continuous—for example, *plane late*, can be the number of hours a plane is late, from 0 to in nity. To simplify matters, and later on to simplify the calculation of conditional probabilities, we consider only discrete nodes having two possible values.

The directed links in a Bayesian network specify the causal or in uential relationships between the variables. In Figure 9.10, both *mechanical failure* and

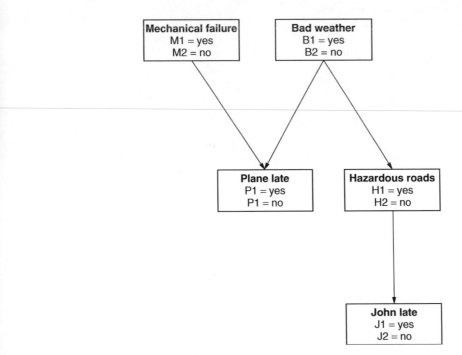

Figure 8.11. A simple Bayesian network.

bad weather are possible causes of *plane late*. Likewise, *bad weather* is the cause of both *plane late* and *hazardous roads*, which, in turn, is the cause of *John late* (John is more likely to be late to work under hazardous road conditions because he drives to work).

It is important to note at this point that the causal connections, as represented by Figure 8.11, are not certain and absolute. For example, the occurrence of mechanical failure and/or bad weather does not necessarily lead to a plane being late, but it certainly does increase the chances of the event *plane late* occurring. Therefore, to represent uncertainty, we need to assign probabilities to each of the nodes to represent the likelihood of a particular event occurring.

Furthermore, we would like to be able to modify these probabilities, in light of the actual observations of events. For instance, let us suppose that we discover that a plane was, in fact, late. Our system, according to intuition, should revise the nodes of the network accordingly to re ect this observation. In particular, we would expect the probabilities of *mechanical failure* and *bad weather* to be revised upward. Not only that, we would also expect the likelihood of the events *hazardous roads* and *John late* to also be increased (due to the fact that *bad weather* has increased). The real power of Bayesian reasoning is that it enables the propagation of probabilities, based on the structure of the interconnected nodes. We will look at a speci c example of this later on to show how a Bayesian network updates probabilities in light of new evidence.

One way to deal with the problem of probabilistic reasoning is to specify the complete joint probability distribution of the Bayesian network. What do we mean by *joint probability distribution*? Let us spend a few moments looking at a brief example of joint probabilities before we continue our discussion on Bayesian reasoning.

A joint probability distribution of a set of random variables $(X_1, X_2, \ldots, X_n)$ is de ned as $P(X_1, X_2, \ldots, X_n)$. For the two-variable case, let us assume two random variables X and Y. We can specify a discrete two-variable distribution by a table of probabilities. Suppose that in a university there are three dormitories and let X denote the dormitory: Dorm1, Dorm2, and Dorm3. Dorm1 is coed with half male students and half female students; Dorm2 is all-male; and Dorm3 is all-female. Let Y denote the student's sex: male or female. We may specify the joint probability distribution as in Table 8.2:

Note that the probabilities in the table sum to 1:

$$\sum_{\text{all } i \text{ and } j} P(X = x_i, Y = y_j) = 1$$

Table 8.2. A Joint Probability Distribution of Dorm (X) and Sex (Y)

Sex	Dorm1 (Coed)	Dorm2 (All-Male)	Dorm3 (All-Female)
Male	0.15	0.40	0.00
Female	0.15	0.00	0.30

We may express a speci c joint probability as $P(X = \text{Dorm2}, Y = \text{Male}) = 0.40$ (40% of the students in the university live in Dorm2 and are male). We may also sum a row or column of the table to obtain a marginal probability. For example, the marginal probability that a student is female can be obtained by summing the values of the second row of the table:

$$P(Y = \text{Female}) = 0.15 + 0.00 + 0.30 = 0.45$$

It is an easy matter to calculate the conditional probabilities from a fully-speci ed joint probability table. Let us suppose, for example, that we observe that a student is female. How do the probabilities of X change, given that the student is female? We need to calculate the conditional probability $P(X|Y = \text{Female})$. From Eq. 8.5:

$$P(X = \text{Dorm1}|Y = \text{Female}) = \frac{P(X = \text{Dorm1}, Y = \text{Female})}{P(Y = \text{Female})}$$

$$= \frac{0.15}{0.15 + 0.00 + 0.30} = \mathbf{0.25}$$

$$P(X = \text{Dorm2}|Y = \text{Female}) = \frac{P(X = \text{Dorm2}, Y = \text{Female})}{P(Y = \text{Female})}$$

$$= \frac{0.00}{0.15 + 0.00 + 0.30} = \mathbf{0.00}$$

$$P(X = \text{Dorm3}|Y = \text{Female}) = \frac{P(X = \text{Dorm3}, Y = \text{Female})}{P(Y = \text{Female})}$$

$$= \frac{0.30}{0.15 + 0.00 + 0.30} = \mathbf{0.75}$$

Figure 8.12 shows graphically the two-node Bayesian network. In this diagram the node *Sex* is in boldface to indicate that it has been instantiated—that is to say, evidence has been observed that the student's sex is female. Based on this observation, the probabilities of X are updated accordingly.

One problem with the use of joint probabilities in the calculation of conditional probabilities is that the complete speci cation of a joint probability distribution will require a great many numbers. For the two-node case, this was a relatively small number—only $2 * 3 = 6$ joint probabilities. In general, however, one would need to specify $n_1 * n_2 * \ldots * n_k$ probabilities, where n_i is the number of

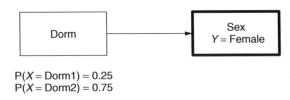

P(X = Dorm1) = 0.25
P(X = Dorm2) = 0.75

Figure 8.12. Two-node Bayesian network with sex node instantiated.

discrete values a node can assume. This number quickly becomes unreasonably large for a Bayesian network with k nodes. For example, in a 12-node Bayesian network, in which each node is binary (e.g., yes/no), one would have to specify $2^{12} = 4096$ joint probabilities. (Indeed, typically all the joint probabilities are not available for all possible combinations, so this method would quickly bog down even the most assiduous person tasked with lling in all the probabilities.)

Fortunately, Bayesian networks are constructed so that certain independence assumptions hold. (Two nodes are independent when the occurrence or nonoccurrence of one of them has no relation or in uence on the other.)* We will have more to say about independence among the nodes of a Bayesian network later on. For now, we note that these independence assumptions will greatly reduce the number of probabilities required to specify the probability distribution among the variables in the network.[11]

To specify the probability distribution of a Bayesian network, one must provide two types of probabilities: (1) the prior probabilities of the root nodes (nodes with no parents) and (2) the conditional probabilities of all nonroot nodes given all combinations of its parent nodes. Let us look at a speci c example. See Figure 8.13, which is the same Bayesian network described earlier.

There are two root nodes, *mechanical failure* and *bad weather*, and their prior probabilities are indicated in Figure 8.13. By **prior probability** we mean the probability of an event occurring before any evidence is introduced. The prior probability of mechanical failure occurring is given by $P(M1) = 0.1$, whereas the prior probability of bad weather is $P(B1) = 0.2$.

In addition, Figure 8.13 includes the conditional probabilities of all nonroot nodes, given all possible combinations of their parent nodes. For example, for the node *plane late*, we must consider all combinations of *mechanical failure* and *bad weather*, its two parent nodes. Hence the conditional probabilities $P(P1| M1, B1)$, $P(P1| M1, B2)$, $P(P1| M2, B1)$, and $P(P1| M2,B2)$ all need to be speci ed. We do not need to specify the conditional probabilities for the event M2, because it is assumed that $P(M2) = 1 - P(M1)$ by Eq. 8.3.

Where do these prior and conditional probabilities come from? If we are fortunate enough, they are based on historical data. For example, we may have records that indicate that 10% of the time a plane will experience a mechanical failure. Similarly, the prior probability of bad weather can be looked up from meteorological data, which shows that 20% of the time bad weather occurs (to ne-tune the system, we could adjust this probability to re ect the time of year—we would expect, for example, that bad weather is more likely to occur during the winter than during the summer).

The conditional probabilities are more dif cult to determine. For instance, $P(P1|M1,B1)$ is the probability that a plane is late, given that there is both mechanical failure and bad weather. This data may be determined from the historical record. If, however, these data are not readily available, or very dif cult

---

*If two events A and B are independent, we may express this mathematically as $P(A|B) = P(A)$. This means that knowledge of B does not convey any additional knowledge in calculating $P(A|B)$. It is the same as the unconditional probability $P(A)$.

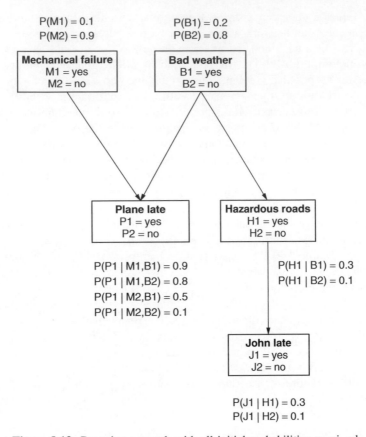

Figure 8.13. Bayesian network with all initial probabilities speci ed.

to obtain, we may seek an expert opinion on what the subjective probability is. A bene t of the Bayesian approach is that it allows one to use both historical data as well as subjective probabilities to determine prior and conditional probabilities. Of course, objective data are preferable, because they are not as subject to the biases and possible contradictions of human expert opinion.

When all is said and done, the ve binary node Bayesian network required only the speci cation of 10 probabilities (2 prior probabilities, and 8 conditional probabilities). The complete speci cation of the joint probability distribution would have required 2^5 or 32 probabilities. For larger Bayesian networks, the savings could be even more dramatic. Indeed, the real power of Bayesian networks is that it allows us to calculate the conditional probabilities from a much smaller subset of probabilities (we will see an example of how the conditional probabilities are calculated shortly). This substantial economy is achieved because of the independence assumptions of Bayesian networks, so that we need consider only the parents, or direct predecessors of the nonroot nodes.

We calculate the prior probabilities of all the nonroot nodes by using the conditional probabilities, together with information about the prior probabilities of their parents. For example, the prior probability of *plane late* can be calculated by using the following formula:

$$P(P1) = P(P1|M1, B1) * P(M1) * P(B1) + P(P1|M1, B2) * P(M1) * P(B2)$$
$$+ P(P1|M2, B1) * P(M2) * P(B1)$$
$$+ P(P1|M2, B2) * P(M2) * P(B2) + \qquad\qquad (8.11)$$

Hence the prior probability can be calculated as follows:

$$P(P1) = (0.9 * 0.1 * 0.2) + (0.8 * 0.1 * 0.8) + (0.5 * 0.9 * 0.2)$$
$$+ (0.1 * 0.9 * 0.8) = \mathbf{0.244}$$

From this calculation the likelihood of a plane being late, given that we know nothing else, is 0.244.

Similarly, the prior probability of *hazardous roads* can be calculated using the formula:

$$P(H1) = P(H1|B1) * P(B1) + P(H1|B2) * P(B2)$$
$$= (0.3 * 0.2) + (0.1 * 0.8) = \mathbf{0.14}$$

Finally, the prior probability of *John late* is calculated using the formula:

$$P(J1) = P(J1|H1) * P(H1) + P(J1|H2) * P(H2)$$
$$= (0.5 * 0.14) + (0.1 * 0.86) = \mathbf{0.156}$$

Note that $P(H1)$ is 0.14, which is the prior probability of H1, and $P(H2) = 1 - 0.14 = 0.86$.

We have now calculated all prior probabilities of the nonroot nodes. They are indicated in Figure 8.14a. We now come to the most interesting aspect of Bayesian networks, the ability to process new evidence as it comes in, and update probabilities of the nodes accordingly. Let us rst suppose that we have discovered that there are hazardous road conditions (i.e., $P(H1) = 1.0$). Figure 8.13b shows how the probabilities of nodes change to re ect this new information.

First, we expect that the probability of *John late* will increase. Because $P(J1| H1) = 0.3$, $P(J1)$ increases from 0.156 to 0.3. We also expect that the probability of bad weather will increase, given that we have observed hazardous roads. We will need to calculate $P(B1| H1)$. From Eq. 8.6 we know that

$$P(B1|H1) = \frac{P(H1|B1) * P(B1)}{P(H1)} = \frac{0.3 * 0.2}{0.14} = 0.429$$

Hence $P(B1)$ increases from 0.2 to 0.429 when we know that there are hazardous roads. Finally, we also expect that the probability of the plane being late to increase, if the probability of bad weather increases. We calculated P(P1) earlier from Eq. (8.3). Substituting P(B1) = 0.429 and P(B2) = 1−0.429 = 0.571 into Eq. (8.11) results in the following calculation:

$$P(P1) = (0.9 * 0.1 * 0.429) + (0.8 * 0.1 * 0.571) + (0.5 * 0.9 * 0.429)$$

$$+ (0.1 * 0.9 * 0.571) = \mathbf{0.329}$$

P(P1) increases from 0.244 to 0.329. The node *mechanical failure* is unaffected by our knowledge of *hazardous roads*; hence its probability is unchanged. See Figure 8.14b for the results of these calculations. The node *hazardous roads* is bold-faced to indicate that evidence has been observed for this node—that is, the node has been instantiated. A newly calculated probability, in light of the

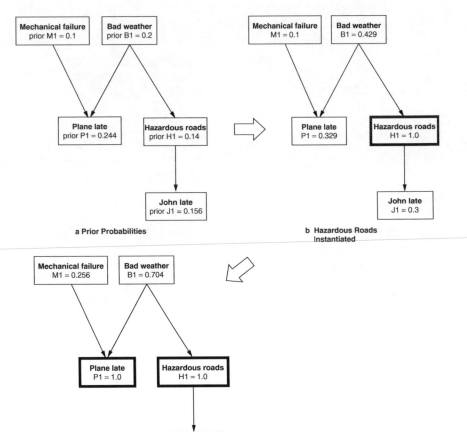

Figure 8.14. Updating a Bayesian network.

evidence *hazardous roads* occurring, is referred to as a **posterior probability** to re ect the fact that a conditional probability is calculated after an event is known. Bayesian networks allow one to consider evidence incrementally—that is, new observations and new pieces of evidence may be observed one by one, and their effects on a Bayesian network are updated each time. Continuing on with our example, we may suppose further that we have, at a later point in time, observed that our plane did, in fact, arrive late. See Figure 8.14c for the updated Bayesian network.

Two nodes would be affected by the instantiation of the node *plane late: mechanical failure* and *bad weather*. We would expect that both their probabilities would increase upwards to re ect this new piece of evidence. Let us rst consider P(M1| P1), or the probability of mechanical failure occurring given that a plane is late. From Eq. (8.6) we know that:

$$P(M1|P1) = \frac{P(P1|M1) * P(M1)}{P(P1)}$$

We know that P(M1) = 0.1, and P(P1) = 0.329. What about P(P1|M1)? To calculate this probability, we rst observe that we initially speci ed P(P1|M1,B1), P(P1|M1,B2), P(P1|M2,B1), and P(P1|M2,B2), or the conditional probability of P1 given all combinations of its parent nodes. Because we are assuming M1, we do not need to consider the two conditional probabilities P(P1|M2,B1) and P(P1|M2,B2). We are left with P(P1|M1,B1) = 0.9 and P(P1|M1,B2) = 0.8. Hence we may use the following formula to perform our calculation:

$$P(P1|M1) = P(P1|M1, B1) * P(B1) + P(P1|M1, B2) * P(B2) \qquad (8.12)$$

$$= (0.9 * 0.429) + (0.8 * 0.571) = \mathbf{0.843}$$

Substituting these numbers yields the following result:

$$P(M1|P1) = \frac{0.843 * 0.1}{0.329} = \mathbf{0.256}$$

The probability of mechanical failure P(M1) increases from 0.1 to 0.256 when it is known that a plane is late.

Similarly, we may calculate P(B1|P1). From Eq. 8.6:

$$P(B1|P1) = \frac{P(P1|B1) * P(B1)}{P(P1)}$$

We know that P(B1) = 0.429 and P(P1) = 0.329. To calculate P(P1|B1), we need to apply the following formula (by similar argument as when we calculated P(P1|M1) by Eq. 8.12:

$$P(P1|B1) = P(P1|M1, B1) * P(M1) + P(P1|M2, B1) * P(M2)$$

$$= (0.9 * 0.1) + (0.5 * 0.9) = \mathbf{0.54}$$

Substituting these numbers results in the nal calculation:

$$P(B1|P1) = \frac{0.54 * 0.429}{0.329} = \mathbf{0.704}$$

As expected, the probability of bad weather also increases, from 0.429 to 0.704.

This example shows how the structure of a causal diagram can be used to propagate probabilities in a Bayesian network. One distinguishing feature of Bayesian networks is the ability to reason about problem structure and propagate probabilities accordingly. In this respect, Bayesian networks are really a form of model-based reasoning (for a review see Chapter 7), a form of inferential reasoning in which problem solving is aided by knowledge of system structure because system behavior is determined from structure. Let us make these ideas more precise and concrete, by considering the types of structures that are possible in Bayesian networks. See Figure 8.15 for three types of structures.

In a linear structure, three variables x, y, and z are linked in a causal chain, in which x causes y and y causes z. If we have evidence for x, it is transmitted to y, which in turn transmits this to z. In the Bayesian network given in Figure 8.14, we were given the linear structure:

```
Bad weather   →   Hazardous roads   →  John late
```

Evidence for *bad weather* would increase our belief in *hazardous roads*, which in turn would increase our belief in *John late*.

Now, let us suppose that we have hard evidence for Y (in this instance, we know for certain that there are hazardous roads). If this were true, knowledge of X would not have any effect on Z (in effect, the instantiation of Y blocks, or overrides, the transfer of knowledge from X to Z). In fact, in this example (Figure 8.14c), when evidence for bad weather increased, the probability of *John late* remained unchanged, because it was already known that *hazardous roads*

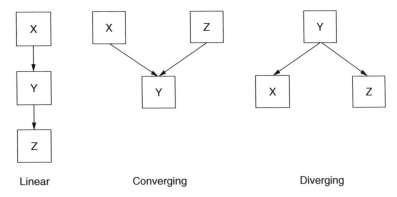

Figure 8.15. Three connection types in Bayesian networks.

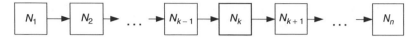

Figure 8.16. Instantiantion of N_k in a linear structure.

was true. In this respect, X (*bad weather*) is independent of Z (*John late*) given Y (*hazardous roads*).

The general case is given by the following. If a Bayesian network is made up of n nodes linked in a linear structure, and if node N_k is instantiated (where $k < n$), then knowledge of nodes N_1 through N_{k-1} would not have any effect on nodes N_{k+1} through N_n (Figure 8.16).

The second type of connection is a converging structure, in which two causes (X and Z) converge on a single effect (Y). Obviously, any evidence of either X alone or Z alone, or both together will affect Z. Moreover, if there is evidence for both X and Z, then the probability of Z is likely to be greater than if we had only evidence for only X or Z alone. Further, if there is evidence for Y, then this would also transmit back to its causes, X and Z. An example of a converging connection in Figure 8.14 is *mechanical failure* and *bad weather*, two nodes that both cause *plane late*. (Note that in our example, we had evidence for *plane late* and this transmitted to both causes by increasing the probability of both *mechanical failure* and *bad weather*).

What about the transmission of information from X to Z? If we have no evidence of Y, then X and Z are independent. (In our example, if we have no evidence for *plane late*, then *mechanical failure* and *bad weather* are independent of one another.) Therefore, evidence of X does not transmit to Z and vice versa, given no evidence of Y. However, if something is known about Y, then X and Z become dependent. For example, let us suppose that we know that a plane is late. Further, let us suppose that we have evidence for *mechanical failure*. We would actually expect the probability of *bad weather* to decrease, because we would reason that it was the mechanical failure that caused the plane to be late, and not the bad weather. In this manner, we have explained away the bad weather as a possible cause. On the other hand, if we have evidence for *plane late*, and we have evidence that would decrease the probability of *mechanical failure*, then, by analogous argument, we would expect the probability of *bad weather* to increase.

The third type of connection is a diverging structure, in which two effects, X and Z, have a common cause Y. Certainly, any evidence for Y would transmit to both X and Z. A more interesting question is whether evidence can be transmitted from X to Z. If Y is not instantiated (i.e., we do not know Y for certain), then, indeed, evidence can be transmitted from X to Z. We observed this to be the case in Figure 8.14 where *bad weather* was the common cause for both *plane late* and *hazardous roads*. When we instantiated *hazardous roads*, this had the effect of updating probabilities of the *bad weather*, which in turn increased our belief in *plane late*. Hence X and Z are not independent when Y is not known for certain. In contrast, let us suppose that Y is instantiated. Then, evidence for X

does not in any way affect Z and vice versa. If, for example, we knew for certain that *bad weather* did occur, then evidence for *plane late* would not transmit to *hazardous roads*, and vice versa. Similar to the case of the linear structure, the instantiated node blocks the transmission of evidence to the other nodes of the Bayesian network.

In a sense, causality (or in uence) and the propagation of uncertainty has been "mathematized" so that probabilities are consistent and correct based on the principles of probability theory and Bayes' theorem. Somehow probabilities must be calculated and updated on the Bayesian network according to the structural elements noted earlier: linear connections, diverging connections, and converging connections. This is the remarkable achievement of Bayesian networks: They employ mathematical algorithms so that probabilities can be appropriately propagated on the causal diagram.

In Chapter 1, we described and de ned the explanatory power of an intelligent user interface, and noted that two qualities contribute to enhancing its explanatory power: transparency, or the ability to understand how a system works, and exibility, or the ability of the interface to adapt to a wide variety of end-user interactions. Bayesian networks, it can be said, excel in both respects. First, Bayesian networks are highly intuitive and graphical. They enable us to model causal factors in a network diagram. Because they are graphical, one can easily observe the effects of new evidence on the nodes of the causal diagram. Hence they allow for a high degree of transparency in the reasoning process. Second, Bayesian networks are highly exible. New evidence can be entered in any order (i.e., nodes can be instantiated in any order), and the Bayesian network will update appropriately. In addition, the Bayesian network will make predictions based on incomplete evidence—it is therefore robust, and does not completely break down if some evidence is unavailable. Furthermore, Bayesian networks can reason from effect to cause, not only from cause to effect. Hence they can perform backward reasoning, which is not possible in other approaches, including the certainty factors approach.

Another bene t of Bayesian networks is that they are an excellent way to represent subjective expert judgments. As we noted earlier, the prior and conditional probabilities speci ed initially in Bayesian networks can represent either subjective expert opinion or objective data. Bayesian networks will process each type equally well. In contrast, other statistical approaches such as regression analysis, are highly data driven, and neglect to consider expert opinion. For this reason, regression models are limited to describing the past but are less successful in predicting the future. Because Bayesian networks allow one to incorporate expert opinion and causal explanation, they are more suitable to tasks requiring the prediction of future events.[12]

DISCUSSION

We have described two different approaches for the representation and processing of uncertain information. The rst technique, the certainty factors approach, was developed as a practical and convenient way of handling uncertainty. Rather than represent uncertainty as probabilities, the original developers of MYCIN felt that the use of Bayes' rule would have produced inaccurate probabilities, because the assignment of conditional probabilities would have been highly subjective.[13]

Because the certainty factors approach is not mathematically correct and lacks theoretical justi cation, the value of the certainty factor should be interpreted with caution. One criticism is that the composite number—a number in the range $(-1, 1)$—is purely artifactual and does not represent the correct probability or likelihood that a hypothesis is correct.[14] However, proponents of certainty factors argue that its uses are primarily (1) to guide a program in its reasoning, (2) to cause the current goal in an expert system to be eliminated from the search space if its cf falls in an insigni cant range $(-0.2, 0.2)$, and (3) to be used as a way to rank hypotheses.[15] Used in this more limited way, such proponents argue that the certainty factors approach can produce good results, achieved with far fewer calculations than the Bayesian approach. MYCIN, after all, was deemed to render reasonably good recommendations in the diagnosis of bacterial infections.

Furthermore, there are many domains in which probabilities are unknown or are simply too dif cult to obtain. Therefore, the question arises as to whether Bayesian networks, and the representation of uncertainty as probabilities, might be too biased to produce meaningful results. Some have argued that the certainty factors approach offers a simple alternative for dealing with uncertainty in expert systems when statistical data are lacking.

In recent years, the AI community has shifted toward a Bayesian approach in dealing with the problem of uncertainty and inexact reasoning. There are two primary reasons for this recent development. First, it has been only in the last few decades that ef cient algorithms have been created to calculate and propagate the probabilities in a Bayesian network. (See, for example, Pearl[16], Lauritzen and Spiegalhalter[17], and others.) For the rst time, real-world problems of realistic size can be solved using these algorithms. Although there is no known algorithm that will work for all types of Bayesian networks, the algorithms that exist today work reasonably well for many types of problems. Research continues today on the development of more algorithms to solve more types of problems. Second, software tools have been created that automatically calculate the probabilities for us. Even in the simple example ve-node Bayesian network described earlier (see Figure 8.14), the calculations are laborious and time-consuming to do by hand. Companies such as Hugin[18] and AgenaRisk[19] have developed software tools that have enabled fast computations even for large Bayesian networks. Researchers and practitioners who are not specialists in Bayesian networks can now build and run Bayesian networks with relatively easy to use graphical user interfaces. Because of these trends, the popularity of Bayesian networks has grown rapidly in recent years. Applications are proliferating in many different domains including medical diagnosis, risk analysis, and equipment fault diagnosis (Microsoft and Hewlett-Packard have famously used Bayesian networks for fault diagnosis). The future of Bayesian networks, and the use of causal diagrams to illustrate inexact reasoning, looks promising.

ENDNOTES

1. See Peter Jackson, *Introduction to Expert Systems*, 3rd ed. Reading, MA: Addison-Wesley, 1999, pp. 166–167, for sources of uncertainty.

2. For a review of these formalisms on uncertainty management see Keung-Chi Ng and Bruce Abramson, "Uncertainty Management in Expert Systems," *IEEE Expert*, 5, no. 2 (1990), 29–48.

3. See Edward H. Shortliffe and Bruce G. Buchanan, "A Model of Inexact Reasoning in Medicine," *Mathematical Biosciences* 23 (1975), 351–379.

4. Jackson, p. 50.

5. Ibid.

6. John Durkin, *Expert Systems: Design and Development*. New York: Macmillan, 1994; see also Michael Negnevitsky, *Artificial Intelligence: A Guide to Intelligent Systems*, 2nd ed. Harlow, England; New York: Addison-Wesley, 2005, p. 78.

7. Much of the discussion in this section is based on the textbook Morris H. DeGroot, *Probability and Statistics*. Reading, MA: Addison-Wesley, 1975. The interested reader should consult a reference on probability theory for a more in-depth understanding of probability theory.

8. Ibid., p. 5.

9. Judea Pearl, *Causality*. Cambridge; New York: Cambridge Univ. Press, 2000, p. 14.

10. There are a number of books to consult for a more technical treatment of Bayesian networks: see, for example, Judea Pearl, *Probabilistic Reasoning in Intelligent Systems: Networks of Plausible Inference*. San Mateo, CA: Morgan Kaufmann, 1988; Richard E. Neapolitan, *Learning Bayesian Networks*. Upper Saddle River, NJ: Pearson Prentice Hal, 2003; and Finn V. Jensen and Thomas D. Nielsen, *Bayesian Networks and Decision Graphics*. New York: Springer, 2007. These books are for the mathematically sophisticated reader. For a more introductory treatment of Bayesian networks, there are a number of tutorials on the Internet. For an introduction to Bayesian networks see also Eugene Charniak, "Bayesian Networks with Tears," *AI Magazine* (1991), Vol. 12, no. 4, 50–63.

11. See, for example, Charniak, p. 51, for a discussion on how the independence assumption will reduce the number of conditional probabilities that need to be speci ed.

12. For a discussion on the bene ts of Bayesian networks, see Norman Fenton and Martin Neil, "Managing Risk in the Modern World: Applications of Bayesian Networks," A Knowledge Transfer Report, London Mathematical Society and the Knowledge Transfer Network for Industrial Mathematics (2007). This report can be found on www.agena.co.uk.

13. Jackson, p. 171.

14. There have been several criticisms of the cf approach. Adams showed that the cf associated with a hypothesis by MYCIN does not correspond to the probability of the hypothesis given the evidence. Adams also showed that it is possible for two hypotheses to be ranked in reverse order. See J. B. Adams, "A Probability Model of Medical Reasoning and the MYCIN Model," *Mathematical Biosciences* 32 (1976), 177–186. Another criticism is that has been used as a measure of change in belief, when it is actually elicited from experts as a degree of absolute belief. See E. Horovitz and D. Heckerman, "The Inconsistent Use of Measures of Certainty in Arti cial Intelligence Research," in *Uncertainty in Artificial Intelligence*, New York:

North Holland, 1986, pp. 137–151. See Jackson, pp. 172–175 for a discussion on the limitations of certainty factors.

15. Jackson, p. 173.

16. Pearl.

17. S. L. Lauritzen and D. J. Spiegelhalter, "Local Computations with Probabilities on Graphical Structures and Their Application to Expert Systems," *Journal of the Royal Statistical Society* 50, no. 2 (1988), 157–224

18. For more information on Hugin, go to www.hugin.com.

19. For more information on Agena, go to www.agena.co.uk.

CHAPTER 9

A FRAMEWORK FOR UNDERSTANDING DIAGRAMMATIC REASONING

In the preceding chapters, we have looked at a number of diagramming notations, and a number of ways of employing diagrammatic reasoning. Our discussion has taken us through many different diagramming techniques, a diverse range of applications, and a number of ways of reasoning with diagrams to help us infer solutions to problems. It is useful, at this point, to take a step back, and reflect on the major themes and undercurrents of diagrammatic reasoning. What are some of the common principles of diagramming? What criteria can we use to judge the quality of a diagram? (In the process of answering these questions, what are the limitations and pitfalls of diagramming?) How can we evaluate the effectiveness of a diagram? Can we classify the diagrammatic reasoning techniques we have learned throughout this book into broader types? Through answers to these questions and others, we will acquire a broader perspective of diagrammatic reasoning and what some of the larger issues are. This concluding chapter provides a framework for understanding diagrammatic reasoning.

First of all, let us consider what some of the common principles of diagramming are. Diagrammatic representations of all kinds share a number of common characteristics. First, they are all visual graphics, as opposed to sentential (or linguistic) representations. As such, they enable indexing by location on a plane—this means that related pieces of information can be grouped to together and arranged thematically. This also allows for a visual rendering of how components of a system are interconnected to one another. Because they are highly visual, diagrammatic representations tap into the human visual information processing system, which is capable of performing a number of perceptual inferences

Diagrammatic Reasoning in AI, by Robbie Nakatsu
Copyright © 2010 John Wiley & Sons, Inc.

quite easily; on the other hand, we cannot perform these same inferences (or we perform them with much more difficulty) when using sentential representations.

Diagrams are primarily, but now always, made up of geometric shapes interconnected by lines or arrows. (One important exception is the Venn diagram, which shows relationships among sets, not through interconnected lines, but through overlapping circles). The geometric shapes can represent any number of things: people, things, concepts, events, activities, decision points, sets, actions, steps—almost any type of entity can be modeled. Different shapes can be used to represent different things on the same diagram. For example, on a decision tree, squares denote decision points, while circles denote chance events. On a basic flowchart, rectangles denote actions and diamonds denote decision points. The meanings of the shapes are frequently conventions that have been adopted by diagrammers over the years. In general, it is better to stick with standard and conventional notations rather than make up your own.

As discussed in Chapter 3, lines are used to represent a linkage between two objects on a diagram. Depending on the diagram, the line can take on a different meaning. It could mean any one of the following six linkage types:

1. Connected to (topology)
2. Precedes in time (sequence and flow)
3. A type of (classification)
4. A part of (composition)
5. Related to (association)
6. Causes/influences (cause and effect)

Lines can be either directed or nondirected. An arrow is typically used to indicate a directed relationship. Some types of linkages are always directed. Linkages of the type (2) *precedes in time*, (3) *a type of*, (4) *a part of*, and (6) *causes/influences* are always directed. For example, the *causes/influences* linkage is always expressed as a directed relationship, with the cause on the open side, and the effect on the arrowhead side of the line:

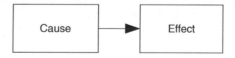

The (1) *connected to* linkage, which is employed in a system topology diagram, can be either directed or nondirected. In a hydraulic system, for example, the linkages may indicate how the water pipes are connected to the components of system (pumps, reservoir, valves, etc). If the water moves in only one direction, then the linkages are directed. On the other hand, in other physical systems, the components are attached to other components with no particular directional orientation in the connections. See, for example, Figure 3.3 for an illustration of how the components of a computer network are interconnected. Information flows in all directions, so that none of the linkages are directed.

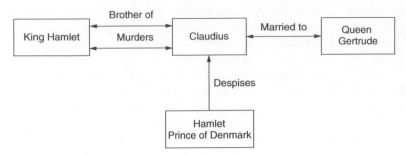

Figure 9.1. A semantic network of unidirectional and bidirectional relationships.

The (5) *related to* linkage can also be directed or nondirected. Figure 3.14 is a semantic network that illustrates the relationships among the characters of Hamlet. Some of the relationships are unidirectional, whereas others are bidirectional. A portion of the diagram in reproduced in Figure 9.1.

In this semantic network, the linkages representing *brother of* and *married to* are bidirectional (they apply in both directions), whereas the linkages *murder* (Claudius murders King Hamlet) and *despises* (Hamlet despises Claudius) are unidirectional. A bidirectional relationship is equivalent to a nondirected relationship, and the arrowheads could just as easily have been omitted.

In general, a single diagram will contain only one type of linkage. A causal diagram will contain a web of cause and effect associations (*causes/influences* linkages), a system topology diagram will contain a description of how the components of a system are connected to one another (*connected to* linkages), and a flowchart will describe a chronological sequencing of events (*precedes in time* linkages). However, if it is necessary to model more than one type of linkage within a single diagram, notation must be used to distinguish the different types of linkages. For example, Figure 3.16 shows an entity-relationship diagram that uses two types of linkages: one to indicate cardinality, and the other to indicate *a type of* linkage. To avoid ambiguity in the notations an (unfilled) arrowhead is used to signify *a type of* linkage. Sometimes directed lines are implied but the arrows are omitted from the diagram. A good example are the decision trees described and illustrated in Chapter 3 (e.g. Figures 3.24 and 3.26). Decisions trees are almost always read from left to right, so that it is not necessary to add the arrows in the diagram. At other times diagrams are read from top to bottom, so again, the arrows may be omitted. For example, hierarchies, including organization charts, inheritance hierarchies, and composition models, can all have their arrows removed without loss of clarity. However, whenever there is ambiguity as to the direction of the relationship, the arrows should be added to the diagram (some diagrammers will include the arrows in all representations of hierarchical relationships, just to be safe).

That is really all you need to know about basic diagramming. When all is said and done, it is really a simple concept: It consists of shapes connected by lines, directed or nondirected (as already noted, there are a few exceptions to this simple definition). From this basic description, its power lies in its ability to take on myriad forms and to be used in many different applications.

Sometimes diagrams are internal representations, created on the fly, to help us understand the real world. We studied in Chapter 2 how humans will sometimes form mental models that are like diagrams in the mind. We form mental models to understand how the components of a system are interconnected (internal connections) or we form mental models to map out how a new system is similar, or analogous to, something more familiar to us (external connections). Because internal representations are formed in a person's head, they are subject to the limitations of the human mind, and short-term memory. As such, they are often incorrect, incomplete, inconsistent, unstable over time, and rife with superstitions and prejudices.

Because of these limitations, we may commit the diagram to some kind of external representation—most typically we draw the diagram and save it to paper or to a computer file. By doing so, we hope to create a more nearly correct diagram than an internal representation would allow. Over time, we may refine the diagram so that it is a more complete, accurate, and consistent description of a target system. Because we have stored it to some external media, we preserve it for future use and reference and don't have to rely on our short term memory. Furthermore, because we may store diagrammatic representations on a computer, programs may be developed that allow them to be modified and manipulated in many different ways. The future of diagrammatic representations is the intelligent user interface in which the diagram will be used in dynamic and powerful ways.

CRITERIA FOR EVALUATING DIAGRAMS

In looking at diagrams of various types and in different application areas, it is obvious that some diagrams are more effective than others. Some diagrams do nothing more than create a picture that does not add significantly to our understanding; other diagrams are much more powerful, and enable us to infer solutions to very difficult problems. In this section, we consider the criteria for judging the quality of a diagram. In particular, here are five qualities of effective diagrams:

1. A good diagram promotes system understanding.
2. A good diagram is unambiguous.
3. A good diagram is parsimonious.
4. A good diagram is relevant.
5. A good diagram enables multitiered descriptions.

A Good Diagram Promotes System Understanding

One of the main reasons we draw diagrams is to help us understand a system better. The conceptual model of the electromechanical thermostat is a good example (Figure 2.5). Though simple, this diagram illustrates the topology of the

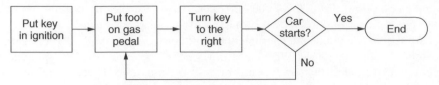

Figure 9.2. A flowchart illustrating how to start a car.

components of an electromechanical thermostat. It enables us to understand and visualize how the device works. Together with the causal model (also discussed in Chapter 2), we are able to see how the components of the device causally interact in a cascading series of events: We may actually run the diagram in our heads to understand the sequence of events that occur whenever, say, we adjust the temperature level of the device upward. A simple verbal description of the electromechanical thermostat alone would have been far less effective in conveying system behavior.

Other diagrams bring very little to the table and provide an information graphic that does not add anything over and above a verbal description. Diagrams such as the basic flowchart given in Figure 9.2 are not really that useful. They could just as easily have been expressed in numbered sentences.

A Good Diagram Is Unambiguous

Notational elements on the diagram should not be overloaded—that is to say, every construct on a diagram should mean only one thing. One example of construct overloading was described in Chapter 3, when we discussed and illustrated influence diagrams. In most standard notations, the directed linkages on influence diagrams are overloaded, because the arrows can denote either sequence or influence. An overloaded diagram would be one like the diagram given in Figure 9.3 (a modified from Figure 3.28). Sometimes an arrow represents influence. An example of influence is the arrow from *Oil* (a chance node) to *Payoff*

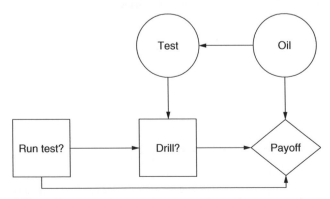

Figure 9.3. An influence diagram with ambiguous notation.

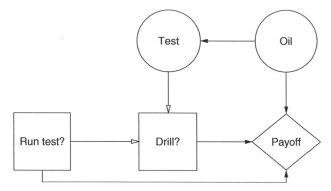

Figure 9.4. An influence diagram with unambiguous notation.

(an outcome node). This linkage means that the presence or absence of oil will influence your payoff. Alternatively, an arrow can signify sequence or a *precedes in time* linkage. An example of sequence is the linkage from *Run Test?* (decision node) to *Drill?* (decision node). This signifies that the decision to run the test is made before the decision to drill. There is also sequence in the relationship between *Test* (chance node) and *Drill?* This indicates that the results of the test are known before the decision to drill or not is taken.

The diagram is disambiguated in Figure 9.4. Here, an unfilled arrowhead represents sequence, whereas a filled arrowhead represents influence. In fact, most influence diagrams do not adopt this notation but instead reason that the context of the diagram makes clear whether a linkage represents sequence or influence. In particular, sequence always occurs when a predecessor node (whether a decision node or a chance event) is linked to another decision node. Unfortunately, this type of reasoning places a great burden on the reader of the diagram who must mentally perform these steps to determine what type of linkage an arrow represents. For the sake of clarity and ease of use, we adopt the principle that every notational element on a diagram should have one and only one meaning.

A Good Diagram Is Parsimonious

All diagrams are abstractions of reality. Accordingly, they are never intended to completely model everything there is to know about a target domain. All good abstractions are selective about what is modeled and include only what is needed and no more. To some, this notion of parsimony goes against the grain of one's desire to create a diagram that is as inclusive and complete as possible. There are a number of reasons why a diagrammer should resist the temptation to create as complete a picture as possible.

First, diagrams that include too much information quickly lose focus and purpose. What is the diagrammer trying to accomplish? What is the message of the diagram? By including too much in a single diagram, the diagram quickly devolves into a jumble of ideas and concepts. Indeed, one of main reasons we

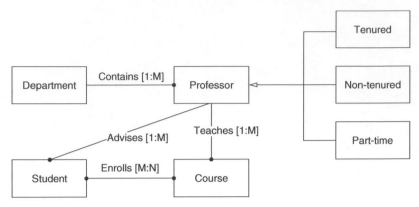

Figure 9.5. An entity-relationship diagram.

diagram is to capture the essence of a domain, not to completely represent it. Second, diagrams that are overladen with ideas and notational constructs are more difficult for users to process and use. The most effective diagrams promote understanding by focusing attention only on what is needed to understand a complex system or what is needed to infer solutions to difficult problems. By including too much information, a user of a diagram must filter out the unnecessary portions of the diagram. In many cases, the user won't bother.

Let us look at a specific example of an entity-relationship diagram, discussed in Chapter 3. An entity-relationship diagram is used to help design a database application. It serves as a blueprint for how the database is actually created—it is really a specification of what the tables are and how they are linked together. Figure 9.5 is the entity-relationship diagram for a university database (from Figure 3.16).

If we wish to create a parsimonious diagram, every rectangle and every notational element should have meaning as to how the database is created and structured. Database designers, for instance, take every rectangle off the diagram and create a separate table for each one. Let us suppose, however, that information about *Department* is unnecessary. If this is the case, we do not need this rectangle and should remove it from the diagram. Furthermore, the diagram models two notational elements: cardinality (see Chapter 3 for a review), as indicated by the lines with the filled circles, and supertype/subtype relationships, as given by the link with the unfilled arrowhead. The cardinalities are used to help link the tables together according to the rules of relational database design and hence are necessary—we should not remove these, for they help us implement the database application. The supertype/subtype relationship on the diagram indicates that a professor (supertype) can be one of type subtypes, tenured, nontenured, and part-time. If it is important to capture information about the three different professor types, then we should leave the notation in the diagram; if it is not necessary, the university domain is over-modeled, and we should eliminate the unnecessary notations. What should remain in the entity-relationship diagram are only the portions of the diagram that will be included in the final database product.

A Good Diagram Is Relevant

A diagram should support the user in some kind of problem-solving task. If the diagram is not suitable to the task, then it is not a good fit, and must be reenvisioned. If the user must work too hard to get the information from the diagram, it is perhaps not the right diagram for the task.

As a first step, the right diagram type—whether illustrating system topology, sequence and flow, classification, composition, association, cause and effect, or logic reasoning—must be created. Even within specific diagram types, there are choices that may be unsuitable. For example, there are different types of diagrams representing sequence and flow. Basic flowcharts are a good choice for representing basic notions of sequence and flow; however, if there is a need to illustrate parallelism in activities (such as might be the case for a project manager who must schedule activities concurrently), then a better choice might be the activity diagram (see Figure 3.8). In still another flowchart, it might be necessary to illustrate who is responsible for particular tasks. If this is the case, swimlanes in the diagram may be created to illustrate responsibility (see Figure 3.9). Likewise, the choices for causal diagrams can run the gamut from a basic directed graph (see Figure 3.18) to a fishbone diagram (see Figure 3.21) to a fault tree (see Figures 3.23 and 3.24). Each of these choices would be suitable for specific types of tasks, and wholly unsuitable for others.

A Good Diagram Enables Multitiered Descriptions

A diagrammer will quickly discover that it is oftentimes difficult to fit a diagram on a single page. Some diagramming notations, especially, take up a lot of real estate, so that it is a challenge to fit everything on a page. Activity diagrams, for instance, are sometimes difficult to draw because they can illustrate parallel actions, and there are only so many parallel paths that can be squeezed onto a single page. Likewise, hierarchic diagrams can contain many levels of nodes that sometimes don't easily fit onto one screen. For this reason, it is important to be able to continue a diagram onto a second page, a third page, and so on.

To combat this difficulty, one technique is to create a multitiered description. By multitiered description, we mean that separate "layers" of diagrams are created. A top-level diagram of a domain provides an overview of the system that needs to be modeled. For example, see Figure 9.6 for a top-level causal diagram of the factors that influence the unemployment rate in the United States. Three types of factors affect unemployment: frictional unemployment, structural unemployment, and cyclical unemployment. Each of these factors, in turn, can be represented by a causal diagram of some kind. (For the causal diagram of cyclical unemployment see Figure 3.18). If necessary, a third layer may be created to represent the details from the second layer.

Besides the fact that this technique allows for more elaborate diagrams that don't fit on a single page, the creation of multiple tiers means that users can drill down into diagrams for more supporting details. If a more aggregated view is sought after instead, the user may go up a level to get a higher-level perspective.

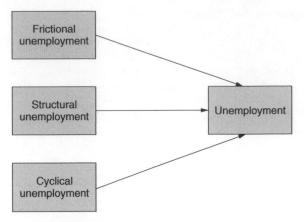

Figure 9.6. Top tier of a causal diagram.

Multitiered descriptions allow the user to control the level of detail needed. They are strongly encouraged, especially when creating diagrams for more complex systems. (To continue a diagram to other pages, an alternative to multitiered descriptions is to use off-page references. See Figures 3.22 and 3.23 for an example of a fault tree displayed over two pages using off-page references.)

COMPARING TWO DIAGRAMS: INFORMATIONAL AND COMPUTATIONAL POWER

In Chapter 1 we described explanatory power. An intelligent user interface that is capable of explaining its actions is said to be one that is endowed with explanatory power. Further, we noted that there are two facets of explanatory power: system transparency, which is related to providing a user with an understanding of how a system works, and system flexibility, which refers to the features of the user interface that make it easy to use, such as the provision of feedback, the ability to back out of changes made to a system, the ability to display different levels of details very easily, and the ability to process uncertain data and information.

   Understanding the difference between transparency and flexibility is important in designing a user interface having maximum explanatory power. This is because system transparency, in and of itself, may be insufficient in creating a system having adequate explanatory power. What we desire, in addition, is the ability to request information and explanations in different ways, depending on our needs and the context of the problem-solving situation. That is to say, it may be possible to request more information from a system (i.e., system transparency exists) but without flexibility, such as the ability to back out of changes, and the ability to easily modify input assumptions without having to start all over again, a user may not bother to seek out transparency, even if it does already exist. In effect, the rigidity of the user interface may hamper and discourage such a user from exploring the system more fully; system transparency is lost on a user.

How do transparency and flexibility contribute to explanatory power, and why is the distinction important? To answer this question, it is useful to view explanatory power as composed of two components, informational power and computational power. Informational power is strictly related to content alone, while computational power evaluates efficiency and usability as well. Interfaces having greater informational power contain superior content, while interfaces having greater computational power have content that can be used and accessed more efficiently and effectively. By this definition, transparency enhances informational power, whereas flexibility enhances computational power.

Larkin and Simon define these notions more precisely in comparing two diagrammatic representations. They define two representations as informationally equivalent "if all the information in one is also inferable from the other, and vice versa."[1] Moreover two representations are computationally equivalent "if they are informationally equivalent and, in addition, any inference that can be drawn easily and quickly from the information given explicitly in the one can also be drawn easily and quickly from the information given explicitly in the other, and vice versa."[2] Using their definition, two user interfaces would be equivalent, in terms of explanatory power, if they are computationally equivalent (which by their definition means they are informationally equivalent as well, because computational equivalence subsumes informational equivalence).

An example will help illuminate the difference between informational power and computational power. Figure 9.7a provides a diagram of TransMode Hierarchy (see Chapter 6 for a review). This diagram is intended to serve as a user interface to the expert system that recommends a transportation mode. The diagram partitions the knowledge base into more manageable chunk, and creates a hierarchic representation, so that the interrelationships among the chunks are made explicit. On the other hand, Figure 9.7b illustrates a flat interface of the same expert system. It is a flat interface because the links among the nodes have been removed; in essence, the structural information is missing. Moreover, the variables are listed in alphabetical order. (One benefit of a diagrammatic representation is that we can group related variables together by location on a plane; to avoid indexing by location on a plane, we simply list the variables in alphabetical order).

The two interfaces are not informationally equivalent—the flat interface is informationally inferior to the hierarchic interface, because it is lacking structural information about how the variables are interconnected. To render the two interfaces informationally equivalent, we must add more content to the flat interface. For example, we can attach a textual explanation to each node that describes how the node is related to other nodes. A user may click on any node on the flat interface to request information about its parent node. For example by clicking on *Shipment Weight* the system informs the user: "The parent of *Shipment Weight* is *Load Type*." Such explanations, in effect, would produce a flat interface that is informationally equivalent to the hierarchic interface.

Clearly, however, the two interfaces are not computationally equivalent. The hierarchic interface possesses a number of advantages over the flat interface in

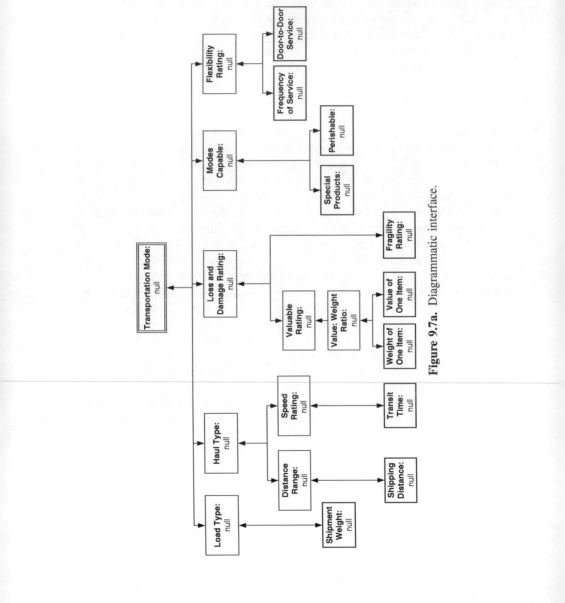

Figure 9.7a. Diagrammatic interface.

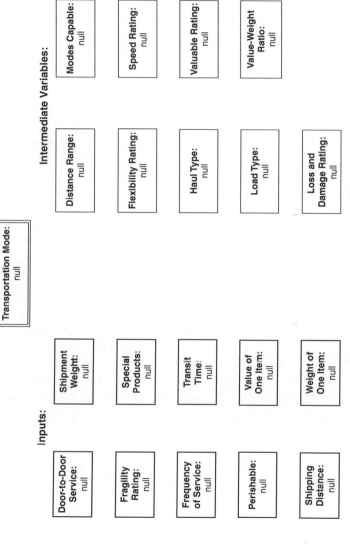

Figure 9.7b. Flat interface.

terms of efficiency and ease of use. It is much easier to see how information is propagated on the hierarchic interface—that is, how changing one node can propagate information, node by node, up the levels of the hierarchy. A user of the flat interface, by contrast, must reconstruct the series of variable that are affected (indeed, the hierarchic structure can be reconstructed from the textual explanations), but it would require much more cognitive effort and time to do so. Hence, even though the two interfaces are informationally equivalent, the flat interface is sorely lacking in terms of flexibility and computational power.

In general, this is the real power underlying diagrammatic representations: not that it contains more informational power but that it can dramatically increase computational power. The human visual information system, in essence, is able to construct all the perceptual inferences on a diagram at little or no cost. (Unfortunately, such visual recognition capabilities are very difficult to simulate by an AI program.) On the other hand, this same human user must painstakingly reconstruct these perceptual inferences under the flat interface; the textual explanations can be used to reconstruct the hierarchic relationships, but they are arrived at a high cost in terms of cognitive effort. The diagram, in effect, produces all these elements for free, and that is why it is so powerful and useful.

Larkin and Simon's framework for understanding informational and computational power can be employed to compare and evaluate two different user interfaces—for example, a diagrammatic interface vs. a non-diagrammatic one. To compare apples to apples (not apples to oranges), one must first ensure that the two interfaces are equivalent in terms of informational power. Then, a controlled experimental study can be conducted in which participants are asked to solve a host of problems. One group is asked to use the first interface, let's say the diagrammatic interface, while the second group is asked to use the second interface, the nondiagrammatic interface. (Of course, participants are randomly assigned to each of the two groups). We would expect the diagrammatic interface group to outperform the nondiagrammmatic interface group on a number of measures:

- The ability to solve problems correctly (accuracy in problem solving)
- The time spent to arrive at a correct solution (efficiency in problem solving)
- The ability to infer solutions to novel or difficult problems
- User satisfaction with the interface, as assessed by a survey instrument

In fact, just such an experimental study was conducted to evaluate the effectiveness of the diagrammatic interface provided by TransMode Hierarchy.[3] A total of 40 participants used a hierarchic interface like the one in Figure 9.7*a* and 40 participants used an *informationally equivalent* flat interface like the one in Figure 9.7*b*. One problem-solving task required the participants to identify the two faulty rules used by the expert system when it reached an incorrect conclusion:

> Due to the poor performance of RAIL carriers in transporting very fragile goods, it has been decided that RAIL should never be chosen when the **fragility rating** is high. Does the system always reach the conclusion that highly fragile goods

[**fragility rating** = high] are NEVER to be shipped by RAIL? If not, can you identify the faulty rule or rules that are executed, which result in an incorrect **transportation mode** = RAIL? Please be as precise as possible in specifying the faulty rule(s), if any such rules exist.

Table 9.1. Results of Experimental Study

	Faulty Rules Found			
Treatment	0 rules	1 rule	2 rules	Total
Flat Interface	17	17	6	40
Hierarchic Interface	6	23	11	40

The results of the experimental investigation are provided in Table 9.1. It is clear that the hierarchic interface facilitated problem-solving performance. Under the hierarchic interface 34 out of 40 participants (85%) were able to correctly identify at least one faulty rule, whereas 23 out of 40 participants (58%) using the flat interface could do so.*

In terms of user satisfaction, the participants overwhelmingly preferred the hierarchic interface to the flat interface. A total of 77 participants preferred the hierarchic system, whereas a mere 3 preferred the flat system. It is not surprising that a great majority of the participants (57 individuals) cited that the interface offered a great advantage in terms of enhancing their ability to visualize or see the relationships among the variables in the system. Other important advantages of the hierarchic interface cited included the logical nature of the interface, resulting in increased comprehensibility (36 participants); ease of use (10 participants); and the facilitation of problem solving (4 participants). When asked to comment on possible weaknesses of the hierarchic system, participants were able to come up with a few responses. The most popular response was that the hierarchic interface was more complex and that more training would be required to learn and use it (28 participants). It is interesting that a few participants (6 individuals) suggested that the hierarchic interface might be harmful in terms of biasing the user toward a certain way of using the system. That is to say, the user of a flat system is more actively engaged in trying to understand the relationships in the variables, whereas the user of the hierarchic system is more likely to passively accept what the system tells him or her to do. However, overall, it was clear that the hierarchic interface was highly preferable to the flat interface.

BEYOND STATIC DIAGRAMS

Throughout this book, we have seen several examples of diagrams. Some of the diagrams were static or not intended to be modified by a user or updated by a

---

*The problems were also scored on a scale of 0 through 10 (10 being a perfect score). The average score of the flat interface group was 4.0, whereas the average score of the hierarchic interface group was 5.65. This difference in the scores was found to be significant ($F = 5.85$, $p = .018^*$).

Table 9.2. Classifying Diagrammatic Representations by the Modifiability of Structure and Information

	Structure Static	Structure Dynamic
Information Static	**I. Static Representations**	**III. Constructive Diagrams**
	Paper-based diagrams (Ch. 3) Rule trace diagrams (Ch. 6)	Dynamic Venn diagrams (Ch. 4)
Information Dynamic	**II. Propagation Structures**	**IV. Constructive Diagrams with Information Propagation**
	TransMode Hierarchy (Ch. 6) Bayesian networks (Ch. 8)	LogNet (Ch. 7)

system. Other diagrams were intended to be used in more dynamic and interesting ways. In Table 9.2 diagrammatic representations are classified by (1) whether the structure of the diagram can be modified and (2) whether the information on the diagram is updated. Whereas Quadrant I diagrams are those in which both structure and information are static, Quadrant II, III, and IV diagrams are more dynamic, enabling us to create diagrammatic user interfaces, and in some cases, infer solutions to difficult problems.

The great bulk of diagrams in use today are **static representations** (Quadrant I in Table 9.2). The diagrams in Chapter 6, for the most part, were static, never really intended to be manipulated in any way. Diagrams such organization charts, basic flowcharts, semantic networks, and entity-relationship diagrams are primarily informational and help us understand systems but are (usually) not intended to be modified by the user. Some of the diagrams presented in Chapter 6.8, such as the rule trace diagrams that show the interrelationships between the conditions and actions in a rule trace (see Figure 6.8) as well as the diagrams that model strategic knowledge (see, for example, Figure 6.14) are nothing more than static representations: They depict how the expert system works and help us acquire deeper system understanding, but are not really dynamic. Because these diagrams are static, they can easily be inserted in a static medium, such as in the pages of a book, on a read-only computer screen, or on a static web page.

On the other hand, **propagation structures** (Quadrant II in Table 9.2), are diagrams that are intended to be the user interface of an intelligent system. As such, the information on the diagram can be modified and updated by a user. Examples of propagation networks presented in this book include TransMode Hierarchy and the Bayesian networks described in Chapter 8. TransMode Hierarchy (see Figure 9.7a) is a diagram that serves as the user interface to the expert system that makes transportation mode recommendations. When input information is entered on the leaf nodes of the hierarchy, the hierarchy transmits and propagates information upward through the diagrammatic structure. Thus a user can visualize and trace a line of reasoning through the knowledge base. Bayesian networks, in a similar manner, employ causal diagrams that can illustrate a network of cause and effect associations (see, for example, Figure 8.14). Probabilities are assigned to each node on the causal diagram and are updated based on the introduction of new evidence and data. While propagation structures are static (the structure itself cannot be modified), the information is dynamic because new information can be propagated on the diagram based on the addition of new evidence or data.

A **constructive diagram** (Quadrants III and IV in Table 9.2) is dynamic in the sense that the structure itself is meant to be modified by the user. A good example is the dynamic Venn diagrams described in Chapter 4. These diagrams can be manipulated through rules of transformation, which refer to rules for combining and manipulating objects on the Venn diagram. Like the rules of algebra, the rules of transformation tell us what a permissible transformation is—how one can transform a Venn diagram, step by step, into another equivalent Venn diagram. Why do we do this? We perform these transformations in to test the validity of a syllogism or to prove logic theorems. It turns out that constructive diagramming can be a very powerful technique for solving difficult problems, such as proving logic theorems.

A **constructive diagram with information propagation** (see Quadrant IV in Table 9.2) is dynamic in a dual sense: both the structure itself can be modified and information can be updated and propagated through the structure. In Chapter 7, we looked at such an example. The system we described is called LogNet, and it supports a network design task: How to create a business logistics network design—that is, how to configure a network of factories, warehouses, and customer zones interconnected by transportation links (see Figure 7.10 for a sample diagram in LogNet). The network design task involves a trade-off between consolidation (merging two or more warehouses into one thereby reducing costs) and decentralization (splitting warehouses into two or more separate locations so that they better serve customers). The diagrams are constructive because they are meant to be actively modified by the user—different network configurations can be drawn (nodes can be added/deleted to the network, and transportation links can be added and deleted to connect and disconnect nodes). By request, the resulting benchmarks (e.g., cost and customer service level) of the network design can be calculated. Furthermore, information propagates in the network, based on how the networks are configured. For example, the inventory carrying cost of a warehouse is updated based on the extent to which inventory is consolidated—the more consolidated the warehouse, the less the (per unit) inventory carrying cost, whereas the more decentralized the inventory the more the (per unit) inventory carrying cost.

All in all, diagrammatic reasoning is really about the use of dynamic techniques, whether through information propagation (Quadrant II and Quadrant IV diagrams) or through constructive diagramming (Quadrant III and Quadrant IV diagrams). This book, in essence, is about illustrating some of these more interesting uses, and going beyond the more traditional and static uses of diagramming. The future of diagrammatic reasoning, and how it intersects with the AI discipline, is about how these techniques might be used to solve difficult, thorny, and seemingly intractable problems. This book has showcased a number of applications, but this is only the beginning and a hint and a glimpse at what else may be possible.

AFTERWORD: DIAGRAMMATIC USER INTERFACES IN AI AND BEYOND

In the beginning, in Chapter 1, we described AI as a field of outsized expectations and unreasonable goals. As a result of the hype surrounding the field, especially in the early years, to many AI has been a disappointment because the quest for a thinking machine was never achieved. However, we argued for a different approach to designing AI systems, a more pragmatic orientation in our objectives and expectations. We argued for the need to be more embracing of the limitations of AI by finding work-around solutions. One approach, in this regard, is to focus on the graphical user interface, and redesign it to take into account the limitations and shortcomings of AI.

We have now come full circle to these original ideas, laid out in the introductory chapter of this book. Having surveyed a wide variety of diagramming techniques and applications, we are now in a better position to look more retrospectively and more critically at the limitations of AI and how they may be addressed with diagrams. A useful point to revisit is the lack of commonsense reasoning, an important limitation of AI systems and a main reason why AI is not further along in its quest to create a thinking machine. Earlier we presented and discussed four components of commonsense reasoning:

- The ability to use multiple representations to the same problem
- The ability to deal with errors
- Self-reflection at a higher level
- Efficient knowledge retrieval

Each of these problem areas has been addressed or touched on, in some form or another in this book, and a diagrammatic solution proposed. If AI systems are to deliver more effective results and be more fully embraced by the user community, we need to understand how to grapple with and find solutions to each of these problem areas. Much more work needs to be done, and diagrammatic reasoning is surely not the only solution to these problems. But a strong case can be made for how diagrammatic representations and diagrammatic reasoning can greatly augment an AI system by grappling with these issues.

With respect to the issue of multiple representations, diagrams of a variety of forms have been proposed and illustrated throughout this book. It is clear that diagramming techniques can be used to create many different kinds of representations and emphasize different aspects of a problem-solving situation. Furthermore, the ability to build multitiered descriptions of a system will go a long way toward creating useful and usable AI systems: Users should be able to request the level of detail that they desire.

Second, we should expect the AI user interfaces of the future to be flexible enough to deal with errors and different forms of user interactions with a system. We have illustrated a number of diagrammatic techniques that can help in this regard. The user interface of TransMode Hierarchy was designed to support a wide variety of human–computer interactions with a system: A user, for example, may enter data in any order, backtrack, test out different scenarios (e.g., perform What if? analysis directly on the diagram), and in general explore a system with ease and without restriction. Another limitation of AI is that so many AI applications are brittle, or completely break down when a slightly different form of a problem is posed to it. AI systems such as Bayesian networks are designed to be robust enough to work even when some evidence is missing or when evidence cannot be asserted with complete certainty. The causal diagram provides a convenient way of entering information on the Bayesian network in a flexible manner and provides a structure for visualizing how probabilities are propagated. In general, the benefit of having a diagrammatic structure as a user interface is that it allows one to interact more flexibly with a system and understand when things go awry.

Third, the ability to understand and reflect at a deeper level on problem-solving strategies that an AI system uses can be greatly aided by a diagrammatic representation of some kind. This subject was dealt with in Chapter 6, when we addressed ways of graphically illustrating strategic knowledge (see Figures 6.14–6.16). Too often, we do not possess a deep mental model of how a system works or knowledge about the methods used to solve problems in a domain. This knowledge needs to be made more explicit because it can give us more confidence in using a system and generate more trust in accepting system recommendations. Otherwise, we are lost when things go wrong. Otherwise, we must operate by blind faith alone. The importance of strategic knowledge and other forms of deep understanding cannot be overstated.

Finally, many of the diagrams that we studied in this book serve as convenient organizational scaffolds to complex systems. They enable us to retrieve information in a more efficient way. Even in a simple knowledge base of 50 rules (like the TransMode knowledge base described in Chapter 6) it can be very difficult to understand how the rules interact to generate system recommendations. Diagrams, such as hierarchic structures, may be employed to partition and organize a complex system. As we noted earlier, it is far simpler to zero in on a specific rule when the system is organized in a diagram or when a multitiered diagrammatic description is created than it is to perform a sequential search through a knowledge base without the help of any diagrammatic aids. We need diagrammatic representations to help us organize our knowledge so that it is easier to retrieve later on.

While the discussion here was squarely focused on the AI user interface, diagrammatic reasoning, in a larger and broader sense, can be employed in all types of technology and in all walks of life. Indeed, as we move further into the new millennium, the need for diagrammatic user interfaces that offer system transparency and flexibility is more urgent than ever. We have evolved into a society in which technology and information overload bombards us from all directions, and keeps us perpetually wired and connected. Moreover, technological innovation is proceeding at a rapid pace, and it is hard to keep up. To cope, the person of the future will need to be supported amid all this complexity and all this technological wizardry. When Arthur C. Clark famously wrote in 1962, "Any sufficiently advanced technology is indistinguishable from magic,"[4] he seems to have prophesied the predicament that we would all face today. While it is an exciting time to live, and to experience the technological revolution firsthand—everything from the Internet to the smart phone to the GPS device—it is also an extremely frustrating time for the user who has to figure out how to get things to work, often to no avail. Unfortunately, technology all too often does not cooperate because it is a black box—mystical, unintelligible, and impossible to modify. Ideally, it should be transparent, visible for inspection, flexible, seamless, and easy-to-use. A diagram is one powerful and convenient way to transform the black box into a glass box. Technology, in short, should not be indistinguishable from magic.

ENDNOTES

1. Jill H. Larkin and Herbert A. Simon, "Why a Diagram Is (Sometimes) Worth Ten Thousand Words," *Cognitive Science*, 11 (1987), 65–99.
2. Ibid.
3. Robbie T. Nakatsu and Izak Benbasat, "Improving the Explanatory Power of Knowledge-Based Systems: An investigation of Content and Interface-Based Enhancements," *IEEE Transactions on Systems, Man, and Cybernetics, Part A*, 33, no. 3 (2003), 344–357.
4. Arthur C. Clarke, *Profiles of the Future*. New York: Harper & Row, 1962

INDEX

Printed and bound by CPI Group (UK) Ltd, Croydon, CR0 4YY

28/10/2024

14581347-0001